The Six-Shooter State

American violence is schizophrenic. On the one hand, many Americans support the creation of a powerful bureaucracy of coercion made up of police and military forces that provide public security. At the same time, many of those citizens also demand the private right to protect their own families, homes, and property. This book diagnoses this schizophrenia as a product of a distinctive institutional history in which private forms of violence – vigilantes, private detectives, mercenary gunfighters – emerged in concert with the creation of new public and state forms of violence, such as police departments or the National Guard. This dual public and private face of American violence resulted from the upending of a tradition of republican governance, in which public security had been indistinguishable from private effort, by the nineteenth-century social transformations of the Civil War and the Market Revolution.

JONATHAN OBERT is Assistant Professor of Political Science at Amherst College, where he has taught since 2014. He has published articles on violence, organizational change, and state formation in the United States at *Law & Social Inquiry, Perspectives on Politics, Studies in American Political Development,* and the *Journal of Policy History*, among others.

The Six-Shooter State

Public and Private Violence in American Politics

JONATHAN OBERT
Amherst College

CAMBRIDGE
UNIVERSITY PRESS

CAMBRIDGE
UNIVERSITY PRESS

University Printing House, Cambridge CB2 8BS, United Kingdom

One Liberty Plaza, 20th Floor, New York, NY 10006, USA

477 Williamstown Road, Port Melbourne, VIC 3207, Australia

314–321, 3rd Floor, Plot 3, Splendor Forum, Jasola District Centre, New Delhi – 110025, India

79 Anson Road, #06–04/06, Singapore 079906

Cambridge University Press is part of the University of Cambridge.

It furthers the University's mission by disseminating knowledge in the pursuit of education, learning, and research at the highest international levels of excellence.

www.cambridge.org
Information on this title: www.cambridge.org/9781316515143
DOI: 10.1017/9781108557740

First published 2018

Printed in the Untied States of America by Sheridan Books, Inc.

A catalogue record for this publication is available from the British Library.

Library of Congress Cataloging-in-Publication Data
NAMES: Obert, Jonathan, author.
TITLE: The six-shooter state : public and private violence
in American politics / Jonathan Obert.
DESCRIPTION: Cambridge, United Kingdom ; New York, NY :
Cambridge University Press, 2018. | Includes bibliographical references and index.
IDENTIFIERS: LCCN 2018017124 | ISBN 9781316515143 (hardback) |
ISBN 9781108454148 (paperback)
SUBJECTS: LCSH: Violence–Political aspects–United States. |
Vigilantes–United States. | Police–United States. | Firearms ownership–United States.
CLASSIFICATION: LCC HV6432 .O24 2018 | DDC 303.60973–dc23
LC record available at https://lccn.loc.gov/2018017124

ISBN 978-1-316-51514-3 Hardback
ISBN 978-1-108-45414-8 Paperback

Additional resources for this publication at www.jonathanobert.com

And the fruit of righteousness is sown in peace of them that make peace.

– James 3:18

Contents

Figures

Tables

Acknowledgments

This book has taken many years to complete, and it never would have reached this point without the generosity, support, feedback, and faith of so many people. This project began as a dissertation at the University of Chicago, where I was fortunate to have a wonderful committee of supportive scholars. John Padgett, John Mearsheimer, Dan Slater, and Paul Staniland have given much of their time and their guidance to this project, which proved crucial in those frequent moments where I wondered whether it would ever see the light of day. Paul Staniland organized a writing group early in the process, and his critical insight, along with the creative and sympathetic advice of Sarah Parkinson and Eric Hundman, allowed me to clarify and articulate my theoretical contribution. Dan Slater and John Mearsheimer, in workshops and in meetings, have been helpful in keeping my ideas honest and clear, and were willing to trust the strange directions this project has taken.

John Padgett has not only been the quintessential advisor – helpful, engaged, supportive, patient, and, most of all, intolerant of bad ideas – but has been a source of unparalleled intellectual guidance, support, and sheer inspiration in every dimension of my academic career. His own scholarship is immensely creative and inspiring on its own, but he has also given me an opportunity to learn at the feet of a true master through collaborative work, scholarly exchange, teaching opportunities, frequent advice, and wonderful conversations. This project simply would have been impossible without his help, and I owe him and his wonderful family my deepest and most abiding gratitude.

Other faculty and staff within the Department of Political Science at the University of Chicago also proved instrumental. I would also like to thank Alex Wendt, who helped me begin this process, as well as Bob Pape, Carles Boix, Patchen Markell, Charles Lipson, Charlie Glaser, Bill Sewell, Bernard Silberman, and Lisa Wedeen, who in workshops and other settings provided memorable and useful feedback on my work. Kathy Anderson has routinely proven her irreplaceability and helpfulness in more ways than I can count.

At Chicago I learned most from my fellow students. My own cohort – in particular, Burak Kadercan, Ian Storey, and Matthias Staisch – included an incredible collection of scholars, who have pushed my work in unpredictable and, for me, highly satisfying directions. Conversations with Ian, Burak, and (especially) Matthias have been the source of many of the best ideas found in this project, and their friendship and brilliance has meant the world to me. Thank you, my friends. Dina Rashad, J. J. McFadden, Jeremy Menchik, Willow Osgood, Marissa Guerrero, Yuna Blajer de la Garza, Keven Ruby, John Schuessler, Jon Caverly, Negeen Pegahi, Chris McIntosh, Michelle Murray, John Stevenson, Takayuki Nishi, Todd Hall, Sarah Johnson, Jade Schiff, Erica Simmons, Morgan Kaplan, Lindsey O'Rourke, Zack Callen, Emily Meierding, David Bholat, Min Hee Go, Brian Fried, Lauren Duquette-Rury, Carolyn Hippolyte, Rose Kelanic, and many others have formed a graduate community of unparalleled inspiration and support. Daragh Grant, in particular, has not only been an invaluable friend but also a continual source of intellectual inspiration, offering incredible feedback, guidance, and a critical eye. Nuno Monteiro, also, has helped immeasurably through his conversations, support, and advice. I am lucky to know both of these scholars.

The Committee on International Relations was also instrumental in providing time and support while completing the early stages of this project. Duncan Snidal and Mark Bradley were incredible directors, while Mimi Smiley, Keisha Yelton-Hunter, Johanna Schloss, Will Gossin-Smith, and E. G. Enbar composed the best staff one could hope for. Instructors in the program – including Michael Reese, Anne Holthoefer, and Qiang Zhou – were always sources of great support and help. In addition to Matthias and Anne, Milena Ang and Diana Kim were wonderful interlocutors, sharing their ideas and passion without reservation. Diana provided important shaping my argument at a key moment, and I treasure her insights and keen historical sensibilities.

I was extremely fortunate in the early days to have a group of fellow scholars to aid in the actual writing of this book – the "Gang of Four" writing group. Chris Haid and Manuel Viedma occasionally and usefully expanded the gang to five, but I must credit Anne Holthoefer, Nick Rush Smith, and Adam Dean with much of what is valuable herein. These three have read and commented on almost every word in this (long) book and have each brought a distinctive voice and a critical eye to its structure, content, and claims. Adam, in particular, has served as one of my most honest and incisive interlocutors, my closest collaborator, and one of my dearest friends. My gratitude to him is without measure.

This book was completed at Amherst College, a wonderfully unique, diverse, and insightful community. The Department of Political Science – Amrita Basu, Kristin Bumiller, Javier Corrales, Tom Dumm, Pavel Machala, Eleonora Mattiacci, Ruxandra Paul, Andrew Poe, Kerry Ratigan, and Austin

Sarat – form an unparalleled group of scholars and friends whose intellectual passion and creativity is never less than inspiring. In particular, Javier and Pavel both provided extremely helpful feedback on portions of this book, while Andrew and Austin have been generous with their time, energy, and support. Tom not only read the entire manuscript, but helped me organize a book workshop in the final push, giving incredible feedback and help on every chapter. Theresa Laizier, Steve Laizier, and Donna Simpter have been instrumental, providing administrative and logistical help and good cheer.

The Dean of Faculty's office at Amherst has provided much support for this project as well. In particular, I'd like to thank Catherine Epstein, Greg Call, Jack Cheney, and Janet Tobin. Elsewhere in the College, I want to acknowledge Vanessa Walker, Dwaipayan Sen, Andy Anderson, Ted Melillo, Adi Gordon, Nusrat Chowdhury, Jan Dizard, and Leah Schmalzbauer, as well as Bryn Geffert, Steve Heim, and Dunstan McNutt at Frost Library and Mary Strunk in the Grants Office. Kevin Sweeney not only read the whole manuscript, but pointed me in some very helpful directions. This project also benefited from conversations with members of the Copeland Colloquium on "The Social Life of Guns," hosted by the College in 2016 and 2017; Jennifer Yida Pan, Chad Kautzer, Nathan Shelton, and Alex Young formed an engaged interdisciplinary sounding board for some of the ideas in this book.

I have had the privilege of working with some wonderful students as well as fantastic research assistants during the writing of this book. Elias Schultz, Joshua Cavé, and Daniel Delgado have done a great job reading portions of this manuscript and helping me with data collection. Members of my First Year Seminar classes, in particular, have been sources of inspiration, forcing me to keep my ideas honest and clear.

Henning Hillman, Hans Joas, Dan Carpenter, Elisabeth Clemens, Anthony Chen, Randall Calvert, Richard White, Dorit Geva, Michael Pfeifer, Larry Isaac, Josh Kertzer, Ben Jones, Bear Braumoeller, Nicholas Parrillo, Ilia Murtazashvili, Meyer Kestnbaum, Audrey Latura, Chris Ansell, Paul Frymer, Chris Smith, Sam Mitrani, Justin Gross, Jeffrey Friedman, Kevin Young, and Ezra Zuckerman have each contributed to this project in a variety of ways. I also want to thank the wonderful staffs at Northeastern Illinois University Library, Northern Illinois University Library, the Chicago Historical Society, Indiana University-Bloomington Library, the University of Illinois-Chicago, the Colorado Historical Society, the Newberry Library, the Huntington Library, the New Orleans Public Library, Tulane University Library, the National Archives and Records Administration, Widener Library, Regenstein Library, Boulder Public Library, Denver Public Library, and Louisiana State University Library for their help locating materials. Audiences at the American Political Science Association, Social Science History Association, and Midwest Political Science Association Annual Conferences, as well as Yale University, the Santa Fe Institute and the Radcliffe Institute for Advanced Study, all provided useful feedback on portions of this manuscript.

I would especially like to thank Richard Bensel, Jim Morone, Tom Dumm, and Daragh Grant for participating in a highly stimulating book conference funded by a Faculty Research Award Program Grant from Amherst College; their feedback has proven absolutely critical in helping refine, reframe, and sharpen every word of this project. Christopher Lura, in turn, provided excellent guidance and copyediting for the manuscript, pointing out numerous areas for improvement and refinement. Thank you all so much for your time and help.

At Cambridge University Press, I'd like to thank Robert Dreesen for his support and faith in this project, as Christina Taylor, Joshua Penney, and Jackie Grant. It has been a pleasure to work with such an efficient and incredible team.

My family and friends have also been sources of help throughout an undertaking we all, I'm sure, doubted would ever be completed. Harley Stroh and Joel Rusnock are the best and most patient friends a person could ask for, while my brother, Simon, my sister, Susy, and their wonderful families have helped in more ways than I could ever acknowledge. My grandma, Jean, and my parents, Mike and Peggy, are exemplars of unconditional support and care – I love all of you so much.

Most of all, however, I need to thank Eleonora Mattiacci and our son, Cosmo. Eleonora is not only my partner, colleague, friend, and inspiration, she is my soul. I cannot imagine life without her. I love you both more than anything.

Note: Portions of Chapter 4 and Chapter 6 of this book were previously published in the following journals:

- "The Co-Evolution of Public and Private Policing in Nineteenth Century Chicago." *Law & Social Inquiry*, (February 2017) https://doi.org/10.1111/lsi.12285.
- "The Six-Shooter Marketplace: 19th Century Gunfighting as Violence Expertise." *Studies in American Political Development*, Vol. 28, No. 1 (April 2014), pp. 49–79.

Abbreviations

AC	*Alexandria Caucasian*
CDP	*Chicago Daily Democratic Press*
CP	*Chicago City Council Proceedings Files, 1833–1871* (Illinois Regional Archives Depository, Northeastern Illinois University)
CTR	*Chicago Tribune*
CWD	*Chicago Weekly Democrat*
CWT	*Chicago Weekly Times*
NDD	*New Orleans Daily Delta*
NOC	*New Orleans Crescent*
NOP	*New Orleans Daily Times-Picayune*
NOR	*New Orleans Republican*
NOT	*New Orleans Times-Democrat*
OC	*Opelousas Courier*

1

Introduction

THE DUAL FACE OF AMERICAN VIOLENCE

On the evening of October 6, 1866, just outside the southern Indiana town of Seymour, several armed and disguised men made their way onto the eastward-bound mail car on the Ohio and Mississippi line. Brandishing pistols, they demanded that the messenger for the Adams Express Company – one of the most important shipping firms in the nation – open the company's safes. The messenger, E. B. Miller, handed over the keys, and the armed men rifled through a small safe in the car, procuring somewhere between $12,000 and $15,000 worth of valuables and money. Miller lacked the keys to the other, larger "through" safe, so the men, noting the box was attached to wheels, rolled it to the edge of the car and pushed it over the side. After binding and gagging the employee, the men pulled the bell signal for the brakes, waited for the train to slow, and jumped off the car into the night. The world's first moving train robbery had – so far – been a success.[1]

After the train stopped and a route agent for the Adams Express Company discovered the bound Miller, he too exited the train and made his way the half mile or so back to Seymour. There, presumably contacting the town constable, he raised a *posse*, which, though finding the unharmed safe near the tracks, was unable to locate the bandits themselves.

The route agent's response was the normal way of handling such an event in the mid-nineteenth century. A victim of a robbery would issue a complaint with the nearest law officer (usually a sheriff or constable), who would then procure a warrant and arrest the suspect. In the event a larger force was needed, the officer would raise a *posse comitatus* of local citizens, who would be granted temporary police powers of arrest. If the suspect was fleeing or posed

1 *Louisville Daily Journal*, October 8, 1866; October 16, 1866.

an immediate risk, in turn, the victim could raise a "hue and cry," through which an officer of the peace and surrounding citizens would be responsible for arresting and detaining the suspect. The failure of the *posse* to find the bandits was unfortunate, but given the amateur participatory nature of law enforcement, perhaps unsurprising.

The story, however, did not end there. The Adams Express Company offered a reward of $5,000 for the capture of the thieves and also enlisted the aid of several private detectives, John Egan (from St. Louis) and Larry Hazen (from Cincinnati), who made their way to Seymour. Once there, they (somewhat surprisingly) were easily able to identify prints from the train leading to the house of Wilkinson Reno, the patriarch of a notorious local family. Though they were able to secure warrants on October 10, the detectives had a strangely difficult time getting local officers to help them with the search of the Reno property.[2]

The detectives undoubtedly knew that Seymour – where the O & M railroad intersected the Jefferson, Madison, and Indianapolis line – had developed a reputation as a den of "cut-throats and highwaymen," largely due to the activities of what became known as the "Reno Gang.[3] The gang – composed of Wilkinson's sons, as well as a number of other affiliates – had already been connected to a counterfeiting and horse thievery ring, as well as a number of bank and safe robberies in the areas surrounding Seymour since the end of the Civil War. The detectives' suspicions immediately centered on three men: Wilkinson's sons John and Simeon, and their associate Frank Sparks. Undeterred by the lack of help among local residents, the detectives arrested the three themselves, taking them to nearby Brownstown for safekeeping.[4]

Despite the arrests, the robbery of October 1866 was only the first foray in a renewed crime spree that would rock the lower Ohio River valley over the next two years. The Reno brothers and Sparks were able to post bail and joined their compatriots in a series of robberies and thefts, including ransacking numerous county treasuries and attempting to rob at least two more trains. In all, the Reno Gang made out with tens of thousands of dollars in banknotes and other valuables, almost none of which was recovered.

The scope of the crimes became a major problem for both the Adams Express Company and local residents. The railroad made it possible not only for the Reno Gang to rob wealth concentrated within specific points of transit but also to escape quickly, thereby outstripping the capacity of local sheriffs and *posses* to mount an effective response. And Seymour, like many areas in the

[2] Rachel Dickinson, *The Notorious Reno Gang: The Wild Story of the West's First Brotherhood of Thieves, Assassins, and Train Robbers* (Guilford, CT: Lyons Press, 2017), 95–96; *Louisville Daily Journal*, October 16, 1866.

[3] *Seymour Times*, August 3, 1865.

[4] Robert Frederick Volland, "The Reno Gang of Seymour" (master's thesis, Indiana University, 1948), 114.

border areas separating north from south after the Civil War, was coping with a number of other challenges. Discharged soldiers and transient laborers frequently made their way through town (becoming prime targets for con artists and thieves), political tensions were running extremely high, and – just as in the South, where the Ku Klux Klan initiated a campaign of terror in Tennessee, Kentucky, and Arkansas, as well as several other states in the run-up to the 1868 elections – Indiana was experiencing a wave of private violence and general disorder.[5]

By mid-1868, both the Adams Express Company and some residents of Jackson County (home of Seymour) began to organize a more robust response to the Gang's activities. In addition to Hazen and Egan, the Adams Express Company enlisted the aid of the famed Chicago-based private security firm, Allan Pinkerton's National Detective Agency, which coordinated a regional hunt for the gang members. Working closely with local sheriffs and police departments, Pinkerton agents arrested several members of the gang in the aftermath of a repeated attempt to rob the O & M line in July 1868, as well as John Reno following a raid on a county treasurer's office in Gallatin, Missouri, in late 1867. (Gallatin was also the site of Jesse James's first robbery the following year.)[6] Perhaps most famously, the agency tracked down several of the gang members (including Frank Reno) to Windsor, Ontario, in 1868, where they worked with the US state department to secure their extradition and transport back to Indiana for trial.[7]

This private detective industry was part of a transformation in policing in the mid-nineteenth century characterized by the growth of new bureaucratic, municipal police departments (replacing the traditional town night watch) and a battery of private detective and security firms emerging in cities throughout the nation.[8] These forces, composed of full-time experts rather than ordinary citizens, patrolled public space, mobilized to suppress ethnic, racial, or labor "disorder", investigated crimes stemming from migration and the growth of the market, and generally oriented themselves to managing the growing cities. Crucially, there were important links between the municipal departments and the private detective agencies; Larry Hazen, for instance, had been a police chief in Cincinnati during the Civil War, while Egan was a longtime St. Louis

5 Emma Lou Thornbrough, *Indiana in the Civil War Era, 1850–1880* (Indianapolis: Indiana Historical Society, 1965), 203–205, 270–272; Allen W. Trelease, *White Terror: The Ku Klux Klan Conspiracy and Southern Reconstruction* (New York: Harper & Row, 1971), 28–185.

6 Volland, "The Reno Gang of Seymour," 151–168; Cleveland Moffett, "The Destruction of the Reno Gang: Stories from the Archives of the Pinkerton Detective Agency," *McClure's Magazine* 4, no. 6 (May 1895): 549–554.

7 Volland, "The Reno Gang of Seymour," 225–253.

8 Eric H. Monkkonen, *Police in Urban America, 1860–1920* (Cambridge: Cambridge University Press, 1981), 49–64; David R. Johnson, *Policing the Urban Underworld: The Impact of Crime on the Development of the American Police, 1800–1887* (Philadelphia: Temple University Press, 1979), 59–64.

municipal detective with experience hunting forgers and thieves across the Midwest.[9] While the Adams Express Company depended on these agents who could easily cross jurisdictions and centralize intelligence, the private detectives, in turn, coordinated their efforts with expert police officers nested in cities like Indianapolis.[10]

Residents of Seymour, on the other hand – apparently deciding that they could not rely on a small force of private detectives – turned to another solution: private vigilantism. Led by a number of eminent citizens (likely including the town's mayor), a group organized the Jackson County Vigilance Committee in the middle of the summer of 1868 to address the crime problem more locally.[11] Despite the efforts of the Pinkerton agents and law officers throughout the Midwest (which had, indeed, yielded a number of important arrests), the committee contended that the "laws of our State are so defective that ... they all favor criminals going unwhipt of justice."[12] Ten days after the gang's train robbery on July 10, 1868, the vigilantes decided to take action: over two hundred hooded figures stopped a train holding three members of the Reno Gang on their way to arraignment in nearby Brownstown, and – while threatening the Pinkerton guards keeping an eye on the men – hung the gang members on a nearby farm.[13] Five days later, three other members of the gang, caught in Illinois and held in Brownstown temporarily until facilities in Seymour could be secured for their arrival, were also killed, again by the Vigilance Committee.[14] Most spectacularly, following the arrest and extradition of Frank Reno and Charlie Anderson from Canada in December later that year (and their reunion with William and Simeon Reno, who had been captured in Indianapolis earlier that summer), the committee attacked the jail in New Albany, Indiana, where the men were being held and lynched them summarily.[15]

The story of the Reno Gang points to a key transformative moment in the history of organized violence in the United States. Indiana in 1868 – situated at both the geographical juxtaposition of the south, west, and north, and at a moment of great social and political upheaval – represents a microcosm of the ways in which the older, republican notion that ordinary citizens were responsible for collective security were decomposing into separate (but relatively equal) public and private forms of violence. On the one hand, both local and state governments throughout the nation were revolutionizing their approaches to organizing coercion; in addition to municipal police forces in

9 *Cleveland Morning-Leader*, February 10, 1862; *Leading Manufacturers and Merchants of Cincinnati and Environs* (New York: International Publishing Company, 1886), 134.

10 Volland, "The Reno Gang of Seymour," 114.

11 *The Wabash Daily Express*, July 13, 1868; ibid., 126–150. Volland contends that the group had been active as early as 1865.

12 ibid., plate xxv. 13 ibid., 197–200. 14 *Terre Haute, Weekly Express*, July 29, 1868.

15 *New Albany Daily Ledger*, December 12, 1868; Volland, "The Reno Gang of Seymour," 254–278.

cities like Indianapolis and Chicago, states were adopting new forms of militia (such as the National Guard, which rose out of the labor and racial struggles of the 1870s). On the other hand, vigilantism – which would crest in the early 1870s before making a comeback in the terrible racial lynching campaigns of the 1880s and 1890s – and the private security industry indicated a shift toward, rather than away from, the notion that private interest should be at the forefront of how violence should be used in society. Private forms of administering punishment, such as citizens' vigilance groups, anti-horse thief associations branches, citizen policing initiatives, and private prosecution societies, would become even more prevalent through the turn of the century and beyond.

Moreover these two nineteenth-century developments – a large-scale increase in public, bureaucratic coercion with an equally large-scale expansion in private forms of violence – set in motion an institutionalized system of coercion that continues to characterize the organization of violence and criminal justice in the United States. The evidence of these two public and private forces working together can be seen everywhere. Private prisons in places like California, for instance, make a profit providing "solutions" to problems they themselves have a vested interest in seeing turned into matters of public criminal law. It is, according to geographer and activist Ruth Wilson Gilmore, impossible to make sense of the "carceral" state without taking into account these private actors.[16] Or consider the fact that a larger-than-ever proportion of those buying guns do so for reasons of personal protection, even as public expenditures on corrections explode and crime rates decline.[17] Even neo-vigilante movements like the Minutemen in Arizona – who "aid" Customs Agents by identifying and apprehending "illegal" migrants from Mexico and Central America – invoke an early American tradition of citizenship in which private actors self-consciously supported the state in law enforcement activities.[18] They build on a rich tradition of tacit cooperation between private

[16] Ruth Wilson Gilmore, *Golden Gulag: Prisons, Surplus, Crisis, and Opposition in Globalizing California* (Berkeley: University of California Press, 2007). Also see Kelly Lytle Hernández, *City of Inmates: Conquest, Rebellion, and the Rise of Human Caging in Los Angeles, 1771–1965* (Chapel Hill: University of North Carolina Press, 2017), 7–15.

[17] Over 60% of those owning a gun do so for reasons of personal protection (a proportion that has increased considerably over the past thirty years). As of 2017, at least 40% of Americans live in a household with at least one firearm. Moreover, expenditures for corrections in American states *also* increased over 141% during that same period (from about 1986 and 2013), outstripping spending on other services like education. www.pewresearch.org/fact-tank/2017/06/22/key-takeaways-on-americans-views-of-guns-and-gun-ownership/, accessed November 29, 2017; Michael Mitchell and Michael Leachman, *Changing Priorities: State Criminal Justice Reforms and Investments in Education*, Center on Budget and Policy Priorities, October 2014, 7.

[18] Harel Shapira, *Waiting for Jose: The Minutemen's Pursuit of America* (Princeton, NJ: Princeton University Press, 2013).

movements organized to use force to ensure moral or legal compliance and state police power.[19]

At the same time, these developments also create a theoretical puzzle for our conceptions of states and the protection they offer. Although it takes many forms and has many gradations, a monopoly over the legitimate capacity to define the organization of violence is for most political theorists the key defining attribute of the state.[20] Violence itself, of course, is a complex concept: some have limited their conception to the physical destruction committed by people intending to harm one another, while others believe violence can also be more indirect – a property, for instance, of inequality or racism (this book generally adopts the former conception).[21] What many political theorists mean when they talk about violence is physical coercion: that is, the state should preserve within its own organizational apparatus (e.g., its own police or military forces) the power to use physical harm to defend against threats and to protect its subjects, and that those same powers should generally be denied to citizens themselves. Hence, even though most states preserve some legal right to, say, self-defense in emergencies (when agents of the state cannot reach a party in danger in time) or the right to physically discipline children, those rights are generally closely circumscribed by the law; in other words, the state is ultimately supposed to have the power to define which groups or individuals can and cannot use physical harm against one another.

This capacity to define the right to use force, however, becomes much more complex in a situation in which *both* the state and nonstate actors effectively coordinate violence independently but in concert with one another. In the United States, private actors like the Seymour vigilance committee used force that was not officially sanctioned by the law, yet did so in order to "enforce" the law. Similarly, though private detective agencies were technically "legal," this was not the result of an explicit authorization on the part of a governing authority – indeed, since many detectives were also deputized by the state, even the supposedly "private" nature of the agencies was somewhat unclear until well into the nineteenth century (as Chapter 4 will show). Moreover, they often operated in a gray area in terms of the actual practices they used; detectives Egan and Hazen, for instance, used citizen's arrest powers to try to detain the Reno brothers and Frank Sparks, but limits of this power were hard to define and were rarely explicitly authorized or challenged by state actors. Instead, they relied on an older, republican conception of state power in which private citizens *themselves* could determine how to use force for protection.

19 Iris Marion Young, "The Logic of Masculinist Protection: Reflections on the Current Security State," *Signs: Journal of Women in Culture and Society* 29, no. 1 (2003): 1–25.

20 For important interpretations, see Anthony Giddens, *The Nation-State and Violence* (Berkeley: University of California Press, 1985), 7–31; Gianfranco Poggi, *The State: Its Nature, Development, and Prospects* (Stanford, CA: Stanford University Press, 1990), 5–25.

21 For a good overview of the debates, see Randall Collins, *Violence: A Micro-Sociological Theory* (Princeton, NJ: Princeton University Press, 2009), 19–25.

The growth of these private forms of violence alongside the bureaucratic development of state police and military agencies had important implications for institutional development in the United States Private violence experts did not *compete* with the state in offering protection, but rather, even as the state increased its bureaucratic capacity to manage force, they collaborated with public officers, sharing personnel and resources.[22] A dual system emerged in which a key duty of state capacity – the responsibility to protect – became distributed to a wide variety of public *and* private actors, legal and "illegal" alike.

Where and how did this dual public and private system arise? The core argument of this book is that this institutional transformation was largely the result of a process I call "jurisdictional decoupling." Jurisdictions are both a set of rules determining the legal distribution of rights, duties, obligations, and responsibilities in particular contexts, as well as the name for geographical units of governance, such as counties, towns, and so forth. Jurisdictional decoupling, in turn, means that the rules helping to define the social order in a given jurisdictional context – the legal expectation, for instance, that members of a town or county ought to be willing to participate in chasing down criminals – are no longer sustained by the actual day-to-day relationships allowing actors (individuals, firms, associations, etc.) to practice social control against others. This process occurred at different times and across different jurisdictions, but it usually led to the same result: older forms of private participation in public security no longer worked the way they once had, splitting public security from private effort, but displacing neither.

Jurisdictions like Jackson County were built on what I am calling a "republican" model – "ordinary" white male citizens were expected to participate in defending their political communities against domestic and foreign threats, and did so at each jurisdictional level. The theory of the republican model is that duty, virtue, and freedom were all intimately linked to the larger concerns of a community, and that the risks and expense of a "permanent" policing apparatus to the economic and political freedom of citizens were too high.

Underlying these rules for social order was a system of control embedded in everyday social relations. White men, for instance, took over the responsibility of protecting their communities, but were able to do so because they were also largely powerful in other aspects of day-to-day social life. To provide enforcement, jurisdictions linked or "coupled" everyday forms of power, based on personal wealth, status, or other ways in which people related to each other,

[22] The term "violence experts" covers those with a commitment to cultivating and using skills in violence (broadly construed) as a primary vocation. It does not necessarily mean "professionalization" in the contemporary sense, although in Chapter 6 I trace the emergence of a class of such experts who developed a careerist and professional identity. See Jonathan Obert, "The Six-Shooter Marketplace: 19th-Century Gunfighting as Violence Expertise," *Studies in American Political Development* 28, no. 1 (2014): 49–79.

to more abstract rules of social order, in which the "duties" and "rights" of citizens were laid out and articulated. Together rules for social order and social relations of social control helped make coercive enforcement appear as though there really was no distinction between public security and private effort.

This ambiguous distinction between private effort and public security was the essence of republican security institutions. County militia, the town watch, and old law enforcement roles like the sheriff, constable, and so forth were the domain of amateurs rather than professionals. In southern and western jurisdictions, private participation in violence was particularly important. Maintaining slavery in the south, for instance, depended on ordinary white citizens being willing to use violence to police and reinforce bondage, and many were required to participate in formally organized slave patrols.[23] Additionally, the continual warfare with native groups in the expanding West and Southwest was largely the domain of local militia units, since the early colonial period had provided the main form of mobilization to seize land and remove tribes.[24] The nation had only a very small standing army at the beginning of the nineteenth century and, before the 1830s, almost no bureaucratic police or violence experts. As such, whether or not residents held republican ideological beliefs, the institutions on which they depended to maintain law and order were characterized by the expectation that, ultimately, citizens were responsible for public security.

The problem was that the link between the rules of social order on which institutions were premised and the relations among actors allowing them to control one another in day-to-day social interactions could fail to work as intended. In Seymour, for instance, the Reno family had a powerful constituency of allies, making it difficult for members of the local community to help officers arrest the Reno brothers. As early Jackson County pioneers, the family had been quite successful putting down roots in the community by becoming active members of the local Methodist church, for example.[25] Moreover, a number of family members speculated in the local real estate market, building close business ties with some of the area's most prominent settlers, while others had a sort of "Robin Hood" reputation, distributing some of the proceeds of their crimes to friends and neighbors in need.[26]

At the same time, it was also clear the Reno family had many powerful enemies both in Seymour and elsewhere. The family had been suspected of using arson to drive the values down on properties they wished to obtain and seem to

23 Sally E. Hadden, *Slave Patrols: Law and Violence in Virginia and the Carolinas* (Cambridge, MA: Harvard University Press, 2001).

24 Peter Rhoads Silver, *Our Savage Neighbors: How Indian War Transformed Early America* (New York: W. W. Norton, 2008).

25 Volland, "The Reno Gang of Seymour," 13–16.

26 Volland, "The Reno Gang of Seymour," 60–80; Robert William Shields, *Seymour, Indiana, and the Famous Story of the Reno Gang* (Seymour, IN: R.W. Shields, 1939), 29.

have engaged in financial chicanery involving mortgage manipulation.[27] These activities created much local animosity – Seymour was a booming frontier railroad center, and many new settlers became quite concerned about the bad reputation that the town was developing. In a system that depended on private participation for punishment and arrest, the family's alliances were enough to shield them from any serious attempts at prosecution, but there were many who would have liked to see them punished nonetheless. In this, they agreed with the Adams Express Company, which found it frustrating to have to rely on local citizens to punish criminals they felt acted more like organized criminal syndicates. Traditional rules concerning law enforcement had decoupled from the relations undergirding control over local social life.

The inability of the local system to "work" – the decoupling between the rules to which residents were subject in terms of organizing law enforcement and the social control relations among residents on the ground – had important effects. In Seymour, those opposed to the gang took the law into their own hands; that is, they mobilized themselves as a *posse* without seeking the imprimatur of the law. They claimed that they were forced to do so because the power of the Reno Gang over many in the area undermined the operation of the county's legitimate legal apparatus. Which, of course, depended on private mobilization.

The Adams Express Company, too, relied on a traditional mechanism – the capacity for individuals to secure special deputization to arrest suspects. The difference was that they hired experts with experience in the new police departments, who served as private investigators for fees. These experts were able to travel across jurisdictions and investigate the Reno Gang's activities throughout the region. Unlike the vigilantes, their adaptation was built on professionalism and expertise rather than popular sentiment.

What caused decoupling? I argue that, in Seymour and elsewhere, two important social developments of the nineteenth century – the Market Revolution and the Civil War – generated new forms of rule instability, physical mobility, and social ambiguity. These phenomena, in turn, upended the link between the the ways in which social order was supposed to be enforced and the capacity for powerful actors to practice actual social control through their everyday social relationships with others. The Market Revolution – that cluster of shifts in industrial production, new kinds of wage labor, and transportation building that characterized the Jacksonian and late antebellum period – created new ways for people to relate to each other. As people moved from place to place and previously marginalized communities gained new rights and took advantage of various opportunities, it was increasingly difficult for traditional political officials in towns like Seymour to control residents. Policing had depended on the personal knowledge of neighbors and acquaintances rather

27 Volland, "The Reno Gang of Seymour," 60–81.

than expert, full-time investigators and officers, but the presence of strangers made this knowledge hard to come by.

The Civil War, on the other hand, produced important shifts in the rules for how society was ordered. In the Reconstruction South, for instance, new constitutional guarantees considerably expanded the political rights of African Americans. However, these rights were not accompanied by shifts in access to day-to-day forms of relational power. Those who did have the resources to control the economic well-being of their communities – usually white people – sought techniques outside the law to enforce their status. Thus, even where people *did* know each other, changes in political rights challenged traditional ways through which they tried to exert their control.

Similarly, the conclusion of the Civil War also led to an explosion in the forming of new territories in the trans–Mississippi West; the problem was that territorial institutions depended on divide-and-rule and the outsourcing of law enforcement to local communities, while the new settlers themselves were increasingly tied to one another through chains of trade, communication, and transportation. As in Indiana, railroads and shipping companies simply could not rely on local sheriffs to protect their highly mobile property. In these kinds of settings, the rules characterizing the order of republican society – based on a principle of private participation in civic protection – were no longer sustained by the kinds of intimate day-to-day social relations that originally allowed such private effort to flourish.

Like residents of Seymour, however, Americans continued to rely on the institutional practices they knew best – the *posse comitatus*, the militia, special deputization, etc. – even in the midst of these transformations. Because the underlying link between rules and relations that originally allowed those practices to work had changed, they began to have new effects. Entrepreneurs like Allan Pinkerton transformed special deputization into an opportunity to develop for-profit policing services; community factions, unable to work within a law enforcement system based on strong local ties of hierarchy, deference, and control, instead used the *posse* outside the law.

Crucially, *public* officials too continued to rely on traditional techniques, leading ironically to institutional change. In the midst of cities in which residents were increasingly anonymous and mobile, deputization continued to provide a mechanism for officials to put police forces on a permanent, professionalized footing. In southern states during Reconstruction, fundamental changes in the professionalism and militarism of domestic policing – induced largely by Republican governors attempting to expand and consolidate their power – paved the way for the collapse of the traditional local militia company and the growth of new kinds of professionalized state police. Whites who regained control of these states in the mid–1870s in hopes of "redeeming" their states did not abandon these institutions, but instead used them to complement the violent private forms of racial control accompanying Jim Crow. These changes in state coercion complemented the growth of quasi-professional and permanent National Guard units in northern states, where labor strife made recourse to traditional amateur volunteer militia untenable.

In other words, Americans did not intend to reorganize their coercive institutions; it was simply that the basis for those institutions had changed in response to massive political and economic changes, and those older practices became the seedbed for new kinds of organizations. Moreover, where previously the public and private security interests of citizens had been seen by most as almost indistinguishable, the organizational split between the public and private forms created categories that allowed Americans to clearly distinguish parochial concerns of capitalists, laborers, and other specific social groups from the shared (but completely imaginary and abstract) "public interest." At the same time, because distinct public and private organizations were actually interlinked through the people who participated in them, these groups only rarely became direct rivals. Instead, more often than not, they aided each other. Participation in violence through vigilantism and marketized private security continued to be quite defensible for Americans who viewed both vigilance and making money as virtues of citizenship.

This argument is important for several reasons. For one, it helps provide an institutional reason for why, exactly, a nation with a powerful legal and political tradition of self-protection – one that only seems to have grown stronger in recent years – could also generate such a massive public security bureaucracy. The puzzle of domestic American violence – from gun crime to mass incarceration, to cycles of collective protest – is often framed as a matter of constitutional distinctiveness (e.g., the legacies of the Second Amendment), social pathology (e.g., racial or class antagonism), or macroeconomics (e.g., neoliberal or capitalist political economy). This book's argument provides, instead, an *institutional* account, suggesting that we need to understand the republican logic of coercion in early jurisdictions like cities, counties, and states in order to make sense of why both self-defense and robust public security could seem so compatible.

For another, this book also helps us reconsider what states actually *do* with regard to their core function of protecting citizens. Much social science scholarship on the state adopts, at least implicitly, the assumption that a strong state is one that maintains a firm hold over violence in society, and that citizens cede the capacity to use force to a central government – in Thomas Hobbes' terms, a "Leviathan" – so that they don't have to rely on their own devices for protection. Reality, of course, is much messier than this: many states universally acknowledged to be "powerful" nevertheless also appear to permit a great deal of control over force to private parties. By examining a series of moments at which the relationship between public and private violence is starkly revealed and by providing a theory to explain why these two kinds of coercion could work together, this book provides a new set of tools to understand some of the realities of how authority over coercion works.

VIOLENCE IN AMERICAN POLITICAL DEVELOPMENT

Scholars have not, certainly, ignored the reality of violence in US state formation. A number of accounts have begun to explore the ways in which, in particular, the late nineteenth-century American state was more active in coordinating and organizing violence than the stereotype of a "stateless" United States had led us to believe.[28] Indeed, these works – in particular the foundational account of political scientist Ira Katznelson, who identifies a uniquely American commitment to "flexible capacity" in the use of violence – challenge the notion, inherited from influential political economists like Robert Bates and Mancur Olson, that centralizing violence in the state is the primary way to ensure the value of protection as a form of public security, and that deviations from this model lead to state failure and anarchic competition.[29]

These political economic approaches treat violence as a form of *protection*, which requires a natural monopoly to function the right way. That is, violence can be used both to extract resources directly from populations through force *and* can be used to *preempt* threats to that ability.[30] For this reason, depending on various constraints (such as the "stationarity" or immobility of the organization made up of violence experts), the capacity to use force will

[28] See William D. Adler and Andrew J. Polsky, "Building the New American Nation: Economic Development, Public Goods, and the Early U.S. Army," *Political Science Quarterly* 125, no. 1 (2010): 87–110; Brian Balogh, *A Government Out of Sight: The Mystery of National Authority in Nineteenth-Century America* (Cambridge: Cambridge University Press, 2009); Paul Frymer, "Building an American Empire: Territorial Expansion in the Antebellum Era," *University of California-Irvine Law Review* 1 (2011): 913–954; Laura Jensen, *Patriots, Settlers, and the Origins of American Social Policy* (Cambridge: Cambridge University Press, 2003); Desmond King and Robert C. Lieberman, "Ironies Of State Building: A Comparative Perspective on the American State," *World Politics* 61, no. 3 (2009): 547–588; William J. Novak, "The Myth of the 'Weak' American State," *The American Historical Review* 113, no. 3 (2008): 752–772; Mark Wilson, *The Business of Civil War: Military Mobilization and the State, 1861–1865* (Baltimore: Johns Hopkins University Press, 2006). For traditional American Political Development literature on the American state, see Richard Franklin Bensel, *Yankee Leviathan: The Origins of Central State Authority in America, 1859–1877* (Cambridge: Cambridge University Press, 1990); Stephen Skowronek, *Building a New American State: The Expansion of National Administrative Capacities, 1877–1920* (Cambridge: Cambridge University Press, 1982).

[29] Ira Katznelson, "Flexible Capacity: The Military and Early American Statebuilding," in *Shaped By War and Trade: International Influences on American Political Development*, eds. Ira Katznelson and Martin Shefter (Princeton, NJ: Princeton University Press, 2002), 82–110.

[30] Scholarship in this tradition includes: Robert H Bates, *Prosperity and Violence: The Political Economy of Development* (New York: W.W. Norton, 2001); Diego Gambetta, *The Sicilian Mafia: The Business of Private Protection* (Cambridge, MA: Harvard University Press, 1993); Frederic Chapin Lane, *Profits from Power: Readings in Protection Rent and Violence-Controlling Enterprises* (Albany: SUNY Press, 1979); Mancur Olson, "Dictatorship, Democracy, and Development," *American Political Science Review* 87, no. 3 (1993): 567–576; Thomas C. Schelling, *Choice and Consequence* (Cambridge, MA: Harvard University Press, 1984); Charles Tilly, *Coercion, Capital, and European States, AD 990–1990* (Oxford: Blackwell, 1990).

likely become dominated by a single actor with a unitary security interest. The resources gained from offering protection are maximized, in short, when violence is monopolized by a single organization or actor.

The upshot of these approaches is that protection is also explicitly a public good, in which certain groups and individuals cannot be excluded from its benefits and the usage of it by one person does not affect its availability to be used by others.[31] The reason for this is that the more successful violence experts are in centralizing force, the fewer cases they will need to actually *use* that capacity, in part because they maintain the predominance of coercive power which is common knowledge to all actors. Thus, deterrence – which is less costly than actually imposing damage – substitutes for the actual use of force, allowing *all* actors within the purview of the violence centralizer to inhabit a more orderly society. Private capacity to use force, then, poses a challenge to this order, and requires the creation of a regime of state suppression to maintain the public good benefits of protection *and* the value of that protection to the extracting state.[32]

The American experience poses an important challenge to this perspective. Rather than incorporate and bureaucratize force within powerful militaries and central police, as many European states did in the process of their formation, Katznelson argues that the United States was able to combine simple state oversight with the outsourcing of key coercive functions to small, easily expandable private and public organizations like militia units, filibusters, privateers, and a small frontier army. The policing and military system of the United States was not "weak" – it was different, capable of quickly aggregating force if necessary (through popular participation) while retaining a skeletal, small permanent force. In large measure, this force was the result of unique peripheral threats, which were highly complex and local and could not be easily addressed within the framework of a centralized military or the constraints of funding imposed by federalism. But, according to Katznelson, the approach was nevertheless quite effective in terms of sustaining state interests: coercive force built around such "flexible capacity," he claims, "not only solved its own multidimensional challenges but also provided answers to the country's great

[31] Austrian school economists and some scholars of spontaneous order don't believe that public security is necessarily a public good and discount the monopoly logic of protection rents. Such accounts, however, also tend to see private and public forms of security as competing rather than mutually constitutive, as in this book. See Edward Peter Stringham, *Private Governance: Creating Order in Economic and Social Life* (Oxford: Oxford University Press, 2015), 113–133; Erwin A. Blackstone and Simon Hakim, "Competition Versus Monopoly in the Provision of Police," *Security Journal* 26, no. 2 (2013): 157–179.

[32] The best descriptions of this logic can be found in Mancur Olson, *Power and Prosperity: Outgrowing Communist and Capitalist Dictatorships* (New York: Basic Books, 2000); Schelling, *Choice and Consequence*; Charles Tilly, "War Making and State Making as Organized Crime," in *Bringing the State Back In*, eds. Peter Evans, Dietrich Rueschemeyer, and Theda Skocpol (Cambridge: Cambridge University Press, 1985), 169–187.

normative question of how to make sovereignty and popular rule compatible. It also helped to solve the practical problem of how to rule over a great variety of people and a vast expanse of territory without compromising the country's unity or sovereignty."[33] The challenge of how to provide protection, which scholars argued was empirically resolved by the construction of a powerful, centralized monopolizer of violence capable of providing for the "public" good, could also be solved by the fusion of private and public coercion through institutions that maintained popular approval and participation.

This was not merely a matter of controlling slaves and removing native groups, though these factors were absolutely critical. States and municipalities in the United States, as historian William Novak and others have emphasized, possessed a great deal of "police power" – or capacity to enact regulations over many domains of social life.[34] Local governments could regulate everything from where to store firewood to the price merchants could charge for certain kinds of goods. According to Novak, this regulatory infrastructure created a powerful form of state authority that, in contrast to the European model, was "organized more horizontally. Power is separated and divided rather than integrated. Jurisdictions frequently overlap, and authority is routinely delegated downward to relatively autonomous sub-units of government."[35] This type of distribution of authority, in turn, allows for open-ended but highly local forms of state intervention.

State formation in the United States thus unsettles the logic of protection rents in several ways. First, it demonstrates empirically that effective enforcement of legal norms and protection of individuals need not require a centralized violence expert. Instead, multiple, fragmented, and often contradictory forms of organized violence can overlap and coexist while still providing effective governance. Moreover, these forms of organized violence can be private or public – as long as the state retains its capacity to coordinate and shape violent activity, the actual infrastructure of violence can take on multiple forms.

Second, the American experience points to the need to look beyond the functional logic of violence as an often costly tool of government extraction to view the ways that popular violence can actually be *constitutive* of state power. Manifest Destiny, the Mexican-American War, and other nineteenth-century expansionary endeavors provided opportunities for participation in violence to

33 Katznelson, "Flexible Capacity: The Military and Early American Statebuilding," 101.

34 On police power, see Markus Dirk Dubber, "'The Power to Govern Men and Things': Patriarchal Origins of the Police Power in American Law," *Buffalo Law Review* 52, no. 4 (2004); Markus Dirk Dubber, *The Police Power: Patriarchy and the Foundations of American Government* (New York: Columbia University Press, 2005); William J. Novak, *The People's Welfare: Law and Regulation in Nineteenth-Century America* (Chapel Hill: University of North Carolina Press, 1996); Christopher L. Tomlins, "Law, Police, and the Pursuit of Happiness in the New American Republic," *Studies in American Political Development* 4, no. 1 (1990): 3–34.

35 Novak, "The Myth of the 'Weak' American State," 766.

help seal and consolidate political membership in the American nation (while also opening up rifts about what kind of nation the United States would be). While the extraction and institutional development associated with violent undertakings have, of course, shaped state bureaucratic development, such developments need not always lead to the dichotomous outcome of either the expansion of state capacity or a descent into violent competition and anarchy. Instead, they can produce a form of popular participation in violence that makes the distinction between private and public interests highly ambiguous. In these forms, volunteer militias, vigilance committees, and even for-profit policing can remain "public" services for participants despite being solely the purview of private individuals.[36]

More profoundly, it was not always clear to Americans that they *should* look to the state for protection. Scholars have demonstrated how deeply embedded direct collective violent action was in maintaining local norms or establishing social boundaries for both Northerners and Southerners.[37] While seemingly autonomous forms of state coercion *did* emerge during the mid-nineteenth century, most scholars of American political development have not addressed the question of whether these forms continued to present fundamental alternatives to state coercion that nevertheless remained compatible with a more powerful regulatory state.

Additionally, scholars tracing the changes in particular coercive institutions in the United States – including municipal police forces, vigilante committees, private detective agencies, and state militias – have rarely placed these accounts into a shared analytic framework, treating them as separate (and often opposed) developments. For example, historian Eric Monkkonen's work on the origins and development of the municipal police in the United States, which argues that such departments were part of the general diffusion of municipal reform agendas in the United States in the late nineteenth century, not only largely ignores the important role that private detective agencies played supplying resources and individuals to municipal police departments in the early years

36 Adam Malka, "The Rights of Men Power, Policing, and the Making of the Liberal State, 1812–1870" (PhD diss., The University of Wisconsin-Madison, 2012), 42–43.

37 Richard Maxwell Brown, *Strain of Violence: Historical Studies of American Violence And Vigilantism* (Oxford: Oxford University Press, 1975); Christian G. Fritz, "Popular Sovereignty, Vigilantism, and the Constitutional Right of Revolution," *Pacific Historical Review* 63, no. 1 (February 1994): 39–66; Paul A. Gilje, *The Road to Mobocracy: Popular Disorder in New York City, 1763–1834* (Chapel Hill: University of North Carolina Press, 1987); Marjoleine Kars, *Breaking Loose Together: The Regulator Rebellion in Pre-Revolutionary North Carolina* (Chapel Hill: University of North Carolina Press, 2002); Pauline Maier, "Popular Uprisings and Civil Authority in Eighteenth-Century America," *The William and Mary Quarterly* 27, no. 1 (1970): 4–35; Michael J. Pfeifer, *The Roots of Rough Justice: Origins of American Lynching* (Urbana: University of Illinois Press, 2011); Christopher Waldrep, *The Many Faces of Judge Lynch: Extralegal Violence and Punishment in America* (Basingstoke, England: Palgrave Macmillan, 2002).

of their development, but also views the adoption of such departments as a somewhat natural step in the modernization of local bureaucratic capacity.[38]

But police departments were fundamentally conservative organizations in the same way that private detective firms were: both build directly on a system that fused private efforts to public interest. That the police became uniquely public institutions while detective agencies were private did not imply that only the former could be authorized agents of coercion. Both institutions were born of an antebellum tradition of coercive organization and both became organizational innovations only when they became distinct from one another. In other words, we cannot tell their stories by separating them. They coevolved and helped shape each other at their very points of origin. Indeed, this coevolutionary process did not stop even after each gained institutional identity: legal devices like the special constabulary deputization and the hiring of private detectives to coordinate with public police continued to blur and unsettle the divide between public and private violence in American cities throughout the nineteenth century.

In short, I argue that a more integrated story is necessary to explain the puzzle of how that force developed over time. The next section outlines the organization of the book, which addresses these concerns directly.

ORGANIZATION OF THE CHAPTERS

Changes in the organization of violence in the nineteenth century United States exhibited important variation in terms of timing and type. However, this variation itself can be partly explained by examining the unique local American jurisdictions like counties or parishes, municipalities, and townships, each with their own types of coercive institutions. This book addresses differences in the creation of the public and private institutionalization of violence across both time *and* space, linking micro- and meso-level examinations of the organization of force in specific counties and towns at particularly critical historical moments, to a macro-level narrative about the effects of the double transition of the Market Revolution and the Civil War on different jurisdictions over time. I take, in other words, a microscope and quickly zoom out to show how local patterns scaled to shed light on regional variation across time.

Chapter 2 lays out a theory of institutional change in coercive enforcement as the decoupling of jurisdictional rules of social order from day-to-day relational forms of social control. This theory is built around two moves: The first move shows that, to be effective, coercive institutions depend on a link between abstract rules for social order and day-to-day forms of social control; I refer to this link as "coupling." In the United States, that link made collective security depend on the efforts of amateur citizen participation, a republican fusion of public and private violence.

38 Monkkonen, *Police in Urban America*.

However, that link could come under threat from developments like the Civil War and Market Revolution. Hence, the second move shown in this chapter traces to trace how the republican fusion was undermined through jurisdictional *de*coupling – in other words, how instability in rules, social ambiguity, and physical mobility operated together to challenge and reorder the rules and relations making up coercive institutions. Together these phenomena created a kind of unsettled social frontier, in which older forms of social control and social order no longer worked together as they once did. Within each key American jurisdiction, in turn, older republican institutions were slowly transformed into a dual system in which the development of explicitly public forms of state violence coincided with a new private system of violence, organized on behalf of firms, communal groups, and individuals.

Chapter 3 introduces the empirical components of the book, demonstrating how the logic of jurisdictional coupling and decoupling worked in two very similar but distinct northern Illinois counties in the early 1840s. On the face of it, this case unpacks the story of a now largely forgotten explosion of vigilantism in the Rock River counties of Ogle and Lee (which for simplicity, I refer to as Ogle-Lee) in northern Illinois, in which local notables mobilized vigilance committees to combat a loosely organized band of horse-thieves and counterfeiters known as the "Banditti" in the late 1830s and early 1840s. However, this case also sheds light on how the link between practical authority and formal institutional rules was supposed to work, and how highly local experiences of physical mobility and social ambiguity could unravel traditional republican institutions.

Comparing the Ogle-Lee experience to nearby Kane County, which faced a similar threat from the Banditti and had virtually identical demographic characteristics, I show that, because of the pattern of their local social relations in Ogle-Lee, office holders lost their capacity to identify a shared people with a unified interest and, consequently, ceased to rely on local legal institutions. In Kane County, on the other hand, office-holders were able to retain their dominance over legal institutions by maintaining what I call "enclosed authority" over non-officeholders. Different patterns of network relations existing within the same kinds of jurisdictional rules, in other words, help explain why Ogle-Lee turned to vigilantism to combat the Banditti while Kane County continued to rely on county courts.

Counties like Ogle, Lee, and Kane (as well as Jackson County in Indiana) were all part of a larger market revolution organized around Chicago, which was quickly becoming the most important city west of New York.[39] Chapter 4 shows how this city's transportation and market system led to radical increases in anonymity and mobility, fundamentally changing the social relations on which the law enforcement rules of the city had been built. As Chicago became

39 William Cronon, *Nature's Metropolis: Chicago and the Great West* (New York: W. W. Norton, 1992).

a focal point for trade and infrastructure, the clear distinctions between social communities and the capacity to delegate enforcement through residential and ethnic segregation to local neighborhoods was compromised. This was particularly evident in those spaces of social mixing and anonymity in the city where local mechanisms of control could work least well – railroad depots, hack driver stands (hack drivers were the cabbies of the nineteenth century), hotels, taverns, and city streets. To manage these areas, which were redefining the idea of public space, city elders turned to new regulations as well as the use of deputization, a classic republican practice of expanding law enforcement capacity. The city saw an explosion in anti–public disorder regulation aimed at precisely these kinds of interstitial zones late in the 1860s, while, in 1853, the Common Council reorganized the city police into a separate administrative department under the control of the mayor and a select committee.

The municipal police in Chicago therefore reflected not a complete organizational novelty, but rather the expansion and transformation of the old watch/constable system in spaces where delegation of enforcement didn't seem to work. Indeed, the case of Chicago demonstrates that the creation of a public bureaucracy for violence, like the municipal police, was an aftershock of the breakdown of the old fusion between public and private forms of protection rather than a fundamental break from a traditional form of communally organized protection.

The concurrent creation of the new private detective industry in Chicago reinforces this point. The private detective industry in the city and the public police force actually grew together – sharing people, ideas, institutions, political authority, and resources – because they both grew from the same assumption that private and public security could be indistinguishable. Private detectives like Allan Pinkerton, William Douglass, and Cyrus Bradley (among many others) gained law enforcement experience in Cook County, which they parleyed into a profitable private careers as fee-for-service detectives for wealthy individuals, railroads, and even towns and cities.

Interestingly, private detectives did not view themselves solely as self-interested capitalists, but rather believed they were serving a public good. Allan Pinkerton, for example, was a vigorous participant in debates over municipal policing, and in the creation of the secret service, effectuated by his close friendship with the former railroad chief George McClellan, became a proponent of a publicly funded national criminal database. Indeed, both municipal police and the private security industry exploded after the Civil War, as veterans returned and harnessed their new skills in violence to the burgeoning demand for order in the postbellum city.

The Civil War and its aftermath had a major effect on rules and relations not only on antebellum coercion in local jurisdictions like counties and municipalities, but also in states. This was particularly true in the South – the focus of Chapter 5 explores the emergence of both a powerful new militia in Southern states under occupation by the North, as well as the growth of large-scale racial vigilantism. During Reconstruction, the South was the site of the most aggressive attempt to expand federal control over violence in its history. As countless scholars have demonstrated, this project of changing and reforming jurisdictional rules – at the federal level – failed miserably, as the end of military occupation in 1876 and the Posse Comitatus Act of 1878 curtailed the use of federal intervention into local disorder in Southern states.

At the same time, despite the collapse of Reconstruction, the freeing of the slaves, and occupation on the part of the Northern Army, Reconstruction led to a highly ironic consequence – whites, who retained most of the social and economic power at the level of day-to-day life, launched a series of effective vigilante crusades against the Reconstruction Era government of the state. Ultimately, after gaining control over the state apparatus, these "Redeemers" did not abandon the important reforms in state capacity pioneered by Republican rule during Reconstruction, but rather bent them to their own efforts at policing the racial order. As a result, the new, powerful public security apparatus designed, in part, to protect freedmen – the state militia – became the National Guard, which worked in conjunction with private, systematic vigilantism in the late nineteenth century to manage the African-American population.

I explore this process by focusing on a critical juncture in the development of state control over violence and in the legal changes in late Reconstruction: the organization of a group of reformers active in Louisiana called the "White League." The White League was a violent, paramilitary racist vigilante group which maintained a highly public presence and was a crucial organizational resource for those who wanted to overturn Reconstruction in the bitter election of 1874. Originally envisioned as a state-wide political party, it quickly gained a military cast, working through Democratic ward and parish committees, as well as through traditional militia organization. As such, it was based on a form of jurisdictional coupling in which the authority of "the people" (as an exclusive category composed of relatively wealthy white men), was coupled to the state's traditions of representative politics, which helped reproduce both the semblance of legitimacy as well as the actual control of wealthy planters. The League, in turn, adapted this form of authority to provide the foundation on which a more coercive and powerful state could be made after casting the Reconstruction government aside in 1876. They did so by helping to reestablish a regime that had the support of both Louisiana's elite capitalist class and the majority of its white residents, one deriving its authority from a broad participatory racial order enforced by both the state and private actors.

This institutional change was possible only because the traditional coupling of white male authority, built through their economic and social relational ties, to the rules of representative institutions was thrown into extreme disruption by Reconstruction (when African Americans and poor whites began to vote in large numbers), upending the capacity for those men to remain firmly under the control of those who belonged to the polity. The violent racial and political struggles in Louisiana parishes (particularly in the northwest and central portions of the state in 1866, 1868, and 1872) were thus interpreted by white Democrats – especially elite landowners and merchants – as a much needed political reform. They were a means, in other words, of correcting the "abuses" of the carpetbagger regimes of Governors Henry Warmouth and William Kellogg. By the time of the Colfax Massacre in 1874, in which over a hundred African Americans were killed in a dispute over political offices in Colfax Parish, the groundwork for a paramilitary political party was in place.

Despite being viewed by most historians as atavistic racists – though they were certainly that – the White League were also self-proclaimed state modernizers: by claiming to reform the abuses of carpetbaggers, they were also inadvertently strengthening the unique power of the state to manage the affairs of what had been the purview of traditional personal social relations. This, in turn, helps us rethink the coercive aspects of the Jim Crow state, which allowed police, sheriffs, and prison wardens to act along with private individuals and firms as arbiters of racial control, bolstering both state and private coercion. The modernizing efforts of the post–Reconstruction South were ultimately rooted in a tradition of private violence that they could not escape, as the horrifying epidemic of lynching in Louisiana and elsewhere after 1880 attests.

Chapter 6 – which explores the rise of the gunfighter – expands the focus onto territorial politics in the trans–Mississippi West. In the aftermath of the Civil War, the federal government engaged in an attempt to incorporate the region by expanding territorial jurisdiction, which, in turn, depended on divide-and-rule forms of control. In this system, local towns and assemblies were responsible for managing their own protection – by electing their own sheriffs and constables, for instance — while federal appointees were in charge of the territory as a whole.

The problem was that these new jurisdictional rules did not map to social relations on the ground, which were increasingly interlinked in a growing market of trade in livestock, grain, and minerals. The growth of the railroad and large cattle drives took place at a vast scale, making it difficult for cattle barons and railroad corporations to protect their property simply by relying on local officers of the peace.

Their response was not to turn to the military, which was engaged primarily in managing territorial incorporation and policing native groups. Instead, they (just like the Adams Express Company) hired private guards, particularly those with a reputation for being effective in their use of violence. In so doing, they also somewhat inadvertently opened up an opportunity for a class of violence experts – many of whom were Civil War veterans, accustomed to violence – to organize themselves into a professional network. This group – including famed gunfighters like Wyatt Earp and Wild Bill Hickok, as well as countless lesser known but skilled purveyors of gunslinging – were consummate market entrepreneurs, working, quite literally, for whomever would offer them a paycheck. Many were wage earners working at the behest of actors who were much more powerful than they, including the Pinkerton's Agency, which opened offices throughout the West in the 1870s and 1880s. Others took advantage of opportunities on both sides of the law, and used their skills both to serve as law officers and armed guards, as well as bandits and horse-thieves.

The market structured every component of the new violent opportunism. For instance, gunfighting became a career in specific locales connecting the railroad to the cattle trail, what I call *entrepôts*. These were the places where skilled experts could build reputations by fighting, which would allow them to find employment and get to know one another, building alliances and rivalries with other violence experts. Through information diffusion and role consolidation, then, gunfighters developed a social network, one that allowed them to more or less adapt to the scale of the market in the West. Once again, as in Chicago and Louisiana, traditional institutions were used in novel contexts, splitting the public dimension of those institutions from the private while privileging neither.

A quick note about the cases. These chapters – which exclusively focus on domestic violence rather than war-fighting – are not randomly chosen, nor are they intended to capture every nuance of change in coercive enforcement in the nineteenth century United States.[40] Instead, they highlight particular, acute *moments* of transformation, when, for instance, the police were invented in a specific historical context, or a new pattern of vigilantism emerged in a state or county. This strategy, though it sacrifices some level of causal generalizability, has the advantage of highlighting in concrete and narrative detail how decoupling actually worked in practice. It also allows me to focus on a larger period of historical change – the mid–nineteenth century – when the institutional patterns that continue to shape contemporary American forms of violence were actually put in place.

More precisely, however, these cases were selected to show how a similar mechanism (decoupling) led to very different outcomes depending on the ways in which republican-style institutions operated at different levels of governance. From counties to territories, the older republican basis for American coercive enforcement was transformed into dual public and private halves, even if what this transformation looked like varied across different places. Moreover, the cases are meant to work together as integrated unit, rendering the nuances of the theory in stark light and tracing a developmental account

[40] For a good general overview of the relationship between war and institutional development in the United States, see David R. Mayhew, "Wars and American Politics," *Perspectives on Politics* 3, no. 03 (2005): 473–493. Interestingly, foreign war, too, reflects some of the arguments in this book. In a context of war against native peoples or one in which "ordinary" citizen violence helped serve the aims of continental expansion, for example, the distinction between "inside" and "outside" could become very ambiguous. And Americans have frequently blurred distinctions between private enterprise and foreign conquest in other ways, as the nation's rich tradition of mercenarism and filibustering attests.

of American violence over time in the vital (and often understudied) West. Northern Illinois counties, the municipality of Chicago, the state of Louisiana, and the territories of the trans–Mississippi West were all transition zones, part of a periphery of American settlement during the nineteenth century where the effects on social life were heightened and accentuated by events like the Market Revolution and the Civil War. While the underlying narratives of these cases turn out to be quite common throughout the nation (for instance, though antedating Chicago's police by a decade, New York City's police department had a somewhat similar origin story, while South Carolina's approach to vigilante mobilization during Reconstruction resembled Louisiana's), these cases reveal decoupling in a particularly clear and, one would hope, compelling way.[41]

At its heart, this book argues that the distinction between public and private forms of violence needs to be *made* rather than assumed. Organized forms of antebellum violence like the militia or the town watch assumed an overlap between public and private forms of security precisely because personal security was viewed in civic terms. Ultimately this overlap functioned because powerful individuals had the capacity to shape the use of violence and the way that violence was understood in local political life. But through the unsettling effects of social frontiers events like the Market Revolution and the Civil War conditions of instability in rules, physical mobility, and/or social ambiguity events like the Market Revolution and the Civil War public and private kinds of security began to become distinct from one another, soon becoming organized into new kinds of institutions. Despite the fact we now recognize private security and vigilantism as private and the police as public, however, these forms of violence have frequently worked together toward similar aims and by sharing personnel, practices, and techniques. In this way, private violence is not only compatible with public state coercion in the contemporary United States, it also may be essential to it.

[41] On South Carolina and Reconstruction, see Stephen Kantrowitz, "'One Man's Mob Is Another Man's Militia:' Violence, Manhood, and Authority in Reconstruction South Carolina," in *Jumpin' Jim Crow: Southern Politics from Civil War to Civil Rights*, eds. Jane Dailey, Glenda Elizabeth Gilmore, and Bryant Simon (Princeton, NJ: Princeton University Press, 2000), 67–87; on police reform in New York (and Philadelphia) see Johnson, *Policing the Urban Underworld*, 12–35. New York even had what appears to be the first American private detective, Gil Hayes, who was also a former member of the city's constable force and who, just like Pinkerton, appears to have transformed his skills in detection into a profit-driven enterprise right after reorganization. See *New York Tribune* October 26, 1843; June 20 1845; ibid., 59–60.

2

Jurisdictional Decoupling as Institutional Change

INTRODUCTION

Making sense of the coemergence and coevolution of public and private violence in the United States is ultimately a question of understanding institutional change. Institutions, made up of rules and relations, translate cultural, legal, and discursive conceptions of violence into empirical, organizational forms. This chapter therefore presents an approach to institutional change – which I call the theory of "jurisdictional decoupling" – that combines a series of claims about how coercion is actually practiced within specific, historical political institutions with an analysis of how those practices evolve over time.

In a nutshell, I contend that change in coercive enforcement often comes as a result of the delinking or decoupling of political jurisdictional rules from the practical, day-to-day network relations that allow people to actually exert influence and power over one another. Institutional rules in jurisdictions help produce the standards that are enforced by organizations like police forces and militias, but they also help generate a sense of social order, in which individuals know how to interact and contend with one another. That knowledge, in turn, is sustained by the social control of ordinary family, social, and economic relationships, which provide the resources and mobilization capacity for enforcement of social norms and expectations. When these two processes become disconnected or decoupled – when, for instance, rules change without a corresponding change in relations (or vice versa) — the use of older rules or relations produce novel effects.

In the United States, the decoupling of older, republican coercive enforcement institutions, such as the militia and *posse comitatus*, in which public security was inextricable from private effort, led to the emergence of a dual system in which distinct public and private forms of coercion *coexisted* and *coevolved*. This meant that police forces and private detective agencies, and the National

Guard and organized vigilance committees, emerged at the same time out of the same institutional root system. Moreover, they continued to evolve together, sharing resources and people.

How did this occur? There were several stages. To begin, in the mid–nineteenth century, a combination of the Market Revolution (responsible largely to shifts in social control relations) and the Civil War (responsible largely for shifts in social order rules) dramatically increased the pace of physical mobility and the level of social ambiguity.[1] In rapidly changing cities like Chicago, states undergoing intense changes in political life, like Reconstruction Era Louisiana, and sparsely settled territories becoming incorporated in a national economy like the trans–Mississippi West of the late nineteenth century, instability in rules, social ambiguity, and physical mobility created what Ann Swidler has called "unsettled" times.[2] The places and contexts in which such phenomena were most prevalent generated a kind of social frontier in which older forms of authority no longer worked as they once had.

Unsettled spaces like these created a rupture between the actual means of social control and abstract conceptions of social order they were supposed to enforce. However, because political and economic elites continued to rely on existing republican practices like deputization and militia mobilization, those practices began to produce new effects, including the creation of "new" distinctly public and private vigilance organizations, detective agencies, gunfighting experts, professional police, and militia units. These coercive enforcement organizations were really just older institutional practices carried into new contexts – vigilance committees were, in essence, militias without a link to a clear sense of public order, and private detectives were essentially older municipal constables with businesses rather than cities as clients. And so forth.

Over time, new networks of security providers emerged, which linked these public and private sectors together and helped to stabilize them – police officers often served as private guards and watchmen (and vice versa), vigilantes maintained close links to new forms of militia, and, in the West, a class of economically motivated violence experts moved easily back and forth between public and private employers emerged. In other words, competition for protection services between public and private forms of violence never really happened because those serving in these various roles were often the *same people*.

This chapter lays out these arguments in detail, beginning with a discussion of how social order and control come together to produce coercive

[1] John Lauritz Larson, *The Market Revolution in America: Liberty, Ambition, and the Eclipse of the Common Good* (Cambridge: Cambridge University Press, 2009), 98–140; Heather Cox Richardson, *West from Appomattox: The Reconstruction of America After the Civil War* (New Haven, CT: Yale University Press, 2007), 8–38.

[2] Ann Swidler, "Culture in Action: Symbols and Strategies," *American Sociological Review* 51, no. 2 (1986): 273–286.

enforcement, and proceeding with a theoretical account of how social relations become decoupled from the rules characterizing institutions. A typographic description of these changes in key jurisdictions in the United States concludes the chapter.

SOCIAL ORDER, CONTROL, AND INSTITUTIONAL CHANGE

How do states and other collective entities produce enforcement? Obviously this is an enormous question, and one that I will not pretend to answer in full. This book only intends to focus on one specific mechanism of ensuring such enforcement: coercive institutions. These institutions, including police forces, militias, armies, and so forth, provide social order by mobilizing potentially violent forms of social control.

Social order and social control are related but distinct concepts. For example, what counts as order is really a question of the various conceptual schemes about how the world works that allow people to articulate desirable and normative ways of life.[3] Take, for instance, Puritan New England: for those living in small towns in Massachussetts and Connecticut in the seventeenth century, order was both religious and political, including strong assumptions about how citizens were supposed to live, and powerful punishments (like banishment) for those who threatened the conceptual underpinnings of the system. Contemporary suburbs, with their homeowners' associations and zoning ordinances, usually have a property-based vision of order, one deeply tied to a need to protect real estate value and maintain control over services like schools and sanitation.

These kinds of order are not simply about peace or cooperation or coordination in an abstract sense (though these provide the language people use to describe social order);[4] instead orders involve a set of concepts that structure how people understand themselves, their responsibilities, and ties with others, properties (which vary by context), time, and place. In this sense, I think of social order as constituted primarily by the rules for social life – we don't always follow them or even fully know what they might be, but rules inform both our standards for behavior as well as our perceptions of right and wrong.

In turn, social control indicates the range of ways in which those who deviate from rules can be punished, restrained, deterred, and so on. Social control is a property of day-to-day forms of interaction; the ways, in other words, how our parents, neighbors, and friends use resources, language, sanctions, and other media to influence and shape our behavior. In the context of this argument, it outlines the relations involved in the organization of coercion. In Puritan New

[3] Mary Douglas, *How Institutions Think* (Syracuse: Syracuse University Press, 1986), 45–53.

[4] e.g., Jon Elster, *The Cement of Society: A Survey of Social Order* (Cambridge: Cambridge University Press, 1989), 1–16.

England, church elders and fathers held social positions of great esteem; in contemporary suburbs, real estate appraisers, homeowners' association board members, and other informal modes help sustain control over the actions of residents. Indeed, scholars have identified multiple forms of social control, including education and welfare systems – each of which have to do with the state – but this book focuses on those which explicitly mobilize violence.[5]

Social order and control are related of course: fathers or clergy members are able to exert influence over those in their families or flocks at least partly *because* of the ways in which legal rules or norms grant them authority. And, conversely, many important legal or social roles are built on ties of kinship or economic affiliation; not everyone was able to become a pastor in a New England town. Both order and control, in fact, need to come together in order to make institutions coercive. Without a potentially harmful form of social control, it is difficult to speak of the enforcement of social order; conversely, forms of social order that do not require coercive enforcement (such as self-enforcing institutions), are not predicated on social control, but simply raw coordination of self-interests.

Nevertheless, making a distinction between social control and social order is important because it allows us to view institutions as constellations of different kinds of sources of power. On one hand, institutions are powerful because they enable people to shape one another's behavior directly through different kinds of relations; on the other hand, this capacity is tied into underlying rules that help inform those actors about who they are and how they should act. Neither rules nor relations are adequate in explaining how institutions work; both must operate together to produce a stable form of enforcement.

Take again the example of the *posse comitatus*, introduced in the account of the Reno Gang in Chapter 1. The name refers, literally, to the "power of the county" – the collective capacity of male citizens to ensure the safety and order of their own communities. In places like Seymour, Indiana, the *posse* involved the temporary deputization of ordinary residents to participate in law enforcement activities like arrests and pursuit under the direction of an authorized officer of the peace. Refusing to cooperate with a *posse* was itself a crime, and the institution was, like the militia or the town watch, considered a civic duty for all able-bodied male citizens.[6]

One way of explaining how and why the *posse comitatus* worked is to focus on how a rule distributing the responsibility for coercion across all residents of a particular area is self-enforcing — how, in other words, the *posse* solves

5 Stanley Cohen, *Visions of Social Control: Crime, Punishment and Classification* (Cambridge: Polity Press, 1985), 2–3.

6 David B. Kopel, "The Posse Comitatus and the Office of Sheriff: Armed Citizens Summoned to the Aid of Law Enforcement," *Journal of Criminal Law and Criminology* 104, no. 4 (2014): 804–851.

a collective action problem.[7] Scholars in law and society who study "local ordering" tend to focus on these kinds of concerns, and explain institutions like the *posse* as the collective result of individual, rational decision-makers understanding the stakes of their participation and agreeing that organizing together in an *ad hoc* manner is preferable to turning to a state or other external actor to ensure protection.[8] According to this argument, residents of Seymour mobilized themselves to investigate the theft of Adams Express Company property following the Reno Gang's first major railroad robbery perhaps because they wished to avoid the costs of hiring a full-time police force, or maybe to make it appear to outside corporations that their town was a safe and hospitable one.

This approach, while often providing clear and straightforward ways of making sense of coercive institutions, has several weaknesses. It ignores the problem, for instance, of how residents define and understand threats. What if residents disagree on the source of danger? Will they only coordinate around threats they all share? How will they know they share those threats? In Seymour, some residents seemed to disagree on how far the investigation should proceed; they "overlooked" evidence, for instance, leading the bandits back to the Reno homestead. Since the Reno family had many supporters in the town, it is not always clear that such a mechanism would work to successfully organize residents in a shared effort.

Similarly, these theories do not pay close attention to the many social ties linking actors together: actors living together are not merely abstract agents, but are also neighbors, kin, co-ethnics, religious affiliates, and so forth. These relations, which usually involve other forms of power, invariably affect how threats are interpreted, while also shaping the interests of the actors involved. In order to explain why the *posse* specifically arose and evolved, we need to know something about how participants understood the problem of order and who affected those understandings, rather than simply that they had a shared interest in self-protection.

Conversely, of course, one could explain the *posse comitatus* in structural or relational terms, as merely a reflection, for instance, of preexisting hierarchies or class configurations in the feudal/early modern world. In this story, for instance, the *posse* would simply be an instrument for powerful residents (like the town constable) to mobilize coercion against threats *they* consider dangerous. In the case of the Reno Gang, we would need to know who the constable's allies were and whether or not he was involved in the Reno family's activities in order to explain the response of Seymour residents to the robbery.

7 Douglass C. North and Barry R. Weingast, "Constitutions and Commitment: The Evolution of Institutions Governing Public Choice in Seventeenth-Century England," *The Journal of Economic History* 49, no. 4 (1989): 803–832.

8 Robert C. Ellickson, *Order Without Law: How Neighbors Settle Disputes* (Cambridge, MA: Harvard University Press, 1991), 167–183.

But a simple structural account cannot explain how something like the *posse comitatus* might take on a life of its own *outside* those social relations, nor can it explain widespread mobilization throughout many years. Indeed, why did the *posse* emerge and not some other form of coercion? Why did it last as long as it did, all the way through the early years of industrial capitalism (and even beyond)? We need to understand both rules of social order and relations of social control in order to make sense of why coercive institutions like the constabulary or shrievalty work the way they do and how they change over time.

The next two sections relate this abstract discussion of social order and social control to the empirical world of American politics in the nineteenth century. First, I show how how jurisdictions in the United States contain core rules for understanding social order, before turning to an exploration of how network relations help produce social control. I then turn to the question of how physical mobility and social ambiguity decouple the links between these rules and relations.

SOCIAL ORDER AND JURISDICTIONAL RULES

Jurisdiction is one of the more complicated concepts in legal theory; formally, jurisdictions are sets of rules determining the legal distribution of rights, duties, obligations, and responsibilities in particular contexts. As such, they specify the patterns through which authority in a governing body is ordered. At the same time, jurisdictions are also territorial divisions within government, like counties and towns. I use the term in both ways.

I do so because a variety of jurisdictions were the organizational basis for authorized violence in the United States. Different jurisdictions each had their own form of coercion: counties had a sheriff and a militia company, states had militia and adjutant generals, and so forth. Within towns and municipalities, other subunits exercised coercive power: when incorporated under general laws, antebellum towns across the United States usually had constables or marshals; when incorporated with charters, cities had more flexibility, creating night watches, systems of deputization, and expanded constabularies.[9] Moreover, from individual conflict to collective warfare, as the scale of violent activity increases, the scale of the jurisdiction responsible for organizing and containing that violence also increases.[10] Wars, after all, are

[9] These institutions did not link into one another seamlessly – the particular responsibilities of each role were partially defined by the constitutional laws of the states or the incorporating acts of the sub-jurisdictions. Republican security roles were generally quite flexible and responsibilities (such as keeping the peace) overlapped among officers active in the same territory.

[10] Douglass C. North, John Joseph Wallis, and Barry R. Weingast, *Violence and Social Orders: A Conceptual Framework for Interpreting Recorded Human History* (Cambridge: Cambridge University Press, 2009), 51–54; Charles Tilly, *The Politics of Collective Violence* (Cambridge: Cambridge University Press, 2003).

not fought by counties, while local riots are only rarely put down by centralized military forces.

Jurisdictions also help provide order by informing residents about what they are supposed to be doing and who is responsible for enforcement. In this sense, jurisdictional relations among actors are often abstract and conceptual; for instance, as a citizen of a particular nation state, I relate to other citizens through a legal category that may ensure equal treatment, access to rights, and so on. Other institutional roles like police officer and militia captain are linked to specific jurisdictions, which provide the regulative content for what those inhabiting those roles are supposed to do.

For the purposes of this analysis, I group jurisdictional orders into two types. *Translocal* jurisdictions like states and territories help organize political authority across a space that is territorially bounded but usually outside the purview of day-to-day interaction or relations. *Local* jurisdictions, like counties and towns, are bounded at the scale of day-to-day interaction. Although overly simplified, of course (translocal jurisdictions always, for instance, are local in some sense, and vice versa), this distinction helps clarify what kinds of social relations and rules might be important to maintaining enforcement. Governing a large state, in which it is impossible for direct personal relations to tie an entire polity together, means relying at least partly on other kinds of relations, such as legal categories.

Jurisdictional politics help shape what coercive actors can do and where they can act. But how they do it depends on how day-to-day relations tie powerful actors to constituents.[11] This means that activities whose effects are attributed to formal political institutions (paying taxes, agreeing to serve in the armed forces, and so on) are often actually due to a social infrastructure of informal power and authority that underlies those institutions (peer pressure, employer expectation, familial authority, and so on). Thus, in order to explain how the abstract rules of jurisdictions work, we also need to understand the way institutional rules intersect with the social control provided by network relations.

SOCIAL CONTROL AND NETWORK RELATIONS

Most scholars assume that participating in violent collective action is difficult – serving in a military organization or arresting a criminal is dangerous and difficult work, which may not be individually beneficial.[12] Political institutions – organized through jurisdictional divisions – putatively help solve these

[11] Day-to-day networks include the personal relationships connecting people to one another as individuals; they do not, for instance, include relationships to abstract fictions like the state or a business.

[12] Mark I. Lichbach, "Rethinking Rationality and Rebellion: Theories of Collective Action and Problems of Collective Dissent," *Rationality and Society* 6, no. 1 (1994): 8–39; Gordon Tullock, "The Paradox of Revolution," *Public Choice* 11, no. 1 (1971): 89–99.

collective action problems for society by outlining conditions under which violence should be used, as well as sanctions for failing to participate as prescribed.[13] The *posse* was one of the primary solutions to this problem in the antebellum period in the United States, though other institutions such as the town watch, militia, constables and sheriffs, and so forth, also played a critical role. Each of these forms of organizing coercion, as we shall see, depended on a fusion of public security to private effort. It was only late into the nineteenth century that distinctive public and private forms of violence emerged to supplant these older traditions.

Moreover, as I argue in the chapters that follow, enforcement depends heavily on the network relations through which people influence and affect one another. And explaining such enforcement is a means to making sense of the cumulative decisions of actors who respond to the social pressures placed on them by rules and relations.

In the *posse*, for example, day-to-day network relationships shape access to tangible resources, such as property, knowledge, and social support, which allow actors who control access to them to influence those who do not and elicit their help in mobilizing violence.[14] These relations also, however, allow powerful actors – pastors, employers, fathers, and so on – to shape social interpretations concerning what threats are important and which can be ignored. When these threats can be described in terms that do not discriminate between personal security and collective security, as I argue was the case in many antebellum communities, solving the collective provision of violence through individual interests simply means recasting those individual interests in collective terms. When powerful actors lose their ability to determine for everyone else what counts as security – perhaps, as in Seymour, by different factions making equally strident claims to representing the public – making this connection can be much more difficult.

Network relations thus provide the day-to-day sinews through which actors affect each other. How, though, do the flows of resources and interpretation shaped by networks transform into actual control? There are two ways this happens.

Concrete control involve the interpersonal influence of powerful individuals with whom one has personal contact. Pastors, teachers, coaches, police officers, and others of whom a person has specific knowledge exercise concrete authority by controlling access to resources and supplying interpretive frameworks in particular, quotidian social interactions. In rural towns like Seymour (and counties like Jackson), the Reno family's direct connections helped shield them from county legal institutions, which depended on precisely these kinds of ties.

13 Yoram Barzel, *A Theory of the State: Economic Rights, Legal Rights, and the Scope of the State* (Cambridge: Cambridge University Press, 2002).

14 Richard M. Emerson, "Power-Dependence Relations," *American Sociological Review* 27, no. 1 (1962): 31–41.

Categorical control, on the other hand, depends on impersonal and remote influences, which may take the form of informal or folk classifying distinctions. For example, racial hierarchies usually transcend personalistic relations; African Americans in the Jim Crow South had relatively less general political authority than their white counterparts simply by virtue of being black. These kinds of relations are structured by (and, in turn, structure) the distribution of resources and interpretation, but they don't depend on particular, individual interactions as much as underlying social schemas. When a white person encounters an African-American person in a system based on racial categories, the classification itself helps shape the flow of social control between the actors.

Categorical and concrete control are not, of course, mutually exclusive – the concrete control of a parent over a child can depend on an underlying system of categorical relations, while concrete interaction between, for instance, African Americans and whites help prop up the categorical distinctions between them.[15]

Moreover, control shouldn't be interpreted to mean the complete power or authority of one actor or group over the actions of others. Instead, it is much closer to what sociologist Erving Goffman has described as an "interaction ritual" – the ways in which the social contexts actors find themselves in provide them with guidelines about how to act (usually to save face), while requiring participants to negotiate particular interactions through their own, often strategic, choices.[16] The simple fact, for instance, of being in church or participating in a family event sets expectations for behavior, but participants may try to subvert or reorder those interactions by acting unpredictably or by adopting roles unsuitable to the moment.

As a result, even in highly enclosed and tight-knit communities, people's actions are merely *influenced* by neighbors, authorities, and family members. We all certainly possess our own sets of interests, preferences, and tastes. At the micro-level, my model sees institutional authority as the result of the strategic actions of particular individuals – business owners, politicians, community leaders, ethnic entrepreneurs, and so on – who are nevertheless situated in particular network positions shaping their outlooks over time. In the words of John Padgett and Woody Powell, "in the short run, actors create relations; in the long run, relations create actors."[17]

My approach to thinking about coercive enforcement, however, also moves us away from the common idea that all institutions are merely the concatenation of individual decisions. One of the key assumptions of this book is that

15 See, for example, Charles Tilly, *Durable Inequality* (Berkeley: University of California Press, 1999), 8–10.

16 Erving Goffman, *Interaction Ritual: Essays on Face-to-Face Behavior* (New York: Pantheon, 1967), 5–9.

17 John F. Padgett and Walter W. Powell, eds., *The Emergence of Organizations and Markets* (Princeton, NJ: Princeton University Press, 2012), 2.

precisely because social order rules and social control relations are distinct, we should be very cautious about treating individual decisions as merely a product of an internal decision-making process. When a person makes a decision, for instance, about whether to follow a rule, part of that decision will reflect the kinds of social control that other actors can exercise against him or her; conversely, when making decisions about making social connections, actors are deeply affected by the sets of social ordering rules (not merely jurisdictions, but all kinds of rules about language, status, and so forth) that help tell them how to interpret and understand the world.

In the sense I am using it, coercive enforcement is the use of social control to mobilize violence or the threat of violence to sustain existing rules, as well as the ways in which those rules help reproduce and order the relations controlling interactions among people. Specific kinds of institutions, like police forces and militias, play a crucial role in helping to produce enforcement in the larger society, and are the main focus of the rest of this book.

One important implication of this way of thinking about enforcement is that the use of violence is not merely used to defend institutional rules, but also reflects and shapes the social relations underpinning those rules. Violence can be used to get people to obey the law, but it can also express collective solidarity, reshape social networks, or allow for participants and targets to reinterpret their social lives.

Another implication of this approach to enforcement is that violence involves a range of social behaviors requiring skill and coordination. As sociologist Randall Collins points out, violence *is* very difficult to achieve, but not necessarily because of the potential harm one might suffer or the costs involved in imposing and resisting physical damage. Instead, committing violent acts of a variety of kinds – arresting, lynching, fighting, shooting – requires overcoming the default emotional practices of our social lives, most of which are oriented toward reproducing the rituals that preserve our interactions with others. According to Collins, only certain unpleasant and rare interactions – those marked by intense fear – reliably generate violence; as a consequence, most people who act violently are simply not very good at it because they are afraid and distraught. Instead, it takes skilled experts to be able to successfully navigate the complex emotional and physical consequences of doing damage to other people, and many have to undergo a training and socialization process (like attending military boot camp) to facilitate its use.[18]

Thinking of violence in this way means exploring the processes through which some people come to be violence experts and examining how the practices used to make violence are negotiated through use over time. The chapters in this book thus address a variety of violent practices – executions, arrests, pitched battles, and gunfights – and show how older ways of making

[18] Collins, *Violence: A Micro-sociological Theory*, 19–29.

violence can be altered into new organizational forms by skilled practitioners like police officers and private guards. At the same time, we need to look at the institutional contexts themselves, to make sense of how, in particular settings, rules for social order shape relations of social control and vice versa. The next section takes up this task.

COUPLED JURISDICTIONS AND INSTITUTIONAL STABILITY

The key claim of this section is that the social order rules of different US jurisdictions – county, town, state, and territory – *presuppose* a corresponding infrastructure of relational control that makes them work. I call this link "coupling." Later I describe what the empirical manifestations of this model were and how it changed over time, but first I lay out the logic of coupling, the crucial building block to understanding coercive enforcement.

The premise of jurisdictional coupling is that rules and relations should reinforce rather than undercut each other in order to supply coercive enforcement. Take the example of rural crime control, for example. In antebellum counties in the Northern and Southern United States, there were very few formal roles and opportunities to easily expand local bureaucracy. Hence day-to-day coercion was the provenance of the sheriff, a few constables, and several deputies. This rudimentary force was enhanced by the *posse* when needed. County jurisdiction assumed that those who occupied the formal roles of the state would be able to mobilize constituents at will. This capacity, I argue, depended on political officials having close, tight relationships with their constituents that allowed them to accomplish mobilization (I go into this form of control in much more detail in Chapter 3). This relationship between the formal roles of political officials and nonofficials coupled practical social authority to the formal expectations of county administration and allowed the sheriff to practice coercion.[19] The social control found in elite networks helped reproduce the social order supplied by the jurisdictional rules of counties and vice versa.

Figure 1 depicts a coupled relationship between a jurisdictional social order (the top part) and relational social control (the bottom). Specifically, individual nodes are people or groups who are coupled through their joint position in a system of social order (created by formal institutional rules) and social control (created by categorical and concrete relations). The specific manner in which these two positions overlap depends on specific jurisdictional type, but in each case successful coupling helps generate authoritative ties linking an individual's relations to the rules to which they are subject, in turn keeping the institution stable.

[19] Cyrus H. Karraker, *The Seventeenth-Century Sheriff: A Comparative Study of the Sheriff in England and the Chesapeake Colonies, 1607–1689* (Philadelphia: University of Pennsylvania, 1930).

TABLE 1. *Jurisdictional coupling and coercive enforcement in the nineteenth-century United States*

		Social order	
		Local jurisdictional rules	**Translocal jurisdictional rules**
Social control	Concrete relations	Counties Enclosed authority (Sheriff/Militia)	States Representative authority (State Militia)
	Categorical relations	Cities Delegative authority (Constable/Night Watch)	Territories Imperial authority (US Military/US Marshal)

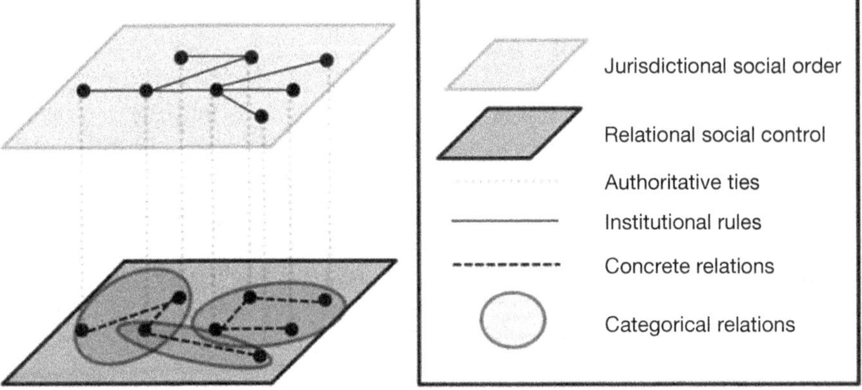

FIGURE 1. Jurisdictional coupling*

*This diagram is adapted from John F. Padgett and Walter W. Powell, eds., *The Emergence of Organizations and Markets* (Princeton, NJ: Princeton University Press, 2012).

As noted, there are two types of relational control and two types of jurisdictional order. These two dimensions define a space in which different kinds of formal jurisdictions can be linked to the hidden forms of authority helping to shape violence within their purview. Table 1 depicts four key jurisdictions in the United States, as well as what I will describe as the logic of the coupling in each jurisdiction during the Antebellum period. In parentheses, it also specifies which security institutions were used in each jurisdiction to organize and coordinate violence. Coupling makes relationships between day-to-day life and abstract rules seem natural and accepted, generating institutional stability; hence, the general concept is applicable to explaining the stable organization of coercion in all kinds of jurisdictions.

This typology also suggests a model through which institutional *change* – or, more precisely, evolution – can occur. That is, a change in either authority or in jurisdiction without a corresponding change in the other coupled component will alter the way in which violence is governed, opening up the possibility for transformation in security institutions.

Moreover, change reflects the transformation of what actors do to pursue security or where they are able to do so and how they mobilize coercive force. This decoupling of social order rules from social control relations is a general mechanism, but in the United States it had very specific effects: it led to the splitting of public from private security and the coevolution of these two principles in American institutional life. The next section shows how we can understand this process of evolution.

THE DECOUPLING OF INSTITUTIONS

This section establishes the point that decoupling in the United States is often the result of instability over institutional rules, as well as physical mobility and social ambiguity. These phenomena together create a kind of unsettled space I call a frontier.[20]

In using the term frontier I am not talking about physical borderlands or invoking Frederick Jackson Turner's famous theory of American political development, in which westward expansion played the key role in diffusing and reproducing democratic institutions.[21] Instead, I am focusing on a class of settings in which the links between rules and relations become particularly fraught. Such spaces often include areas near borders and borderlands – as Chapter 3 and Chapter 6 highlight – but just as often they took place in cities and rural areas in which older forms of authority were undermined by increases in physical mobility or social relational ambiguity. Frontiers should be interpreted widely, as political or public spaces, as moments in which rules change dramatically, or as particular contexts in which civic membership or belonging are transient or shifting. Even specific times of the day (such as night) can be interpreted as a frontier.[22]

[20] Swidler, "Culture in Action: Symbols and Strategies."

[21] This view – as well as Turner's definition of the frontier as an advancing line of settlement – have been deeply and correctly criticized by historians and social scientists for its teleological bent and blindness to existing native communities, who occupied the supposedly empty land into which Turner's settlers flowed. Leonard Thompson and Howard Lamar, "Comparative Frontier History," in *The Frontier in History: North America and Southern Africa Compared*, eds. Howard R. Lamar and Leonard M. Thompson (New Haven, CT: Yale University Press, 1981), 3–13; Patricia Nelson Limerick, *The Legacy of Conquest: The Unbroken Past of the American West* (New York: W. W. Norton, 1987).

[22] E.g., Richard Hogan, "Carnival and Caucus: A Typology for Comparative Frontier History," *Social Science History* 11, no. 2 (1987): 139–167; Murray Melbin, "Night as Frontier," *American Sociological Review* 43, no. 1 (1978): 3–22; James Ron, *Frontiers and Ghettos: State Violence in Serbia and Israel* (Berkeley: University of California Press, 2003).

Frontiers or unsettled spaces (I use both terms interchangeably in this book) can lead to institutional change because they undermine the link between these components of institutional authority. This can occur through changes in rules or changes in relations. When the rules governing social life become unstable – for instance, when the category of who gets to vote is expanded to include people of color, women, or people aged eighteen – concepts of social order may no longer clearly map onto the actual distribution of power or influence in social life.

Similarly, rapid increases in physical mobility due to transportation innovations like new rail or road connections might mean that an influx of newcomers into towns and cities challenge and rearrange traditional social networks without directly changing traditional institutional rules; indeed, much of the anxiety about urbanization had to do with the loss of intimacy and familiarity that came with the growth of cities as old corporate and neighborhood charters no longer operated the way they used to. And social ambiguity – people whose identities or connections do not fit within the categories society uses to classify them – challenge the control that classification can provide, particularly when those classifications tacitly underpin institutional authority. Rules based on one set of relations can become *decoupled* as those relations change, just as new rules might be decoupled from relations that remain the same.

Decoupling, in turn, opens up the space for change in coercive enforcement. How? As with all kinds of social action, coercive enforcement is risky, laden with unpredictable effects and inadvertent byproducts. Individuals tend to use tried and true practices, even in institutional contexts that have changed. When actors continue to rely on older rules in a world where social relations have changed, or continue to have access to older relations in a world of altered rules, traditional practices of social control and social order no longer produce the same kinds of effects they once did. Older rules can be deployed in new contexts and older relations can take on new meanings.

An example will help explain how this process works. Prior to around 1850, cities like New York and Philadelphia (much like counties) depended heavily on local information provided by neighbors of offenders and victims to help solve and prosecute crimes. Rather than a centrally organized police department, with territorial divisions, the whole system was based on the delegation of local social control among neighbors and the willingness of ordinary individuals to initiate both civil *and* criminal matters before the court.[23]

This system, however, had a difficult time coping with the increased levels of physical mobility associated with the coming of the railroad and the creation of zones of social intermixing. Historian David Johnson, for instance, describes the emergence of a network of criminals linking Chicago, New York, Philadelphia, and other cities together after 1840, allowing new crimes based on anonymity

23 Allen Steinberg, *The Transformation of Criminal Justice: Philadelphia, 1800–1880* (Chapel Hill: University of North Carolina Press, 1989), 24–33.

(such as swindling) to diffuse throughout the nation (this network, incidentally, became the basis for contemporary organized crime outfits).[24] A mismatch between the jurisdiction and social relations began to emerge as existing rules were no longer propped up by the tight-knit ethno-cultural networks that allowed neighborhoods to largely manage themselves.

Crucially, city elders in cities like Chicago in the mid-1850s, as I show in Chapter 4, did not stop using the existing rules for deputization. Indeed, they relied on it ever more, deputizing a wide variety of actors to manage these new unsettled spaces. These officers, however, no longer relied on ethno-cultural ties to help police, but instead began to develop new organizational forms. Some, like Allan Pinkerton, became entrepreneurs, converting the old fee-for-service model into a profit-making scheme by, in part, pursuing precisely the intercity criminals identified by Johnson. Political elites, on the other hand, used deputization to create large bodies of full-time officers, who now worked as professionals for the city rather than for local elites or private guards. These actors were the product of old rules being applied in a world where relations had changed; as a result, a new form of policing (split into a public and private component) began to evolve in the years around the Civil War, when these spatial mismatches became common in American cities. Over and over again, ancient law enforcement roles – the militia, the sheriffs office, the constable, and so on – were transformed into something new rather than abandoned and replaced.

This leads to an important assumption, one that I adopt throughout this book: political and economic elites almost never *try* to abandon their traditional practices of coercive enforcement, having little incentive to abandon the status quo arrangements that provide them with so much power and authority. Instead, the growth of a whole variety of new institutions – including police forces, professional private detective agencies, mercenary gunfighting violence experts, vigilance committees, and so on – were the inadvertent byproduct of attempts (often of elites) to preserve the status quo in conditions where older rules have been decoupled from relations or vice versa. Institutional change is often, somewhat paradoxically, a conservative phenomenon.

If unsettled frontiers decouple existing sets of rules and relations, why don't anarchy and chaos ensue? After all, if some actors use deputization to become public police officers and others use it to develop profit-making detective agencies, why don't these new organizations begin to compete with the state directly over protection services? Why do we see the kind of collaborative relationships between public and private forms of violence that characterize much of American history?

The main reason has to do with the fact that often those involved in this change are those who previously controlled the use of coercion, who have

24 David R. Johnson, "The Origins and Structure of Intercity Criminal Activity 1840–1920: An Interpretation," *Journal of Social History* 15, no. 4 (1982): 593–605.

institutional memory, resources, and skills that others lack. That is, precisely because political and economic elites continue to rely on older rules and relations to produce enforcement, many of those involving themselves in explicitly public forms of coercion are *also* those involved in private enforcement, often on the side. Close relationships between the new professional police and private detective agencies are possible because many of the same people move back and forth between these different jobs. Vigilance committees – particularly those oriented toward the reform of the public – may be private groups, but they often work hand in hand with putatively public officers of the law or National Guard units. There is little competition between public and private violence – at least in the case of the United States – because changes in the organization of coercion reflected preexisting social rules and relations.

Why did we see the emergence of this collaborative relationship in the United States and not in many European states, then? The United States is an unusual case not because it had a monopoly in frontiers – after all, given the way I have defined them, frontiers are really quite common. Instead, it is unusual because of its institutional history, the way in which a well-defined set of republican rules allowed public security to be the responsibility of a wide swath of private individuals connected through day-to-day network relations. In absolutist monarchies in Europe, which relied not on civic republicanism but instead on elite classes of warriors who controlled violence through concentration and specialization, the emergence of physical and social frontiers entailed fierce competition and fighting. In these states, the expansion of mercantilism, imperial competition, and, ultimately, the Industrial Revolution did decouple the traditional quasi-feudal rules of absolutism from the day-to-day social control of agrarian households, but the result was that already elite bands of soldiers competed with one another over territorial domination.[25]

England, on the other hand, had very similar traditions of republican law enforcement to those found in the United States – and underwent strikingly similar changes as industrialization unsettled older relations between day-to-day social relations and the traditional jurisdictional rules of English governance. As a result, just as in the United States, the first steps toward public, bureaucratic police at least initially coincided with the invention of private thief-taking and prosecution societies.[26]

[25] Richard Lachmann, *States and Power* (Cambridge: Polity Press, 2010), 15–65. In her influential account of the growth of state coercion, Janice Thomson argues that North America did, indeed, undergo a process of state monopolization of violence resembling the pattern of European states, which she argues took the form of increasing legal control over filibusters and mercenaries in a context of international competition. Her argument, however, focuses primarily on *external* defense rather than internal law and order, about which she has little to say. Janice E. Thomson, *Mercenaries, Pirates, and Sovereigns: State-Building and Extraterritorial Violence in Early Modern Europe* (Princeton, NJ: Princeton University Press, 1994), 7–20.

[26] Douglas W. Allen and Yoram Barzel, "The Evolution of Criminal Law and Police During the Pre-modern Era," *Journal of Law, Economics, and Organization* 27, no. 3 (2011): 540–567.

At the same time, the compatibility between public and private forms of coercion was entrenched to a degree not seen in England. Social change in the nineteenth-century United States involved the constant creation and rearrangement of new jurisdictional rules, deep and persistent forms of physical mobility, as well as complex exchanges among those with different ethnic, racial, and social backgrounds to an extent not found almost anywhere else. The complexity of this frontier experience led to fully private vigilantism and profit-seeking forms of policing that were unusual in England, where even private prosecution societies largely operated within a well-defined legal framework.[27]

The key point, then, is not merely that history matters, but rather that existing configurations of rules and relations actively constrain the conditions under which transformative change in coercive institutions occurs. That change, in turn, usually involves the continued use of traditional forms of social control under conditions where the rules constituting social order have changed or vice versa. Rules and relations alike are sticky and slow-moving properties of social life, but they can (and often do) move at different rates. Because both are properties of institutional authority, this divergence often means bits and scraps of older institutional rules and relations continue to play a role, even as the link between those properties has shifted. In this sense, frontiers provide the spark, but the existing institutional frameworks determine how far the change will spread and what it will look like.

To transform this abstract theoretical discussion into one of practical relevance means identifying empirical instances of coercive enforcement and identifying how frontiers and decoupling worked in practice. The next section specifies how this theory can help us explain the empirical puzzle of fragmented, coevolutionary public and private forms of violence in American political development in the late nineteenth century.

THE EVOLUTION OF PUBLIC AND PRIVATE VIOLENCE

The United States inherited security institutions from England based on a republican model of citizenship.[28] I am using republicanism here strictly in an institutional rather than ideological sense; that is, most jurisdictions in US politics relied on private male citizens to participate directly in the provision of public security and required that they served, when needed, in institutions

[27] Craig B. Little and Christopher P. Sheffield, "Frontiers and Criminal Justice: English Private Prosecution Societies and American Vigilantism in the Eighteenth and Nineteenth Centuries," *American Sociological Review* 48, no. 6 (1983): 796–808. Interestingly, a similar form of legal but private prosecution also emerged in New England in the early nineteenth century. See Ann-Marie Szymanski, "Stop, Thief! Private Protective Societies in Nineteenth-Century New England," *The New England Quarterly* 78, no. 3 (2005): 407–439.

[28] T. H. Breen, "English Origins and New World Development: The Case of the Covenanted Militia in Seventeenth-Century Massachusetts," *Past & Present* 57, no. 1 (1972): 74–96.

like the *posse comitatus*, the militia, the slave patrol, the night watch, and even as official officers of the peace like sheriffs and constables.[29] The rules for each of the jurisdictions in American political life – the counties, municipalities, territories, and states – essentially fused public enforcement to the social control already part and parcel of American informal social relations of the family and community. The household, for instance, was seen as an extension of the state's police power, and racial and gender categories were key in allowing for public security to essentially be the provenance of white male property owners.

At the same time, these rules and relations were never static. From the outset, the expansion of American political institutions into new territories and the flux of social relations through immigration and trading produced a struggle over how to actually sustain the link between public security and private effort. While many social relations and jurisdictional notions were relatively stable, locked into strong cultural norms of deference, ethnic and kinship responsibilities, and a powerful patriarchal logic of authority, from the outset the American experience involved deep exposure to the disruptions of the frontier.

In the mid–nineteenth century, however, the frontier accelerated in new directions. Older forms of territorial jurisdiction and networks encountered a new market society, a revolution in technology and transportation, and the Civil War, which completely reordered the idea of a republican system of coercive enforcement. These new frontiers had the effect of rendering private and public interests in security *distinct*; no longer, for example, were the security interests of warehouse or factory owners or white men considered indistinguishable from those of workers or other businessmen or members of other genders or races. Instead, they were now obviously particular and private. At the same time, however, a new kind of specifically public interest in protection *also* emerged, one that encompassed all members of a community. The demand that everyone, regardless of their particular racial or economic classification, deserved protection grew hand in hand with the demand of powerful private interests that they be able to protect themselves. Decoupling, in short, transformed the republican unitary security system to a modern dual system by reorganizing the public and private forms of coercion upon which the former were based. The first step in understanding this transition, therefore, is unpacking what I mean by public and private.

[29] H. Richard Uviller and William G. Merkel, *The Militia and the Right to Arms, Or, How the Second Amendment Fell Silent* (Durham, NC: Duke University Press, 2002), 40–68; Karraker, *The Seventeenth-Century Sheriff*, 147–159. Naturally, Americans *disagreed* over the terms of this service, particularly when it came to federal institutions. For the most part, however, the actual lived practices of republican governance in local jurisdictions were taken-for-granted for much of the antebellum period.

PUBLIC AND PRIVATE SECURITY

Public security involves the protection of open, general collectivities, while private security is the protection of particular individuals or closed off collectivities. Public security is usually administered by a government or in terms that reflect civic identity (state). Private security, in turn, can be for pecuniary aims (market) or can be a matter of protecting some enclosed collective like a particular racial class or social group (society).[30] Private and public are used here as what Brubaker calls categories of analysis rather than practice, meaning I am using prior definitions rather than simply accepting the vocabulary that actors used to describe their own participation – many who believed themselves to be acting on behalf of the public interest (such as most vigilantes and some private security officers) represented particularistic and private interests as well.[31] Only over time, in fact, did the division between public and private security become clear to participants themselves.

Republican security institutions had linked these two forms of security by blurring the distinction between them. Through participatory institutions like the militia and the *posse comitatus*, individual citizens would protect themselves in collaboration with their neighbors and fellow community members.[32] Providing security was not the specialized function of experts, but rather an expected duty of otherwise private individuals. This system was supposed to both avoid the costs involved in maintaining a bureaucratic military and to protect against tyranny from a standing army. Moreover, it helped to ensure the powerful regulative capacities of the local state in the United States, since protecting the public welfare often explicitly meant personal sacrifice and surveillance by governing officials. For many civic republicans it was not possible to conceive of true private security outside of a community, nor could one conceive of a just form of public security that did not protect individuals.[33]

30 For shifting terrain of how public violence and security was interpreted in American jurisprudence, see Joshua M. Stein, "The Right to Violence: Assault Prosecution in New York, 1760–1840" (PhD diss., University of California, Los Angeles, 2009), 103–137.

31 Rogers Brubaker, "Categories of Analysis and Categories of Practice: A Note on the Study of Muslims in European Countries of Immigration," *Ethnic and Racial Studies* 36, no. 1 (2013): 1–8.

32 Gautham Rao, "The Federal Posse Comitatus Doctrine: Slavery, Compulsion, and Statecraft in Mid-Nineteenth-Century America," *Law and History Review* 26, no. 1 (2008): 1–56.

33 John Todd White, "Standing Armies in Time of War: Republican Theory and Military Practice During the American Revolution" (PhD diss., The George Washington University, 1978), 24–40. Also, see the debate on civic republicanism and the Second Amendment: Wendy Brown, "Guns, Cowboys, Philadelphia Mayors, and Civic Republicanism: On Sanford Levinson's The Embarrassing Second Amendment," *The Yale Law Journal* 99, no. 3 (December 1989): 661–667; Lawrence Delbert Cress, "An Armed Community: The Origins and Meaning of the Right to Bear Arms," *Journal of American History* 71, no. 1 (1984): 22–42; Sanford Levinson, "The Embarrassing Second Amendment," *The Yale Law Journal* 99, no. 3 (1989): 637–659; David C. Williams, "Civic Republicanism and the Citizen Militia: The Terrifying Second Amendment," *Yale Law Journal* 101 (1991): 551.

Take, for example, the matter of private property, a traditional bedrock for republican responsibility. Indeed, in classic republican conceptions of the state, proper defense of the political community *depends* on a link between state power and property because those private individuals who own property have a vested interest in supporting the kind of free political community that will protect their claims. Conversely, then, for property to continue to be secure (particularly from a tyrannical state), a civic republican order requires property owners to come together to be willing to participate in the common protection of their civic communities. Public security and private effort to protect property are inextricable from one another.

At the same time, what *counts* as private property has never been absolute, but has instead depended upon many factors – the law or cultural norms, for instance, or perhaps political entrepreneurs who have decided that some private matter is, in fact, actually a concern for the larger community. Seizing land through eminent domain to build a highway is one kind of negotiation over what counts as private, but so is determining which intoxicating substances can be controlled or whether people can be owned as slaves. When rules for how society is to be ordered become unstable, or when relations are compromised by new forms of physical mobility or social ambiguity, attempts to redefine property and to alter what should be protected as such can gain new life. In these cases, the property of some particular group – slaveholders, drinkers, and so on – may no longer seem compatible with a larger public interest, challenging the bedrock principle upon which the republican fusion of public security and private effort rests.[34]

In a crucial sense, civic republican security institutions have never simply been a matter of spontaneous voluntary participation in shared self-preservation. Historically, they were about power. Locally powerful actors, in particular, mobilized individuals into participating in their own security. Church leaders, business owners, political officials, and family elders not only controlled resources that helped them sanction and motivate such participation, they also helped interpret the threats against which that mobilization was directed.[35] The rules for jurisdictions like counties and towns actually *depended* on this kind of informal mobilization, since the coercive force they employed was usually activated in response to events rather than as a preventative and permanent feature of the state. Republican security institutions, like other republican conceptions of political order, were explicitly hierarchical and tried to enable those with an unequal share of resources to have an unequal level of jurisdictional responsibility in defining threats and activating a response.

34 Stuart Banner, *American Property: A History of How, Why, and What We Own* (Cambridge, MA: Harvard University Press, 2011), 1–22.

35 Edmund S. Morgan, *Inventing the People: The Rise of Popular Sovereignty in England and America* (New York: W. W. Norton, 1989), 153–173.

In practice, this meant that the actual organizations that provided security – the militia, the night watch, and so forth – were embedded in other organizations in society. Militia captains were often wealthy landowners or prosperous artisans, for instance, elected by men who worked with and for them (as well as their friends).[36] These same individuals frequently held some form of law enforcement or political office, which just served to link their own personal resources and networks to enforcement of laws and regulations – which they themselves often helped make. The social and economic stratification of American society provided much of the hidden capacity for Republican institutions to actually work.

For instance, one of the most important places this link between the personal and private use of violence played out was slavery. Once the slave economy took hold in the American South, the need for highly local and decentralized forms of coercion came along with it. Reproducing discipline among slaves, monitoring them as workers and coresidents, and maintaining social and legal subordination was the task not only of the state but also of the private white citizen. In her pathbreaking work on slave patrols, Sally Hadden demonstrates how institutions like the slave patrol – built on top of the county militia – integrated white citizens in slaveholding areas into a shared institutional form of coercion.[37] More informally, however, the collective need to protect against the constant threat of revolt meant that "all whites, by virtue of their skin, had 'police power' over blacks."[38] Thus, while specific figures crucial to the management of slave labor like overseers and drivers frequently resorted to violence, private white individuals also enjoyed wide latitude in the legal right to assault slaves in day-to-day life.[39]

Another key site in which the lines between public and private violence were blurred was the household. As Marcus Dubber has argued, the household was the fundamental unit of social order in traditional legal thinking about police power, and men were expected within their private households to help produce physical discipline toward the public good.[40] In practical terms, this meant that men were legally authorized to use violence within the family in order to reinforce governing authority. This could take the form of the unwritten law – in which a man was able to kill anyone with whom his wife was having an affair – as well as the discipline of children and women (the right

36 Fred Anderson, *A People's Army: Massachusetts Soldiers and Society in the Seven Years' War* (New York: W. W. Norton, 1984), 41–48; Ronald L. Boucher, "The Colonial Militia As a Social Institution: Salem, Massachusetts 1764–1775," *Military Affairs* 37, no. 4 (1973): 125–130.

37 Hadden, *Slave Patrols*.

38 Michael Stephen Hindus, *Prison and Plantation: Crime, Justice, and Authority in Massachusetts and South Carolina, 1767–1878* (Chapel Hill: University of North Carolina Press, 1980), xix.

39 Andrew Fede, "Legitimized Violent Slave Abuse in the American South, 1619–1865: A Case Study of Law and Social Change in Six Southern States," *The American Journal of Legal History* 29, no. 2 (1985): 126–132.

40 Dubber, *The Police Power*, 6–7, 31–32, 60–62.

of chastisement) directly.[41] By the mid–nineteenth century, legal reformers and women began to challenge this link by seeking protections against domestic abuse, but the key principle that private violence could have a legitimate place in the household to the service of public ends lingered on.[42]

A final, and perhaps decisive, arena in which this dynamic played out was in relations with native peoples. From the earliest period of English settlement through almost of the end of the nineteenth century, ordinary residents of the colonies and, later, states were engaged in a long-term process of territorial expansion and incorporation. While facilitated by the federal government (which provided much of the legal and institutional infrastructure through which these claims to "settler sovereignty" could be made), it was ultimately often backwoods and borderlands residents throughout the middle border, the Old Southwest, and ultimately across the Mississippi who were largely responsible for expropriating land and engaging with Indian groups (as well as the other empires attempting to shore up control over parts of the continent).[43] This struggle was highly decentralized, extensive, and vicious; historian Peter Silver traces the deep level of fear those living in the borderlands felt during periods of conflict, noting how the unpredictability of Indian attacks required settlers be on constant war footing.[44] The response of settlers was the adoption of republican institutions like the militia as a necessity; such institutions provided a pathway for an aggressive form of personal state-building for settlers, who would use individual attacks and killing campaigns to terrorize and devastate native communities.[45]

Of course, there was never anything resembling a perfectly harmonious link between elite interests and regular citizens, nor was the control of powerful people ever complete. Not only did ordinary white men frequently shirk their responsibility to participate in slave patrols and community watches or to

41 ibid., 31–32; Robert M. Ireland, "The Libertine Must Die: Sexual Dishonor and the Unwritten Law in the Nineteenth-Century United States," *Journal of Social History* 23, no. 1 (1989): 27–44; Reva B. Siegel, "'The Rule of Love:' Wife Beating as Prerogative and Privacy," *The Yale Law Journal* 105, no. 8 (1996): 2117–2207.

42 Laura F. Edwards, "Law, Domestic Violence, and the Limits of Patriarchal Authority in the Antebellum South," *The Journal of Southern History* 65, no. 4 (November 1999): 733–770; Hendrik Hartog, "Lawyering, Husbands' Rights, and "the Unwritten Law" in Nineteenth-Century America," *The Journal of American History* 84, no. 1 (1997): 67–96.

43 Paul Frymer, "'A Rush and a Push and the Land Is Ours:' Territorial Expansion, Land Policy, and U.S. State Formation," *Perspectives on Politics* 12, no. 1 (2014): 119–144; Aziz Rana, *The Two Faces of American Freedom* (Cambridge, MA: Harvard University Press, 2010), 99–113; Lisa Ford, *Settler Sovereignty: Jurisdiction and Indigenous People in America and Australia, 1788–1836* (Cambridge, MA: Harvard University Press, 2010), 17–29.

44 Silver, *Our Savage Neighbors: How Indian War Transformed Early America*, 66.

45 Ford, *Settler Sovereignty*, 117–120; Benjamin Madley, *An American Genocide: The United States and the California Indian Catastrophe, 1846–1873* (New Haven, CT: Yale University Press, 2016), 173–230.

discipline their families, but organized political movements tried to consolidate and centralize coercive power in the state to make up for private failures, much to the chagrin of opponents. During debates over the adoption of the constitution, for instance, Anti-Federalists were adamant about the need to preserve a militia tradition and to reserve for the states the ultimate control over coercion; at the same time, a series of rebellions in Pennsylvania organized by backwoods yeoman farmers against urban economic elites demonstrated to their Federalist opponents that militia were often inadequate and needed to be supplemented by a professional federal military. By the early nineteenth century, this debate reached a stalemate, as, in the aftermath of reforms instituted by Secretary of War Henry Knox, a small but robust professional class of military officers took over the bulk of the nation's foreign security needs, serving as more a skeleton force capable of expanding to include local militia units if needed. And despite the continuing nostalgia for the universal militia on the part of Anti-Federalists and, later, Democrats, in reality the institution went into serious decline in the 1820s and 1830s; participation rates dropped, funding was cut, and a crop of volunteer organizations grew in its stead. The republican ideal of a citizenry as army was always, to some degree, more theoretical than actual.[46]

At the same time, other older civic republican institutions, such as the *posse comitatus*, the constabulary, and the shrievalty, continued to operate much as they always had through the first decades of the nineteenth century. And even the volunteer militia continued to operate according to the assumption that there was no real contradiction between public security and private effort. Indeed, volunteer units participated in a suprising large number of domestic policing incidents in decades before the Civil War and, crucially, formed the backbone for the small wars of conquest the country fought against Native Americans and Mexico in the 1830s and 1840s.[47] In this sense, they quite broadly reflected the ambiguous boundaries between public and private that continued to characterize American political institutions of all types during this period.

What ultimately reshaped the relationship between the rules characterizing Republican institutions and the close, tight-knit social network relations that preserve this ambiguity was the acceleration of processes of rule instability, physical mobility, and social ambiguity in the mid–nineteenth century.

[46] Richard H. Kohn, *Eagle and Sword: The Federalists and the Creation of the Military Establishment in America, 1783–1802* (New York: Free Press, 1975), 46–47; Richard W. Barsness, "John C. Calhoun and the Military Establishment, 1817–1825," *The Wisconsin Magazine of History*, 1966, 43–53; William H. Riker, *Soldiers of the States: The Role of the National Guard in American Democracy* (Washington: Public Affairs Press, 1957), 36–40.

[47] Kenneth Otis McCreedy, "Palladium of Liberty: The American Militia System, 1815–1861" (PhD diss., University of California, Berkeley, 1991), 235–264.

These, in turn, were a product of a number of simultaneous social, political, and economic transformations: in particular, the Market Revolution and the Civil War.

The effect of the Civil War on the rules and social relations in the United States was profound: it completely reorganized both Northern and Southern society, socialized men across the nation into the practices of bureaucratized violence, created local threats to order in cities that prompted police reform, and spurred migration west. Indeed, it is hard to overemphasize the extent to which the War transformed American social life at every level.

Most simply, the Civil War led to the creation of a wide variety of new rules. In the Reconstruction South, the Fourteenth and Fifteenth Amendments had the effect of upending who was able to participate in political life by expanding suffrage and civil rights protections to African Americans, even as whites maintained control over local economic and social resources. In the West, in turn, the War encouraged an explosion of territorial expansion – indeed, during the War itself, six new territories were formed with the strong support of the Lincoln administration and organized according to an imperial template, with the federal government maintaining control over crucial and important roles in the territorial administration.[48] All of a sudden, however, Anglo-American settlers were moving in to the Dakotas, Colorado, New Mexico, and Arizona, building economic and social bridges across those jurisdictional divides, undercutting the top-down and segmented form of imperial authority practiced by the federal government. Both Reconstruction-era constitutional changes and western expansion created the potential for decoupling by calling into question whether or not new rules for political life would be enforced through social control relations on the ground.

In turn, the Market Revolution (which, according to Charles Sellers, mostly antedated the War and very likely played a role in initiating it) involved a widespread reorganization in social relations.[49] The Revolution included the creation of new transportation and economic interlinkages, the unsettling of craft logics of production by industrialization, the expansion of commodification, and a host of other related economic developments. It too transformed American social and jurisdictional life, creating scales of social interaction that were previously unheard of, and introducing fundamental changes in how American families, neighborhoods, religions, and so on linked inhabitants together. In areas like northern Illinois and Chicago, these changes meant that traditional republican practices of enforcement in towns and counties that depended on local knowledge and delegation to tight, interconnected

48 Richard W. Etulain, "Abraham Lincoln: Political Founding Father of the American West," *Montana: The Magazine of Western History* 59, no. 2 (2009): 3–93.

49 Charles Sellers, *The Market Revolution: Jacksonian America, 1815–1846* (Oxford: Oxford University Press, 1994), 202–268.

communities would no longer work as intended. Thus, when actors continued to use older practices (such as the *posse comitatus* or deputization) those practices began to allow for divergent private and public forms; private security and vigilantism began to coexist with a more professionalized policing apparatus. Patterns of social control, in other words, gradually decoupled from the jurisdictional order they were supposed to help sustain, leading to organizational transformation.

The double transition of the Market Revolution and Civil War thus deeply affected republicanism in the United States. In a context of new social relations, reorganized political statuses, and expanding jurisdictions into new territories, the interests of powerful men no longer seemed to represent other members of society. The people's security, for instance, could hardly be defined solely by wealthy white men in a world where freedmen could vote, for example. Similarly, it was difficult for locally powerful people to motivate their neighbors to police themselves in the name of a vaguely defined public interest if the residents of their neighborhoods were moving in and out with abandon and did not share the kinds of close ties that would make such proclamations definitive. By losing their grip on what counted as the public interest, the claims of some of these people began to look more partisan – limited, for instance, solely to the interests of property owners or white voters instead of other members of society. This, in turn, became the basis for the separation out of a distinctly "private" interest.

In addition, however, new spaces created by these interactions provided new, overlapping forms of identity as well — and this, in turn, allowed for the construction of a public that was neither one nor the other, but *both*. In the cities, this took the form, for instance, of interactions in spaces like train stations and saloons that mixed individuals not only by ethnicity but also by class. This made it possible to identify interests that were *shared* by various elements of society by "abstracting" individuals away from those categorical markers that made them a distinct part of a subgroup.[50] When these effects could no longer be managed within the formal framework of republican forms of coercion, elites created institutions reflecting the new division of interests into distinct public and private clusters. But these institutions, themselves, were always built using the rules and resources that had come before. I now turn to a closer examination of these institutions in different jurisdictions in the United States.

50 Philip J. Ethington, *The Public City: The Political Construction of Urban Life in San Francisco, 1850–1900* (Cambridge: Cambridge University Press, 1994), 58–85; Lisa Keller, *The Triumph of Order: Democracy and Public Space in New York and London* (New York: Columbia University Press, 2009), 39–61; Mary P. Ryan, *Civic Wars: Democracy and Public Life in the American City during the Nineteenth Century* (Berkeley: University of California Press, 1997), 31–43.

INSTITUTIONAL CHANGE IN AMERICAN VIOLENCE

The building blocks of the United States were the local, overlapping and fragmentary jurisdictions inherited and adapted from England. Table 1 indicates the four most important. Each included a formal set of social order rules and a model of social control relations. Jurisdictional decoupling thus reorganized the existing fusion of public security to private effort at each level, beginning in the mid–nineteenth century and extending through the twentieth. This process depended on i) the preexisting republican institutions within each jurisdictions, and ii) the forms of social control used at that level to motivate those institutions. I begin with counties and then turn to cities, states, and territories.

Counties and Enclosed Authority

Jurisdictional Social Order

Counties, rather than towns, were the most salient political jurisdiction for most antebellum Americans, both North and South.[51] Traditionally, these had been the local extensions of central authority (in England, they were based on the notion of the shire, which was the King's local jurisdiction of administration) rather than serving as entities of local autonomy. In the United States, county government was thus an extension of the state – counties all had, more or less, the same sets of officials who were responsible for collecting taxes, administering the county court, and maintaining local roads, and so on.[52] Counties had a plural executive (often called a board of supervisors or trustees) rather than a single head – these councils were (and are) composed often, but not always, of members selected from subdistricts into which the counties were divided (e.g., townships and towns). Because nineteenth-century counties in the United States (especially in the west and even south) often covered large swaths of territory and were the focal jurisdiction for much market and infrastructural activity, the political offices of the county were almost from the outset the provenance of wealthy, large-scale landowners. Counties almost always had minimal bureaucracy and rarely possessed much authority to make dramatic administrative changes.

[51] David Thomas Konig, *Law and Society in Puritan Massachusetts: Essex County, 1629–1692* (Chapel Hill: University of North Carolina Press, 1979), 36; Albert Ogden Porter, *County Government in Virginia: A Legislative History, 1607–1904* (New York: AMS Press, 1966).

[52] John A. Fairlie, *Local Government in Counties, Towns and Villages* (New York: The Century Company, 1906), 57–58, 75–137. County government in the seventeenth and eighteenth centuries was much more important in the South than in New England, where locally autonomous towns predominated. Ann Durkin Keating, "Governing the New Metropolis: The Development of Urban and Suburban Governments in Cook County, Illinois, 1831–1902" (PhD diss., University of Chicago, 1984), 8–9; Konig, *Law and Society in Puritan Massachusetts*, 36–37.

The primary law officer of the county was the sheriff. Sheriffs, elected officials who earned money primarily through fees and who were attached both to county commissioners and to court judges, had many responsibilities in addition to keeping the peace, including executing warrants, collecting taxes, and holding sales of seized property. They were supplemented by constables, who acted as quasi-sheriffs at the town level. As noted in the introduction, it was sheriffs and constables who were also responsible for arresting offenders identified by the court and mobilizing the *posse*. These groups would very often be composed of neighbors of the victim or of relatives and friends of the constable or sheriff, but they were not usually organized in advance. In most jurisdictions, the sheriff could also mobilize the local militia, which was organized at the level of the county as well and was composed of all free white males inhabiting the county as the *posse*. In the south, most slave patrols were organized along militia lines at the county level.[53]

As Elijah Haines explained in his 1855 legal manual, such officers of the peace in the early nineteenth-century United States were understood to combine two different types of roles – they were both ministerial (in the sense that they were responsible for administering legal writ) and they were original (in the sense that they had their own unique function as conservators of peace).[54] The actual powers of arrest or forcible confinement granted to officers of the law in the United States were (and are) almost the same as those granted to regular citizens; the main difference has to do with the consequences of arresting someone in error and a set of legal responsibilities mandating an officer arrest the suspect when witnessing a criminal act.[55] The real coercive power of sheriffs and constables came when they were able to mobilize local citizens to engage in violence, not when they themselves were engaged in it.

Sheriffs were therefore *coordinators* rather than *practitioners* of violence. Although they were expected to arrest offenders, their role was usually identifying and interpreting threats rather than enacting coercive power. Indeed, in common law, arrest authority was technically the purview of anyone who witnessed a crime – the duties and responsibilities of sheriffs were different in that they could act on warrant (and were less vulnerable to false arrest prosecution), but the coercive expectations of sheriffs were basically the same as the citizenry. Sheriffs were authorized to deputize individuals to act on their behalf, who in turn would earn a portion of the sheriff's fees.

53 Karraker, *The Seventeenth-Century Sheriff*, 63–159; Hadden, *Slave Patrols*.

54 Elijah M. Haines, *A Practical Treatise on the Powers and Duties of Justices of the Peace and Constables, in the State of Illinois with the Necessary Forms of Proceeding, Embracing Also, a Collection of Original and Selected Forms, for Popular Use in the Transaction of Business* (Chicago: Keen & Lee, 1855), 387.

55 David A. Sklansky, "The Private Police," *UCLA Law Review* 46 (1998): 1185.

Relational Social Control

Counties depended on concrete personal relations among elected officials and other residents rather than regulation to facilitate coercion. Specifically, lacking the option of creating a bureaucracy, antebellum counties in most rural districts in the United States were organized to provide *ad hoc* mobilization based on threats identified by powerful leaders, who, in turn, relied on their own personal networks rather than abstract regulations and division of authority to mobilize popular participation. I claim that a particular form of social network organization – known as enclosed authority – provided officials with an interpretive monopoly over local policy in county government and gave them the power to mobilize individuals to act. In Chapter 3, I discuss the specifics of this form of control more in depth and show how to measure it using network analytic metrics.

Enclosed authority basically fuses the interests of the county commissioners – who, much like a group of oligarchs, control the workings of county policy through the commissioner system – to a hidden skeleton of influence controlled by them. Although county officials were often also wealthy relative to their coresidents, it was this pattern of social relations rather than possession of material resources that allowed the system to work. Commissioners don't need to construct a bureaucracy of coercion or rely on voluntary participation (contra the myth of frontier democracy) because they are, ideally, located in a position where they can both control crucial resources *and* interpret how nonofficials are supposed to respond to disorder. Participatory democracy in counties in the United States was based, in other words, on inequality.

Decoupling and Institutional Change

Of course, this system of coupled enclosed authority and county jurisdiction hardly ever worked precisely as intended, since individuals frequently tried to subvert the network positions of powerful political officials by building cross-cutting alliances to other, nonattached elites. For the most part, as long as the county commissioner system was in place, elite actors could find a way to manage such attempts at undercutting control, but when commissioners disagreed with each other or with other county officials about some manner involving the application of coercion *and* were threatened by cross-cutting alliances from below, their control broke down and the private interests of the commissioners could become starkly different from the public interest in protection.[56]

[56] Some important forms of private violence, including county seat wars and early vigilance committees, emerged from these kinds of conflicts. See Nathaniel Pitt Langford, *Vigilante Days and Ways: The Pioneers of the Rockies, the Makers and Making of Montana and Idaho* (Chicago: A. C. McClurg & Co, 1912), 479–481; James A. Schellenberg, "County Seat Wars: Historical Observations," *American Studies* 22, no. 2 (1981): 81–95; Stephen J. Buck, "To Hold the Prize: The County Seat War in Du Page County, 1867–1872," *Illinois Historical Journal* 85, no. 4 (December 1992): 194–208.

In the mid–nineteenth century, new transportation and market links began to transform conceptions of social order and practices of social control in many rural counties throughout the country (particularly those in the Midwest and Mid-Atlantic). For example, not only did the nation's rural transportation infrastructure undergo a revolutionary change in access and development, but between 1800 and 1860 the number of counties in the United States increased five-fold, paving the way for would-be elites to try to carve their own spheres of influence in local settlements across the nation.[57] At the same time, this process also destabilized the efficacy of local law enforcement institutions by creating intense local competition for tax revenue and execution fees.

Institutional change in terms of coercion came slowly and unevenly to counties. But when it did, it usually meant distinguishing specifically public from specifically private forms of violence. Vigilante movements, for instance, were frequently organized at the county level, as were the claims societies and horse-thief protection societies pervasive in the Midwest and far West in the late nineteenth century.[58] But while these groups claimed to act in the public interest, they were also admittedly and explicitly private organizations. In the Southwest, counties became some of the first places to see the professionalization of the sheriff's role, as gunfighter experts in violence transformed the coordinating role of the sheriff into a practitioner role. In the South and nonurban East, on the other hand, traditional forms of sheriff practice continued much as they always had until the end of the nineteenth century.[59]

Municipalities and Delegative Authority

Jurisdictional Social Order

Cities had a very different institutional history than counties. As units preserving a certain amount of local autonomy, most towns in the United States (most of which were located in New England during the colonial period) resembled specially chartered cities rather than the town-as-parish division found in England. This meant that most towns possessed a great deal of control over the scope of local police regulation, extending governmental oversight to moral regulation, market transactions, and, in Puritan colonies, church membership.[60] As city charters became more prevalent in the late eighteenth

[57] 428 counties were listed in the 1800 census; in 1860, the number increased to 2,127. On new transportation links, see Cronon, *Nature's Metropolis*, 63–91.

[58] Brown, *Strain of Violence*, 305–319; Little and Sheffield, "Frontiers and Criminal Justice"; Patrick B. Nolan, *Vigilantes on the Middle Border: A Study of Self-Appointed Law Enforcement in the States of the Upper Mississippi from 1840 to 1880* (New York: Garland, 1987).

[59] Bruce Smith, *Rural Crime Control* (New York: Institute of Public Administration, 1933), 48–63.

[60] Novak, *The People's Welfare*; Jon C. Teaford, *The Municipal Revolution in America: Origins of Modern Urban Government, 1650–1825* (Chicago: University of Chicago Press, 1975).

century, much of this police power was retained, usually under the guidance of a common or municipal council (elected by wards), with a unitary executive at the head.

The city's main coercive institution was the constable/watch system. The constable or town marshal, usually (though not always) a political appointee of the city council and paid on the basis of a fee-for-service model, possessed many of the same duties as the sheriff did within county jurisdictions: tax collection, the execution of warrants, supervising elections, and so forth. Constables usually worked explicitly for the council, though they were also attached to the justices of the peace office. They too could call on onlookers or local residents to aid in arrests in case of need and were able to deputize officials (often at the request or approval of the council) to operate on their behalf. Frequently, the constable system was extended so that each ward had a constable under the unitary control of a town marshal.[61]

In addition to the constable or marshal, towns and cities usually possessed a watch, composed of small patrols of men who were conscripted or who volunteered to roam the streets of the town at night and, occasionally, during the day to check for fires, ensure that shopkeepers were following regulations, and so forth. The watch – usually made up of ten or twenty men, scattered throughout the city's environs – were not necessarily empowered with special arrest powers, though they were expected to respond to cries for help and to report crimes in progress. They did not execute warrants, however, and were paid a daily fee (which was usually small). In Boston, most of the night watch in the 1810s and 1820s were small business owners, many of whom appreciated the opportunity to make extra money on fees and who began to serve repeatedly in the role.[62] Other cities, such as Chicago, only activated a watch for limited periods of time of crisis, such as the periodic burglary epidemics that would hit the city. In addition to the watch, the city often authorized special watchmen or constables for public events like elections. During riots, these men would often be called into action to restore order, usually under the supervision of the constable or county sheriff.[63]

Relational Social Control

Cities did not depend on personal relationships to maintain control – instead, they relied on expansive and abstract regulatory or police power. This power in turn involved specifying (often at great detail) the expectations of residents of the city.

[61] Roger Lane, *Policing the City: Boston, 1822–1885* (Cambridge, MA: Harvard University Press, 1967), 3–13; Monkkonen, *Police in Urban America*, 30–37.

[62] Lane, *Policing the City*, 9.

[63] Gilje, *The Road to Mobocracy: Popular Disorder in New York City, 1763–1834*, 278–281; Lane, *Policing the City*, 26–37.

Enforcement of these regulations was not bureaucratic, however. Ironically, because cities were usually too large for personal monitoring of observance of these regulations, most cities delegated enforcement to local neighborhoods. Local citizens, in essence, would bring complaints to the justice of the peace or to the local alderman, who would issue a warrant and adjudicate the matter locally. In Philadelphia (and other cities) most of the alderman were esteemed members of the local community and much of their work involved essentially using the imprimatur of the law to help settle local squabbles.[64] This system basically located coercive power in the neighborhoods themselves, where personal relations *could* help manage social control. In Chapter 5, I operationalize and measure patterns of delegative authority in Chicago during the crucial years of the 1850s.

This system of delegative authority depended, then, on a substratum of relationships among residents in city neighborhoods that were cohesive. Ethnic ties usually served this function, and much law enforcement, as I argue in Chapter 5, was a matter of internal management of disputes within solidaristic communities. At the same time, in order to avoid the politicization of these local ethnic ties into parties that would threaten to force redistribution of tax revenue toward poorer communities, city councils in places like Chicago drew ward boundaries to divide ethnic neighborhoods and protect property owners. Robin Einhorn has termed this a "segmented system" of political economy.[65]

Decoupling and Institutional Change

Although delegative authority worked fairly well as long as ethnic or class-based groups could be contained in distinct communities that cross-cut ward boundaries, political mobilization along these lines began in earnest in the 1840s and 1850s. The causes for these disruptions in the division of urban life into smaller islands providing their own security is complex, but a series of ethnic riots, a robust nativist movement, along with the Civil War, blurred the social categories organizing enforcement in many northern cities.[66] At first, these unsettled spaces were most obvious in areas where members from distinct communities interacted with one another, like saloons and train stations. These, in turn, soon became public places in a way that confounded earlier attempts to maintain social gradations in city life. But they also created a public security threat to which city councils responded by expanding and fusing the constable/night watch institutions and making them permanent divisions in city government.

64 Steinberg, *The Transformation of Criminal Justice*, 38–55, 103–106.

65 Robin L. Einhorn, *Property Rules: Political Economy in Chicago, 1833–1872* (Chicago: University of Chicago Press, 1991).

66 Steinberg, *The Transformation of Criminal Justice*, 119–149; Lane, *Policing the City*, 26–38, 85–141.

Because the breakdown of delegative authority also affected the powerful market actors who were, in many ways, the power behind the scene in the common councils, this extended policing power *also* led some constables and deputies to transform themselves into entrepreneurs, catering to this market. At first, this simply meant substituting private firms for the city as the provider of fees (even without giving up official roles as deputies), but eventually people like Pinkerton became important sources of expertise in the coveted skill of detection and often ended up working for cities as well.[67] In addition, firms began hiring their own watchmen, many of whom secured a special constable status granting them public powers of arrest. During the 1860s and 1870s, the modern American private detective industry and the hiring of watchmen became just as vital to the provision of security in American cities as did the police departments, which diffused throughout American cities during the same period. These two entities – the private security industry, organized along market terms, and the municipal police, organized as a bureaucracy – jointly provided security in the city in response to the decoupling of delegative authority from municipal social order.

States and Representative Authority

Jurisdictional Social Order

States were considered a locus of sovereignty in the United States before the Civil War and were quintessential republican institutions.[68] They were and are based, usually, on a unitary executive and representative assembly. Governors gradually became elected officials in each state (some, such as Massachusetts, had relied on elections from the outset) first by the assemblies themselves, and later by state residents.

The primary coercive arm at the state level was the militia – the governor was the executive in charge of mobilizing the state militia and in ensuring its administration via the adjutant or some other office. Militia were not only a constitutional requisite, they were considered the key institution within the republican framework for national security as well; consequently, Congress, could also mobilize the militia of the states, over which the president was commander.[69]

Governors could and did request federal military aid – something they often considered preferable to mobilizing their own residents to, say, suppress

67 Johnson, *Policing the Urban Underworld*, 62–65.

68 Larry D. Kramer, "Putting the Politics Back into the Political Safeguards of Federalism," *Columbia Law Review*, 2000, 252–268; Forrest McDonald, *States' Rights and the Union: Imperium in Imperio, 1776–1876* (Lawrence: University Press of Kansas, 2000), 19–22.

69 Jerry Cooper, *The Rise of the National Guard: The Evolution of the American Militia, 1865–1920* (Lincoln: University of Nebraska Press, 2002), 11–22.

local disorder, a costly and sometimes politically unpopular duty.[70] When the issue was one of state defense against native communities, on the other hand, militia mobilization was often a popular way of harnessing settler anti-Indian prejudice and sentiment.

Finally, in some states, the governor or assembly was responsible for appointing militia captains in the counties. Invariably, these appointments involved identifying locally influential and popular men who, nevertheless, could be relied on as political allies vis-à-vis the ruling faction or party.

Relational Social Control

Since states were sovereign, they were based, ultimately, on a form of authority that made them the repository of the people's will. The key mechanism that had sustained this link between the will of the people and the capacity for the state to enact coercion were the representative institutions that allowed select, powerful individuals to embody the preferences and political demands of those who elected them and were known to them.

This concrete form of authority, in turn, implied the personalistic organization of local influence within the context of party politics. Since the franchise was quite heavily restricted, particularly in the South, many elected officials were wealthy and socially influential. Factions and parties were fairly unorganized until the 1820s and 1830s, and even when Jacksonian Democracy began to replace the restrictive franchise with a more organized system of party-based patronage, this did not undermine the local connections that made a given individual a good representative of his particular district. Even through the changes in the party system in the 1840s and 1850s, small-scale ward clubs and so forth (which aggregated into larger state organizations) helped reproduce this older logic of personalism, a key tenet of republican authority.[71]

The formal militia, which was also based on this representative logic, had fallen into a period of decline after the War of 1812.[72] However, this only applied to the universal militia; the *volunteer* militia exploded in popularity, particularly during the 1840s and 1850s in cities in the Northeast and Midwest.[73] These units, which involved a group of like-minded men electing a captain and forming what amounted to a fraternal organization to hold dances

[70] Robert W. Coakley, *The Role of Federal Military Forces in Domestic Disorders, 1789–1878* (Washington, DC: Center of Military History, US Army, 1989); Daniel A. Kenney, "Seizing Domestic Tranquility: National Military Intervention in America, 1866–1940" (PhD diss., Brandeis University, 2010), 10–35.

[71] Richard Franklin Bensel, *The American Ballot Box in the Mid-Nineteenth Century* (Cambridge: Cambridge University Press, 2004), 168–185.

[72] McCreedy, "Palladium of Liberty," 184–194; Riker, *Soldiers of the States: The Role of the National Guard in American Democracy*, 21–40.

[73] McCreedy, "Palladium of Liberty," 278–324.

and marches, were integrated as full-fledged entities within the formal state militia. Moreover, they were very often organized on the basis of exactly the same ward and ethnic clubs that provided the personal relationships at the heart of the party system. While these groups did not always serve in a coercive capacity, they did help couple personal influence and personal networks – which were, by definition, exclusive and restricted – to a system whereby they could nevertheless represent the people's coercive power in general.[74]

Decoupling and Institutional Change

The supposition that specific groups of organized men (usually white, wealthy men) could represent the people in general was undercut by changes in formal rules about political participation. In particular, expanded suffrage decoupled the traditional logic of personal authority from the formal coercive institutions of the state.

After the Civil War, however, this crisis became acute. This was particularly true in Southern states, where military occupation laid a completely new and foreign layer of coercive power in the hands of Reconstruction governors, and where the expansion of suffrage completely undermined the restrictive myth of the white male as the representative ideal for society as a whole. This was not merely a matter of new interests challenging older ones within the framework of stable electoral institutions, but rather decoupling the coercive logic of personal control from those institutions that were supposed to protect that control.

On one hand, in many Southern states, many whites converted their personal political ties, forged in party politics, and their experience with wartime violence into an organized, private vigilante crusade to reestablish the link between white men and their representative authority and state institutions. These vigilante groups were numerous – the Ku Klux Klan, the Knights of the White Camelia, the White League, and so on – but they all, under the aegis of powerful elites, combined an attempt to reintroduce racial boundaries with a political attempt to redeem the state from the corrupt and impure Reconstruction governments.[75]

On the other hand, these very attempts at reform were a key part of the reorganization of the legal norms that guided public militia organization. Commercial and industrial elites in the north and agrarian interests in the south converged on the need for a public solution to the problem of class and race "disorder."[76] By the late 1870s, states were beginning to professionalize their militias and nationalize them: the National Guard and, eventually, the

74 Marcus Cunliffe, *Soldiers & Civilians: The Martial Spirit in America, 1775–1865* (Boston: Little, Brown, 1968), 179–254; Harry S. Laver, "Rethinking the Social Role of the Militia: Community-Building in Antebellum Kentucky," *The Journal of Southern History* 68, no. 4 (2002): 777–816.

75 Trelease, *White Terror*, xv–xlviii. 76 Cooper, *The Rise of the National Guard*, 44–64.

state police reflected attempts by the state to forge a public alternative to forms of violence (vigilantism, private guards, and so on), which many residents began to despise. At the same time, in the South, in particular, but also in some Midwestern and Western areas, private coercion remained a crucial part of the organization of force and helped sustain the authority of economic and social elites. Organized, systematic vigilantism, professional militia, and even state constabularies characterized the organization of violence in these states.[77]

Territories and Imperial Authority

Jurisdictional Social Order

Territorial governance in the antebellum and postbellum United States was essentially a hybrid administrative structure. Initially most territories were under the control of a military commander, whose primary function was the management of native groups. The military administration of territories was organized around a system of forts and departmental subdivisions. Eventually, as settlers moved into the territory, it was organized into a political unit and the military commander would be replaced by a governor, appointed by the president with the approval of Congress, and a territorial assembly, elected by residents.[78]

Complementing the military/governor system were counties and towns organized and chartered by the local assemblies and, occasionally, simply willed into being by local settlers. These counties and towns resembled those in states, but were very circumscribed in terms of coordination at the level of the territory, since local interests were only represented in the relatively disempowered assembly.[79]

Coercive power in the territories thus contained an element of local control (sheriffs, marshals, and so on were all present in local territorial jurisdictions) but was managed primarily through the military and the US marshal, the agent of the federal court and the only law enforcement official with territory-wide authority. The US marshal was responsible for a variety of duties, including executing federal warrants, investigating postal robbery and counterfeiting, monitoring the borders, and, most controversially, arresting fugitive slaves. Like

77 Michael J. Pfeifer, ed., *Lynching Beyond Dixie: American Mob Violence Outside the South* (Urbana: University of Illinois Press, 2013); Smith, *Rural Crime Control*, 126–179.

78 Julian Go, *Patterns of Empire: The British and American Empires, 1688 to the Present* (Cambridge: Cambridge University Press, 2011), 45; Matthew G. Hannah, "Space and Social Control in the Administration of the Oglala Lakota ('Sioux'), 1871–1879," *Journal of Historical Geography* 19, no. 4 (1993): 412–432.

79 Richard White, *It's Your Misfortune and None of My Own: A New History of the American West* (Norman: University of Oklahoma Press, 1993), 177–178.

sheriffs, marshals worked for fees and relied on a system of deputies for much of the implementation of the process they were expected to serve.[80]

The US Army, however, was a much more important actor from the standpoint of political and territorial incorporation. The military played a crucial role in managing the boundaries between Indian and settler populations, addressing border enforcement, and promoting infrastructural development. While the Army and its soldiers were, naturally, highly important economic actors in the Southwest and West, their role was primarily political. Moreover, while military units occasionally aided in law enforcement duties in the territories, these were considered secondary to the national job of managing the territories as political units. As a professionalizing force (particularly in the aftermath of the Civil War), the US Army regarded itself less and less as a mediator of domestic discord.[81]

Relational Social Control

Scholars have carefully drawn links between the logic of American administration of territories and British-style imperialism. The territorial system was based on a logic of abstract imperial authority. Imperial authority, in turn, was a strategy of *divide et impera* – what political scientists Daniel Nexon and Thomas Wright have depicted as a hub-and-spoke system.[82]

First, the primary class of officials responsible for administering the state were political appointees from Washington. Their authority was based on their relationship with the core actors in the federal government rather than relationships with local white or native residents. They maintained a relatively centralized control over important political decisions in each territory and were easily able to engage with and coordinate with one another.[83]

Second, local residents (both natives and, to a lesser extent, settlers) were only loosely coordinated with one another, particularly across territorial boundaries. Instead, they were supposed to be "tutored" in the ways of American politics by state officials, who maintained, essentially, monopoly control over their political access.[84] This was part of the reason, for example, that the

80 Frank R. Prassel, *The Western Peace Officer: A Legacy of Law and Order* (Norman: University of Oklahoma Press, 1972).

81 Shelley Bowen Hatfield, *Chasing Shadows: Indians Along the United States-Mexico Border, 1876–1911* (Albuquerque, NM: University of New Mexico Press); Robert M. Utley, *Frontier Regulars: The United States Army and the Indian, 1866–1891* (Lincoln: University of Nebraska Press, 1984); Robert Wooster, *The Military and United States Indian Policy 1865–1903* (Lincoln: University of Nebraska Press, 1995); Robert Wooster, *Nelson A. Miles and the Twilight of the Frontier Army* (Lincoln: University of Nebraska Press, 1996).

82 Daniel H. Nexon and Thomas Wright, "What's at Stake in the American Empire Debate," *American Political Science Review* 101, no. 02 (2007): 253–271.

83 Earl Spencer Pomeroy, *The Territories and the United States, 1861–1890: Studies in Colonial Administration* (Philadelphia: University of Pennsylvania Press, 1947), 62–108.

84 Stefan Heumann, "The Tutelary Empire: State-and Nation-building in the 19th Century United States" (PhD diss., University of Pennsylvania, 2009), 69–106.

government established reservations – to stop native groups from crossing jurisdictional boundaries and upsetting the divide and rule logic of the empire. As reflections of the core power of the US federal government, the military *was* empowered trans-jurisdictionally. The US Army thus engaged in a wide variety of activities that went far beyond the mere protection of settlers, including infrastructural development, providing resources to native groups, and so on.[85] They were responsible for territorial incorporation as a whole.

Decoupling and Institutional Change

The major threat to imperial political control in the territories came from the market incorporation of the trans–Mississippi West, particularly after the Civil War. Railroads, the cattle industry, and mining extraction were all oriented toward *integrating* rather than *dividing* the territorial system into a shared economy.[86] As a result, the opening of the trans-Mississippi frontier involved creating links between jurisdictions that were informal and undermined the logic of imperial authority.

At the central level, economic actors often tried to coordinate their activities with the federal government, and many of the railroad barons and mining company owners had close personal relationships with policymakers in Washington. But at the local level, divide and rule was cross-cut by the reorganization of authority through the building of market ties among communities on the ground and the presence of powerful, translocal employers. This meant that local law enforcement, responsible for much of the property crime translocal market interests were concerned about, became a focus of contention: outside economic actors wanted sheriffs and marshals who would cooperate with them, but the local roots of these institutions combined with resentment against railroads and big mining companies, meant that they often did not function as market incorporating actors wanted.[87]

Hence, not only did local law enforcement agents became important allies for big business in the West, but those firms also hired a veritable army of private experts – both formal, authorized agents of the law and simple private watchmen – to protect their interests. As demonstrated skill in violence became more important as a criteria in finding employment, these individuals, in turn, were knitted into a class, occupying and transforming traditional law enforcement roles and professionalizing them in addition to easily moving between private and public employment. The military, particularly after the Posse Comitatus Act of 1878, focused more exclusively on managing the boundaries of the United States and expanding of its imperial authority overseas.

85 ibid., 107–157.

86 Richard White, *Railroaded: The Transcontinentals and the Making of Modern America* (New York: W. W. Norton, 2011), 507–517.

87 White, *Railroaded*, 414–452.

Both a powerful, private form of violence organization – mercenary gunfighting – as well as the public expansion of military and the US marshals characterized the system of coercion in late nineteenth-century territories.

PUTTING THE PIECES TOGETHER: FRAGMENTED VIOLENCE IN THE UNITED STATES AND DIFFERENT CLAIMS TO PROTECTION

These snapshots demonstrate that decoupling led to the emergence of a public and private organization of violence in each of the jurisdictional building blocks of the American state. Public and private actors often collaborated rather than competed in providing protection, sharing resources and personnel. Just as state-organized bureaucratic coercion expanded for the first time in the United States in the late nineteenth century, so too did the claims of explicitly private individuals, firms, and communities to be able to use force to protect themselves.

Of course, it is important to remember that this transition toward a public-private coevolution occurred in fits and starts. For instance, although almost every county had a sheriff and constable system through most of the nineteenth century, according to Richard Maxwell Brown's data, only around 6 percent experienced vigilance committee mobilization in the antebellum years.[88] Even the spread of police departments was somewhat erratic, reflecting idiosyncratic and local adoption rather than a uniform top-down policy on the part of state or federal government.[89]

Nevertheless, the cases presented in the following chapters offer both an interlinked narrative of how this dual public and private system emerged over time in the United States as well as a way of exploring the causal mechanisms associated with jurisdictional decoupling. The first two cases address changes related to a growing market society and, as such, address changes in social relations. Starting from the earliest and most local case – that of a vigilance movement in several counties in 1840s Illinois – I show the local pattern of concrete social network ties characterizing enclosed authority decoupled from the rules of the county jurisdiction in Ogle-Lee, paving the way for the private enforcement of the law. Though it took the form of communal violence, this enforcement, I show, was a direct result of the pressures induced by anonymity and the need for defending insecure property in a frontier induced by a new market society. In nearby Chicago, which witnessed the birth of

88 Brown, *Strain of Violence*, Appendix 3. This is likely a very conservative estimate, since Brown almost exclusively used county histories rather than newspapers to compile his sample. Moreover, it does not include the pervasive and common miners' courts, squatters associations, claims clubs, and smaller committees of vigilance established in many rural communities during periods of rapid settlement.

89 Monkkonen, *Police in Urban America*, 49–64.

TABLE 2. *Change in coercive enforcement in the nineteenth-century United States*

			Result of decoupling	
Case	Jurisdiction	Period	Public	Private
Northern Illinois	County	1839–1845	Sheriff's Department	Sporadic vigilantism
Chicago	City	1850–1872	Municipal Police	Private security
Louisiana	State	1866–1878	National Guard	Systematic vigilantism
Trans–Mississippi West	Territory	1866–1900	US Military	Mercenary gunfighting

both a public bureaucratic police force and the modern, market-based private security industry over the next two decades, I explore the ways in which the railroad and the growth of public places within the city created the problem of urban strangers, decoupling the system of delegating social control to ethnically homogenous and economically heterogenous neighborhoods from the rules of municipal government.

I then examine the decoupling of rules from relations by focusing on the political shifts engendered by the Civil War. In Louisiana, new political rights for African-American males decoupled the logic of representative rules from the social control relations in day-to-day life, which were still built on the concrete power of whites over blacks, leading (as in northern Illinois) to vigilante violence. Moving west from Louisiana into the territories of the West and Southwest, in turn, the federal government imposed a set of rules on inhabitants that relied on the local provision of enforcement and a strategy of divide-and-rule. These rules, however, decoupled from the actual relationships on the ground in the West, where a powerful form of market incorporation linked actors the federal government intended to keep separate, thereby paving the way (as in Chicago) for a market-based form of private mercenary gunfighting to fill the enforcement gap.

Table 2 depicts this logic of case selection, depicting how the various cases presented in this book work together to establish the mechanism of decoupling across jurisdictional levels and time periods. In each case, the end result was the creation of a dual public and private system of coercive enforcement.

At the same time, advantage of the typographic approach adopted in this book is that it allows us to make sense not only of these specific cases, but also to connect them to a master logic of American coercive organization. The United States in the nineteenth century *never* had a cohesive, centralized security policy, but rather depended on a system of fragmented, overlapping jurisdictions. This meant that private and public interests were fused together into a larger republican institutional framework, one sustained by powerful actors at each level.[90]

90 Novak, "The Myth of the 'Weak' American State."

Decoupling of rules for social order from relations of social control created new kinds of organized coercion in specific places, like Chicago and Louisiana, but those changes concatenated through other levels and other overlaps among jurisdictions to reshape the state provision of violence as a whole. The division of the social world in the United States in the late nineteenth century into distinct market, state and society domains of social life (broadly defined) is usually viewed as a general organizational revolution, but it was also one with specific referents in the organization of coercive enforcement.[91] Thus, I can use the theory presented here to explain the popularization of the private detective industry in Chicago in the early 1850s, but I could also extend it to demonstrate how, given Chicago's place in a national market, the effects of that innovation spread throughout the country.

The unraveling of public from private security meant that the continued reliance on private violence – whether to manage factories, protect railroads, or reinforce racial hierarchies – complemented public and bureaucratic forms of violence emerging at the same time. Bureaucratization of state coercion in the United States also meant privatization; the two organizational responses to decoupling were interlinked from the outset. Moreover, in the legal domain, the rights of the state to monopolize violence were layered onto the older right for individuals and firms to protect their lives and livelihoods, having the effect, ironically, of actually sharpening those private claims. It had become possible to imagine both a powerful security state as well as private, individual protection as not only commensurate, but also mutually reinforcing.

91 Charles Perrow, *Organizing America: Wealth, Power, and the Origins of Corporate Capitalism* (Princeton, NJ: Princeton University Press, 2009), 217–228.

3

Bandits, Elites, and Vigilantes in Antebellum Illinois

INTRODUCTION

In his famous 1838 address to the Springfield Lyceum, Abraham Lincoln spelled out the dangers of mob rule for American politics. Responding, in part, to a private attack on a group of gamblers in Vicksburg, Mississippi, in 1835 that had become a public symbol of frontier disorder, Lincoln argued that the "mobocratic spirit, which all must admit, is now abroad in the land" would lead to the collapse of "the strongest bulwark of any government ... the *attachment* of the people." Lincoln's complaint was that this spirit undermined the core value of the American system: "the capability of a people to govern themselves," a capability that was born in the emotional resonances of the revolution, but which now required "reason, cold, calculating, unimpassioned reason" to "furnish all the materials for our future support and defence."[1]

For Lincoln – and for many Americans of the time – public order was a fragile thing. The 1830s and 1840s not only witnessed the growth of a newly invigorated vigilance movement throughout the Mississippi Valley, but also anti-abolition riots and lynchings throughout the lower Midwest, as well as ethnic clashes in cities like Philadelphia and New York.[2] Moreover, crimes taking advantage of a growing market, such as swindling, confidence artistry, and counterfeiting, seemed to be more common, and many felt a sense of unease about the direction of the nation.[3]

[1] Abraham Lincoln, "Address to the Young Men's Lyceum of Springfield, Illinois," in *Speeches and Writings, 1832–1858*, vol. 45, Library of America (New York: Literary Classics of the United States, 1989), 28–36. For background on the Vicksburg lynchings, see Waldrep, *The Many Faces of Judge Lynch*, 27–35, and Pfeifer, *The Roots of Rough Justice*, 18–20.

[2] Paul A. Gilje, *Rioting in America* (Bloomington: Indiana University Press, 1996), 60–86.

[3] Lawrence M. Friedman, "Crimes of Mobility," *Stanford Law Review* (1991): 637–658.

However, the way Lincoln thought about addressing this unease is revealing; namely, he did not propose a turn to more and better soldiers, nor did he wish to unravel the sovereignty of popular opinion as the key to governmental legitimacy. He did not, in other words, agree with Tocqueville's famed advice that American officials develop "an armed force which, while remaining subject to the wishes of the national majority, is independent of the peoples of the towns and capable of suppressing their excesses."[4] Instead, he steadfastly argued that private citizens needed to maintain their vigilant reverence for the law in their own communities and recommit themselves to a shared vision of the public based in deliberation and civic accountability.

Most have interpreted the Lyceum speech to be a warning primarily about the mobocratic spirit of the slave power.[5] And, indeed, the struggles of mob rule were inseparable from the question of slavery. In November 1837, the abolitionist editor of a newspaper in Alton, Illinois, Elijah Lovejoy, had been killed by a mob attempting to destroy his press.[6] This case (along with several others) became national news and demonstrated to observers like Lincoln that the private defense of slavery was enervating the rule of law and infecting the nation with a plague of suppressive violence.[7]

But the problems of disorder exceeded the racial conflict bubbling up from below the Mason-Dixon line. Right in Lincoln's backyard – in the Rock River Valley of northern Illinois, an area including Ogle and Lee counties – was a large and powerful Regulator movement. These Regulators, which included of a number of the area's most notable local residents, waged an intense vigilante campaign to rid the area of a group of suspected criminals colloquially termed the "Banditti." The Banditti were, much like the Reno Gang of Indiana, supposedly involved in horse-thievery, counterfeiting, and gambling. And, again much like the Reno Gang, many of the Banditti had powerful social connections and were themselves quite well-established settlers, creating a dilemma for a law enforcement system based on personal connections.

In the summer of 1841, the Regulators organized a wave of extra-legal "law enforcement," leading to the deaths of two suspected murderers and horse thieves, as well as one of the largest murder trials in U.S. history (108 people were charged with participating in the lynching of two suspected local horse-thieves). Yet in nearby Kane County – which was *also* subject to Banditti activity, was also composed of very similar types of settlers from the same northeastern states and cities as those inhabiting the Rock River Valley, and had virtually identical political institutions and legal culture – there was no comparable vigilante mobilization. More puzzling, both areas had powerful

4 Alexis de Tocqueville, *Democracy in America*, ed. J. P. Mayer, trans. George Lawrence (New York: Harper Perennial Modern Classics, 1969), 278.

5 Christopher Waldrep, "The Constitution According to Abraham Lincoln," *Journal of the Illinois State Historical Society* 93, no. 2 (2000): 208–214.

6 Edward Beecher, *Narrative of Riots at Alton* (New York: Dutton, 1965).

7 e.g., *Boston Liberator*, November 24, 1837.

and strong legal institutions, which were used frequently by all classes of society to arbitrate conflicts. So why did these legal institutions seemingly break apart in the Regulator mobilization of Ogle and Lee and not in a neighboring county?

This chapter addresses this question by exploring the decoupling effects of the new market society on institutional life in the Old Northwest in the 1830s and 1840s. The area, like most of the lands in Illinois being settled by immigrants and migrants from the east following the removal of the local Indian groups in the early 1830s, was organized along traditional republican lines, with an expectation that local actors would participate directly in law enforcement. The growth in speculation in land and increases in the sheer physical mobility of people living in the region, however, created conflicts among local settlers while unraveling the day-to-day social networks were supposed to allow powerful actors to use those republican institutions to maintain order.

As a result, like many other counties, Ogle and, later, Lee had multiple factions of influential leaders, many of whom held important political roles. Normally, this was not a problem, since county government in frontier areas like northern Illinois essentially allowed influential leaders to use their own factional networks to help accomplish the work of governing. Kane County (against which I compare Ogle County and Lee County throughout this chapter), for instance, *did* possess the kinds of enclosed, tightly knit networks that allowed for local governance to couple with social control.

But in Ogle and Lee, these factional networks were not mutually exclusive; many local residents had business, friendship, or kinship ties to leaders who themselves weren't tied together. When conflicts erupted between residents, as they frequently did in these kinds of communities, this created a crisis for the legal system and made it difficult for leaders to tamp down on conflicts and leading to mobilization of *posses* without legal authorization. In Kane, conversely, elites were able to maintain their control over legal institutions and relied, instead, on the courts to adjudicate conflicts. Vigilantism in Ogle and Lee did not result from a weak or absent legal regime, but rather from the inability of existing rules to keep up with changes in social relations.

Ogle and Lee were not the only places in Illinois undergoing vigilantism during these years – in addition to the anti-abolitionist riots in Alton, there were violent anti-Mormon mobilizations in Hancock County from 1839 through 1845, and anti-bandit activities in several counties in the southern section of the state from 1846 through 1849.[8] The northern Illinois Regulators, however, offer an exemplary case. Not only were most of the participants from the northeast (an area traditionally lacking a tradition of violent vigilantism such as that witnessed in the Rock River valley), but the basis for the group's operations was also directly located on the new transportation corridor connecting Chicago

[8] Brown, *Strain of Violence*, 309–310.

to the northern Mississippi.[9] In other words, focusing on this movement demonstrates how life on the settlement frontier of the Old Northwest was being upended at the extremely local level by large-scale economic change, even among those who shared cultural and kinship ties.

Before turning to the activities of the Regulators, however, it is essential to first understand something of the legal institutions in place in rural, mid–nineteenth century Illinois. It is to this issue I now turn.

VIOLENCE AND ENFORCEMENT IN THE OLD NORTHWEST

Although it had been a state since 1818, Illinois was still on the very periphery of the nation through the first decades of the nineteenth century. A series of conflicts in the late 1820s with the neighboring Winnebago Indians in the northern districts had led to both treaty concessions and hard feelings among the tribes in the area, who had been forced to leave Illinois and cross the Mississippi River, leaving the northern section of the state open to squatting. In the spring of 1832, under a Sauk chief called Black Hawk, a group of Fox, Sauk, and Kickapoo followers decided to relocate in the still sparsely settled Rock River region on the basis of a disputed concession. This incursion, in turn, provoked a furious response on the part of Illinois residents, who organized a large-scale militia that (in cooperation with the US Army) nearly eradicated the Black Hawk band.[10]

The Black Hawk War is emblematic of the process by which settlers in borderlands areas themselves engaged in coercion. As Paul Frymer and others have recently shown, federal land policy essentially decentralized the responsibility for both economic and political development to local residents.[11] In practice, this transformed "state formation" into a process of settler colonialism, through which local residents not only policed neighboring native groups, but also essentially organized legal, social, and political institutions from the ground up.

This played out partly in settlement patterns. Following the war, settlers (primarily from the northeastern and midwestern states) began making their way into the fertile pastures of the nearby plains. There were some older settlements dating to the Indian years – especially those associated with the pioneering homesteads of John Dixon and John Phelps, which together would end up forming the heart of Lee County and Ogle County, respectively – but most new migrants (almost all of whom were from the northeastern

[9] Douglas K. Meyer, *Making the Heartland Quilt: A Geographical History of Settlement in Early-Nineteenth-Century Illinois* (Carbondale: Southern Illinois University Press, 2000), 68.

[10] James Edward Davis, *Frontier Illinois* (Bloomington: Indiana University Press, 2000), 193–198.

[11] Frymer, "'A Rush and a Push and the Land Is Ours:' Territorial Expansion, Land Policy, and U.S. State Formation."

and midwestern United States), simply squatted on land they considered unpossessed, clearing small farms, and waiting for the government to officially open the area up for sale. Despite these economic idiosyncrasies – which, as we shall see, would prove critical – Illinois had the same kinds of settlement patterns found elsewhere in much of the rural north – most residents lived on small farms, there were a couple of larger settlements (located near rivers), and a small class of large landowners dominated social and economic life.[12]

Residents brought with them strong views of how local government was supposed to work. Most rural areas in the belt of land running from New England across through Minnesota and Iowa were settled by easterners and European immigrants with well-articulated ideas of how to enact justice, fully committed to preserving the institutions they knew well.[13] Moreover, economic and social stratification helped prop up this system; between 1849 and 1870 in Jacksonville, Illinois, for instance, approximately 50 percent of total wealth was in the hands of 10 percent of property owners, which was similar to the distribution of land ownership in northern Illinois.[14] Moreover, many of these wealthy residents were regional boosters, who, despite political differences, frequently worked together to manage local governance and economic affairs.[15] In the Ogle-Lee area, as well as further east in Kane, local residents were strongly committed to trying to bring transportation infrastructure to the area, building schools and colleges, and forging links with commercial elites in Chicago and elsewhere.[16]

Most official governance in these newly settled rural areas involved counties and their subdivisions: townships.[17] In Illinois, counties administered the local legal system (the state courts were based around a circuit system), maintained

[12] For evidence, see Appendix A. (All appendices for this book are available online at www.jonathanobert.com.)

[13] David J. Bodenhamer, "Law and Disorder on the Early Frontier: Marion County, Indiana, 1823–1850," *The Western Historical Quarterly* 10, no. 3 (July 1979): 323–336; Terry Wilson, "The Business of a Midwestern Trial Court: Knox County, Illinois, 1841–1850," *Illinois Historical Journal* 84, no. 4 (1991): 249–267.

[14] Don Harrison Doyle, *The Social Order of a Frontier Community: Jacksonville, Illinois, 1825–70* (Urbana: University of Illinois Press, 1978), 104.

[15] ibid., 122–123.

[16] Henry Boss, *Sketches of the History of Ogle County, Ill., and the Early Settlement of the Northwest* (Polo, IL: Henry R. Boss, 1859), 53–57, 59–75; Henry B. Pierce, Arthur Merrill, and William Henry Perrin, *The Past and Present of Kane County, Illinois* (Chicago: Wm. Le Baron, Jr. & Co., 1878), 221–269.

[17] There were important differences in the legal capacities and responsibilities of governance among, for instance, New England towns, southern counties, and the township/county system found in much of the Midwest. At the same time, all of these local jurisdictions usually relied on the kinds of minimal regulatory control found in Illinois counties. See Fairlie, *Local Government in Counties, Towns and Villages*, 18–53.

real estate and probate records, and collected revenues.[18] They were, however, primarily non-bureaucratic – decision-making in counties was centered in the commissioner system, a group of three elected officials responsible for managing all of the county's important financial and non-criminal legal matters. These officials, particularly after county commissioners' courts were created in 1819, simultaneously had wide discretion over both policy-making as well as legal arbitration – they combined a judicial and legislative roles at the local level.[19]

How was the law actually enforced, then? As noted previously, the main officers of the peace in Illinois counties were the sheriff and constable, who were responsible for serving warrants, aiding the justice of the peace (local criminal courts were also organized around the county level in Illinois), maintaining the general peace, and collecting taxes. Under the constitution, the sheriff was an elected position, although he was be capable of appointing deputies under certain conditions; constables were similar figures with precinct (township) level authority.[20] The day-to-day activity of the Illinois sheriff and constable primarily consisted of serving process and completing chores assigned by the justice of the peace, although, in cases of danger or riot, they were also capable of calling out the power of the county and had powers of arrest, enforceable by legal sanction against those refusing to cooperate.[21]

18 The following discussion builds on John A. Fairlie, "County and Town Government in Illinois," *Annals of the American Academy of Political and Social Science* 47 (May 1913): 62–78.

19 According to the 1819 statute (Sec. 9), the county commissioners' court would "have jurisdiction in all cases where the matter or thing brought before the said court relates to the public concerns of the county collectively, and all county business: and the said court shall have power to punish for contempts as other courts may do, and have all the power necessary to the right exercise of the jurisdiction with which said court is or may be vested according to law'; reprinted in *The Revised Laws of Illinois* (Vandalia, IL: Greiner & Sherman, 1833), 142–143.

20 See "An Act to provide for the election of Justices of the Peace and Constables," in *The Revised Code of Laws of Illinois* (Robert Blackwell, 1827), 255–259. Like sheriffs, constables could arrest offenders and were responsible for serving legal process: "[W]hen any felony or breach of the peace shall be committed in his presence," said an 1827 statute, the constable was expected "to apprehend the person committing the same, and bring him before some justice of the peace, to be dealt with according to law: to suppress all riots and unlawful assemblies, and to keep the peace, and also to serve and execute all warrants, writs, precepts, and other process." Before 1826, they were assigned to particular justices (the role became elective after 1826). "An Act Concerning Justices of the Peace and Constables" (Sec. 49) in *The Revised Laws of Illinois*, 399.

21 Sec. 137 of the Criminal Code of Illinois of 1839 made it illegal for any male adult to refuse service in a *posse* in aid to an officer of the peace. Reprinted in *The Public and General Statute Laws of the State of Illinois* (Chicago: S.F. Gale, 1839), 224. *Posse* service was intended primarily for aid during the arrest portion of punishment, particularly in regard to searching for fugitives. According to 1827 legislation, sheriffs "were to execute and return all writs, warrants, process, orders, and decrees, or every description that shall or may be legally directed and delivered to him, within the limits of his county, under pain of contempt of the court from which such writ, warrant, process, order, or decree may have issued; and for the service of such process, and for keeping the peace, such sheriff or coroner may call to his aid the power of the

At the same time, actually mobilizing law enforcement – and, essentially, all manner of county governance – usually was actually a matter of personal connections among local residents. But what kinds of relations were important? In order to provide officials with the kind of interpretive monopoly that would allow them to mobilize residents into enforcing the law, political officials needed to be able to control the ways in which nonofficials interfaced with county government. They depended on tight-knit patterns of network relations among political officials and nonofficials I call "enclosed authority."

Enclosed authority allowed political officials to control circuits of information by ensuring that elites have their own constituents, which they did not share with other elites with whom they were not themselves connected. When we examine the overall social network – friendship, familial, economic, and so forth – within an early county, we should expect to see either that political officials each have their own "fiefdoms" or that all residents are deeply entangled in a common network in which all residents, essentially, know each other. If there are factions, those factions should be relatively distinct, so that members of one group are relatively separate from the other. Political elites are able to implement policy without a bureaucracy, collect taxes, build roads, and enforce laws, because they can reliably mobilize constituents they know, constituents who have no real options for exit by defecting to another official not otherwise known to the elite. Socially powerful actors should *also* be politically powerful, holding important posts and taking responsibility for bringing their own networks into the governing process.

Why was enclosed authority so important in county government in the nineteenth century? First, by rendering constituents subservient to officials who themselves shared relations, it made it much more difficult for them to join other factions should they be reticent to participate in violence or be sympathetic with the targets of violent action. Second, it also made it possible for officials possessing of such ties to interpret and enforce what counts as a public threat; since in these kinds of structures, actors' social, economic, and political ties tend to overlap (e.g., members of a family also tend to be in business together and share political affiliations) it is much easier for all actors to agree that what powerful individuals see as threatening actually poses a problem.[22]

In theory, enclosed authority helped protect republican conceptions of public security ultimately depending on the efforts of private individuals. In practice, of course, these kinds of patterns of social relationship meant that every citizen's responsibility to participate in violence also meant

county when necessary." "An Act Concerning Sheriffs and Coroners" (Sec. 5) in *The Revised Laws of Illinois*, 374.

[22] This can be operationalized in terms of flow betweenness, a measure I employ in the empirical analysis later in this chapter. See Stephen P. Borgatti, "Centrality and Network Flow," *Social Networks* 27, no. 1 (2005): 55–71.

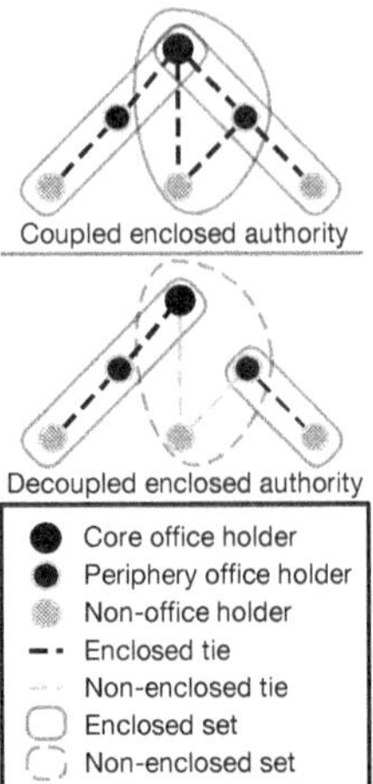

FIGURE 2. Enclosed authority and jurisdictional coupling

acting, at least in part, in accordance with the wishes and demands of the politically powerful, often without having the recourse to turn to other powerful actors.

Moreover, while the ideal type for republican governance in local administration involved enclosed relations dominated by the "best" members of local society, the reality was that enclosed authority was never absolute. Indeed, by the 1830s town and county governance had strayed far from the tight-knit, patriarchal jurisdictions on which much early English settlement had been based. Less wealthy residents, women, African Americans, and even children increasingly sought relief from the presumption of enclosed forms of authority through their use of the law and, at times, their willingness to mobilize against elite authority.[23] Patterns of deference and elite authority (linked to family and work) still played a crucial role in mobilizing law enforcement, but this capacity was always subject to resistance and renegotiation.

The top panel of Figure 2 depicts how enclosed social relations were supposed to couple county government to social authority (I use the words core and periphery here as short-hand for the most important officials in the county's core administration, including sheriffs, commissioners, and others, versus those who are township officials, such as constables and local justices of the peace). In every case when non-officeholders (either core or periphery) have a relationship with more than one officeholder, those officeholders also have a relationship. County leaders are able to maintain high levels of control

[23] Laura F. Edwards, *The People and Their Peace: Legal Culture and the Transformation of Inequality in the Post-Revolutionary South* (Chapel Hill: University of North Carolina Press, 2009), 286–297; Kars, *Breaking Loose Together*, 1–6.

over their constituents (an enclosed set of individuals), making it possible to mobilize coercion when necessary and to interpret threats for the population.

Conversely, the network depicted on the bottom panel – in which non-officeholders have ties to officeholders who themselves are not linked – essentially subverts the interpretive monopoly of the officeholder over what counts as a public security threat and undermines his or her capacity to mobilize coercion (the only path linking the local officeholder to the core officeholder is a tie that goes through a non-officeholder). This mixture of non-enclosed and enclosed ties makes it difficult for officeholders to fuse private interests of individuals with a notion of shared, communal security.

Most of the time in Illinois, officials had no problem getting residents to participate in potentially dangerous service seen as important for maintaining social order, such as joining *posses*.[24] For example, in a survey of Illinois county histories, I was able to identify sixteen cases in which suspects fled after committing a murder between 1819 and 1860; in twelve of those cases, *posses* were organized to help aid in the pursuit.

One early example of such mobilization is an 1834 case in McDonough County in western Illinois, when a member of the truculent McFadden family killed a neighbor with whom he had a long-standing disagreement concerning some property. The neighbor, John Wilson, had been helping the constable, Nelson Montgomery, serve some process at the main family farm concerning an unrelated matter when he was shot by David McFadden, who was hiding in his own house across a field. "A crowd of excited people at once proceeded out to the scene of the murder," arrested David's father, Elias (the target of the original court process), and engaged in a "search ... for the unknown murderer." After finding some broken glass and footsteps, the crowd – by now an authorized *posse* – arrested David and "in company with his father, brought [him] to town and placed [him] under guard."[25]

This story captures the key dimensions of how mobilization actually worked on the ground – in serving the original warrant, Montgomery drew upon the aid of someone known to him; when the situation turned dire, neighbors and others nearby gathered to investigate and ultimately participate. Finally, the constable used *ad hoc* deputization to legalize the proceedings and complete the arrest. The social system undergirding this process involved local knowledge, social hierarchy, and the expectation of participation – in other words, enclosed authority.

At the same time, this system was quite fragile. During the mid–nineteenth century, a number of problems associated with the growth of the market in land and the developing transportation systems began, in some rural counties in

24 For example, see the *Illinois Free Trader*, March 10, 1843.

25 S. J. Clarke, *History of McDonough County, Illinois: Its Cities, Towns and Villages, with Early Reminiscences, Personal Incidents and Anecdotes, and a Complete Business Directory of the County* (Springfield, IL: Heritage Books, 1878), 47.

Illinois and elsewhere, to undermine the enclosed nature of political authority. At the local level, these problems, in turn, threatened to decouple republican law enforcement institutions and promote explicitly private forms of violent social control.

Banditti and Conflict on the Illinois Prairie

The most important challenges settlers in northern Illinois confronted were economic. The 1830s was a period of great turbulence in the US economy; a massive expansion in the middle part of the decade, fueled by booming cotton exports and specie circulation, that helped consolidate many of the previous decade's incipient shifts toward the market and speculative economy, came crashing down in 1837, when one of the largest financial panics in American history began. The recession that ensued led to the collapse of much of the nation's banking infrastructure and, particularly on the frontier, led to a massive crisis in both confidence and currency.[26] In Jackson County in Iowa, for instance, taxes had to be "paid in coon-skins," which William Warren, the collector, "accepted at 50 cents a piece and took ... to Galena, where he sold them for 75 cents or $1."[27]

Moreover, the area itself was becoming important because of the role it played connecting Chicago to the northern Mississippi. As geographer David Meyer and historian Timothy Mahoney have shown, the town of Galena (at the border of Illinois, Iowa, and Wisconsin) was crucial in the development of the local economy in the late 1830s; a lead mining center, the town helped drive migration into the area, a major precipitating factor behind the Black Hawk War, while also providing a key western link in the region's urban market.[28] By 1839, the Rock River Valley lay square in the middle of the still sparse but vital northern transportation network.[29] Settlers, strangers, travelers, and sightseers all made their way on the rivers and roads in this section of northern Illinois, bringing with them economic opportunity and, potentially, danger.

A primary concern for many of those moving into the region was the fact that they had very insecure rights to the farmland they occupied; most land in the area wouldn't be available for sale until 1843.[30] At the same time, government sales of lands in Illinois, Iowa, Wisconsin, and Missouri created the opportunity

[26] Davis, *Frontier Illinois*, 268–275.

[27] Cited in Susan K. Lucke, *The Bellevue War: Mandate of Justice Or Murder by Mob?* (Ames, IA: McMillen, 2002), 21.

[28] Meyer, *Making the Heartland Quilt*, 84–87; Timothy R. Mahoney, "Urban History in a Regional Context: River Towns on the Upper Mississippi, 1840–1860," *The Journal of American History* 72, no. 2 (1985): 318–339.

[29] Meyer, *Making the Heartland Quilt*, 68, 200–201.

[30] See Charles A. Church, *Past and Present of the City of Rockford and Winnebago County, Illinois* (Chicago: S.J. Clarke Pub. Co, 1905), 49–51.

for fortunes to be made overnight in the sale of real estate, which induced a high level of speculation. In Illinois from 1835 to 1837, for instance, James Davis notes that at least 500 new towns were laid out, while new transportation entities like the Illinois Central Railroad, which controlled a great deal of real estate, engaged in market-building strategies that included planting new settlements.[31] Much of this speculation was organized by outside investors who sought to buy lots in bulk and turn them for a profit, creating a rift with more permanent local settlers. These residents, in turn, formed local associations – called claims clubs or settler associations – to help combat some of this speculation.[32] These groups used legal means, political mobilization, and – occasionally – violence to protect themselves against these supposed outside interlopers.

For instance, in DuPage County just west of Chicago, local settlers in an area known as the Big Woods formed a Claim Protecting Society in 1836 to defend locals against land sharks, predatory real estate speculators (often from the east) who tried to outbid locals for prime lots.[33] This pattern repeated itself in claims clubs in Wisconsin and Illinois, most of which created constitutions and procedures for establishing the informal control of squatters of land claims against potential jumpers.[34]

Associations in the Rock River region were somewhat notorious for their use of violence. In Rockford in 1838, a claim "jumper" (a common term for a squatter) was working on a building on land claimed by another when a group representing the association came to the property and destroyed the structure, bringing the pieces into the town and dropping them off in front of the home of a man they suspected of being complicit with the jumper. Similarly in 1844 at nearby Twelve-Mile Grove, when two men named Pierce and Andrus attempted to build on the same plot of land, they got into a fight that led to the death of Pierce. Other such cases occurred throughout northern and western Illinois in the 1830s and early 1840s.[35]

Not all claims societies, however, were the same. Although in some areas, claim clubs were highly coercive; in others, the societies were forms of bringing

31 Davis, *Frontier Illinois*, 210; Paul W. Gates, *The Illinois Central Railroad and Its Colonization Work* (Cambridge, MA: Harvard University Press, 1934), 27–41, 225–250.

32 Davis, *Frontier Illinois*, 214.

33 C. W. Richmond and H. F. Vallette, *A History of the County of DuPage, Illinois* (Chicago: Scripps, Bross & Spears, 1857), 41.

34 Ilia Murtazashvili, *Political Economy of the American Frontier* (Cambridge: Cambridge University Pres, 2013), 69–70. Of course, what counted as an "outsider" was a contested category in a world of physical mobility. Indeed, many other fights were among settlers themselves; "many bloody combats occurred between belligerent parties" who themselves lived in DuPage, and "sometimes the party in the wrong was driven from the field by the rightful claimant, assisted by his neighbors." Richmond and Vallette, *A History of the County of DuPage, Illinois*, 40.

35 Charles A. Church, *History of Rockford and Winnebago County, Illinois: From the First Settlement in 1834 to the Civil War* (Rockford, IL: W. P. Lamb, 1900), 77–79.

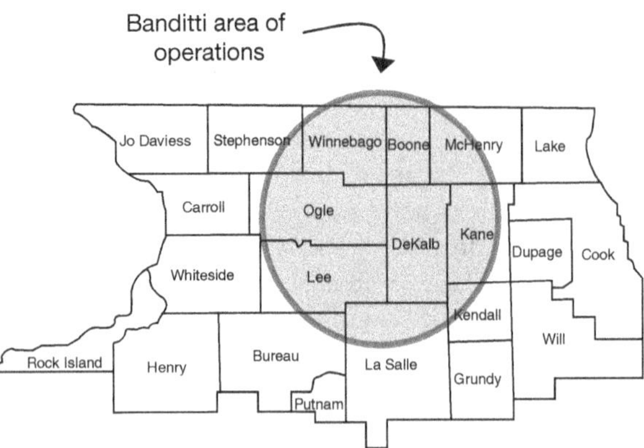

FIGURE 3. Northern Illinois

disparate groups together and operated to deter rather than practice violence. The clubs in Kane County largely fit this mold – they practiced little violence and instead seem to have largely helped local landowners coordinate against outside real estate market pressure.[36] Indeed, the Kane committees were largely committed to bringing an end to violent conflict; in 1837, a committee composed of several influential residents helped bring to an end a fight over some timber-rich land between James C. Hanks and Thomas Deweese, who had "knocked Hanks down with a stone," by awarding the claim to victim. This decision seems to have been met with little resistance on the part of Deweese.[37]

Another problem undermining social order and control among settlers in the 1830s was the development of an organized network of criminals taking advantage of the expanding market economy of the frontier, including horse theft and counterfeiting. As Stephen Mihm depicts in his brilliant book on nineteenth century counterfeiting, the ability to make money – literally – became a key means through which many were able to participate in this economy of highly unstable and decentralized currency, particularly in the frontier areas where banknotes were in short supply and banks themselves often nonexistent. In Ohio, Kentucky, and Illinois in the 1830s and 1840s, a large band of skilled counterfeiters (many of whom had roots in Canada, where much of the earliest counterfeiting operations had originated), composed of men like James Brown, William Taylor, John Craig, and many others, began to ply their trade to satisfy the demand for currency by fabricating a wide variety of notes.[38] This trade involved the construction of links among skilled specialists

[36] Davis, *Frontier Illinois*, 213–217.

[37] R. Waite Joslyn, *History of Kane County, Ill.*, vol. 1 (Chicago: Pioneer Pub. Co., 1908), 62–63.

[38] Stephen Mihm, *A Nation of Counterfeiters: Capitalists, Con Men, and the Making of the United States* (Cambridge, MA: Harvard University Press, 2009), 157–208.

across the Mississippi Valley and elsewhere, and quickly became a matter of national concern by the early 1840s.

Counterfeiting and forgery accentuated a generalized anxiety about how to exist in a world of long-distance trade, credit, and anonymity. The transformation of the market was as much a rural as urban experience. Gambling, which had become increasingly popular on Mississippi riverboats in the 1830s, soon became symptomatic of a sick economy as well, as the distinctions between the "legitimate" and "illegitimate" economy in a time of market expansion became quite blurry. Counterfeiters naturally helped fill the gap by providing currency, but they also became targets of those anxious about the vulnerability of the new economic system.

This trade in counterfeit banknotes quickly fused with another criminal concern, also rooted in the relative anonymity and physical mobility of the Old Northwestern frontier: horse-stealing. The most valuable property many in rural areas owned were horses, and as transportation networks became more sophisticated in the 1830s and 1840s, so did illegal exploitation of that mobility. In the upper Midwest, the actual organization of horse-theft involved a large network of agents (some estimates include up to three hundred individuals, although this is pure speculation) spread out through Iowa, parts of Missouri, the Rock River region, and points beyond.[39] Transport was based on a very simple mechanism – a stolen horse would be secreted away at the house of an unsuspected ally, who would then smuggle the horse (often in return for false notes) to a nearby ally, who would do the same, and so forth.[40] The chain would allow stolen animals, who were rarely in the open, to be moved quickly to markets where buyers were desperate for good horseflesh and unlikely to ask questions about ownership. It was clandestine, efficient, and difficult to detect – as long, that is, as participants could maintain their own good reputations in the places where they actually lived.[41] The very transportation and financial network facilitating aboveboard market transactions could be used to shuttle stolen property to and fro.

The fact that these crimes were *organized* also reflected the complexities of market society: like counterfeiting, much horse-stealing was perpetuated by actors who did not prey on their neighbors directly, but rather used clandestine networks for widen the scope of their activities. This did help hide illicitness from local purview but also increased uncertainty over who, exactly, one

[39] M. Luckett, "The 'Wide Awake Citizens': Anti Horse-Thief Associations in South Central Wisconsin, 1865–1890," *The Wisconsin Magazine of History* 91, no. 2 (2007): 16–27.

[40] See *The New Yorker*, May 30, 1840.

[41] See M. Mott, *History of the Regulators of Northern Indiana* (Indianapolis: Indianapolis Journal Co., 1859); J. W. Murphy, *Outlaws of the Fox River Country* (Hannibal, MO: Hannibal Print. Co., 1882); O. Fritiof Ander, "Law and Lawlessness in Rock Island Prior to 1850," *Journal of the Illinois State Historical Society* 52, no. 4 (1959): 526–543; Wilson, "The Business of a Midwestern Trial Court."

could trust.[42] The scope and interlinks of crime networks allowed many local participants to develop local reputations as "honorable" while also profiting from smuggling and theft.[43]

One of the best sources of information about the world of crime in the frontier Midwest is indicative of this anxiety: Edward Bonney's *Banditti of the Prairie*, a somewhat sensationalist but essentially accurate first-person account of a search for the robbers (and killers) of several prominent citizens in Illinois and Iowa in 1845.[44] Bonney, a confederate of Joseph Smith's during the brief Mormon period of occupation in Nauvoo, Illinois, in the early 1840s, had recognized a cap found at the scene of one of the earliest crimes as one belonging to a member of the LDS church named Thomas Hodges. Hodges, along with a number of family members and friends, was, in turn, part of a branch of the criminal network centered in the Mormon capital.[45] Bonney, who demonstrated an uncanny familiarity with the underworld (indeed, he himself was later accused of counterfeiting), engaged in a shocking exposé of the habits, activities, and organization of the criminals. His long journey to hunt down the killers brought him on an adventure through Tennessee, Missouri, Ohio, Indiana, and Illinois, where he (ultimately) came in contact with members of the organization in the Rock River valley.

Bonney details the ways in which horse thieves and counterfeiters worked in concert, sharing information, personal and family connections, and resources. Banditti used coded language and passed on references to those "of the right stripe" in order to allow them to make their way across the frontier underworld. They teamed up to execute burglaries and robberies, and relied on each other to secure get a ways and provide shelter and food.

For instance, in July 1845, a well-known pioneer named Colonel George Davenport (after whom Davenport, Iowa, was named) was murdered in his home by a group of burglars who had, apparently, used a farm owned by "Old

42 Herman Melville's famous 1857 novel *The Confidence-Man* – a fable of anonymity and opportunism set on the nearby Mississippi River – is particularly symptomatic of this unease. Indeed, Melville appears to have gained much of his inspiration for the story from an 1840 trip to Galena.

43 The term "banditti" had been in use for many years to describe brigands and robbers, primarily in Europe, although there was a newfound fascination in literature on robbery in general in the 1830s (see Charles MacFarlane, *The Lives and Exploits of the Banditti and Robbers of All Nations* (Philadelphia: R.W. Pomeroy, 1836)). In the United States, the term had also been applied to Loyalist partisans during the American Revolution (Harry M. Ward, *Between the Lines: Banditti of the American Revolution* (Westport, CT: Praeger, 2002), ix.

44 There are several editions of the book. I rely most heavily on Edward Bonney, *Banditti of the Prairies, Or, The Murderer's Doom, A Tale of the Mississippi Valley and the Far West* (Philadelphia: T. B. Peterson & Bros., 1855).

45 The Mormons were, indeed, frequently accused of being involved in counterfeiting, banditry, and horse-stealing. John Lee Allaman, "Policing in Mormon Nauvoo," *Illinois Historical Journal* 89, no. 2 (1996): 85–98; Bill Shepard, "The Notorious Hodges Brothers: Solving the Mystery of Their Destruction at Nauvoo," *John Whitmer Historical Association Journal* 26 (2006): 260–286 and Mihm, *A Nation of Counterfeiters*, 181–185, 200.

Grant" Redden in southeastern Iowa as their base of operations.[46] Bonney, in fact, was able to get a lead concerning who had killed Davenport – a makeshift band that included several friends of the Hodge brothers – by convincing a stranger familiar with the suspects to go to the Redden house and report back on what he had heard. By sharing secrets with Redden, the stranger and, later, Bonney himself were able to convince him that they were part of the brotherhood of frontier criminals.

At the same time, the success of the Banditti also depended on anonymity; indeed, many of the counterfeiters and horse thieves in Bonney's account adopted aliases and explicitly avoided robbing neighbors and friends. In addition to the very useful currency they brought into circulation, such selective predation made it possible for many of them to become esteemed members of local communities. Thus, despite already having been arrested for counterfeiting in New Orleans, James Brown served as a justice of the peace in the mid-1830s in his hometown of Boston in the Cuyahoga River Valley of Ohio.[47] Moreover, confederates like William Latta and others were also influential local citizens and business owners. Time after time, Bonney encountered ostensibly honest innkeepers and tavern owners who offered him information about where to procure and sell stolen horses or counterfeit currency.

What Bonney discovered was that while the Banditti were linked into a tight-knit network, it was a network concentrated in a few key areas: eastern Iowa and southern Wisconsin, northern Indiana, Kentucky, northern and western Ohio. In these places – similar, as we shall see, to northern Illinois – counterfeiters and horse thieves put down roots and established a more long-term pattern of predation. Beginning in about 1837, branches of the network established home bases in rugged towns like Bellevue, Iowa, where a hotel owner named W. W. Brown, with close ties to the organization, began to aid and abet their activities. They used the transit opportunities of the Mississippi River to facilitate horse shuttling, and seemed to travel along with the massive migrations of the Mormons across Ohio, Missouri, and Illinois in the 1830s. Until the late 1840s, in addition to counterfeiters like John Craig and Ebenezer Gleason, notorious characters such as Robert Birch, William Fox, John Baxter, as well as families like the Driscolls, Brodys, Reddens, and Aikens created an underground infrastructure for the Banditti network to evolve and thrive.

By the late 1830s, Banditti and associates from the upper Midwest – including the Brody and Driscoll clans, William Taylor, Ebenezer Gleason, Norton Royce, and William Bridge – began made their way to the Rock River and Fox River Valleys in northern Illinois. These migrants, in fact, "were among the first settlers" who "as a consequence, had the choice of locations," undoubtedly allowing them a certain amount of flexibility in exercising their

[46] Bonney, *Banditti of the Prairies*, 56. [47] Mihm, *A Nation of Counterfeiters*, 172–179.

own squatters' rights.[48] Some, like Gleason and Taylor, were affiliates with James Brown and his counterfeiting operation and made DeKalb County their base of operations; others, including the Brodys and Driscolls, had a background in horse thievery, and had been cast out of Ohio by a group of vigilantes in the Cuyahoga River Valley known as the "Black Canes." They (along with William Bridge and Norton Royce) also moved into DeKalb as well as Ogle, where they set up their own claims. Others, including other Brown associates like William Crane and Valentine Gleason, moved into Lake County in the late 1830s and 1840s, while yet others moved closer to Chicago in Kane, particularly near the settlement of Hampshire.[49] These experienced horse thieves and counterfeiters soon began to link the region into the larger network of Banditti operations, using the road network connecting the mining country in Wisconsin to the Mississippi to the West.[50]

In addition to the Brody-Driscoll clan headquartered at Dement and Monroe townships in eastern Ogle, another group of Banditti, the Aikens-Bridge group, dominated life at Washington Grove in Pine Rock Township in the central part of the county. In 1835, the Aikens family moved to the region from Ohio in the aftermath of the Black Hawk War, in which Thomas Aikens (the eldest) had served.[51] The family's connection to the Banditti was rooted in a local conflict over claims. When Samuel Aikens and several of his sons first arrived in Ogle, "they were regarded as rather good men." The problem came, as with so many, over claims disputes: "When speculation in claims became the ruling passion," argued historian H. F. Kett, the Aikens "joined the frenzied mob, and invested heavily, expecting to realize handsome returns. But the wheel of fortune suddenly reversed its motion, and they lost heavily." Because of their good reputation, "when they became victims to the claim speculating mania, they carried with them a number of their neighbors and acquaintances." This local resentment seems to have alienated the Aikens from their neighbors, and the sons, Thomas, Charles, and Richard, "became reckless, and finally identified themselves with the outlaws" allowing their "houses and barns" to become "places of concealment."[52]

These men were not outcasts; instead, they were closely integrated into local political, economic, and social life of the area. Charles and Robert Aikens, for instance, started the first blacksmith shop in Ogle County and had very active

48 *The History of Ogle County, Illinois* (Chicago: H. F. Kett & Co., 1878), 351.

49 The typical line of travel for the shuttling horses and banknotes was "from Brodie's Grove to Gleason's at Genoa, Henpeck, now Old Hampshire, in Kane county, thence north through McHenry county into Wisconsin." Joslyn, *History of Kane County (Vol. 1)*, 141. Also see Mihm, *A Nation of Counterfeiters*, 198, and CDD, September 21, 1845.

50 *The History of Ogle County*, 351.

51 Eugenie Cynthia Taylor, "Captain Thomas Avery Akins and Margaret Ross Akins: Boulder Pioneers and Early Valmont Settlers (Part 1)," *Boulder Genealogical Society Quarterly* 35, no. 3 (August 2003): 99–100.

52 *The History of Ogle County*, 353.

economic ties with a number of other local residents while others, like William Bridge, had reputations for legal and political prowess.[53] Indeed, "some of the gang of villains ... so conducted themselves before the public that they had been clothed with positions of trust," according to one local historian.[54] In Lee County, several who would later be associated with the crime outfit were even elected justice of the peace and constable, supposedly allowing them to help orchestrate getaways and cover up for allies by arranging witnesses.[55] The weigh stations in the Banditti trade were "in charge of men who, to all outward appearance, were honest, hard-working, settlers"; indeed, the whole trade depended on the appearance of propriety.[56]

The twin problems of property insecurity and bandit activity came a head in 1840. Although the precise details are difficult to reconstruct, several things seem clear. First, there was an acute uptick in problems over property rights. The future governor of Illinois, Thomas Ford, who was circuit court judge in Ogle at the time, writes that a body of members of a "fraternity" – whom he did not name – got involved in claim jumping, forcing those who saw "themselves left without legal protection, and subject to the depredations of the dishonorable and unscrupulous ... resolved to protect themselves with force."[57] "Every neighborhood" in turn "was signalised (*sic*) by some brawl of this kind," and "the old peaceful, staid, puritan Yankee" became consumed by a "mobocratic spirit."[58]

Second, in late 1840 or early 1841, Norton Royce and several confederates – Franklin Dewey and Samuel Thatcher – were caught and charged with counterfeiting.[59] On the night of March 21, 1841, as they and two or three other Banditti awaited trial in the jail at Oregon, the newly completed courthouse caught fire. By midnight, a general alarm had been raised and the town mobilized to put out the blaze; supposedly as the townspeople reached the burning building, which was very close to the jail, the imprisoned outlaws were "already up, dressed and apparently watching and waiting for their 'hour of delivery.'"[60] The fire, however, did not reach the jail, and the prisoners were unable to secure an escape.

53 Taylor, "Captain Thomas Avery Akins and Margaret Ross Akins: Boulder Pioneers and Early Valmont Settlers (Part 1)," 101.

54 *The History of Winnebago County, Ill., Its Past and Present* (Chicago: H. F. Kett & Co., 1877), 263.

55 Lee County had a smaller vigilance movement in 1844 that I do not address in this chapter. *History of Lee County* (Chicago: H. H. Hill & Co., 1881), 296–302, 416–417.

56 *The History of Winnebago County*, 263.

57 Thomas Ford, *A History of Illinois: From Its Commencement as a State in 1818 tp 1847* (Chicago: S. C. Griggs & Co., 1854), 254.

58 ibid., 255.

59 Rodney O. Davis, "Judge Ford and the Regulators, 1841–1842," *Selected Papers in Illinois History* 2 (1981): 28.

60 *The History of Ogle County*, 380.

Nevertheless, as Ford recounts, even though Royce, Dewey, and Thatcher did end up getting convicted, they had "managed to get one of their confederates on the jury, who refused to agree to a verdict, until the eleven others had threatened to lynch him in the jury room." Meanwhile, "the other prisoners obtained changes of venue, and were never convicted."[61]

These events signaled something ominous to the residents of the Rock River valley. On one hand, the Banditti were mysteriously powerful, and capable of exploiting the holes in the county court system and (just like the Reno Gang in Seymour) avoiding punishment. On the other hand, again akin to Seymour, some of their neighbors were also, at least notionally, attempting to prosecute and combat suspected members within the courts. The fact, however, remained that without some kind of clear division of power in county politics, the actual mechanisms of enclosed authority – the *posse*, the amateur officers of the peace, the assumption of popular participation in punishment – would no longer work to produce a coherent public interest.

In April 1841, a group of fifteen primarily Scottish and Canadian settlers in White Rock township – right in the midst of criminal country in Ogle county – decided to organize what was called a "lynching club" to administer popular justice to some of the worst offenders.[62] They apparently used military organization and terminology, dividing themselves into companies, each of which was under the command of a Captain who loosely coordinated their activities across county lines.

The idea of the lynch clubs quickly caught on and groups in Winnebago, Lee, Boone, McHenry, and DeKalb organized their own companies of lynchers, now called collectively the Regulators.[63] The key motive of the groups, which, as we shall see, ultimately included some (though crucially not all) of the most important residents of the county, was quite straightforward: "[S]o numerous had the outlaws become," claims Kett, "it was impossible to enforce the laws

[61] Ford, *A History of Illinois*, 247.

[62] For histories of the Regulator movement and the Banditti in northern Illinois, see Davis, "Judge Ford and the Regulators, 1841–1842"; David Grimsted, "Né D'Hier: American Vigilantism, Communal Rebirth and Political Traditions," in *People and Power: Rights, Citizenship and Violence*, ed. Loretta Valtz Mannucci (Milan: Grafiche Vadacca, 1992), 75–113; Robert H. Jones, "Three Days of Violence, the Regulators of the Rock River Valley," *Journal of the Illinois State Historical Society (1908–1984)* 59, no. 2 (1966): 131–142; *The History of Ogle County*, 350–380; Boss, *Sketches of the History of Ogle County*, 57–59; *The History of Winnebago County*, 262–276; Church, *History of Rockford and Winnebago County*, 174–187; Lewis M. Gross, *Past and Present of DeKalb County, Illinois* (Chicago: Pioneer Pub. Co., 1907), 65–73, 185–186; Henry Boies, *History of DeKalb County, Illinois* (Chicago: O. P. Bassett, 1868), 78–84; Frank Stevens, *History of Lee County, Illinois*, vol. 1 (Chicago: S. J. Clarke Pub. Co., 1914), 355–359, 369–376, 387–391; *History of Lee County*, 93–100, 296–302, 416–417, 633–639; Pierce, Merrill, and Perrin, *The Past and Present of Kane County*, 426–428; Joslyn, *History of Kane County (Vol. 1)*, 138–141, 462–467.

[63] Gross, *Past and Present of DeKalb County*, 66. There were two to three companies from Ogle County, one from Dixon in Lee County, at least two from McHenry, DeKalb, and Winnebago each.

against them. Some of their members were justices of the peace; some were constables, and none of the early grand and petit juries were free from their presence. The first sheriff of the county was a sympathizer with, if not an actual member of the clan."[64] In these conditions, with a law that failed to work for at least some residents of a county, the only recourse seemed a turn to summary justice, mobilizing together to "visit every known or suspected person, and notify them to leave the country within a given length of time."[65]

Of course, it was precisely because they lacked the force of *authorized* law that the Regulators turned to this strategy. The first victim was John Harl, who had supposedly helped organize the theft of a neighbor's horse; he was whipped thirty-six times as punishment for his complicity in the activities of the Banditti.[66] So impressed was Harl by the moral probity of the lynchers that he decided to join them, in order, he claimed, "to prove that I am an honest man."[67] The Regulators went onto administer increasingly severe punishments to suspected miscreants, targeting allies of the Bridge, Aikens, and Driscoll families.[68]

In response, the alleged Banditti began to send threatening notices to members of the Regulators, as well as making attempts to physically intimidate them. One early leader of the Regulators named John Long lost his mill to a suspicious fire, causing him to resign, while his successor, S. Wellington, similarly quit after receiving a notice inscribed with a skull and crossbones.[69] The next Regulator leader, John Campbell, also a resident of White Rock, similarly received a threatening notice, which he ignored, choosing instead to escalate the campaign against the Banditti.

64 *The History of Ogle County*, 369. 65 ibid., 356.

66 Apparently "a deacon of the church inflicted the most vigorous strokes"; Church, *History of Rockford and Winnebago County*, 176. According to the 1840 census, Harl lived in Ogle County.

67 *The History of Ogle County*, 356.

68 *The History of Ogle County*, 359. A Baptist preacher named Asa Daggett who lived in the northwestern corner of DeKalb, near the border with Winnebago and Ogle counties, was allegedly involved in the theft of a horse from a man named Fish who lived near Rockford in Winnebago. Taken by a group of one hundred Regulators to Payne's Point in Ogle, he was originally sentenced to 500 lashes by the Regulators despite the presence of some dissenters who felt that Daggett may have been innocent. Phineas Chaney, a White Rock resident, managed to get the sentence reduced to ninety-six lashes, still an extraordinarily harsh punishment. Daggett survived the ordeal but fled Rock River to Indiana, only to return to Boone County sometime in the 1840s. Church, *History of Rockford and Winnebago County*, 176. Daniel Ross, Thomas Aikens' brother-in-law, was tortured by the Regulators sometime shortly thereafter by being "made to hold on to the limb of a tree just high enough to allow his toes to rest upon the ground. Whenever he attempted to let himself down, the prompt and vigorous application of the cow-hide on his seat of honor, compelled him to take the old position." Boss, *Sketches of the History of Ogle County*, 58.

69 Gross, *Past and Present of DeKalb County*, 67.

On Sunday, June 27, 1841, two men confronted Campbell at his home sometime in the early evening, shooting him just outside of the gate near his barn. By the next morning, much of the Rock River region had received news of the killing and a group of Regulators began to plan for revenge, mobilizing "every man that could go" to hunt for the criminals and "to avenge Campbell's death."[70] Suspicion seems to have immediately settled on the Driscolls. Despite the fact that John Driscoll was arrested by William Ward, sheriff of Ogle, some of Campbell's neighbors went to fetch him from the jail in Oregon, while others seized his son William, bringing both to Washington Grove – near the Aikens' house in Ogle County, where a crowd of Regulators and spectators had gathered.

Having convinced (or intimidated) the rest of the crowd into agreeing with a popular tribunal, the Regulators began to arrange what can only be described as a pastiche of an "official" trial, complete with a "justice" (E. S. Leland), "jury" (at least 120 Regulators who formed a semicircle around a large tree, which probably substituted for the bench), and even "counsel" (the "people" were represented by Jason Marsh, while the prisoners were defended by Charles Latimer). In their own testimony, however, the Driscolls refused to confess to the crime. This did not seem to matter to the "jury," who (now down to either 111 or 106, presumably free of dissenting voices) unanimously declared the defendents guilty and ordered their execution.[71] After giving the Driscolls a couple of hours to confess their sins to attending clergy, the Regulators divided themselves into two groups, armed themselves, took aim, and summarily shot John Driscoll and his son.[72]

News of the lynching quickly spread, gaining coverage throughout the country. Much of the sentiment toward the killing of the Driscolls was sympathetic – as Rodney Davis points out, most seemed to agree with the editor of the *Free Trader* that the Regulators were sober and moral and that "a more respectable assemblage of individuals could hardly be convened in the northern part of Illinois."[73] Local opinion, however, was more divided. In his issue on July 1, 1841, Philander Knappen, the editor of the *Rockford Star*, a Democratic weekly, printed a statement condemning the use of lynch law by the Regulators, arguing that "if two or three hundred citizens are to assume the administration of lynch law in the face and eyes of the laws of the land, we shall soon have a fearful state of things, and where, we ask, will

70 *The History of Ogle County*, 362

71 *Illinois Free-Trader*, July 9, 1841. As the *Chicago American* (August 6, 1841) claimed, "all ... appears done ... with the *forms* of a legal proceeding and execution, though a deliberate usurpation of the powers of courts of law," even though conceding this formalism did not provide "justification" for the punishment.

72 *The History of Ogle County*, 366; *The History of Winnebago County*, 271; *Chicago American*, April 3, 1841.

73 See Davis, "Judge Ford and the Regulators, 1841–1842," 29; *Illinois Free Trader*, July 9, 1841.

it end if mob law is to supersede the civil law? If it is tolerated, no man's life or property is safe; his neighbor who may be more popular than himself, will possess an easy, ready way to be revenged by misrepresentation and false accusation."

Ultimately a group of the Regulators was charged with killing the Driscolls in September, but since "no direct evidence was adduced" during the proceedings, the trial jury (which seems to have included at least one member of the vigilance organization) unsurprisingly returned a not guilty verdict.[74]

In the aftermath of the killing, other suspects in the murder of John Campbell fled – William Bridge, for example, made his way toward Marshall County where he stayed with a member of the Redden family, the same group that would shelter Davenport's killers a few years later. Two other Driscoll brothers – Taylor and David – left the area as well.[75]

If anything, however, the Banditti seem to have increased their activity rather than caved to the Regulators. In 1843, for instance, William Bridge, William McDowell, and Charles Oliver apparently went on a spree in Rockford in Winnebago County, robbing stores and stage coaches, while Thomas Aikens, by this time apparently a full-fledged member of the Banditti fraternity, joined up with Robert Birch and William Fox in Warren County to steal horses.[76] According to most historians, it was only with the conviction of Davenport's killers in 1845 that the "reign of terror" of the Banditti in northern Illinois came to an end.[77] By this point, the northern Illinois Regulators had gone down as one of the largest and most famous vigilante movements in American history, an exemplar of what Richard Maxwell Brown has called "constructive" vigilantism, the use of illicit force to help promote social order and reestablish the law.[78]

Vigilantism and the Breakdown in Enclosed Authority

But why, exactly, did the Regulator movement occur when it did in northern Illinois? Why, instead of turning to legal institutions, did the "old, staid" Yankee settlers of the region mobilize privately to punish the supposed killers of Campbell?

Superficially, this story looks straightforward – due to corruption and weak court institutions, there was a crime that authorized law enforcement seemed unable to handle, and the good citizens mobilized to redress the wrong done in a sober but extra-legal manner. Indeed, many traditional explanations for

[74] Davis, "Judge Ford and the Regulators, 1841–1842," 30; *The History of Ogle County*, 378–379.

[75] ibid., 369. Taylor was later charged for the murder of Campbell, but was acquitted. *Argument of Isaac N. Arnold, of Chicago, in Defense of Taylor Driscoll, on His Trial for the Murder of John Campbell* (Chicago: Geer & Wilson, April 1847).

[76] *The History of Ogle County*, 373–375. [77] ibid., 376. Also, CDD, September 21, 1845.

[78] Brown, *Strain of Violence*, 119–120.

vigilantism, which focus on class conflict, social deviance, cultural difference, and so forth, would highlight these dimensions to explain the lynching of the Driscolls.[79] The problem with this approach is that not only does this story have little to do with class or cultural diffference (many of the alleged Banditti themselves were landowners who came from the same kinds of places as other migrants), but also that the local state can hardly be described as absent. To understand the causal dynamics of this story, it is necessary to compare the way enclosed authority worked in Ogle-Lee with another, similar case: Kane County.

Put simply, networks in Ogle and Lee were just different from those in Kane – political officeholders were less likely to uniquely control non-officeholders through enclosed relations. This, in turn, made it much more difficult for the legal system to actually do what it was supposed to do: resolve disputes among residents. Alleged members of the Banditti were involved in a complex cycle of court cases against other residents, many seemingly involving property dispute claims. As a result, not sure that they would be able to get a conviction in the Ogle county court, residents simply used the traditional practice of law enforcement – the *posse comitatus* – to execute a punishment *outside* the law. The *posse*, in form if not legality, constituted the basis for vigilantism.

In Kane, on the other hand, despite the fact that there were Banditti in the area, local network relations *did* facilitate enclosed authority on the part of political officeholders, thereby helping them mobilize legal enforcement in an effective way. County government worked as it was supposed to in Kane, allowing the court system to resolve disputes without perpetuating an endless cycle of conflict.

This comparison provides a useful way to tease out the actual mechanisms facilitating vigilante mobilization because it acts something like a natural experiment, allowing us to control for other possible reasons why vigilantism might emerge, such as differences in class, background, or politics.[80] For instance, both Kane and Ogle-Lee were composed of similar kinds of settlers, largely from New York, Massachusetts, Canada, and Ohio. Both areas voted Whig and had similar kinds of concerns with western infrastructural development. In both areas, an elite controlled a great deal of the available land – indeed, the top one hundred buyers of land owned over 30 percent of the available claims in Kane, Ogle, and Lee counties alike. In both Kane and Ogle-Lee, political office holder elites were wealthier than average residents, owning on average over three times the land of their non–political officeholding fellow residents.

79 See, for example, ibid., 95–133 I address a number of alternatives more directly in Appendix A (available at www.jonathanobert.com).

80 Appendix A discusses this comparison in depth.

In other words, despite being similar on almost every dimension – social, economic, political, cultural, and especially legal (since both areas possessed rich and strong traditions of law enforcement) – and despite facing a similar threat from the same group of actors, Kane and Ogle-Lee had very different responses to the Banditti panic based on the one area they were dissimilar: their levels of enclosed authority.

Social Relations and Enclosed Authority among County Officials

The most basic finding from an analysis of the network relations in each county is also one of the most striking: political officials in Kane had strikingly higher levels of enclosed ties than those in Ogle-Lee.[81] That is, when two officials in Kane shared an economic, social, or kinship tie to a common non-officeholder (that is, they shared an indirect tie), I found that 52 percent of the time they also had a direct tie to each other. In Ogle-Lee, on the other hand, when two officials shared a relationship with a non-official, only 30 percent of the time did they also have a direct tie to each other.

This difference is even more striking when we compare the most important core county officials (those who held county-level office or who linked local jurisdictions to the state center). In Kane, 62 percent of important officials' relations to non-officials were enclosed, while in Ogle a mere 34 percent were. This indicates that political officers in Kane were much better able to exercise monopoly interpretive control over non-elites in general, and provides evidence that there were some important social structural differences among the counties.[82]

In practice, this meant that political officials in Kane County composed a tight-knit, enclosed group, while those in Ogle-Lee had overlapping networks with non-officials, dividing their authority and undercutting enclosed authority.

Much of this seems to have stemmed from the division of Lee from Ogle County in 1839. When Ogle was originally organized, Oregon, the home territory of pioneering settler John Phelps, was selected as the county seat, which meant that it would be the center of all governmental business. At the same time, John Dixon and his friends and allies opposed this move and successfully managed to get its slate elected as commissioners in the first county election in 1836.[83] The whole valley then witnessed a three-way legal battle

[81] To evaluate these different patterns of enclosed authority, I rely on a set of network data gleaned from genealogical resources, county histories, and court records. These resources are described in Appendix A (available at www.jonathanobert.com).

[82] When I determine the proportion of each individual officeholder's network of indirect ties enclosed by direct ties – constructing a kind of enclosure index for each officeholder – I find that the differences between means of the distributions of Ogle-Lee and Kane are significant at the .05 level; (two-tailed t-test $p = 0.0472$).

[83] *The History of Ogle County*, 300.

TABLE 3. *Network clusters and county membership in Ogle-Lee*

		Full network (n = 116)		Main component (n = 85)*	
	Algorithm type:**	Girvan-Newman	Louvain	Girvan-Newman	Louvain
Direct ties	Rajski's index	0.424	0.615	0.560	0.471
	Number of clusters (Q)	5 (0.506)	37 (0.532)	5 (0.506)	5 (0.534)
Indirect ties	Rajski's index	0.247	0.523	0.256	0.406
	Number of clusters (Q)	25 (0.095)	41 (0.461)	18 (0.093)	14 (0.460)

*Direct tie network.
**Optimized at Q.

between the regions most influential settlers – John Phelps, John Dixon, and Virgil Bogue – each of whom wished to secure the location of the county seat for the new county of Ogle near to their own settlements. Phelps (who had a number of important political connections to Illinois elite) won the first round, and the county capital was located near his home in Oregon; but Dixon, no slouch in terms of his own connections, managed to secure a secession from Ogle in 1839 which led to the formation of Lee.[84]

The problem was that while the new jurisdictional boundary separating out Lee from Ogle reflected, to a large degree, the factions and alliances among county officials themselves, the links between non-officials and officials did not reflect these boundaries. Non-officials in Lee and in Ogle had many links to officials in both counties who did not themselves share a social, economic, or kinship tie. This is evident in Table 3, which gathers several measures of network factions in Ogle-Lee and measures their relationship to county boundaries using the Rajski index. Relying on two widely used community detection algorithms – the Louvain algorithm and the Girvan-Newman algorithm, both of which try to unpack subgroup cliques or factions within network data – the table shows how well those network structures correlate with county membership (on a scale of 0 to 1, with 1 showing perfect correlation). In the case of direct network ties between officials, the factions seem to anticipate county membership fairly well in both the full network (which includes all the officials in the sample, whether or not they are tied to other actors) as well as the main cluster of actors who have social ties to one another (the main component). On the other hand, when we look just at how

[84] Royal Brunson Way, *The Rock River Vally: Its History, Traditions, Legends, and Charms* (Chicago: S. J. Clarke Pub. Co., 1926), 155–159.

those officials are tied together through a third party, the association between links within a faction and county membership are significantly less.[85]

This all indicates that county boundaries reflected an attempt to settle jurisdictional boundaries around social factions among officials themselves – but that these very boundaries were unable to contain the links among non-officials and officials, links that cross-cut jurisdictions and undermined the interpretive monopoly of the county officials. In other words, not only were the ties unenclosed, but the social network that did exist was decoupled from county boundaries.

In Kane County, on the other hand, the political elite were part of a tight-knit group whose control largely mapped onto the county jurisdiction. Kane had undergone its own secession crisis in 1841 as a section of Kendall County was carved out from the older county borders.[86] Despite the fact that the secession was unpopular in Kane, however, those officials who were part of the new county seem to have been extremely marginal. Indeed, a group of petitioners reflecting a number of the most influential local residents (including at least one law officer) had coordinated to try to fend off attempts by their assemblyman A. R. Dodge to divide the jurisdiction.[87] Unlike Ogle-Lee, in other words, the redrawing of county boundaries in Kane did not decouple enclosed social relations from the officials in charge of making the rules, largely preserving rather than dividing political authority.

And, as a result, Kane's political class had no trouble controlling its law enforcement officers. In Kane, three out of four sheriffs were linked by enclosed ties to the rest of the county officials. For instance, James Risk – the sheriff serving during the 1841 events – was deeply enmeshed in the inter-elite network. And, other Kane sheriffs – particularly James Herrington, the first sheriff of the county, but also Benjamin Fridley, his replacement, who went on to become one of the most important political figures in Kane – were key elites themselves and possessed strong enclosed relations to other political officials or who had clearly defined constituencies.[88] Indeed, later historians praised officers of the peace like Fridley as being "instrumental in freeing the country from the presence" of Banditti, using their legal acumen and courtroom procedures to combat the counterfeiting and horse-stealing menace.[89]

85 This is evidenced by consistently higher scores in the Rajski Index, which tells us how much of the information in a particular classification is retained within the other (in other words, how much does belonging to a particular faction carry over into membership in a particular county).

86 See Edmund Warne Hicks, *History of Kendall County, Illinois: From the Earliest Discoveries to the Present Time* (Aurora, IL: Knickerbocker & Hodder, 1877), 221–222.

87 *Chicago American*, May 5, 1841. Crucially, neither of the only two officials (Pierre Allaire and Archibald Sears) who both served in Kane and then seceded to Kendall were indirectly connected to any other official.

88 Appendix A (available at www.jonathanobert.com) describes the data used to make this claim.

89 Joslyn, *History of Kane County (Vol. 1)*, 141.

In Ogle-Lee, on the other hand, law enforcement officers were much more marginal. Only two out of the first seven sheriffs in the two counties possessed enclosed ties to the county elite; moreover, neither of these two, Horatio Wales and Aaron Porter, were in office during the events of early 1841 at the height of the vigilante activity. Indeed, Ogle, in particular, had had a troubled history with its sheriffs. In 1838 Wales had taken over as sheriff from William Mudd, a mysterious local figure who seems to have had a number of problems with the law himself and was almost certainly connected in some way with the Banditti (his name appears in court records as an affiliate of William Bridge, for example, and he seems to have been forced to resign in disgrace).

Mudd disappeared from Ogle County sometime before 1840, but Wales only stayed sheriff for two years, replaced in 1840 by William T. Ward, the man confronted by the Washington Grove group during the hunt for Campbell's killer. While Wales was deeply enmeshed in the core of the Ogle County governing faction, Ward himself seems not to have had powerful allies among the county elites, particularly the group surrounding John Phelps and his allies. In other words those responsible for executing the law in Ogle were, on the whole, peripheral figures within the social networks of other political officials.

The fact that sheriffs had very different levels of enclosed authority helps explain why law enforcement was less effective in Ogle than Kane. In Kane a strong infrastructure of enclosed authority existed among political officials, which meant that conflicts among these officials could be arbitrated precisely because they weren't subject to defection on the part of their constituents. Moreover, when necessary, political officials could reliably mobilize a powerful constituency to use violence to enforce the law. Taken together, then, these factors demonstrate that the legal system in Kane worked as intended: cutting off complex disputes and allowing political officeholding elites and others to manage their problems without resorting to informal *posse* mobilization.

In Ogle and Lee, on the other hand, a social order based on county governance, in which enclosed ties were to play a preeminent role and through which private individuals were expected to unproblematically prop up public security, had become decoupled from the ways in which residents actually interacted with each other. Political officials in these counties, for whatever reason, were unable to successfully prosecute Banditti crimes, while at the same time some very powerful local notables were cut out from the governance process. It was these individuals who begin to dominate the Regulator movement.

John Phelps, Claims, and the Regulators

The Regulators' attack on the Driscoll family was most immediately a result of the killing of John Campbell. At the same time, Circuit Court Records in Ogle County and Kane County reveal that there were some deeper problems involving property disputes among residents in Ogle that were not found in Kane, disputes that may have helped determine who actually joined the Regulators (Appendix A, available online, discusses these disputes in depth).

A critical clue has to do with John Phelps, the aforementioned early pioneer to Oregon in Ogle County, one of the most important property owners in the area, and a member of the Regulators. Phelps had come to what would later be Ogle County in 1834 to start a farm and ferry. A native of Virginia, Phelps had bounced around the Mississippi Valley in the 1820s and early 1830s, shuttling whiskey, tobacco, and cotton from New Orleans up to mining settlements like Galena.

During these adventures, Phelps had much direct experience with violence. As soon as he turned eighteen, for instance, thinking "of nothing else but the glory and fame [he] would acquire in the service of [his] country," Phelps joined an expedition against the Creek Indians and participated in the Battle of New Orleans during the War of 1812. After making his way to the Old Northwest, he again joined the effort against the Winnebago Indians in 1827 as part of a company mobilized to guard White Oak Springs (near Galena), where he had built a store. And during the Black Hawk War, he helped raise a militia company in Schuyler County, participating in the burning of a native settlement near Rock Island. It was following the war that Phelps decided to organize a ferry near Ogle, to take advantage of trade between Chicago and the northern mining districts.[90]

In many ways, Phelps was a quintessential settler "colonialist" – an entrepreneurial actor with an interest in and commitment to using personal force to seize land, forge economic connections, and drive out rivals.[91] In this, he also embodied the republican ethos of his time: he saw very little distinction between the efforts he took to preserve his own property and stake, and the greater public interest. This background may not have determined his willingness to ally with the Regulators during the Banditti panic, but it certainly provided him a set of practical skills that would be useful in the mobilization against the Driscolls.

In what would become Ogle County, Phelps quickly established himself as both a powerful and controversial figure. He and John Dixon, the other key figure in the region, fought over the location of the roads leading west from Chicago, in addition (as noted) to the county seat of Ogle. Moreover, while he grew in influence – Phelps expanded his farming interests and quickly developed other trading and commercial enterprises – he also increasingly became entangled in a large number of legal proceedings, including some with other important local figures. From 1838 to 1841, for example, Phelps was a plaintiff in twenty-one cases in circuit court against sixteen different

90 "Narrative of John Phelps," www.rootsweb.ancestry.com/~tnsumner/phelps.htm, accessed November 10, 2016.

91 Walter L. Hixson, *American Settler Colonialism* (New York: Palgrave Macmillan US, 2013), 4–6, 71–80.

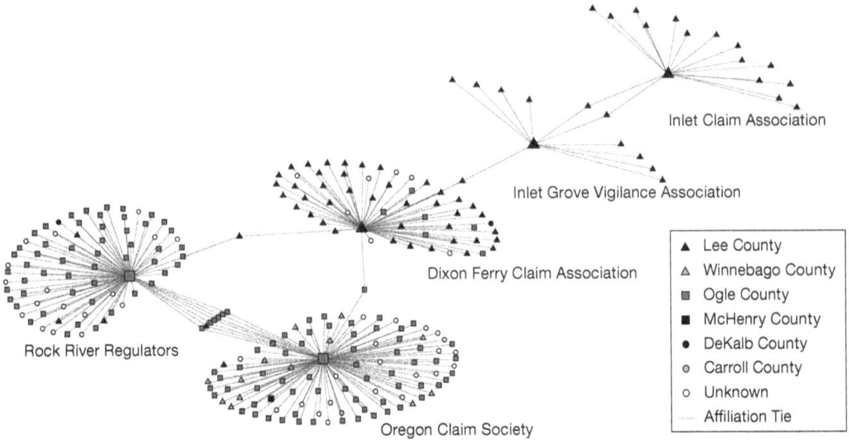

FIGURE 4. Membership in claims associations and vigilante organizations (1835–1845)

defendants, including three Ogle County officials (one of whom, Samuel Hitt, was among the wealthiest individuals in the county); he was also a defendant in twelve cases, including one against a county official. While a wealthy and well-connected man at the local level, Phelps confronted a much more complex and factionalized set of social conditions, making it difficult for him to dominate the politics of the county in the manner he expected.

This seems to have been a particular issue with regard to claims. That is, despite his prominence, Phelps did not belong to the influential Oregon Claim Society, the most important claim club in Ogle (at least thirteen of the forty-seven county officials from Ogle were members of the club). Instead, it seems as though the Regulators were a kind of "private enforcement" coalition composed of those, like Phelps, excluded from the prestigious local clubs. Thus, despite the fact that Ogle was the epicenter for the Rock River vigilantes (of the eighty-five vigilantes for whom I could locate county residency, 68 percent [or 8%] were residents of Ogle County), there was very little overlap between it and the Society – indeed, a mere 7 of the 106 members appear on both membership lists (see Figure 4 for a graphical depiction of membership affiliations). Part of this undoubtedly has to do with the fact that the Oregon Claim Society (1839) was founded two years before the Rock River Regulators (and, hence, members who otherwise might have joined the Regulators could have moved away), but the pattern suggests that rather than a temporary, *ad hoc* group, the Rock River Regulators were organized on much the same logic as the other quasi-legal societies – as an attempt by a local group of elites to mobilize their constituents to enforce some kind of legal claim. The Rock River Regulators, in other words, seem suspiciously similar to a very violent claims association.

Evidence for this can be seen in Table 4, which summarizes some of the data regarding officials who were members of the two most important local claims organizations (in addition to the Oregon group, I include another important claims society headquartered at Dixon in Lee County to help provide a control), and compares it to that of the Regulators. This demonstrates that, essentially, the Regulators were, like the claims associations, primarily extensions of the day-to-day social networks of important actors who belonged to them. On average, over 20 percent of the contacts of an official who belonged to a claims club or to the Regulators were themselves members of the group (see column "Avg. tie proportion (members)" for figures for each group), while, under 10 percent of the contacts of nonmember officials were members (see column "Avg. tie proportion (nonmembers)").[92]

Table 4 also includes some very suggestive information about the average landownership and the network relations of officials who belonged to the various organizations. This chart, for instance, shows that there was no real difference in the wealth of Regulators as opposed to those belonging to claims associations; even though the median Regulator's wealth was significantly less than that of the median Oregon claims association member, he was not less wealthy than members of the Dixon association.

However, in terms of their social relations with other officials, Regulators were, on average, more socially *marginal* than members of the other organizations. This is evident in the average flow-betweenness measure for officials who were members of each group, with both of the claims societies having more central members than the vigilantes. Flow-betweeness is a concept network analysts use to describe actors whose position in a network is critical for the flow of information from other members of the network; for my purposes it is a useful measure because it demonstrates that the informational center of the Ogle-Lee network was made up of members of the Oregon and, especially, Dixon claim associations.[93]

At the same time, while marginal in the overall network, those who joined the Regulator movement nevertheless had powerful enclosed networks amongst themselves; while the average proportion of ties that were enclosed for nonvigilantes in the Ogle-Lee county network was a mere 19 percent, for the Regulators over 45 percent of their indirect ties to other officials were, on average, enclosed.[94] The relatively authoritative social networks of Regulators versus other officials in Ogle-Lee both explains how they were able to mobilize nonofficials so easily, as well as why they went outside the

[92] Assuming unequal variances, the two-tailed t-test scores for each difference of means of proportion contacts who were members for officials who belonged to the organizations and for those who did not is significant at the .01 level.

[93] See Linton C. Freeman, Stephen P. Borgatti, and Douglas R. White, "Centrality in Valued Graphs: A Measure of Betweenness Based on Network Flow," *Social Networks* 13, no. 2 (1991): 141–154, and Borgatti, "Centrality and Network Flow."

[94] Assuming equal variances, this difference in means is significant at $p = 0.0044$ (two-tailed t-test).

TABLE 4. *Networks and quasi-legal enforcement*

	Total	Officials	Acres owned (Med.) (Total)	Acres owned (Med.) (Officials)	Avg. centrality* (Members)**	Avg. tie Proportion (Members)**	Avg. tie proportion (Non-Members)***
Oregon Claim Society	89	18	300	320	0.678	0.244	0.073
Dixon Claim Society	59	12	160	159	1.293	0.256	0.094
Rock River Regulators	106	6	158	436	0.302	0.232	0.021

*Normalized Flow-Betweeness Centrality; Network Avg.: 0.5620; sd.:0.9388; max.: 6.7500; n=116.
** Ogle-Lee Officials who belonged to a specific organization.
*** Ogle-Lee Officials who did not belong to a specific organization.

institutional framework of the county government to do so; individually they possessed strong social mobilization capacities and interpretive monopoly, but their marginality and the lack of enclosed infrastructure across the county as a whole made it difficult for them to rely on the courts. They would be the actors, in other words, most likely both to perceive the crisis of public authority (since they themselves were not in charge) as well as to respond with the traditional mobilization of private effort toward a now fractured public end. And this, as scholars like Nicholas Smith and Philip Ethington argue, is a key component of vigilante politics?[95]

The rivalry between the Oregon claims group and the Regulators becomes especially stark when we link these membership data to patterns of legal conflict. Over thirty-seven of the members claims associations participated as plaintiffs in cases against Ogle residents from 1837 to 1842, while 23 percent of the Regulators were active plaintiffs. Those conflicts, moreover, were often mutual; the Rock River Regulators and the Oregon Claims Association members, for example, together were involved in approximately twenty-seven cases against each other.[96]

Hence the key distinguishing factor for those joining the Regulator movement was their rivalry with the major claims clubs in the area. Those who joined the regional Regulator movement were, like John Phelps, marginal actors in county politics, but powerfully connected to networks they could use to mobilize their constituents for violent activity. The problem, from the standpoint of the legal institutions of northern Illinois, was that county jurisdiction was no longer embedded in actual social authority across the board; instead, small pockets of powerful elites who possessed enclosed and strong ties to one another in a context where other elites did not have these kinds of ties meant that these powerful but marginal actors were likely to try to act outside the law when legal institutions failed to work as they wanted.

In Kane, none of these factors existed. There, the enclosed nature of social ties across the system of county government meant that the court system actually worked as intended. And marginal but powerful factions within the government never really emerged, meaning that not only did claims associations work to manage property disputes informally, there was no constituency of powerful actors deeply disaffected with legal process in the county. Indeed, as a local historian of Kane describes it, when a committee drew up a local claims constitution in 1835, "the common sense, law and logic, as well as patriotism, contained in the constitution were instantaneously recognized to be the very things demanded" by the local "crisis" in property disputes and

[95] Ethington, *The Public City: The Political Construction of Urban Life in San Francisco, 1850–1900*; Nicholas Rush Smith, "Rejecting Rights: Vigilantism and Violence in Post-Apartheid South Africa," *African Affairs* 114, no. 456 (2015): 341–360.

[96] This represents 12% and 16% of all the cases the Oregon Claims and Regulators members respectively participated in from 1837 to 1842.

"were adopted with unparalleled enthusiasm." Indeed, "the thing worked like a charm," claims the historian, as "the moral as well as the physical power of settlers' associations' [in Kane] was so great that if a speculator presumed to bid on a settler's claim, he was certain to find himself 'knocked down and dragged out."'[97] Given the relatively unanimity of the claims clubs in Kane and the unified power of the elite, however, actual violence almost never seems to have occurred.

In other words, while there is no direct evidence to suggest that the Driscolls were targeted because, for example, they were squatting on valuable land or had had other direct difficulties with the Regulators concerning property, the membership of the vigilante movement suggests that they acted something like a rival claims association, concerned (at least in part) with trying to protect and ensure property rights. What made them different from other claims clubs was that the Regulators were composed largely of those excluded from holding political office. With the Banditti seeming to have allies among those in power, their only option was to mobilize outside the law.

HOW DID OGLE-LEE BECOME DIFFERENT?

Still, how did Ogle-Lee *become* different? Why did their patterns of enclosed authority differ from those of Kane, where a very similar set of conflicts and conditions also existed, even down to a struggle over county boundaries and the presence of a band of criminal actors? The origins of the particular differences in social networks between these two areas is difficult to explain – migration to the two areas took place in very similar ways and even involved individuals from the same counties in New York. One possible reason is that individuals who selected Lee and Ogle were not able to move to their first-choice location; the Black Hawk War, for instance, may have delayed settlement by those most concerned with protecting their property, while Kane, which did not participate in the war, may have attracted more legally and politically astute settlers. But this answer is inadequate flow-betweenness both Kane and Ogle, for example, had almost identical distributions of wealth as measured in landowning patterns, and there is no indication in the historical record of concern by settlers after 1835 of local natives (most of whom had been forced out of the state by the military after the war).

A better answer is that the frontier in the 1840s in Illinois was a highly fluid and ever-changing environment, in which older patterns of social life were being called into question and complex new networks were forming in rural areas with a rapidity that was virtually unprecedented. Because there were two centers of power in the area – John Phelps and John Dixon – who did not themselves get along, new residents ended up cultivating relations with both,

[97] Joslyn, *History of Kane County (Vol. 1)*, 67.

unsettling the ability for either to strictly dominate county politics.[98] Indeed, over time, it seems that a counterweight to Phelps's power emerged both in Ogle County government and in the Oregon Claims Society. As a result, as claims disputes increased and the court system was unable to address either civil *or* criminal matters, the killing of John Campbell became a crisis that couldn't be resolved through authorized institutions. The decoupling of traditional law enforcement rules from the actual relations of elites on the ground allowed politically marginalized but powerful actors to take the law into their own hands. The local legal institutions in Ogle and Lee were no weaker than those in Kane, but the underlying social networks allowing them to work were not in place.

Instead, in Kane, conversely, no serious rivalries among elites split the allegiances of newcomers. The court system worked, Banditti crimes were prosecuted, and claims societies largely remained mechanisms for local protection rather than factional armies. And early settlers seem to have mostly worked together to boost economic investment and development in the area.[99]

What was the role of the Banditti in this system, then? It appears as though Banditti were at least loosely allied with a politically powerful faction that opposed John Phelps and likely had conflicts with him and his allies over claims disputes. To Phelps and his allies, the combination of political exclusion and conflict with other residents was intolerable, and in the aftermath of several precipitating events, he and his network mobilized themselves into an organization resembling, in many ways, the claims societies littering the Illinois prairie. The spread of vigilantism thus followed the patterns of network ties among this faction, which had been largely excluded from formal control in county governance. In Kane, not only did the Banditti not appear to have had any access to the corridors of power, but county legal institutions also could reliably be used to prosecute cases against them. Vigilantism was, in short, an attempt at trying to reassert a community identity in a context in which enclosed authority no longer worked as it once did.

CONCLUSION

This chapter has made two basic arguments: First, counties in the nineteenth-century United States had minimal bureaucracy for law enforcement and instead relied on political officials being able to exert enclosed authority over residents in order to mobilize them when necessary. Second, when those relations decoupled from the rules of county administration – as it did in the frontier counties of Ogle-Lee – even though actors would turn to local legal institutions, they could no longer work as intended. The response on the part of some notables was to engage in the same kinds of behaviors that they always

98 *The History of Ogle County*, 314–315.

99 Pierce, Merrill, and Perrin, *The Past and Present of Kane County*, 222–223.

had – *posse* mobilization – but in a private rather than public fashion. This was the root of sporadic, nineteenth-century vigilantism in the Old Northwest.

The Regulator movement was not isolated; in Illinois, Iowa, Indiana, Missouri, Ohio, and Kentucky, there were at least nineteen separate vigilance committees formed between 1835 and 1850. According to the list compiled by Richard Maxwell Brown, around 38 percent of all the vigilance activity in the nation in these years could be found in areas where the Banditti were known to operate.[100] Moreover, the area continued to be plagued by horse-stealing throughout the rest of the century, leading local residents to adopt quasi-public anti–horse thief associations to share information, offer rewards, and even participate in *posses* if necessary.[101]

More significantly, these experiences in antebellum vigilantism created a kind of schema or template for communal, particularized extra-state violence in the years to come. Lynching, "whitecapping" (moral regulation by vigilantes dressed in white masks and costumes), and night-riding (terroristic vigilantism on the part of masked groups of mounted men) would become staples not only of the Reconstruction South, but also of the Midwest and Southwest in the 1880s and 1890s. Even rural areas of Pennsylvania, New York, and New Jersey witnessed the organization of "white cap" groups during these decades.[102]

Not every county, of course, suffered from these kinds of vigilante mobilizations. Most of rural New England, for instance, was spared from more violent forms of extra-legal vigilantism, partly because Yankee communities possessed a long-standing commitment to deference and hierarchy.[103] But the area also relied much more on town-based governance than on counties, which helped reembed already strong legal norms in smaller, tight-knit communities.[104] Other counties in the Midwest and West were simply much more like Kane than Ogle

[100] Brown, *Strain of Violence*. Another eight or nine movements were located in Mississippi and Alabama, which were related to but distinct from the core anti-horse thief/counterfeiting mobilization elsewhere on the Rock River Valley.

[101] Luckett, "The 'Wide Awake Citizens'," 20–22; *Ottawa Free Trader*, April 27, 1861. These groups became a fairly common site across the great plains in the years following the Civil War. Hugh C. Gresham, *The Story of Major David Mckee, Founder of the Anti-Horse Thief Association Together with the History of the Anti-Horse Thief Association and the Anti-Thief Association* (Cheney, KS: Self-published, 1937), 48, 57–64.

[102] Sally L. James, "American Violent Moral Regulation and the White Caps" (B.A., William & Mary College, 1969), 47–48, 57–64.

[103] Michael J. Pfeifer, "Introduction," in *Lynching Beyond Dixie*, ed. Michael J. Pfeifer, *American Mob Violence Outside the South* (University of Illinois Press, 2013), 11.

[104] Anne Szymanski has noted how, even in New England, a recourse to private forms of protection was more likely in the frontier and periphery of the region. Places with concentrated industry developed a reliance on factory discipline, private guard labor, and public police just like larger cities throughout the nation. See Szymanski, "Stop, Thief! Private Protective Societies in Nineteenth-Century New England," 415–417.

or Lee – the effects of new economic transformations were assimilated within local social hierarchies. At least one important implication of this analysis is that macro-level challenges to the social order and social control are not enough to explain micro-level responses on the part of actual residents; instead, we need to examine how the networks tying these communities together (the meso-level) actually worked in practice.

The northern Illinois Regulator movement is important to this book's larger argument, however, because it casts the dilemma confronting the republican fusion of public security to private effort in stark terms. In the 1830s and 1840s, most Americans in the north, south, and west lived in settings much like those found in northern Illinois: rural areas with inhabitants who were expected to participate directly in coercion on behalf the law. The market, however, posed a profound challenge to this logic all over the nation. New relationships between employers and employees, the expansion in the importance of banking and credit (along with the concomitant commercial instability), the growth of new kinds of transportation infrastructure, and novel forms of crime all made the traditional usefulness on enclosed relations as a means of adjudicating disputes more tenuous. And this meant that, even if they didn't witness the spectacular lynchings seen in Ogle County and elsewhere, by the early twentieth century most rural counties began to rely on some combination of a more bureaucratic and professionalized sheriff's department that was expected to handle most policing duties, along with explicitly private voluntary and informal support among residents.[105]

At the same time, the Banditti and the claims associations both reflected the new instabilities in social relations engendered by the expansion of the market. The claims associations – and their darker, vigilante cousins – reflected a community struggle not only over abstract legal concepts like property rights, but also the kinds of day-to-day social relations allowing residents to control and influence each other's behavior. Indeed, what, exactly, counted as a property in a world where older, participatory forms of law enforcement no longer could be securely linked the influence and interpretive authority of traditional social elites, for whom property was a key part of that power? How could such property not only be protected, but also defined? The Banditti, in fact, used these interpretive and social instabilities in highly fluid and remote settings like the Rock River Valley to become active market participants, offering important resources (counterfeit currency and stolen horses) that could offer them forms of power unavailable in older, settled regions in the east. In an important sense, the problem of social order identified by Abraham Lincoln in

[105] Kopel, "The Posse Comitatus and the Office of Sheriff"; David N. Falcone and L. Edward Wells, "The County Sheriff as a Distinctive Policing Modality," *American Journal of Police* 14, nos. 3/4 (1995): 123–149.

his Lyceum speech was connected not only to the effects of slavery on "free" labor, but also on the growing dislocations of the market itself.

This market revolution thus tied areas like the Rock River Valley into a larger world of unstable jurisdictional rules, physical mobility, and social ambiguity. However, these rural areas also bled over into and were structured by the metropolises at the heart of the market revolution, such as nearby Chicago. As I now show, this city too confronted a crisis in coercive enforcement, one generated by presence of "strangers" and the breakdown of delegative authority. It was here that the real organizational effects of decoupling began to emerge, with the invention of two new kinds of coercion: the municipal police and the private detective industry.

4

Pinkertons and Police in Antebellum Chicago

INTRODUCTION

In 1843, Allan Pinkerton moved to Kane County, Illinois to start a cooperage. A Scottish immigrant and Chartist refugee, Pinkerton had made his way to Illinois via Canada in the early 1840s, and in Dundee he found a thriving settlement filled with Scots and political fellow travelers, as well as an environment hospitable to his business. His social commitments to his new town were put to the test in 1847 when he discovered, inadvertently, a counterfeiting operation set up (likely by members of the Banditti) on an small patch of land on the Fox River later nicknamed "Bogus Island." Returning with Sheriff Noah Spaulding, Pinkerton then aided in the arrest of the criminals. This event proved to be Pinkerton's first foray into police work in what would become the most storied career in detection in US history.[1]

On one hand, Pinkerton was simply behaving as many people in frontier Illinois would – he involved himself directly in the protection of his community. Indeed, as I explored in the last chapter, the law enforcement institutions of rural America in the antebellum era deeply depended on everyday people mobilizing to address criminal threats.

On the other hand, Pinkerton had also, seemingly despite himself, discovered how to transform an instinct for uncovering criminal behavior into a way to make a profit. As a result of helping the sheriff capture the counterfeiters on Bogus Island, H. E. Hunt and I. C. Bosworth, both well-known members of the Kane business community, asked Pinkerton to help continue the fight against local counterfeiters (presumably offering him some sort of pecuniary compensation). His efforts, in turn, resulted in the prosecution of one of the key members of the Montreal-based counterfeiting ring that had formed the

[1] Allan Pinkerton, *Professional Thieves and the Detective: Containing Numerous Detective Sketches: Collected From Private Records* (New York: G. W. Carleton & Co., 1883), 24–25.

core of the Banditti, John Craig.[2] Pinkerton quickly gained an appointment as deputy sheriff under Spaulding's successor, Luther Dearborn, and built a local reputation as someone with investigative talents.[3]

By the early 1850s, policing became a full-time occupation for Pinkerton. He moved to Chicago (still a raw frontier town), became a deputy sheriff in Cook County under Cyrus Bradley, and worked with the US Treasury to uncover postal fraud and to investigate counterfeiting cases. It was a short step from these activities to the creation of his own firm of private investigators, which could manage the increasing demand from both municipal governments and private firms for detective services in Chicago.

Pinkerton's new detective agency was not the only change in Chicago policing in the early 1850s. Almost concurrently, the Common Council of Chicago was transforming the watchmen and constable system the city had relied upon for managing order through the 1840s into a bureaucratic municipal police. The creation of a police department in 1853 and, following the so-called Beer Riots in April 1855, the consolidation of the night and day watch created, for the first time, a salaried, full-time force of skilled violence experts who would bear the brunt of the policing duties for the city as a whole.

The simultaneous emergence of public and private forms of policing in Chicago in the 1840s and 1850s is best understood as the result of the decoupling of social relations from the rules of municipal government. Similar to Ogle County and Lee County, the expansion of the market generated new kinds of instability in rules, physical mobility, and social ambiguity, thereby unsettling the link between how coercion was supposed to work in the city and the reality of social control on the ground.

However, the market form of private violence – the private security industry – developed in municipalities like Chicago because of the way rules coupled to relations differed from the institutions found in rural counties like the Rock River Valley. Rather than relying on tight-knit and enclosed forms of authority, city elders tried to *delegate* control to local neighborhood elites who were able to rely on local (often cultural) ties to fellow residents to help enforce the law. Ethnic categories helped organize the city's population into different districts, each of which was then responsible largely for its own policing. The result was supposed to follow quintessentially republican principles – there was no bureaucratic police, but rather neighborhood constables who were able to help resolve disputes locally, without bringing central city elites into the problem of enforcement.

Due to the growth of the railroad and the emergence of dense, multi-ethnic neighborhoods in the early 1850s, however, public areas marked by social ambiguity and physical mobility began to develop, undermining delegation.

[2] Pinkerton, *Professional Thieves and the Detective*, 26–52.

[3] Franklin Morn, *The Eye That Never Sleeps: A History of the Pinkerton Detective Agency* (Bloomington: University of Indiana Press, 1982), 21.

To address these concerns, political and economic elites turned to traditional practices – in particular, the option of expanding powers of arrest to both city employees and private individuals through special deputization. Because the social context in which these traditional practices were being used had changed, however, what was a republican form of law enforcement now had unexpected consequences. From the standpoint of some skilled police like Allan Pinkerton, who envisioned ways to transform the capacity to investigate crime into a service to sell to firms and governments, special deputation allowed for private entrepreneurship. From the standpoint of municipal government, special deputization paved the way to the formation of a permanent, bureaucratic and public police force. Both cases stemmed from the decomposition of older forms of social order into constituent public and private elements.

Due to their shared ancestry in a system of deputization, public and private police did not become rivals, but instead coevolved, sharing people, rules, and resources throughout the nineteenth century. The law enforcement changes of these decades were neither far-reaching bureaucratic reforms intended to modernize the provision of services, nor were they attempts by city government to monopolize coercion. Instead, both the public police and private security industry, as revolutionary as they turned out to be, were actually conservative attempts to preserve traditional republican institutions in changing social conditions.

Before demonstrating how, exactly, these distinct public and private policing institutions emerged, this chapter first lays out the republican conception of policing the city, focusing on the ways in which social control was delegated to smaller communities within the urban jurisdiction.

REPUBLICAN SECURITY, POLICE POWER, AND DELEGATION IN THE NINETEENTH-CENTURY AMERICAN CITY

The origins of the "new police" in the United States have almost always been described as a modern shift away from the logic of self-help and self-enforcement, but scholarly work has rarely traced how preexisting institutions shaped the development of municipal police and private alternatives.[4] In the

4 Most accounts of the origins of American policing explain reform as a significant shift in the power of the state. Marxist accounts (e.g., Sidney L. Harring, *Policing a Class Society: The Experience of American Cities*, 1865–1915 [New Brunswick, NJ: Rutgers University Press, 1983]; Robert Weiss, "An Interpretation of the Origin, Development and Transformation of Private Detective Agency Policing in the United States, 1850–1940" [Dissertation, Southern Illinois University, 1981]), for example, identify the growing problem of class control for urban industrialists in the mid–nineteenth century as central in explaining why elites turned to new policing strategies. Modernization approaches (e.g., Lane, *Policing the City*; Steven Spitzer and Andrew T. Scull, "Privatization and Capitalist Development: The Case of the Private Police," *Social Problems* 25, no. 1 [1977]: 18–29) focus on on how industrialization and ethnic conflict generated new threats and forms of property crime, and led civic leaders to call for more robust

United States, those extant self-help institutions were based on a republican logic of security.[5]

Just as in counties, coercive enforcement in towns and cities was based on a link among personal property, defense, and civic virtue. The town constable and watch, the primary law enforcement arm in seventeenth–and eighteenth–century English and American towns and municipalities, for example, was often viewed in republican terms.[6] Constables represented the principle of locally embedded civic virtue and thrift: as citizens selected to serve the community as executors of the law were therefore responsible for serving warrants and process to friends and neighbors, constables were ideally citizens who had reputations for honesty and integrity who did not use government office to line their wallets. This reputation for virtue – which was not always warranted in practice, of course – would allow them to keep the peace with a minimum of local resistance and cost. Additionally, the constable was supposed to reflect local social status and hierarchy. Ideally, the occupant would be a man of some means and an authoritative presence in the local community rather than a career politician or a shiftless opportunist. The watch – also composed of citizens who were expected to serve occasionally to keep an eye on the order and peace of the local village – followed the same republican logic. Like those in counties, these municipal institutions fused private efforts to public enforcement of locally agreed upon norms and *ad hoc* mobilization.[7]

Law enforcement in municipalities both required that private citizens adopt public responsibilities and fed into a widespread antebellum commitment to fiscal probity and minimal taxation. For example, as scholars like Robin Einhorn have emphasized, for much of its early history, municipal politics in

public forms of social control and, ultimately, the centralization of violence by state professionals. Institutional approaches (e.g., Philip J. Ethington, "Vigilantes and the Police: The Creation of a Professional Police Bureaucracy in San Francisco, 1847–1900," *Journal of Social History*, 1987, 197–227; Keller, *The Triumph of Order: Democracy and Public Space in New York and London*) focus on the crisis of legitimacy confronted by urban governments in the antebellum years as the source for the reorganization of municipal law enforcement. Some scholars do insist on the primacy of public-over-private policing, claiming that reforms of the nineteenth century ultimately marginalized older private alternatives. See Monkkonen, *Police in Urban America*.

5 See Francis Dodsworth, "'Civic' Police and the Condition of Liberty: The Rationality of Governance in Eighteenth-Century England," *Social History* 29, no. 2 (2004): 199–216; Karraker, *The Seventeenth-Century Sheriff*, 152–159; Joan R. Kent, *The English Village Constable, 1580–1642: A Social and Administrative Study* (Oxford: Clarendon Press, 1986), 15–23, 282–296; Jean Mather, "The Civil War Sheriff: His Person and Office," *Albion: A Quarterly Journal Concerned with British Studies* 13, no. 3 (1981): 242–261; Monkkonen, *Police in Urban America*, 33–35; Samuel Walker, *Popular Justice: A History of American Criminal Justice* (Oxford: Oxford University Press, 1980); Williams, "Civic Republicanism and the Citizen Militia."

6 Dodsworth, "'Civic' Police and the Condition of Liberty," 204–205.

7 Malka, "The Rights of Men Power, Policing, and the Making of the Liberal State, 1812–1870," 27–44.

Chicago were organized to preclude redistribution and deflect political conflict among social classes, thereby preserving the republican goals of minimal cost and minimal bureaucracy.[8] Through what she calls the "segmentary system" – in which political jurisdictions like wards were drawn according to real estate rather than communal boundaries – providing public goods like streets and sanitation were the responsibility of those who gain directly from such efforts. This had the effect of dampening partisanship and preserving the capacity for a small municipal bureaucracy to manage city affairs.

While segmentation deflected conflicts over redistribution, it also reinforced the importance of local communities for actual enforcement of regulations. That is, actual policing capacity was delegated to local actors. Local residents had to report crimes to courts – constables and, later, night watchmen rarely engaged in aggressive patrol with the hope of ferreting out criminal behavior.[9] Cities were too big to allow a small clique to dominate both political life as well as maintain personalistic connections to their less-powerful coresidents; thus, constables and night watchmen were, more often than not, residents of local wards and neighborhoods who actually did possess the kind of local knowledge necessary to allow them to manage problems among people they knew directly. The net effect of this delegative system was that antebellum Chicago political and business elites did not really attempt to define a single notion of public security for a municipality, but rather allowed smaller, micro-communities within the city to determine their own versions of how to protect themselves.

Of course, Chicago itself had been actually built to be a city of the market, strategically located to take advantage of the transportation advantages afforded by Lake Michigan. Built on the site of Fort Dearborn, which was burned to the ground by a group of Potawatomi natives during the War of 1812, the city quickly became one of the most important market center in the Old Northwest. Incorporated in 1837 as a city (when the population was under 4,000), the city grew at an incredible rate, as efforts to develop a canal connecting the Great Lakes to the Mississippi prompted investment and speculation. By the late 1840s, almost 30,000 residents had moved into the city, and these micro-communities were bursting at the seams.

During this entire period, the practice of delegating authority in Chicago depended on two components: first, there was a tightly interconnected core of political elites who occupied the key roles within the main city administration (the mayor, the city councils, the key supervisory roles) and who appointed and approved a small staff of constables, using regulation to identify and define the good "police" of the city; second, there were (ideally) small communities organized in such a way as to promote self-enforcement from whom the constables were usually drawn. In Chicago in the 1830s through early 1850s, these local communities were organized around ethnic lines, with an internally

[8] Einhorn, *Property Rules*, 15. [9] Steinberg, *The Transformation of Criminal Justice*, 41–55.

powerful elite maintaining control over co-ethnics so the city wouldn't have to provide direct enforcement. Communities, in turn, were divided into spatially distinct communities, with ethnic categories helping to delegate local policing.

The growth of the railroad and an influx of migrants, however, unsettled ethnic spatial segregation and undermined this neat solution to the problem of public order. Chicago became full of places like saloons, public streets, train depots, and other public spaces in which people from different walks of life and ethnicities would mingle. The frequent movement of people into unfamiliar areas where they didn't know anyone produced new and often unstable forms of social authority; physical mobility, associated with life in a burgeoning and exciting metropolis, was creating tremendous ambiguity over social membership.

The unsettling of spatial boundaries in the city had two effects. On the one hand, it created an intermediary category of individuals – strangers, wanderers, vagrants, and so on – to whom it was difficult to delegate, precisely since they did not necessarily have close ties to co-residents. From the standpoint of city elders, this seemingly indistinguishable group of strangers was more a mass and (ironically) homogenous public than a community ordered by ethnic and residential categories in which each neighborhood could more or less manage its own affairs. On the other hand, the interests of a given group within society was now, also, clearly distinct from those of other groups; the security interests of, say, a warehouse owner could no longer be assumed to be the very same as his employees or as those of a railroad magnate, or any other number of special interest groups in the city. They were (as were other special interest groups) most interested in protecting their own explicitly private property.

Anonymity and mobility were thus highly dangerous in a republican system of security. Not only was there no guarantee that local actors would take the responsibility for countering threats from those with whom they shared no kinship or social ties, but it was also difficult to clearly link private interests to the pursuit of public welfare in a context where the boundaries of the community itself were called into question. As a result, the unsettled spaces of the city posed a significant challenge to the system of delegating security cheaply and effectively to local communities.[10]

[10] For the problem of anonymity in the nineteenth-century city in general, see Sandra Frink, "'Strangers Are Flocking Here': Identity and Anonymity in New Orleans, 1810–1860," *American Nineteenth Century History* 11, no. 2 (2010): 155–181; Lyn H. Lofland, *A World of Strangers: Order and Action in Urban Public Space* (New York: Basic Books, 1973); Richard Sennett, *Families Against the City: Middle Class Homes of Industrial Chicago, 1872–1890* (Cambridge, MA: Harvard University Press, 1984). Of course, the public spaces also were the site of new, often complex forms of social ordering, but these actually reflected an adaptation the fundamental problem of transient interaction. See, for example, Mona Domosh, "Those 'Gorgeous Incongruities': Polite Politics and Public Space on the Streets of Nineteenth-Century New York City," *Annals of the Association of American Geographers* 88, no. 2 (1998): 209–226.

Despite this challenge, political and economic elites did not abandon republican institutions. Instead, they continued to try to use the constabulary role by relying on special deputization, which gave special police powers to private individuals for a given time or for a given jurisdiction. Special deputization provided a great deal of flexibility in making the old system work under changed conditions. Indeed, it provided the crucial link between the traditional republican system and the dual organization of public and private violence, as I demonstrate in this chapter.[11] However, precisely because the spatial foundations of the delegative system changed, these efforts no longer produced an integrated constabulary. Instead, two distinct institutional clusters began to develop: a public police force, funded by the city and responsible for protecting individual citizens, and a private security industry, responsive to economic clients and committed to protecting property. The components of the republican system – bureaucracy and entrepreneurship, public and private interest – decomposed into different forms, allowing a robust private security industry to emerge side-by-side with its public alternative.

Private detectives like Allan Pinkerton and public police officers were rarely rivals in Chicago because they were, very often, the *same* people, moving from one job to another. Not only did these individuals move back and forth between roles as new opportunities arose, they also, occasionally, held multiple such roles at the same time. No longer was policing delegated to local communities and amateurs; instead, throughout the 1850s and 1860s in Chicago it was dominated by specialists who had both public and private policing duties.

DELEGATION IN PRACTICE

How was the republican system implemented in municipalities in practice? And how did particular places marked by ambiguity and mobility actually reshape that system? This section unpacks how policing was organized in Chicago by examining the role of ethnic segregation and elite cohesion in the policing of

[11] Special deputization had been used in England since at least the mid–eighteenth century, enabling the powers and privileges of the constableship to be delegated to private actors for some period of time or some limited jurisdiction. By the early nineteenth century, the municipal government of London, which had a surfeit of private patrol and prosecution associations, regularly deputized private watchmen – the hybridization of public and private interests through special deputization reinforced its appeal as a republican institution. Moreover, mobilizing often middle-class men as specials was a key line of defense against the Chartist protests in the 1830s and 1840s, clearly identifying it as a participatory form of maintaining traditional social hierarchies and order. See Clare Leon, "The Mythical History of the 'Specials': Sorting Out the Fact from the Fiction," *Liverpool Law Review* 11, no. 2 (1989): 187–197; Leon Radzinowicz, *A History of English Criminal Law and Its Administration from 1750*, vol. 2 (New York: Macmillan, 1957), 194, 205–207, 215–224; R. E. Swift, "Policing Chartism, 1839–1848: The Role of the 'Specials' Reconsidered," *The English Historical Review* 122, no. 497 (2007): 669–699.

the city, tracing how spaces of intermixing and civic disorder challenged the traditional operation of the constableship.

The formal rules of the 1837 city charter of Chicago, like other American cities in the 1830s and 1840s, allowed flexibility in the crafting of regulations to help police the public welfare of the city without prescribing a specific bureaucracy to help enforce those regulations. Legally, enforcement for provisions lay in part with the aldermen and mayor themselves, as well as the officers they appointed. A high constable was elected in addition to the mayor and was granted the same responsibilities as a sheriff within the city limits; both the high constable and the council could appoint city constables and deputy constables to aid in the collection of fines and the enforcing of various regulations.[12] All these officials were, at first, paid through fees for services, allowing enforcers to link their own entrepreneurial instincts with their public service as police.[13] Initially, constables were appointed by the Common Council, though this changed in 1847 when each ward gained the ability to elect its own constable.[14]

The council occasionally appointed seasonal forces of night watchmen and even authorized construction of a Watch House in 1845, but such appointments were contingent on momentary outbreaks of disorder and did not reflect a continued commitment of the city to the creation of a full-time staff of policemen.[15] When the night watch was expanded and made into a permanent operation in October of 1849, it was still firmly under the control of the mayor and was primarily organized to detain those "found ... at unusual hours" and "under suspicious circumstances," as well as to arrest drunk and disorderly persons in public places; the simple fact that those so arrested were supposed to be personally presented in front of the mayor for individual examination limited the degree to which police could police private spaces like the home and business, each of which were to be under the patriarchal control of the father and master, respectively.[16]

[12] Edmund J. James, ed., *The Charters of the City of Chicago* (Chicago: University of Chicago Press, 1898–1899), 40, 70–71.

[13] Einhorn, *Property Rules*, 146.

[14] *Chicago Daily Journal* March 12, 1845; John J. Flinn, *History of the Chicago Police: From the Settlement of the Community to the Present Time* (Chicago: W. B. Conkey, 1887), 58. In 1841, a charter amendment abolished the high constable and replaced it with a salaried city marshal (James, *The Charters of the City of Chicago*, 115). During the 1840s, the council itself came to be seen as police with duties to maintain the order and peace of the cities. (e.g., Common Council Proceedings [CP] 1849: 5783).

[15] CP 1843: 1523A; CP 1844: 2271A; CP 1845: 2521A; CP 1845: 2544A; CP 1847: 3875A; CP 1848: 4608A.

[16] CP 1849: 5672A. This act still presupposed that the night watch might not be needed throughout the year, since they were to be appointed "from time to time." In 1851, the watch was finally permanently established as a noncontingent force. See CP 1851: 463A.

Though it was left unsaid in the charter, the deputies appointed by the constable were not necessarily intended to be public officials.[17] Special constables began to appear in the 1840s, and after the consolidating act of 1851, which reinforced the importance of the special assessment for the city's fiscal system, these private/public specials became even more integral to the operation of the police.[18] This system, composed of elected constables, a city marshal, a small, quasi-permanent night watch, and the sheriff and his deputies – in all a group of perhaps 20 individuals – represented the totality of organized law enforcement in Chicago in 1850, a year when the population of the city reached around 30,000. Despite this very small number of law officers, the city nevertheless had many laws in need of enforcing; the charter of 1837 had, for instance, included ninety-two separate sections with regulations covering a huge swath of behavior, including market exchange, storage of firewood, use of guns, use of streets and public spaces, and provisions for schooling and other services; moreover, this core regulatory apparatus was modified and expanded at least 182 times in the years before the consolidating act of 1851, when a new charter supplanted the old.[19]

The net result was a paradox: There were many, many regulations that nevertheless were supposed to be enforced through communal participation. How did the council get local residents to cooperate in this enforcement?

The answer has to do with the role of ethnic categories and social stratification as forms of practical authority in both the political institutions and the day-to-day life of residents of the early city. That is, while at the very top of government, a tightly interconnected cluster of elites used regulations to articulate the legal expectations for residents, the implicit assumption was that sanctions and monitoring would reflect *local* relations of common knowledge and influence based on the activity of the ward level constable and the justice of the peace; these local relations in a city like Chicago, the site of such explosive immigration from the 1840s through 1870s, put a premium on language and shared membership. Ethnic categories – being Irish, or Swedish, or German – were as much based on the patterns of local residency allowing for the diffusion of local information and the self-policing of communities as they were on actual identities of people (many of whom, such as the many Prussians and Bavarians moving to the city in the late 1840s, would not have necessarily seen themselves as sharing anything other than language). In this way, the making of ethnicity and the delegation of authority went hand in hand; the early city was divided in a patchwork of distinctive ethnic neighborhoods, the differentiation of which

[17] Einhorn, *Property Rules*, 146–147.

[18] CP 1845: 2832; CP 1849: 5672. Also see Flinn, *History of the Chicago Police*, 57–61.

[19] Numbers calculated from James, *The Charters of the City of Chicago* and Common Council Proceedings files. Also see Novak, *The People's Welfare*, 3–18.

provided a way of ensuring compliance to the directives issued at the center by simple delegation.[20]

The construction of ethnic boundaries meant that internal forms of hierarchy, reflecting ties based on kinship, nativity, and religious identity, also provided a form of social discipline. For example, Irish communities of canal workers, such as those at Bridgeport in the 1840s, were not known for their peacefulness, but the myriad fights and disputes local residents engaged in (particularly those between what local papers inaccurately called the "Corkmen" and "Ulstermen" factions) only rarely became threats to others outside the work camps because local elites managed to arbitrate disputes.[21] Religious figures, local notables, as well as the shopkeepers and professionals who shared ethnic identity with the workers but had a vested stake in the maintenance of local social hierarchy, managed to monitor and organize these local immigrant communities internally.[22]

At the micro-level, then – the level of day-to-day contacts among individuals – many Chicago immigrants moved into areas where they had the opportunity to reproduce their traditional lives without too much external interference.[23] In his study of Swedish immigration to Chicago, for instance, Ulf Beijbom shows how most settlers prior to 1850 selected homes that, though nestled in a primarily Irish area near what would become Kilgubbin, nevertheless were within close spatial proximity to St. Ansgarius, the Swedish Lutheran Church. This provided both a focal point for the religious livelihoods of Swedes in Chicago, as well as a means of establishing moral regulation of their day-to-day lives in a strange city.[24] Keeping a small police force in the midst of an elaborate regulatory government depended on precisely this kind of local control.

[20] Ethnic residential patterns were often cast explicitly in political terms. See, for example, Mabel McIlvaine et al., *Reminiscences of Chicago During the Forties and Fifties* (Chicago: R. R. Donnelley & Sons Company, 1913), 55–56.

[21] There were, of course, some exceptions, such as the 1838 LaSalle riot, which involved local militia mobilization. Michael F. Funchion, *Chicago's Irish Nationalists, 1881–1890* (New York: Arno Press, 1976), 10–11; La Salle Centennial Committee, *La Salle, Illinois: An Historical Sketch*. (La Salle Illinois: La Salle Centennial Committee, 1952), 24–25.

[22] Their influence, though rooted in neighborhoods even, at times, ascended to the level of political representation at the ward level: at least two out of six wards elected German aldermen in the early 1840s, for example. ibid., 24; Andrew Jacke Townsend, "The Germans of Chicago" (PhD diss., The University of Chicago, 1927), 17.

[23] See *Historic City: The Settlement of Chicago* (Chicago: Department of Development & Planning, City of Chicago, 1976), 20–27; Vivien M. Palmer, "The Primary Settlement as a Unit of Urban Growth and Organization" (PhD diss., The University of Chicago, 1932), 110–118; Bessie Louise Pierce, *History of Chicago: The Beginning of a City, 1673–1848*, vol. 1 (New York: Alfred A. Knopf, 1937), 179–186.

[24] Ulf Beijbom, *Swedes in Chicago: A Demographic and Social Study of the 1846–1880 Immigration*, trans. Donald Brown (Stockholm: Läromedelsfölagen, 1971), 58–62.

How did the residential segregation of the city promote policing with a city government that was explicitly organized, as Robin Einhorn demonstrated, to protect the interests of powerful real estate interests through dividing the city into wards based on property?[25] Four factors are important.

First, internal economic stratification helped make local elites sympathetic to the real estate interests lying behind the segmentary political economy. Local notables – property owners, businessmen, shopkeepers, and so forth – were both fully invested in the booster economy of the city and active in community politics and policing, supporting those they knew and trusted to help preserve the local peace.[26] In a sense, delegated policing depended on the presence of *intra-community* stratification precisely because local notables would have similar interests to those in the core of city power in the Common Council and could be trusted to manage their local communities in such a manner as to avoid complicated public threats. In other words, self-policing took place within social categories like ethnicity while also depending on variation in economic power within those categories.

Second, ethnic communities possessed their own mechanisms of communicating to the city council, mechanisms that were mediated through local notables. Petitions, for example, were a key way in which these communities sought to communicate their demands for public service or security to the Common Council. Between 1837 and 1851, we have records for eighty-seven such petitions (or reports on such petitions) brought before Common Council concerning police matters.[27] Moreover, these petitions often reflected demands that would help preserve rather than threaten local autonomy – local notables would nominate a fellow resident, for example, to be appointed as constable to help manage local affairs.[28] For immigrant communities, the appointment of constables with linguistic skills was strongly preferred. In 1845, for example, a group of Germans requested that N. A. Berdel be appointed constable, presumably because of his linguistic capabilities, while a more explicit request was made in August of 1854 for someone who could "execute various writs" efficiently in German in the environs of the dense immigrant community of the Northside.[29]

Third, precisely because jurisdictions divided and segmented communities that were supposed to be quite ethnically homogenous and economically stratified, it was possible for local communities to define for themselves what security for residents would actually look like, rather than to try to hash out

25 Einhorn, *Property Rules.*

26 Palmer, "The Primary Settlement as a Unit of Urban Growth and Organization," 100–104; Ruth M. Piper, "The Irish in Chicago, 1848–1871" (Master's thesis, The University of Chicago, 1936), 6–8, 10–17, 47–53; Townsend, "The Germans of Chicago," 24–40.

27 Common Council Proceedings Files. 28 e.g., CP 1849: 5529A; CP 1849: 5430A.

29 CP 1845: 2455A; CP 1854: 758A.

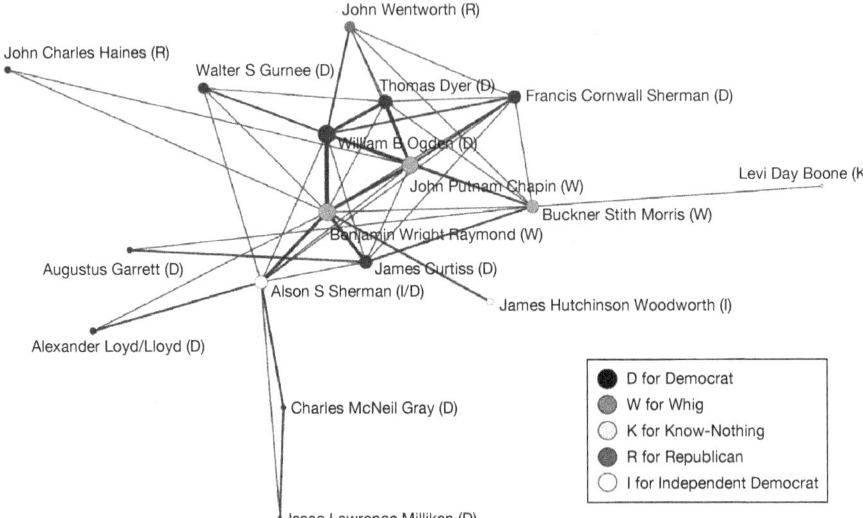

FIGURE 5. Mayoral co-affiliations (1835–1868)
Showing the first seventeen mayors of Chicago. Width of line proportional to the number of shared organizational affiliations. Size of node proportional to 1-mode eigenvector centrality.

a shared definition of the "public good" of protection in the abstract. This means, in other words, that many infractions of the law were never actually prosecuted in the courts – instead, they were managed informally, through local social networks. For these kinds of disputes, not even constables were required.

Fourth, the city's government was itself dominated by an elite drawn from earliest settlers (many of whom moved from New York and Massachusetts) who used close personal connections and dominance of economic life to help manage intra-governmental conflicts. For example, the first seventeen mayors of Chicago (from 1837 through 1859) shared extensive membership affiliations within the city's many economic and social organizations.[30] Not surprisingly, these mayors were all connected to one another via the myriad business and social enterprises in the city during its first decades. Figure 5 depicts the relationship among early Chicago mayors as a network composed of ties of organizational co-memberships: the wider the tie, the more memberships in organizations shared by the individuals; the larger the node, the more centrally connected the node is to other central nodes (eigenvector centrality).

[30] A. T. Andreas, *History of Chicago: From the Earliest Period to the Present Time*, vol. 1 (Chicago: A. T. Andreas, 1884). I included church memberships, philanthropic co-service, militia company membership, and so on, as social"; I included business and booster relationships as "economic." Although I coded for membership in governmental bodies as well, I exclude those in the following analysis since I am more interested in the social embedding of political actors.

Indeed, serving as mayor meant enjoying a camaraderie with other political elites, regardless of party. Only one of the mayors in question – Levi Boone (1855–1856) – was weakly tied to the rest of the political elite through organizational memberships, while the rest of the mayors were interconnected with one another (each mayor shared organizational memberships with over five other mayors on average, while over 32% of possible inter-organizational ties among mayors were actually present).[31]

These inter-mayoral contacts reflect the closure of the most economically powerful Chicagoans within city government – not only were early mayors and political leaders of Chicago among the wealthiest residents of the city (in contrast to latter economic elites, who tended to disdain political office), they were also linked to one another through a kinship and business ties.[32] Moreover, economic elites actively tried to protect their position in the city by marrying and doing business with one another; one estimate holds that in 1863, almost 32 percent of the residents making $10,000 annually shared kinship ties.[33] Over time, the familial network of elite actors became even more closed off to new entrants, particularly among the highest earning group.[34] Hence, while most of Chicago's early political elites were self-made or came from less privileged backgrounds than many of their compatriots in the East, they pursued a similar strategy of protecting their status through building family alliances.

This strategy accentuated the distance between the privileged core of Chicago and the working/immigrant classes.[35] While a kind of *noblesse oblige* did lead leaders like William Ogden to, occasionally, personally supervise lower-class lifestyles through the surveillance activities of groups like the Relief Society, these activities were rarely based on actual personal deference of the working

[31] Moreover, over 62% of two-star ties in the network are also enclosed triads, implying that actors knew each other across multiple organizational settings. In terms of basic metrics, the average distance of this converted one-mode network is 1.86 while the diameter is 4. By any measure this is a structurally cohesive, highly connected set of actors.

[32] Donald S. Bradley and Mayer N. Zald, "From Commercial Elite to Political Administrator: The Recruitment of the Mayors of Chicago," *American Journal of Sociology* 71, no. 2 (1965): 153–167; Einhorn, *Property Rules*, 39–44; Frederic Cople Jaher, *The Urban Establishment: Upper Strata in Boston, New York, Charleston, Chicago, and Los Angeles* (Urbana: University of Illinois Press, 1982), 492–498; Bessie Louise Pierce, *History of Chicago: From Town to City, 1848–1871*, vol. 2 (Chicago: University of Chicago Press, 1940), 305–306; Rima Lunin Schultz, "The Businessman's Role in Western Settlement: The Entrepreneurial Frontier, Chicago, 1833–1872" (PhD diss., Boston University, 1985), 391–396.

[33] Jaher, *The Urban Establishment*, 495. [34] ibid., 497.

[35] Craig Buettinger, "Economic Inequality in Early Chicago, 1849–1850," *Journal of Social History* 11, no. 3 (April 1978): 413–418, traces the incredible level of inequality in Chicago in the late 1840s, estimating a GINI Coefficient of around .89.

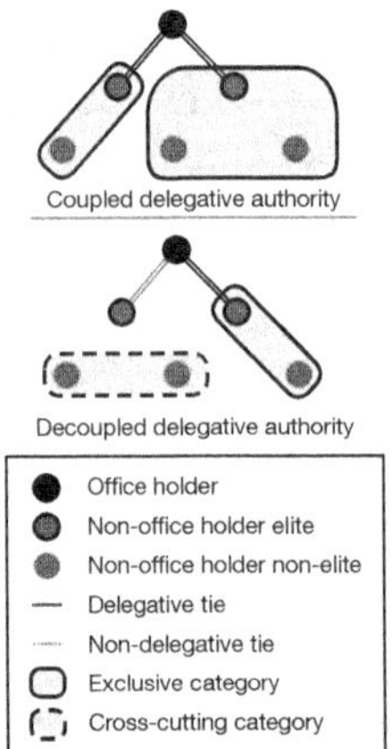

FIGURE 6. Delegative authority and jurisdictional coupling

classes and immigrants toward political elites.[36] Instead, close links among Chicago's elites allowed them to control who did and did not have access to the inner corridors of municipal power, while essentially allowing others to fend for themselves.

The overall picture of delegated policing was thus: a system of practical authority based in islands of ethnic homogeneity and economic stratification cross-cut by jurisdictional boundaries that inhibited political demands on the city for a unified system of public protection. The formal rules of the municipal government allowed local communities to essentially monitor themselves and shifted the onus of actual enforcement downward, allowing immigrants to find a home in communities that were defined around ethnic boundaries.

The top panel of Figure 6 depicts this set of social relationships – officeholders have connections to powerful people in local communities who, in turn, use their ethnic ties to other residents to help manage conflict. Authoritative delegative ties, in other words, link governing institutional rules to day-to-day relations when the categories ordering the social lives of residents (in this case, ethnicity) map onto residential segregation, allowing local elites to take over the burden of local policing. Decoupling occurred when cross-cutting forms of interaction (in this case, places marked by social ambiguity) undermined the ability of those co-ethnic elites to sanction and monitor their neighborhoods, as depicted on the bottom panel of the figure. When the boundaries ensuring delegation were called into question, it became very difficult for delegation to actually work.

36 Kathleen D. McCarthy, *Noblesse Oblige: Charity and Cultural Philanthropy in Chicago, 1849–1929* (Chicago: University of Chicago Press, 1982); Pierce, *History of Chicago (Vol. 1)*, 185–186.

HOW DELEGATED POLICING BROKE APART

By the late 1840s, Chicagoans were profoundly concerned about the efficacy of their policing institutions. This was due to several key changes occurring in the city, changes related to the growth of the city's economy and its effect on social relationships. First, residents increasingly began to discuss the presence of strangers in the city, the growth of traffic on city streets, and the creation of a sense of anonymity and bustle. This was, for the most part, seen as a positive change because it indicated growth and prosperity – the *Chicago Weekly Democrat*, for example, reported on the ways in which the presence of "more strangers passing through our city" helped prove "the importance of the city in a commercial point of view."[37] But the presence of strangers and traffic had ambiguous effects; while Chicago boosters actively courted the economic traveler and investor, the papers also noted an increase in the number of "rogues" interspersed among the crowds; newspaper accounts began to note how horse thieves and counterfeiters could quickly adopt a complex series of pseudonyms and exploit relatively new forms of evading local law enforcement by taking advantage of the anonymity afforded by the growing city.[38]

Second, and related, the issue of security for Chicago became intertwined with a specific sector of the economy: transportation. As noted, Chicago's centrality in the nation's transportation system in the late 1840s grew to a degree virtually unprecedented in American history.[39] These changes in the transportation industry led to perceptions among residents that rogues and villains were able to use the newfound physical mobility to avoid local punishments, as well as a growing concern that important business travelers and future investors were often confronted by conmen, corrupt cab drivers, and hotel thieves preying on the tourist infrastructure developing in the city.[40] Strangers to the city were not themselves always considered dangerous, but they were often seen as vulnerable.[41]

Another development that lead social categories to become less useful for delegation had to do with the growth of mobilized political sentiment

[37] CWD, May 1, 1851. Also CDP, February 21, 1853.

[38] e.g., CDP, April 2, 1853; CDP, January 21 1853. For the spatializing of disorder in other cities, see John C. Schneider, *Detroit and the Problem of Order, 1830–1880: A Geography of Crime, Riot, and Policing* (Lincoln: University of Nebraska Press, 1980); Stein, "The Right to Violence," 96.

[39] David Young, *The Iron Horse and the Windy City: How Railroads Shaped Chicago* (DeKalb: Northern Illinois University Press, 2005), 20–48.

[40] Ted Robert Mitchell, "Connecting a Nation, Dividing a City: How Railroads Shaped the Public Spaces and Social Understanding of Chicago" (PhD diss., Michigan State University, 2009), 18–36, 67–76, 137–160.

[41] Amy Richter demonstrates how this vulnerability was often interpreted in gendered terms, which provoked responses by railroads to establish order on the trains. Over time, this helped pave the way for a new understanding of the publicness of railroad spaces. See Amy G. Richter, *Home on the Rails: Women, the Railroad, and the Rise of Public Domesticity* (Chapel Hill: University of North Carolina Press, 2005), 20–25.

among both immigrant groups and nativist organizations in the 1850s. During the late 1840s and early 1850s, a large number of benevolent societies, aid groups, and fraternal associations emerged within the mostly poor Irish and German communities, many aimed at providing a safety net. Often these groups were organized through the Catholic church and involved social traditions of drinking and relaxing that were anathema to many of the Protestant white Americans, a number of whom started to advocate for the "Maine Laws" aimed at banning or limiting alcoholic consumption. Indeed, ethnicity was less and less useful as a form of delegation just as it became more politically important as a way of mobilizing people.

Each of these changes posed a threat to the delegated policing system. As categories based on nativity became simultaneously more *ambiguous* through intermixed social spaces at train stations and on city streets, as well as more *salient* as ways of dividing the populace, the ability to simply segment residents into mutually exclusive, self-policing islands was undermined. Instead, residents began to have to confront the question of who, exactly, constituted the "real" Chicago. And this, in turn, meant that Chicagoans were forced to recognize new categories of citizens that did not fit neatly into ones defined by ethnic or linguistic background.

CHANGES IN THE SPATIAL ORGANIZATION OF THE CITY

The breakdown in ethnic segregation was related to several changes in the spatial organization of the city. For instance, during the early 1850s, a number of specifically public places of intermixing were constructed: railroad depots, hotels, and theaters, all of which either brought strangers together in places at a remove from the embedded social networks of their neighborhoods or allowed visitors to the city to intermingle with locals. This, in turn, considerably changed the way in which residents thought about the sources of danger and threat.[42]

Through the 1840s, the papers only rarely covered crime in Chicago itself. In part, perhaps, this was because crime itself was uncommon, but it also was likely due to the fact that enforcement of criminal laws only rarely required the activation of the municipal constabulary or Cook County shrievalty. For example, I examined a sample of seventy-three issues of the *Chicago Daily Journal* from January 1 to March 31 in 1845, when the population of the city reached 12,000.[43] In total, not counting coverage of the Circuit Court (which met at predetermined times), only four of these issues (5%) contained information about criminal events and arrests in Chicago itself. On the other hand, thirty of the issues (41%) contained a news article about crime elsewhere in the nation.

By 1855 (when the population of Chicago hit 80,000 and some older ethnic neighborhoods were rapidly becoming less segregated), coverage of local arrests

[42] Arthur L. Stinchcombe, "Institutions of Privacy in the Determination of Police Administrative Practice," *American Journal of Sociology* 69, no. 2 (1963): 150–160.

[43] This includes almost all the issues still in existence for the period in question.

was much more prevalent, reflecting the consolidation of a permanent staff of violent professionals actively arresting offenders in the city, as well as the creation of a police court in which arrested offenders could be quickly tried. Of the seventy-six issues of the *Journal* I examined from January 1 to March 31 of that year, 53 percent (forty-three issues) contained Chicago crime coverage, while coverage of crime outside the city remained fairly constant (47% or thirty-six issues).

At the same time as reports of crime increased, the spaces associated with crime were explicitly public ones. In all, I was able to catalogue 387 violent events of a variety of types (murders, armed robberies, fights, and so on). Of those, approximately 213 included information about the locale in which the crime was committed. Table 5 indicates frequency of location types.

As is evident from the table, the vast majority of violence receiving publicity in the press took place in either public places or in areas associated with tourist infrastructure – streets, saloons, boarding houses, and so forth. From the outset the burgeoning police department engaged not in policing general disorder, but rather focused on those areas where such disorder would create an explicitly public threat.

In addition, the structural foundations of delegation were eroding. In particular, areas that were no longer characterized by the residential segregation crucial to delegating policing began to develop in the city. This, in turn, involved the decoupling of the practical forms of authority found in the neighborhoods from the requirements of the municipal system of delegation.

To explore these changes, I constructed a sample of over 1,800 different residents of the city using the 1856 Gager City Directory, which collected data on nativity, occupation, and length of residency in addition to physical address.[44] This data, collected as a result of the 1855 city census (and was completed, very likely, with an eye to enumerating and locating concentrations

44 My sampling strategy was twofold: first, I selected four major thoroughfares at random (Wells, Randolph, Michigan Street [now W. Hubbard] and Michigan Avenue) and collected all enumerated addresses on those streets; second, I selected residents of several key proto-neighborhoods areas and collected data on all residents I could locate who lived within relatively arbitrarily defined boundaries. This provided the mix of randomness and systematicity necessary to reconstruct meaningful but not fully determined local economic and ethnic networks for residents. This also presents a simple alternative to traditional measures of residential segregation such as most of those based on Simpson's diversity index, since it takes for its unit of analysis the average diversity of individual social networks within an arbitrarily sampled spatial unit rather than the diversity of neighborhood clusters within a unit; arguably, this provides a more direct means of identifying diversity in actual interaction patterns than relying on spatial clusters alone, the boundaries of which often reflect precisely the underlying social patterns we are trying to measure. See Otis Dudley Duncan and Beverly Duncan, "A Methodological Analysis of Segregation Indexes," *American Sociological Review* 20, no. 2 (1955): 210–217; Homer Hoyt, *One Hundred Years of Land Values in Chicago: The Relationship of the Growth of Chicago to the Rise of Its Land Values, 1830–1933* (Chicago: University of Chicago Press, 1933); Palmer, "The Primary Settlement as a Unit of Urban Growth and Organization"; Olivier Zunz, *The Changing Face of Inequality: Urbanization, Industrial Development, and Immigrants in Detroit, 1880–1920* (Chicago: University of Chicago Press, 2000).

TABLE 5. *Location of local violent events in Chicago newspapers (1853–1856)*

Location type	Number of events
Street	62
Saloon	38
House	35
Boarding house	19
Brothel	10
Depot	7
Boat	4
Bridge	3
Dock	3
Hotel	3
Dance house	2
Lake shore	2
Polling station	2
Shanty	2
Store	2
Auction house	1
Barbers shop	1
Beach	1
Bridewell	1
Coffee house	1
Construction site	1
Gambling house	1
Grocery	1
Park	1
Police station	1
Poor house	1
Post office	1
Prairie	1
Printing press	1
River	1
Steamboat landing	1
Theater	1
Wharf	1
Wood	1
Total	213

Data from *Chicago Tribune*, *Chicago Daily Journal*, *Chicago Daily Democrat*, and *Chicago Daily Times*.

of potentially dangerous immigrants at the very height of local Know-Nothing nativism) is tremendously useful – it allows me to geocode physical addresses of residents and thereby reconstruct networks of those with whom individuals would likely have had day-to-day contact based on spatial proximity. As

TABLE 6. *Personal networks in select Chicago neighborhoods (1856)*

Neighborhood	N	Avg. economic stratification	Avg. ethnic heterogeneity	Proportion of elite ties intraethnic (%)	Delegative capacity score
1 Southwest	190	0.627	0.587	32	1.04
2 Sands	425	0.683	0.746	24	0.937
3 Northwest	126	0.609	0.321	83	1.288
4 North Lake	109	0.579	0.567	37	1.012
5 Downtown	523	0.627	0.724	21	0.903
6 Westside	479	0.681	0.751	18	0.930
Total/Avg. (s.d.)	1852	0.634 (0.041)	0.616 (0.165)	36 (24)	1.018 (0.142)

Data from 1856 Gager City Directory.

such, I defined a "tie" between two actors as being present if they lived within 750 feet of one another. Then, using loosely defined definitions of "community" as plausible historic neighborhoods, I calculated the average levels of heterogeneity and homogeneity among the ethnic and class ties across individuals living in each community using the standard index.[45]

This data, in turn, can be used to identify how well a given neighborhood might be able to handle the responsibilities of delegation. On one hand, delegation requires tight-knit ethnic ties; such neighborhoods should be relatively homogenous. On the other hand, delegation also depends on elites within those homogenous ethnic communities, who coordinate with city officials and manage local conflicts. Table 6 captures the data from the residential survey to capture both these phenomena – ethnic heterogeneity (based on nativity) and economic stratification (based on a threefold division of the prestige of occupation).[46] The two measures work together to create the *delegative capacity* of local neighborhoods – the more economically stratified and the less ethnically diverse the networks of local residents, the more they are able to "self-police."[47]

On the first measure of delegative capacity, economic stratification, most neighborhoods were similar. This meant that, on average, individuals in each

45 This index is the classic Blau fractionalization index: for a group i where p_i a proportion of the group, fractionalization is $1 - \sum_{i=1}^{n} p_i^2$. This roughly measures the probability that two actors drawn randomly would come from different groups.

46 The occupation prestige scheme was adapted from the classifications designed in 1976 by the Philadelphia Social History Project. See Theodore Hershberg and Robert Dockhorn, "Occupational Classification," *Historical Methods Newsletter* 9, nos. 2–3 (1976): 59–98.

47 The Delegative Capacity score is simply *AverageEconomicStratification* + (1 – *AverageEthnic Heterogeneity*).

neighborhood were likely to be in contact with others who had either lower or higher status occupations than themselves. Wealthy Chicagoans were not isolated into enclaves, but were engaged in day-to-day contact with the less wealthy and less powerful.

However, the same equitable distribution across the city did not apply to the other source of delegative capacity: ethnicity. Some areas in 1855 – the southwest (composed of a large number of Irish residents), the northwest side (made up of Germans) and the north lake area (also German) – were characterized by less ethnically fractionalized personal networks on average, in which many of one's contacts shared one's own nativity and, likely, religious background and even kinship ties. Other areas, however, including downtown (where many of the city's Yankee elite had moved during the 1840s) and the notorious vice district just north of the river known as the Sands, were much more fractionalized, implying that interethnic interactions were common among residents. From the standpoint of the capacity for policing to be delegated within island communities, this posed a problem for city elders.

This becomes particularly evident if we look at the relations in different neighborhoods of well-off residents, those most committed to the protection of their personal property and the maintenance of the delegated policing system. Table 6 depicts the average proportion of ties among the highest income earners in each neighborhood who matched that individual in terms of ethnicity. In the northwest German community, over 83 percent of such ties were intraethnic, providing another way in which powerful local residents could help sustain self-policing. In the downtown and westside communities, on the other hand – precisely those areas where the traditional American elite was active – ethnic identification only rarely provided a subsidiary way for wealthy actors to help control other residents.

In other words, individuals at the top of the economic ladder in some places were less able to maintain the kind of control that would allow them to manage a delegated police power. The core of the city was densely populated, highly diverse, and increasingly anonymous (the map in Figure 7, for example, depicts relative scores of delegative capacity in the neighborhoods in question). By 1855, the city was undergoing a transition from being composed of an archipelago of little ethnically homogenous and economically diverse security islands to a mixed zone of some highly isolated and insulated communities (e.g., Northwest side's Little Germany) and other, deeply mixed areas (e.g., the Sands).

Moreover, ethnicity was becoming highly politicized, making it much more difficult for elites to rely on cultural ties to delegate policing. In St. Louis, New Orleans, Baltimore, and Cincinnati in the 1840s and 1850s, the massive influx of immigrants created a political backlash among native residents, leading to the creation of powerful local Know-Nothing movements and resulting in

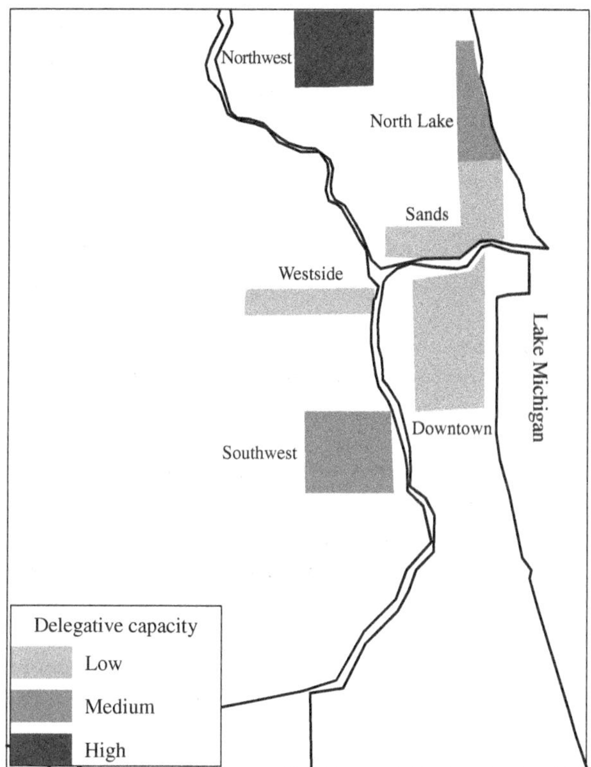

FIGURE 7. Delegative capacity in select neighborhoods (1855–1856)*
*Divisions between levels are based on natural breaks calculated through Jenks optimization.

violent collective disturbances targeting immigrant communities.[48] In Chicago, where the proportion of immigrants was as high as anywhere else in the country, the *Chicago Tribune* began to argue that it was the Irish Catholics, in particular, who posed a threat to the "good order" of the city, claiming that "a very

[48] David Grimsted, *American Mobbing, 1828–1861: Toward Civil War* (Oxford: Oxford University Press, 1998), 184–193. Scholars like David Fearon and James Laitin, among others, have demonstrated how the construction of ethnic boundaries (often through the cultivating of violent confrontation) reflects the strategic calculations of political elites who try to forge a coalition, marshal support, or avoid costly compromises or conflicts. Such calculations were undoubtedly in play for both the Know-Nothing party leaders and ethnic notables, for whom organizing cleavages around the issue of ethnicity (as opposed to class or sector) could prove personally advantageous. See James D. Fearon and David D. Laitin, "Violence and the Social Construction of Ethnic Identity," *International Organization* 54, no. 4 (2000): 845–877; James D. Fearon and David D. Laitin, "Explaining Interethnic Cooperation," *The American Political Science Review* 90, no. 4 (1996): 715–735; Kanchan Chandra, "Ethnic Bargains, Group Instability, and Social Choice Theory," *Politics & Society* 29, no. 3 (2001): 337–362.

large proportion ... of the riots and bloodshed which have grown out of and in opposition to Native Americanism, may easily be traced to the fatal mistake which is continually being made by the Catholic priesthood of this country in telling their spiritual children that their allegiance and obedience is due, not to the laws and institutions of their adopted country, but to the mandates and instructions of their ghostly superiors."[49]

Crucially, one major problem nativists had with some of the newcomers was related to their capacity to serve as the vessels of delegation. Know-Nothingism in Chicago, for instance, was not opposed to all immigration; instead supporters were worried that Irish and other Catholic foreigners would be unable to exercise the kind of self-management necessary to operate in a republican system. "Those Romish adherents," wrote the nativist paper *Watchmen of the Prairies*, "would prefer that the Pope should enjoy the honors of temporal sovereignty than that the people should enjoy the right of self-government."[50] Those groups which could manage their own affairs were commended; the *Tribune*, for example, was strongly supportive of both Swedish and Jewish immigrant communities because of their putative self-sufficiency.[51] Ethnicity was still useful as a way to delegate authority, but for certain groups with supposed allegiance to a foreign power, such networks could be construed as a means of undermining local social order.

This issue came to a head, however, over the issue of drinking in public saloons. Saloons both played an increasingly important role in ethnic life in Chicago and elsewhere during the 1840s and 1850s, and were the frequent site of violence.[52] In its report on the "Liquor Traffic of Chicago" in 1854, the local branch of the Maine Law temperance association assailed the saloons as sites of prostitution and gambling, "where time is wasted, morals destroyed, and the ignorant and unwary are robbed of their last dollar."[53]

At the same time, these public places of intermixing were also key institutions for the articulation of a new ethnic politics, one that drew on links between the growing parties and party leaders; nativist papers repeatedly linked "drinking hells" to the Irish vote.[54] As such, for nativists across the country, the problem of violence in saloons was both a danger to the public order – in the sense that saloons were zones of intermixing – as well as a threat to the political rule of the traditional ruling elite – in the sense that they were hotbeds of partisan mobilization.

49 December 12, 1853. 50 March 12, 1850.

51 Bruce McKittrick Cole, "The Chicago Press and the Know-Nothings, 1850–1856" (Master's thesis, The University of Chicago, 1948), 62–65.

52 Perry Duis, *The Saloon: Public Drinking in Chicago and Boston, 1880–1920* (Urbana: University of Illinois Press, 1983).

53 CDD, January 30, 1854.

54 Duis, *The Saloon*; Cole, "The Chicago Press and the Know-Nothings, 1850–1856," 56–58.

In Chicago, this crisis led to an alliance between the forces of temperance and Know-Nothingism, producing a fusion slate for the 1855 municipal elections. This alliance was predicated on defeating the combined politico-social threat of Catholics, drinking in saloons, and public disorder. Much of this supposed disorder was illusory: the *Tribune*, for instance, breathlessly fabricated tales of Irish riots at both groggeries and Protestant churches, which it claimed were intended to suppress the Know-Nothing vote.[55] Nevertheless, the *perception* of public danger had changed; precisely as ethnicity became a partisan issue, it ceased to operate as a means through which ruling elites could delegate policing to neighborhoods. Indeed, the Know-Nothings won the municipal in part based on these exact fears.

SPECIAL DEPUTIZATION AND THE EMERGENCE OF THE PUBLIC AND PRIVATE POLICE

Despite their severity, city elders did not respond to these threats by radically transforming the existing law enforcement system. Instead, their initial responses built on the republican logic of public interest through private effort, trying to preserve rather than overthrow the key principles of the constable/watch system.

Chicago's press and politicians began to debate means of responding to these changes. In 1851, Edward Bonney, the author and private investigator famous for his pursuit of members of the Banditti in northern Illinois in the 1840s, wrote the Common Council, laying out the case for the creation of an independent police in Chicago. Arguing that "Chicago is now considered about the safest place of refuge for rogues in the Union," and that "it is in cities and large towns and along the lines of the principle thoroughfares, that desperadoes concentrate as places most congenial to their habits and criminal careers," the city required a police force "clothed with the same power to do criminal business that the regular police constables now are."[56] This police force, argued Bonney, could be organized privately and paid through fee for service by employers. In turn, of course, Bonney generously offered his expert services to the city.

The Common Council did not take Bonney up on his offer – primarily because he was not a resident of the city – but they recognized that the problem of public disorder centered on the dimensions Bonney identified: the

[55] ibid., 56.

[56] CP 1851: 1290. Bonney appeared to be referring to the independent police organized in St. Louis in 1846, an obscure quasi-private entity granted municipal policing powers. See Marshall S. Snow, "The City Government of St. Louis," chap. IV in *Municipal Government: History and Politics*, ed. Herbert B. Adams, vol. V, Johns Hopkins University Studies in Historical and Political Science (Baltimore: John Hopkins University Press, 1887), 165; Maximilian Ivan Reichard, "The Origins of Urban Police: Freedom and Order in Antebellum St. Louis" (PhD diss., Washington University, 1975), 259–260.

emergence of anonymous places like hotels and depots where criminals took advantage of the failure of local knowledge and sanction. As the council's Committee on Police pointed out, "[T]he time is quickly approaching if it has not already arrived when conventions of the Scientific, the Mercantile, the Political and Religious Communities of the Union, which give character to the cities in which they are had will assemble frequently in our midst and they will naturally expect, as they would have the right to demand, to conduct their deliberations unmolested by unauthorized visitors and to receive those civilities for the transaction of their business for which other cities have been so justly praised."[57] Policing was becoming a matter of ensuring the public good.

Bonney's solution, however, took for granted that private effort could be linked to public interest without contradiction. Indeed, the approach to reforming law enforcement actually taken by the Common Council also reflected a commitment to changing the republican system incrementally. Some changes had come to the policing infrastructure of Chicago during the late 1840s and 1850s, for instance, but these were almost always oriented around strengthening the constable and watch system.[58] For example, the council occasionally appointed seasonal forces of night watchmen and even authorized construction of a watch house in 1845, but such appointments were contingent on momentary outbreaks of disorder.[59]

In particular, however, city elders expanded the use of deputization to special cases, a practice with deep roots in English and American legal history.[60] Some special deputies were involved in other municipal services: Pound Masters, Bridge Tenders, Tax Collectors, and a Special Sanitary force, for instance, all began to receive special constabulary powers.[61] More frequently, however, the mayor appointed specials to deputize already employed watchmen and private guards. While there was some precedent for the mayor and council allowing such appointments in response to individual petitions by business owners, the power was implicit until June of 1855, when the council passed an ordinance explicitly enabling the use of specials for businesses. Noting that "many of our railroad and manufacturing companies, lumber, and other dealers find it necessary to employ private watchmen" who would be "much more serviceable to their employees and beneficial to the city of invested with police powers," the ordinance allowed the mayor to appoint watchmen as specials who "shall profess the same power and authority as the regular police of the city."[62]

57 CP 1855: 294.

58 Sam Mitrani, *The Rise of the Chicago Police Department: Class and Conflict, 1850–1894* (Urbana: University of Illinois Press, 2013), 14–23.

59 e.g., CP 1843: 1523A; CP 1844: 2271A; CP 1845: 2521A; CP 1845: 2544A; CP 1847: 3875A; CP 1848: 4608A.

60 Radzinowicz, *A History of English Criminal Law and Its Administration from 1750*, 202–232.

61 e.g., CP 1852: 0388A; CP 1855: 0611A; CP 1858: 0786A; CP 1865: 0803A.

62 CP 1855: 0623A.

TABLE 7. *Private special constable commissions in Chicago (1840–1871)*

Type of organization	Number of specials hired
Railroad	27
Lumber yard	6
Brick yard	5
Theater	5
Emigrant aid society	4
Storage & commission	3
Church	2
Coal	2
Fire engine company	2
Planing mill	2
Alderman	1
Baker	1
Boarding house	1
Brewer	1
Butcher	1
Ferryman	1
Hospital	1
Land agent	1
Machine Works	1
School	1
Ship builder	1
Wood dealer	1

Data from Common Council Proceedings Files; oaths only included.

Table 7 depicts some of the businesses who hired and used special deputies. Firms with specific, spatially defined property interests subject to the problems of anonymity and physical mobility – the railroads in particular – hired the bulk of deputies. Although these firms were usually less concerned with public drinking or disorder than wealthy elites and some political officials, the erosion of the social structural foundations of delegation nevertheless made it increasingly difficult for them to rely on an amateur constabulary.[63] Hiring specials was simply a way of using traditional institutions to address a growing threat.

The city also used special deputies in response to collective disorder. This was most obvious in the case in the Lager Beer Riot in 1855, the most serious threat to the extant system of policing Chicago had seen. The event was precipitated

[63] Spitzer and Scull, "Privatization and Capitalist Development: The Case of the Private Police," 21–22.

by the prosecution of a group of primarily German saloon owners for serving liquor without paying the massive licensing fees imposed by the new Know-Nothing mayor, Levi Boone. The micro-level story is complex, but the upshot was that a demonstration of the saloon forces on the day of the prosecution induced a police crackdown, which then led to a retaliatory spiral and, by Chicago standards, a severe riot, in which several people were killed and a policeman lost his arm. The majority of the participants in the demonstration were Germans, who had been mobilized through the organized efforts of ethnic elites in the northern section of the city.[64]

The Lager Beer Riot was the culminating event of the tensions which had accompanied the rise of ethnic politics in Chicago. For some of Chicago's "native American" elite, the event emblematized the threat jointly posed by saloons as public places associated with disorder and the newfound ethnic (Catholic) resistance to native control over politics. It demonstrated, as nothing else yet had, the ways in which delegated policing was failing to work for communities that nativists had decided were incapable of self-governance. "The attempt made by the Germans to over-awe a court of justice, and to resist the laws of the city, all for 'lager beer,'" proclaimed the *Tribune*, "has infused a deep seated and invincible determination in the minds not only of the Americans, but of all the Law and Order citizens of the place, that they shall be *made* to respect and obey our laws."[65]

To manage the crisis, Mayor Boone appointed 201 special officers (including luminaries like Allan Pinkerton), who were deputized to help keep the peace during the riots, and mobilized several local militia units to aid the special deputies and the city watch in restoring order.[66] In his debriefing to the Common Council, the mayor remarked with pride how he was quickly able to produce "a force so strong that none would be rash enough to oppose it," composed of both regulars and specials, all "men of indomitable courage and firmness, proving themselves eminently worthy of the trust that had been reposed in them."[67]

However, the riot also reframed the public debate over law and order in the city; indeed, as scholars have pointed out, ethnic rioting led to calls for policing reform in cities throughout the country.[68] Indeed, in many ways, the riot was electorally advantageous for the Know-Nothing party; in Chicago, the Common Council, under the slim control of the party (and with the support of the *Chicago Tribune*) began deliberations on restructuring the existing police

[64] Richard W. Renner, "In a Perfect Ferment: Chicago, the Know-Nothings, and the Riot for Lager Beer," *Chicago History* 5, no. 3 (1976): 14–16.

[65] *Chicago Tribune*, April 24, 1855. [66] CP 1855: 2434A. [67] CWT, May 10, 1855.

[68] Gilje, *Rioting in America*, 138–139; Dennis C. Rousey, *Policing the Southern City: New Orleans, 1805–1889* (Baton Rouge: Louisiana State University Press, 1996), 62–80.

force and creating a new consolidated police department.[69] The republican system that had guided Chicago's first twenty years was well on its way to decomposing into something new, even as both political and economic actors continued to turn to traditional techniques and practices.

THE CREATION OF THE POLICE

Partly in response to the Lager Beer Riots in 1855, the Common Council reorganized the police, combining the night and day watch and adding new regulations to help ensure control over the force. This reorganization has been interpreted as a major organizational innovation for the municipal governance of Chicago. [70] The ordinance that created the new department was passed by a close eight-to-seven vote on April 30, 1855, and involved the expansion of the existing force, its reorganization into police districts, and the creation of a more clear-cut internal hierarchy.[71]

Forming this police force was, at heart, a political compromise by a Know-Nothing party that could control barely half the electoral votes in the city and – as the election the next year would prove – actually possessed only fleeting control over city governance. As a result, the force reorganization still largely reflected the republican foundations of delegative law enforcement rather than a clear attempt to transform the existing system. It was fundamentally conservative, intended to shore up the power of the Common Council still largely in the hands of real estate and other economic elites, rather than to construct a large new administrative body.

For one thing, the new force established in 1855 actually represented only an incremental bureaucratic shift. Not only had there been an administratively separate police department in place since 1853, but Boone had also already spelled out the need to combine the day and night police in his inaugural

69 Steve Wilkinson has argued that when electoral victory in fragmented societies only requires majority support, majority-interest parties have an incentive to allow ethnic riots to occur (even when they could suppress them), partly as a way of deterring counter-mobilization and consolidating support. The problem in Chicago was that the local city government would have been incapable of preventing a riot to begin with, since the participation of friends, family, and co-ethnics of the rioters themselves likely would have been required to suppress or preempt the conflict. See Steven I. Wilkinson, *Votes and Violence: Electoral Competition and Ethnic Riots in India* (Cambridge: Cambridge University Press, 2006), 4–9.

70 In an important recent account, for instance, Sam Mitrani claims that through the reorganization, "the police were transformed from an unorganized, undisciplined, and poorly defined group of citizens into a well-ordered hierarchy organized along military lines and clearly differentiated from the rest of the population by their uniforms." This, he argues, marked "a crucial founding moment" in the modernization of the city's coercive capacity. Mitrani, *The Rise of the Chicago Police Department*, 28.

71 CP 1855: 0293A.

address, well before the Beer Riot.[72] Moreover, in anticipation of the need to enforce a new Sunday closing law, he had already dramatically expanded the existing police force through special deputization almost immediately after taking over the mayoralty.[73] The official transformation in 1855 was more a matter of quantity than quality; the force was expanded and made more directly subject to mayoral control, but the essential regulatory structure and rulebook of the force was kept in place. While the size of the force was expanded to ninety-six in the spring of 1855, there were at least fifty-two members of the watch who had served the city by the end of 1854; this expansion was significant but not necessarily transformative.

For another, the reorganization of the police did not supplant older republican institutions, but rather coexisted with them. For instance, the constable remained a key law officer in the wards, special deputies continued to be appointed as supplements to the public police force, and the fee structure continued in place for non-police law officers until well into the 1860s.[74] Moreover, other traditionally republican institutions (such as the Cook County sheriff) remained highly active participants in law enforcement, and important political figures like Anton Hesing (a leader of the German community) viewed the role as a crucial stepping stone in their public careers.[75] Indeed, the ordinance expanding the powers of deputization to include businesses was actually passed the month *after* the reforms of 1855, indicating that special constables were seen as just as valuable in addressing the problem of law enforcement as paid police.[76]

There were other points of continuity with earlier forms of policing. For instance, the personnel of the new police force included many who had held earlier law enforcement roles. The special deputies who served during the riot, for instance, provided the core for the new police force; twenty-nine of these deputies were hired by the police department in the following years. Moreover, of the ninety-six officers who took oaths to serve in Boone's police in the spring of 1855, forty-six (47%) had served in some policing capacity during the height of the republican system of constables and watch.[77]

Indeed, the *Tribune* complemented the new captain of the force, Cyrus Bradley, as a reputable member of the old order, in which party politics was secondary to the aims of promoting the city's overall business class. Bradley had "long been known to us as one of the most efficient conservators of the peace and good order of the city," and, as one whose "name has already become a terror to evildoers," he would best be able to ensure the public would be protected.[78]

72 CDD, March 13, 1855. 73 Einhorn, *Property Rules*, 164.

74 *Journal of the Proceedings of the Common Council*, December 11, 1871.

75 CTR, September 28, 1860. 76 CP 1855: 0623A 77 For the oaths, see CP 1855: 2436A.

78 CTR, May 18, 1855. The Democratic *Chicago Weekly Times*, naturally, criticized this very reputation, claiming that the new police was another way to pad the pockets of the Bradley family. For the *Times*, the police's new salary structure and elimination of a separate night watch

From the outset, police rosters also reflected the continuing importance of ethnicity as a political category. Of the forty members of the original police force for whom I was able to locate information on ethnicity, approximately 90 percent were natively born Americans, many of whom were involved in Know-Nothing politics.[79] This was a major source of contention for the *Times*, which complained about a "know-nothing and do-nothing police" that focused on persecuting poor Irish women rather than solving important crimes.[80] When control over city government reverted to the Democrats in 1856, the new mayor, Thomas Dyer, in turn completely overhauled the force: of the ninety-eight members listed on the new roster, only nine were also on the previous year's list.[81] In addition, approximately three-fourths of those on the new force were Irish or Germans, leading the *Tribune* to retaliate in a series of editorials about the incompetence of police officers in the city, even accusing some of running "rumshops."[82]

The permanence of the Chicago police was not a foregone conclusion, however, particularly as the Know-Nothing party disintegrated and the Democrats began to have access to the patronage power of appointing the force. As late as the 1860s it remained unclear how the use of special deputization and the consolidation of the new department would play out over the long run, and whether the municipal police would be the only security option available to political and economic elites. Just as municipal reforms were creating the seed for a new kind of public policing infrastructure, so too was a private alternative emerging, one built on the same incremental approach to change and reliance on traditional republican institutions, but with similarly revolutionary effects.

THE CREATION OF THE PRIVATE SECURITY INDUSTRY

The new security industry in Chicago represented the other half of the transformation of the republican system in the 1850s. Just as with the new police, it was the availability of special deputation for private security purposes that fed into the creation of a new industry (for example, ten of those who served during the Lager Beer Riots later became private detectives or watchmen). The shared ancestry of the public police and the private security industry in an older republican tradition helped ensure that over time the two entities would coevolve rather than emerge as competitors and rivals.

was a financial boondoggle, which meant that "over one half of the total income of the city is to be expended in carrying out a system of police, the benefits of which will be inferior to those of the present system." CWT, May 10, 1855.

79 Mitrani, *The Rise of the Chicago Police Department*, 30–31. There were approximately 96 members of the reformed police in 1855.

80 *Chicago Daily Times*, June 14, 1855.

81 CP 1856: 1446A.

82 CTR, April 22, 1856; Cole, "The Chicago Press and the Know-Nothings, 1850–1856," 94–95.

Unlike the police, however, which reflected the public side of the old republican institutional logic, this new industry emphasized private interests and incentives. Guard and detective firms were organized by entrepreneurs to confront the increasing problem of theft, as well as the class of threats (such as swindling and fraud) associated with social anonymity that Friedman has called "crimes of mobility."[83] Though public police were also responsible for addressing property crimes, the need for agencies that could move across jurisdictional boundaries became key in a world with fast and integrated transportation networks.[84] The unease created by the Lager Beer Riot likely accentuated this general sense of disorder in Chicago.

There were two sides to the emergence of this new industry: the first were the entrepreneurial firms organized to provide security and detective services to private firms; the second were watchmen and "merchant police" forces organized *en masse* by companies themselves to protect property.

Allan Pinkerton exemplifies the first development. Pinkerton's early experience as a deputy sheriff made seamless the transition to viewing the organization of violence as entrepreneurial activity. As a deputy, Pinkerton received fees based on performance, the same system that remunerated city and county constables. Deputies like Pinkerton had traditionally done the brunt of actual policing work for sheriffs, whose activities mainly involved serving process, and as a deputy in a county with some of the most well-developed railroad infrastructure in the world in 1853, Pinkerton's duties also frequently took him across the region, which allowed him to cultivate a wide range of contacts.[85] Because, outside the politically fraught and minuscule US Marshals Service, there was no national police force in the United States at the time, Pinkerton's conversion of his normal thief-taking duties to a national scale meant creating a new, private firm to take advantage of the rewards such arrests could provide. His decision to organize the North-Western Detective Police Agency, the first such agency in Chicago, with lawyer Edward Rucker in March of 1855 (just days before the election that brought Levi Boone to power in the city) was a simple one, adapting the skills and connections he had established as a deputy to service clients.[86] Some of the firm's earliest clients, unsurprisingly, were railroads.[87]

The private detective industry built on the traditional republican constable system in two ways. First, it relied on contracts and fee schedules.[88] This meant that the kinds of services provided by private security were limited in scope and

83 Friedman, "Crimes of Mobility."
84 Katherine Unterman, *Uncle Sam's Policemen: The Pursuit of Fugitives Across Borders* (Cambridge, MA: Harvard University Press, 2015), 35–42.
85 Morn, *The Eye That Never Sleeps*, 35–39. 86 CTR, March 2, 1855.
87 CTR, November 5, 1856.
88 Spitzer and Scull, "Privatization and Capitalist Development: The Case of the Private Police," 19–21.

focused only on particular problems confronted by clients. Second, it relied on *ad hoc* deputization.[89] Private detectives frequently worked closely with local courts and were allowed to participate directly in arrest.[90] Detectives also relied on the common law, by which average citizens could arrest offenders of felonies committed in their presence on their own authority.[91]

Pinkerton's firm was the first, but not the only, private security firm to emerge out of the ferment of antebellum Chicago. Cyrus Bradley – Pinkerton's former boss and the city marshal under Levi Boone – formed the private Detecting and Collecting Police Agency with a number of other police officers after the Know-Nothing party was defeated in 1856 and Dyer restructured the police department.[92] Though rivals, both Bradley and Pinkerton provided detective services calibrated to address the same problems in finding criminals in anonymous settings.[93]

By 1860, a second kind of service was being offered in Chicago, one that was aimed at saturating vulnerable areas – especially business and warehouse districts – with watchmen. These watchmen, sometimes known as merchant police, formed a privately funded, geographically limited alternative to the kind of patrol municipal police services were increasingly expected to provide for the general public across the city.[94] Private police services were offered by George T. Moore's Merchant Police as well as Pinkerton's Preventive Police patrol, also founded in 1858, a force that was active in patrolling retail and public areas through the 1860s.[95] In 1858 alone, for example, the Pinkerton Preventive Patrol arrested fifty-three people for a variety of infractions. These groups formed a corps of paid watchmen available for selective patrol, capable of using force if necessary to protect their client's property.[96]

The new guard industry was also promoted by non-security firms who hired their *own* watchmen without going through a merchant police service.[97] Railroads and some of the larger manufacturers had employed their own watchmen beginning in the early 1850s, but by the end of the decade the pattern of hiring permanent guards was set, particularly in the transportation and industrial sector. For instance, as evident in Table 8, which presents the numbers of individual guards identified in city directories who were hired to work for different firms, every sector of the economy increased the number of guards it

89 US Senate. 52nd Congress, Second Session, *Investigation in Relation to the Employment for Private Purposes of Armed Bodies of Men, or Detectives, in Connection with Differences Between Workers and Employers*, S.Rep.1280 (1893), 235–23.

90 William Pinkerton and Robert Pinkerton, *Annual Report of Pinkerton's National Detective Agency to American Bankers' Association* (American Bankers' Association, 1895), 6–14.

91 Henry Warrum, *Peace Officers and Detectives: The Law of Sheriffs, Constables, Marshals, Municipal Police and Detectives* (Greenfield, IN: William Mitchell Printing Co., 1895), 85–86.

92 CTR, May 10, 1856.

93 Johnson, *Policing the Urban Underworld*, 65.

94 Other cities – Baltimore, Philadelphia, and St. Louis in particular – had experience with these groups before Chicago; see Johnson, *Policing the Urban Underworld*, 60.

95 CTR, October 6, 1858.

96 Morn, *The Eye That Never Sleeps*, 29–30.

97 Schneider, *Detroit and the Problem of Order, 1830–1880*, 62–63.

TABLE 8. *Number of private watchmen employed in Chicago firms (1851–1870)*

	Firm type						
Year	Industry	Transportation	Retail	Recreation	Office	Wholesale	Total
1851–1855	3 (50%)	3 (50%)	0 (0%)	0 (0%)	0 (0%)	0 (0%)	6
1856–1860	3 (6%)	36 (80%)	1 (2%)	1 (2%)	1 (2%)	3 (6%)	45
1861–1865	28 (20%)	84 (60%)	1 (0%)	11 (8%)	0 (0%)	16 (11%)	140
1866–1870	100 (28%)	183 (51%)	8 (2%)	20 (6%)	9 (2%)	42 (12%)	362
Total	134 (24%)	306 (55%)	10 (2%)	32 (6%)	10 (2%)	61 (11%)	553

Data from City Directory of Chicago, 1851–1870.
Note: Row percentages in parentheses; totals do not add to 100% because of rounding.

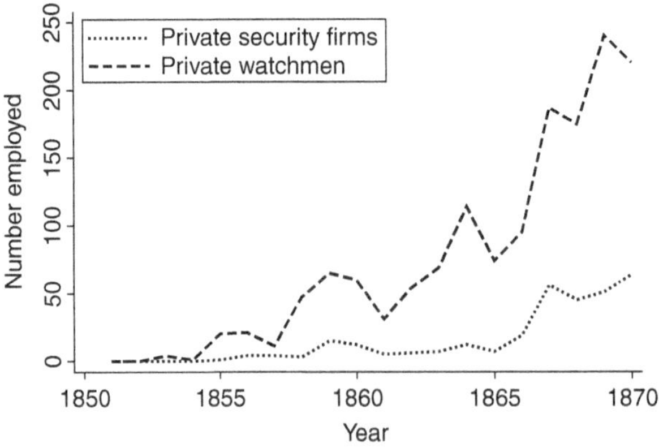

FIGURE 8. Trends in private security employment in Chicago (1851–1870)
Data from *City Directory of Chicago*, 1851–1870.

hired after the war. In particular, the new, large sectors – railroad and heavy manufacturing, factories and stock yards – which had much physical property to protect relied most directly on their own private armies of watchmen.

Figure 8, in turn, depicts the annual number of individuals I could identify in the city directories who were employed as private guards or by private security firms from 1851 through 1870. The trend lines are fairly straightforward: firms had begun hiring private guards prior to the Civil War, but the years between 1860 and 1870 saw a dramatic escalation in their number. By the mid-1870s – when the Pinkerton firm began redefining its operations through anti-banditry in the West and labor suppression in the East – the private security complex was well-entrenched across the nation.[98]

[98] Weiss, "An Interpretation of the Origin, Development and Transformation of Private Detective Agency Policing in the United States, 1850–1940."

THE COEVOLUTION OF PUBLIC AND PRIVATE POLICING

The use of traditional republican institutional practices like special deputization to address new threats to social order and the gradual extensions of those mechanisms to serve the ends of political and economic elites ultimately led to the creation of both the public and private security industry. But, crucially, the new divide between what counted as public and what was private only stabilized over time, and was a product of reorganization of the networks linking these state and market forms of law enforcement.

Ironically, during the early years of both the private security industry and public police department, it was not even clear whether either or both would survive. In the late 1850s, for example, Chicago papers began a debate over whether the municipal police were actually an effective means of managing the city's criminal problems. Democratic papers and politicians decried the adoption of policing duties by specialist private firms and private watchmen rather than neighborhood police, arguing that "it is the business ...of a private police everywhere to affrighten the people and make them think they are unsafe unless a private police is maintained."[99] While it, also, often emphasized the need for a publicly funded police, the *Tribune*, in turn, considered private detectives like Pinkerton and Cyrus Bradley as heroes.[100]

Though this debate carried on for several years, public and private security alternatives flourished, often cooperating with one another and sharing resources. For example, Pinkerton guards frequently cooperated with Chicago police in identifying public threats.[101] Moreover, Pinkerton's agency was itself even hired by the city to investigate certain crimes, such as a notorious grave-robbery scandal involving city officials in 1857.[102] The boundary between public and private security was quite ambiguous, particularly in the early years of the new police department, and private detectives frequently saw themselves as public-minded officials. Moreover, many police officials – such as city constables – continued to operate on the basis of fees and personal rewards.

Part of what allowed this dual system to work was the fact that public police and private security agencies were tied to one another through their experiences in older republican institutions. Indeed, private policing quickly became an attractive option for those who lost their jobs with the public police. Special deputization was a seedbed for both types of careers, and it linked public actors to private security professionals.

There are several ways of demonstrating this dynamic. I begin by exploring how occupants of different protection agencies in Chicago moved back and

99 CDD, June 30, 1857.

100 For the general debate, see Johnson, *Policing the Urban Underworld*, 62–67; CWT, June 14, 1855; July 19, 1855; November 1, 1855; and CTR, December 28, 1855; January 16, 1856.

101 CTR, June 25, 1864; December 19, 1863; March 18, 1869.

102 CTR, November 9, 1857.

forth between occupational positions.[103] By examining who these individuals were and what kinds of jobs they held, as well as what activities they participated in, it is possible to examine the interconnections among security experts serving in Chicago during the period before and after the Civil War (from approximately 1845 through 1871).

Most members only belonged to one organization throughout their careers. However, some were much more active – 450 of the 3,799 people identified in this study (around 12%) belonged to different security organizations at some point. Table 9 depicts the number of individuals who moved from job to job. By treating the flow of security providers from one organization to another as a social network, in other words, it is possible to identify both how those providers related to each other as well as identify whether particular roles were important in linking them together.[104]

When we look at the level of individual careers, serving as a member of the special police played a key role for the most important of security officers. Of the total number of security providers identified in the dataset, I focus on 388 who were the key players in the network – those for whom we have comparable records over time and who were members of multiple organizations.

Some summary information about the career trajectories of these individuals is presented in Table 10, which records the frequency with which an organization assumed a particular position within the career trajectories of the actors in the set (the numbers in the columns reflected the number of individuals in the sample to whom the role position applies). The most active seedbed for

103 For this analysis, I collected data on almost 3,800 individuals active as watchmen, policemen, sheriffs, constables, and private detectives in Chicago from 1845 through 1871 (for the purposes of this book, I only focus on inter-organizational mobility from 1845 through 1860). I culled these data from a wide variety of sources, including official rosters and records of oaths, newspaper articles, and city directories.

104 One way of unpacking this process involves examining what organizations were crucial in knitting different types of actors together. Indeed, those receiving special deputization did indeed provide pathways for police to move to different types of organizations. Drawing on the influential notion of brokerage articulated by Gould and Fernandez, I identify those organizational nodes acting on liaisons in the inter-organizational network; that is, those that are uniquely positioned to connect nodes with different kinds of attributes. This analysis reveals that those receiving special deputization did indeed broker relationships among different types of organizations; the position of being a special deputy played an important role first in allowing those who had served in the city watch to join the older municipal constabulary from 1845 to 1850, and then for those who members of the police force to become private detectives and vice versa in the crucial years of the late 1850s. Both brokerage roles exceeded the number of times the special constabulary was predicted to play the role by a factor of three, with the expected value derived from an assignment process in which similar numbers of ties were distributed among partitions at random. See Roger V. Gould and Roberto M. Fernandez, "Structures of Mediation: A Formal Approach to Brokerage in Transaction Networks," *Sociological Methodology* 19, no. 1 (1989): 89–126.

TABLE 9. *Links between security institutions in Chicago (1845–1871)*

	Destination									
Origin	Police	Private detective	Special police force	Municipal (other)	Sheriff	US Marshal	US (other)	County (other)	Private firm	Municipal constable	County constable
Police		39	28	23	16	2	5	0	94	57	14
Private detective	51		2	1	1	0	1	0	16	3	3
Special police force	44	5		6	1	0	0	0	20	20	1
Municipal (other)	31	1	0		3	0	0	0	1	9	3
Sheriff	13	3	3	2		0	4	1	2	10	9
US Marshals	1	0	0	0	1		1	0	1	0	0
US (Other)	2	2	1	2	1	0		0	2	3	2
County (other)	0	0	0	0	1	0	0		0	0	1
Private firm	82	16	16	1	1	0	1	0		7	4
Municipal constable	53	4	12	10	12	1	3	0	10		25
County constable	15	3	1	3	6	0	0	1	8	29	

*Data from Common Council proceeding files and City Directories of Chicago (1845–1871).
Includes those moving from position to another within five-year windows.

TABLE 10. *Career trajectories of important actors (1845–1871)*

	Starting position	Intermediary position	Last position	Any position	Average position
Police	150	30	119	299	1.57
Municipal constabulary	52	22	37	111	1.74
Private detective firm	38	17	43	98	1.84
Sheriff	14	12	19	45	1.89
Special police force	**19**	**15**	**22**	**56**	**1.95**
Private firm	71	16	80	167	1.74
County constabulary	26	11	31	68	2
Municipal (other)	13	7	23	43	2.21
US (other)	2	4	12	18	2.33
US Marshals	3	0	1	4	1.75
County (other)	0	0	1	1	3

$N = 388$; Avg. Trajectory Length: 2.35 (s.d.: 0.67); Max: 6.

security careers was the police force: of the 388 individuals, approximately 39 percent began their trajectories as police. On the other hand, the special police force served as the most active *intermediary* position for security experts in Chicago; approximately 27 percent of those who were special police officers held the role between holding two other positions.[105] This again hints at the importance of traditional republican deputization in facilitating brokerage between modern security jobs.

Not only did traditional republican roles like that of the special deputy connect the private industry to the public police in general, but a group of very influential individuals occupied both public and private security institutions at various points in their careers. To explore this, I trace the careers of six of the most well-known individuals active in Chicago's police and private detective system in the timeline presented in Figure 9. In this figure, each line represents the career of an individual through time, while the shaded regions represent different types of security institution in which the actor in question participated. The timeline bar in the middle represents a divide between public and private institutions, while the small vertical bars in the chart indicate that the two actors were linked together as partners in a criminal case at a given point.

The figure demonstrates several things. First, early ties between these actors, often forged during shared public service, paved the way to a future career as a private detective. Cyrus Bradley and Bartholomew Yates, having known Pinkerton as a deputy and witnessed his success, decided

105 Only 10% of those who served as police, on the other hand, used the job as an intermediary stepping stone in their careers.

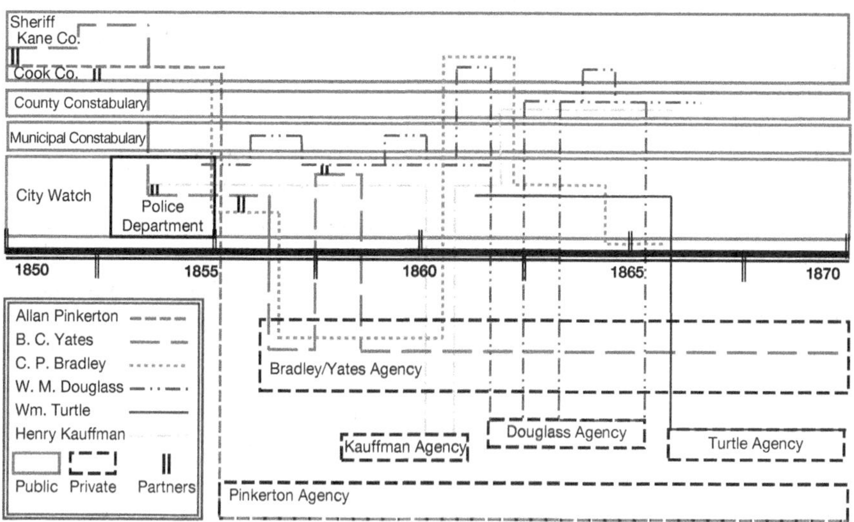

FIGURE 9. Selected career trajectories of Chicago violence experts (1850–1870)

to become private detectives after having lost their jobs in the turnover of the 1856 election.

Second, these actors also moved throughout their careers between public police to private service. Yates, Bradley, Henry Kauffman, and William Douglass all served as police as well as in other county or municipal roles. Douglass, in fact, *linked* multiple roles together at one time, apparently serving, for instance, as both a police detective and a municipal constable in 1859, and later combining service as county constable with his private position as head of his own agency. This, in turn, helped lock in a longer-term pattern in American policing whereby law enforcement became the purview of a wide variety of actors and in which public and private police frequently cooperated and shared information and resources.[106]

CONCLUSION

The creation of unsettled spaces – saloons, hotels, and railroad depots – in antebellum Chicago undermined the delegation of policing to ethnically homogenous and economic stratified nineteenth-century communities. As a result the older components of the republican constabulary institution – the entrepreneurial incentives, the organized watch, the notion of private participation, and so on – were repurposed to new ends as political and economic

[106] Morn, *The Eye That Never Sleeps*, 164–183.

elites continued to rely on them in a context where they would no longer work. Special deputization, in particular, both set in motion and mediated a process of inter-organizational mobility by occupants of police and private security roles.

The decoupling of social relations in neighborhoods from the rules of delegation was a direct result of the growth of the market and the new railroad infrastructure. Indeed, New York, Boston, Philadelphia, and St. Louis – which, along with Chicago, were the most important market centers in the northern United States – all experimented with public and private forms of policing in the 1840s and 1850s.[107] Moreover, the specific sequence of events leading to police reform in each of these cities were shockingly similar; ethnic conflicts (often riots) generated a crisis in civic relations that, in turn, drove each city's governing council to expand its deputized police force and consolidate its town watch.[108] Other cities – such as Detroit – mirrored Chicago even more closely. Even as some of the city's ethnic communities (particularly the Germans) remained largely autonomous and self-policing, a massive and sudden influx of immigrants and the emergence of public spaces like depots and saloons in the 1850s and 1860s led Detroit's city council (as well as sever entrepreneurial businessmen) to transform older law enforcement institutions into new public and private police organizations.[109]

Chicago's status as a premier frontier metropolis, however, makes particularly clear the ways in which anonymity and publicness undermined a system of republican participation and delegation. In this context, figures like Allan Pinkerton were both forward looking, in that they took advantage of an explosive market, as well as conservative, in that they operated within preexisting institutional rules. As such, the transformation they achieved in terms of building a vast network of police departments and private detective agencies was inadvertent rather than a grand attempt at state-building, engendered by the use of older practices in the midst of a revolution in social relationships.

At the same time, despite the fact that the nation was becoming more economically and infrastructurally interconnected, sectionalism and political disagreements over the all-important issue of slavery were tearing at seams. The Civil War and its radical political effects, therefore, joined with the market revolution as a second key process challenging coercive enforcement in American jurisdictions during the nineteenth century. While Chicago played

107 David R. Johnson, *American Law Enforcement: A History* (St. Louis: Forum Press, 1981), 12–35.

108 Allan E. Levett, "Centralization of City Police in the Nineteenth Century United States" (PhD diss., The University of Michigan, 1975), 61, 77–81, 90–93, 95–96.

109 Schneider, *Detroit and the Problem of Order, 1830–1880*, 15–86.

a key role in the war – Allan Pinkerton and Cyrus Bradley, for instance, both found opportunities to link their own private careers with the struggle of the Union, the former most famously serving as a key player in setting up the Secret Service – its effects were most profound in the South, where much of the fighting took place and where the transformative effects of Reconstruction were most keenly felt. The next chapter examines this process, and the crisis induced by the expansion of new political rights to African-American males in Reconstruction Louisiana.

5

Racist Vigilantism as Reform in Reconstruction Louisiana

INTRODUCTION

In September of 1862, George Augustus Sheridan, a young Yale graduate from Massachusetts, was visiting family near Chicago when he decided, apparently on a whim, to join one of the newly formed regiments called up to fight in the Civil War. A hotbed of Northern sympathy, the city had quickly emerged as a center in the mobilization of the Union Army and Sheridan was just one of thousands of young men enticed into military service in the 88th Illinois Infantry, nicknamed "The Second Chicago Board of Trade."[1]

Sheridan, proved himself an able commander, quickly making his way through the ranks (he replaced his company's first captain, George W. Chandler, when Chandler was made major).[2] But, like so many others, he also experienced the full brutality of combat. After a winding path through various encounters and adventures, he was wounded at Chickamauga Creek in Georgia in 1863, one of the bloodiest battles of the war. Despite this trauma, the political options open to Republicans and Union veterans in the states under Reconstruction law convinced him (and thousands of other Northerners) that opportunity and power lay in the conquered region.[3] He decided to go further south, to Louisiana.

An opportunity quickly arose in northeastern Louisiana, where he was elected sheriff of Carroll parish, apparently on the strength of his "oratorical

[1] Jasper N. Reece and Isaac Hughes Elliott, eds., *Report of the Adjutant General of the State of Illinois*, vol. V, Containing Reports for the Years 1861–1866 (Springfield, IL: Phillips Bros., 1901), 246.

[2] A. T. Andreas, *History of Chicago: From the Earliest Period to the Present Time*, vol. 2 (Chicago: A. T. Andreas, 1885), 244.

[3] *The National Cyclopaedia of American Biography*, vol. 3 (New York: James T. White & Co., 1893), 134.

gifts."[4] He didn't last long in Carroll, however, moving to New Orleans the next year after being appointed by Republican Governor Henry Warmouth as adjutant general of the Louisiana Militia, the highest position in the force.[5]

Though it sounded prestigious, in 1868 control over the state government had shifted toward a more radical wing of the Republican party, and this job had become highly politicized. The general assembly, caught up in a myriad of political squabbles, had refused to fund the force. Indeed, in his Annual Return to the US Adjutant, Sheridan quipped, "[T]the effective militia force of this State for the year... consisted of one Adjutant General; he was well organized, thoroughly drilled, and moderately well-equipped."[6]

Although a highly regarded soldier, he and Governor Warmouth were confronting a profound crisis: the postbellum militia, in the hands of Reconstruction governors, was no longer viewed by many white Southern residents as bearing any relationship to a unitary public security interest at all.[7] Sheridan and Warmouth were both emblematic of the so-called carpetbagger – Northern opportunists who were riding on the back of military victory to political conquest. And, indeed, both *were* involved in a project of trying to centralize Southern political institutions (including both the Republican party and the state administration) in order to forge an alternative to the older elite-driven politics of the antebellum South. One of those institutions, the militia, was at the center of the debate – and by appointing Sheridan, Warmouth was exerting control over a body increasingly seen by Republicans as vital to ensuring that their strongest constituency, newly freed African Americans, under threat from a ferocious counter-mobilization, could vote.

The issue ultimately involved the collapse of the older social categories of race, slavery, and aristocracy that had propped up Southern states before the War. Anti- and pro-Unionist groups, each claiming to act on behalf of a public were active in many Southern states, contending with one another for control and each claiming the other was illegitimate. Each, in a way, reflected the older notion that the militia was private service, but no longer was that service unambiguously seen as linked to public security.[8]

At the heart of these questions was the issue of power. The traditional planter and commercial elite of Louisiana had confronted economic disaster during the war, as confiscatory policies and emancipation threatened both the labor and

[4] NOR, April 9, 1868; ibid.; http://bioguide.congress.gov/scripts/biodisplay.pl?index=S000341 (accessed December 4, 2016).

[5] NOC, January 8, 1860.

[6] NOT, February 12, 1870; Evans J. Casso, *Louisiana Legacy: A History of the State National Guard* (Gretna, LA: Pelican Publishing, 1976), 217.

[7] Carole Emberton, *Beyond Redemption: Race, Violence, and the American South after the Civil War* (Chicago: University of Chicago Press, 2013), 156–158.

[8] Trelease, *White Terror*, 39–40.

property bases of their livelihood.[9] For many whites in Louisiana, the problem of disorder was rooted in their political weakness; while they continued to dominate social and commercial activities in New Orleans and throughout the state, they confronted a political context in which they were unable to use state policy to support a viable labor system. The *Shreveport South-Western* analyzed the situation thusly: "If the negroes had been left to themselves, the kindly relations existing between them and their former masters would probably have never been disturbed" and "the new system of labor would have been inaugurated with a feeling on the part of the citizen that he must yield to the inevitable necessity of emancipation." The problem, was that "mischievous people from other sections have sedulously inculcated in the negro's mind a feeling of distrust" and, backed up by African-American troops, "urge(d) the negroes ... to assert their claims to the rights of the ballot box." Along with most other whites in the South, "we believe," continued the editor, "that this is a government of white men, and that they alone should make and execute its laws."[10]

African Americans and their allies, of course, refused to accede to this proposition and continued to mobilize for political access. The net result was that between 1866 and 1878, the South was the scene of an almost unrivaled violent contest for power on the part of disenfranchised whites, African-American freedmen, and Northern carpetbaggers like Warmouth and Sheridan. In Louisiana, a series of vicious street battles and rural massacres rocked the state; New Orleans, the scene of a series of deeply contested elections, witnessed armed political confrontations in 1872 and 1873, while in rural parishes like Boissier, Caddo, and Colfax, chaos took the form of massacres of mostly African-American citizens.[11] This struggle not only centered on issues of who was "worthy" of political representation and what kind of state was going to protect the residents of the former Confederacy, but also, most practically, on how violence itself would be organized in the aftermath of the bloodiest war the country had ever seen.

9 Scott P. Marler, *The Merchants' Capital: New Orleans and the Political Economy of the Nineteenth-Century South* (Cambridge: Cambridge University Press, 2013), 154–155, 176; Chester G. Hearn, *When the Devil Came Down to Dixie: Ben Butler in New Orleans* (Baton Rouge: Louisiana State University Press, 2000), 206–212; Joe Gray Taylor, *Louisiana Reconstructed, 1863–1877* (Baton Rouge: Louisiana State University Press, 1974), 342–346.

10 November 1, 1865.

11 James K. Hogue, *Uncivil War: Five New Orleans Street Battles and the Rise and Fall of Radical Reconstruction* (Baton Rouge: Louisiana State University Press, 2006); James H. Ingraham, Robert H. Isabelle, and Joseph S. Soude, *Report of the Committee on Grievances to the Radical Republican Convention* (New Orleans: New Orleans Republican, July 1867); LeeAnna Keith, *The Colfax Massacre: The Untold Story of Black Power, White Terror, and the Death of Reconstruction* (Oxford: Oxford University Press, 2008); George C. Rable, *But There Was No Peace: The Role of Violence in the Politics of Reconstruction* (Athens: University of Georgia Press, 1984), 75–78.

In order to demonstrate how antebellum ways of organizing violence were transformed by Reconstruction into both an expansion in the state's capacity to use force and a statewide explosion of private vigilantism, this chapter explores the growth of a white supremacist movement in Louisiana in 1874 called the White League. The White League was both a political party *and* a militia, both a vigilante group *and* a new kind of military force organized to help propel anti-Union forces to electoral victory. To examine this group, I first show how the older logic of the militia, the key means of mobilizing force at the level of the state in the antebellum period, was systematically subverted and reorganized by Reconstruction into a pattern of vigilantism centered in New Orleans and extending throughout the state. Specifically, as rules for who got to participate in the political process began allowing African Americans and mixed-race Creoles to vote and become prominent members of the police and militia force, older, vested elites were cut off from traditional sources of political power. The traditional fusion of political order to economic and social control was, in short, decoupled. In response, these elites turned to their economic and social networks, which they mobilized into an extra-legal militia, organized to take back, by force if necessary, the reins of political power.

The White League, organized in both local militia-vigilance companies and coordinated through a hierarchical political party, was primarily an effort at racial control. But this effort, crucially, was also tied up in questions of class and politics: Reconstruction threatened the traditional planter and commercial elite of Louisiana not merely by shifting rules about who belonged to the civic community, but also by creating the threat of mobile, politically empowered laborers. By accusing the Republican party of corruption, and then transforming that critique into a effort at racial purity in the political system, this elite hoped to relink its economic and social power to enact control over state coercion. That coercion, in turn, could be used to police both racial and economic boundaries.

In addition, this chapter shows that, despite vigilantism, Reconstruction-era reforms and the movement toward Redemption somewhat ironically led to an important expansion in state control over violence. That is, while the federal government was forced to withdraw its military and bureaucratic presence from Louisiana in the late 1870s, the institutional legacies of the era remained in state capitals across the South. In the face of resistance, Reconstruction Republican governors continued to turn the militia to address the threats of crime and disorder in both New Orleans and the outlying parishes. By staffing the militia with a combination of ex-Confederate veterans, African Americans, and professionals like Sheridan and James Longstreet (a West Point graduate, as well as an important Confederate army general who had joined with the Republicans after the war), all while centralizing command and control under the executive, Reconstruction governors were able to transform the force into a much more formidable and professionalized state National Guard. In the years following the collapse of Republican rule, Redeemer conservative whites simply adopted the new militia organization by appointing their own political allies, thereby paving the way to a rejuvenated and powerful National Guard in the 1880s.

Prior to examining the legacies of Reconstruction on state formation and private violence, however, I first turn to explain how antebellum states organized their militia, which in the South largely involved those institutions involved in control over slavery.

REPRESENTATIVE AUTHORITY, THE STATE MILITIA, AND THE OLD SOUTH

Louisiana was of the South and of the West. A jurisdiction born both out of Jefferson's titular purchase as well as the conquest of the War of 1812, its long tenure of French and Spanish control mean that by statehood in 1812, Louisiana had already become both a critical market center (connecting the Mississippi River Valley to the Gulf) and an important agricultural economy – with cotton- and sugar-growing regions, as well as a cattle-raising prairie in its southwestern region. In some areas – particularly the Delta – it closely resembled parts of Mississippi and Alabama, with large slaveholding plantations and a large number of Anglo-American settlers, who (like the French before them) had warred with natives in the region (such as the Chickasaw) and established a deeply violent race-based political economy. In other areas, such as New Orleans, the state possessed financial and market services only found in the South in states like Virginia and South Carolina. In still other places, like the Attakapas region of the west, Louisiana was like Texas, a wild, grasslands prairie, with small-scale slaveholders and a frontier economy based on cattle trading. Although its transition to joining the United States was by no means seamless – older French Creole and Acadian (Cajun) residents frequently resented and resisted the onslaught of American political institutions – by the eve of the Civil War, its complexity allowed Louisiana to appear as culturally Southern as any other state in the union, while also maintaining a frontier, territorial tradition.

States were not only the root system for political authority in the US constitutional system, they were also the key locus for organizing collective force via the militia, a quintessential republican fusion of public interest with private interest.

The militia, like the *posse comitatus* in counties and towns, was based on the principle of popular sovereignty over the means of coercion. As noted in Chapter 2, the militia was supposed to cultivate civic virtue and protect the political autonomy of states, towns, and villages. At the same time, the link between the private efforts of these citizens and the general public welfare *actually* depended on a subset of individuals capably claiming they could adequately represent the public good. I call this link representative authority.[12]

Representative authority, like the enclosed authority of the county, was based on concrete personal relations of co-residents in a town or village. Those who supposed to participate in militia mobilization, however, were not merely residents of a neighborhood or a town; they were citizens. They were supposedly the strongest and most capable members of society – official militia membership was, consequently, in most places limited to white male citizens, a particularly useful factor for slave owners who depended on non-slaveholders to help them police the slaves on their plantations.[13] Such men were supposed to "represent" the interests of the whole because they were the most powerful and important members of their class; their interests were basically seen as identical with the good order and functioning of the entire public welfare.[14]

Figure 10 depicts this basic logic graphically. Representative authority is ensured by the participatory access of only some individuals (both at capital core and the local periphery of the state jurisdiction) in order to represent those (women, children, minorities, and so on) with whom they are concretely connected (these are the non-official elites, which in this context merely means any male with full suffrage rights). This is the representative set, that group which stands in for the interests of the whole. Authoritative representative ties, in turn, reflect situations when socially and economically powerful individuals are also able to successfully claim the right to uniquely represent their own day-to-day "clients" (families, other genders, other races) by having monopoly access to avenues of political power like voting and formal participation.

The militia was (in theory) supposed to include the mobilization of those within the representative set in the name of protection of all those included

[12] Edmund S. Morgan provides the most compelling argument concerning the link between the ideology of popular sovereignty and the reality of elite control in the Anglo-American politico-military system. Morgan, *Inventing the People*, 47–54, 167–170.

[13] These racial exclusions only appeared, interestingly, after the Revolutionary War period; in colonies like South Carolina, slaves and other African Americans were often mobilized into militia companies in order to defend isolated communities against attacks by native residents and soldiers from Spanish or French imperial outposts. See Lyle D. Brundage, "The Organization, Administration, and Training of the United States Ordinary and Volunteer Militia, 1792–1861" (PhD diss., University of Michigan, 1959), 6–8. In Louisiana, mixed-race Creoles had been allowed to serve in the militia during the War of 1812, though, in the midst of a series of slave panics in the 1820s and 1830s as well as the looming effects of the Haitian Revolution, this service was restricted. Roland Calhoun McConnell, *Negro Troops of Antebellum Louisiana: A History of the Battalion of Free Men of Color* (Baton Rouge: Louisiana State University Press, 1968), 102–110.

[14] ibid., 101–102; Ricardo A. Herrera, *For Liberty and the Republic: The American Citizen as Soldier, 1775–1861* (New York: New York University Press, 2015), 64–84; R. Claire Snyder, *Citizen-Soldiers and Manly Warriors: Military Service and Gender in the Civic Republican Tradition* (Boulder, CO: Rowman & Littlefield, 1999), 93–94.

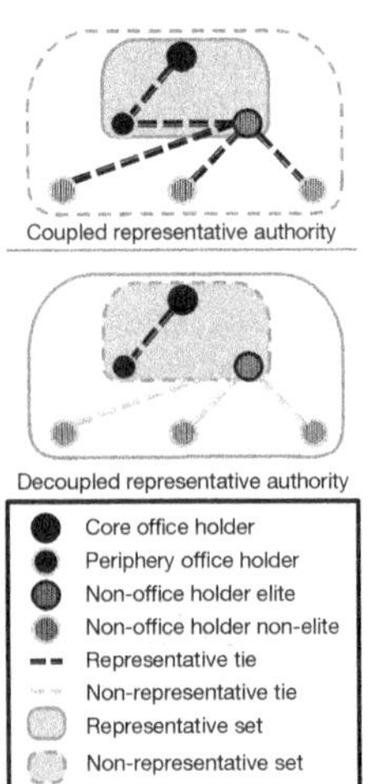

FIGURE 10. Representative authority and jurisdictional coupling

in the social system. Formal shifts in this boundary – as, for instance, in the expansion of voting to include previously non-included groups – unsettled the link between the militia as a form of popular mobilization for the purposes of coercion and the political control of that mobilization by the previous representative set. The bottom panel is a schematic of this decoupling process – rules for who gets access to political institutions have changed (who, in other words, can act as a representative has been expanded), but older forms of control (who is actually tied to whom in terms of employment, for instance) that have not. Although oversimplified, this is meant to represent the fact that, while Reconstruction brought upon new political rights, on the ground most African Americans were poor and, despite newfound ownership of their own labor, still largely depended upon wealthy white bosses for work; this situation preserved racism as a form of categorical control on the ground, even as the state was in the hands of more sympathetic Republicans.

In Louisiana, the war and Reconstruction unsettled the link between antebellum rules for political access and day-to-day forms of social control in two ways. To begin, it led to changes in rules for access that dramatically increased the ambiguity of social relations. Most significantly, the newfound voting and participatory rights of African Americans – particularly after the Black Codes were rolled back and the Freedmen's Bureau was established in the late 1860s – gave them the chance to ally politically with groups of sympathetic whites, threatening to undermine the role of racial boundaries as a form of ordering political life.[15] To Anglo-American whites in Louisiana, this seemed to open up

[15] Stephen Kantrowitz, *Ben Tillman and the Reconstruction of White Supremacy* (Chapel Hill: University of North Carolina Press, 2000), 48–53.

a treacherous new phase in social life; while a free, mixed-race community had, for many years, been relatively able to pursue prosperity and security in New Orleans and its environs, this group had always been the target of suspicion as well as rules of political exclusion.[16] The shock to the underlying system of social control induced by changes in these rules was like that resulting from the market and transportation revolution in Chicago in the 1850s – social status became ambiguous and contested, with older alliances and settled social hierarchies thrown into question.

In addition, the detachment of African Americans from the system of slavery and the support of the Freedmen's Bureau allowed them to gain new forms of economic leverage. Most importantly, they could now not legally be compelled to work; it was possible, at least in theory, for them to bargain for wages or engage in contract negotiations with plantation owners and other employers.[17] They also became physically mobile, granting them a previously unavailable exit option from intolerable local conditions. [18] This physical mobility terrified white planters and provided a major inducement in the 1870s and 1880s to leverage crop tenancy to entangle agricultural workers (particularly in cotton areas) in debt and thereby trap them on the land.[19] Both new property and labor rights and physical mobility thus injected a challenging ambiguity and dynamism into existing economic arrangements.

These challenges – increased social ambiguity and newfound economic leverage – transformed organized coercion in Louisiana by compelling elites to look for new ways to counter economic and racial threats, and by leading them to use extra-legal militia mobilization cast in racial terms to pursue this aim. Before explaining why this solution appealed to them, however, it is necessary to explore the relationship between vigilantism and the militia in the South.

THE MILITIA AND VIGILANTISM IN THE SOUTH

The Southern militia was, like militia in the North, viewed as essential to the protection of communal interests. Many scholars have noted that the official militia went in to a steep decline in the early nineteenth century and that,

[16] Joseph Logsdon and Caryn Cossé Bell, "The Americanization of Black New Orleans, 1850–1900," in *Creole New Orleans: Race and Americanization*, ed. Arnold R. Hirsch and Joseph Logsdon (Baton Rouge: Louisiana State University Press, 1992), 207–209.

[17] John C. Rodrigue, *Reconstruction in the Cane Fields: From Slavery to Free Labor in Louisiana's Sugar Parishes, 1862–1880* (Baton Rouge: Louisiana State University Press, 2001), 67–77.

[18] The famed "exoduster" movement in Louisiana in 1879 was a late but important example of this newfound physical mobility (and one that was a response to local persecution and violence rather than a cause of it). See Morgan D. Peoples, "'Kansas Fever' in North Louisiana," *Louisiana History* 11, no. 2 (1970): 121–135.

[19] Howard A. White, *The Freedmen's Bureau in Louisiana* (Baton Rouge: Louisiana State University Press, 1970), 115–117, 121–122. The Freedmen's Bureau was often sympathetic to the problem of labor shortages due to mobility. See Taylor, *Louisiana Reconstructed*, 324–329.

particularly in the Deep South (outside of South Carolina and Virginia), the universal militia was largely moribund by the 1830s.[20] At the same time, recent work has demonstrated not only that a rich *volunteer* militia tradition emerged in Southern towns and cities from the 1830s to the outbreak of the Civil War, but that crucial official institutions like the slave patrol were themselves integrated into militia companies.[21] Indeed, the local militia company, in form if not name, and the rituals associated with musters, were the most important avenue through which Southern men were mobilized into the Confederate military, in addition to providing a way of linking residents together in shared patriotic events.[22]

Much more important, however, in the South, the militia was also essential to the policing of slaves. In most Southern states, the patrol was organized as a subsidiary of the local militia muster; units of patrollers were drawn from the militia and then assigned to particular geographic beats.[23] Just as with the general militia, men of most classes were expected to participate even when they did not own slaves themselves.[24] Just like the militia, slave patrols in Louisiana reflected local hierarchies – influential local notables (not necessarily slaveowners themselves) often served as captains of the patrols.[25]

Of course, not every Southern county or parish had a large enough slave population to merit an extensive patrol system, but managing slave populations was increasingly considered a crucial dimension of the police power of the state and became a responsibility that tied all white Southern men into shared coercive service.[26] By the 1850s, concerns over slave insurrection and the problem of fugitives had reached a crescendo; thus, even as participation militia itself receded into the background for many Southerners, participation in the patrols did not.[27]

It is hard to overstate how much the presence of slavery connected a particular vision of public security to the violent participation of private white citizens. Louisiana, like other Southern states, was frequently gripped by fears of a general slave insurrection; local disturbances in 1804 and 1811 combined with more general fears in the aftermath of Nat Turner's 1831 rebellion heightened the sense among many whites that African Americans needed to

20 Riker, *Soldiers of the States: The Role of the National Guard in American Democracy*, 27.

21 McCreedy, "Palladium of Liberty," 195–226.

22 See Harry S. Laver, *Citizens More Than Soldiers: The Kentucky Militia and Society in the Early Republic* (Lincoln: University of Nebraska Press, 2007), 20–47.

23 Hadden, *Slave Patrols*, 43–47. Local law officers were also frequently responsible for managing patrols.

24 ibid., 75.

25 E. Russ Williams, "Slave Patrol Ordinances of St. Tammany Parish, Louisiana, 1835–1838," *Louisiana History* 13, no. 4 (1972): 399–412.

26 Malka, "The Rights of Men: Power, Policing, and the Making of the Liberal State, 1812–1870," 145–158.

27 See, for example, *Shreveport South-Western*, December 3, 1856; *Carrollton Sun*, July 18, 1869; NDD, January 18, 1850.

be terrified into submission.[28] Because violence was integral to the political economy of slavery and created a legal space in which private violence was necessary for the public order, personal willingness to engage in violence and exposure to violent practices became part of day-to-day life for many in the South. On one hand, this took the form of highly coercive interactions within the household; managing slaves, which was a matter of public interest, induced white owners and drivers to use sexual coercion, whipping, confinement, and humiliation to maintain control in private spaces.[29] On the other hand, as scholars like Kenneth Greenberg point out, slavery also compelled white men to adopt standards of honor amongst themselves to distinguish themselves from slaves. Because slaves could not have honor and, concomitantly, could not defend it, part of what constituted a man's public identity was his willingness to duel or fight to protect his public face.[30] Interpersonal private violence was essential both to maintain economic order among slaves and social order among white men.

The other side of the militaristic tradition in the South were the volunteer companies. While Louisiana, like other states, had abandoned a universal militia after the War of 1812, such companies had become integral to the civic life in urban areas. These groups had emerged in the 1830s and 1840s as Anglo Americans moved into the New Orleans and sought a means for both cultivating civic belonging and maintaining their vision of law and order.[31] In addition to mobilizing for national crises like the Mexican War, groups like the Washington Artillery, the Southern Rifles, and the Louisiana Greys constituted the militia in New Orleans in the 1850s.[32] These militia units were also involved in the antebellum political struggles of the city, and were mobilized at least five times to address problems of public disorder in the decade preceding the Civil War.[33] On the eve of the Civil War, most of the major towns and cities in

[28] James H. Dormon, "The Persistent Specter: Slave Rebellion in Territorial Louisiana," *Louisiana History: The Journal of the Louisiana Historical Association* 18, no. 4 (1977): 389–404.

[29] Peter H. Wood, *Black Majority: Negroes in Colonial South Carolina from 1670 through the Stono Rebellion* (New York: Knopf, 1975), 271–284; Philip D. Morgan, *Slave Counterpoint: Black Culture in the Eighteenth-Century Chesapeake an Lowcountry* (Chapel Hill: University of North Carolina Press, 1999), 385–395; Fede, "Legitimized Violent Slave Abuse in the American South, 1619–1865." These practices of control bled into patriarchal authority more generally. See Edwards, "Law, Domestic Violence, and the Limits of Patriarchal Authority in the Antebellum South."

[30] Kenneth S. Greenberg, *Honor and Slavery* (Princeton, NJ: Princeton University Press, 1998), 34–35.

[31] Powell A. Casey, "Early History of the Washington Artillery of New Orleans," *Louisian Historical Quarterly* 23 (1940): 471–484.

[32] Robert C. Reinders, "Militia in New Orleans, 1853–1861," *Louisiana History* 3, no. 1 (1962): 33–42 William Miller Owen, *In Camp and Battle with the Washington Artillery of New Orleans: A Narrative of Events during the Late Civil War from Bull Run to Appomattox and Spanish Fort* (Boston: Ticknor & Company, 1885), 1–3.

[33] Reinders, "Militia in New Orleans, 1853–1861," 39.

the state had a rifle company or elite militia; Opelousas had its Rifles, St. Mary had a Pelican Guard Company, and so forth.[34]

The volunteer militia helped knit the social and civic lives of residents together. In New Orleans in the 1850s, for example, there were French, Swiss, Spanish, and German units, as well as several units populated by commercial elite.[35] These units were particularly important reflections of the military commitments of the commercial and planter class in Louisiana. On the eve of the Civil War, for example, of the 223 soldiers and staff listed as belonging to the four companies of the Washington Artillery, twenty-five (or 11%) would also join or were already members of New Orleans' two most exclusive social clubs, the Pickwick and the Boston, while another 16 were relatives of members.[36] Other members of the unit included important commercial players like H. M. Isaacson, W. B. Krumbhaar, and C. H. C. Brown, each of whom would go onto important civic and social roles in the post-war city. Militia unit parades and target exhibitions were some of the most celebrated sources of entertainment, as were the balls held by the units.[37]

The South was thus the site of a particular strong connection between private effort and (often) competing conceptions of public order. One side of this was the kind of vigilantism becoming common in the 1830s and 1840s.[38] Much of this vigilantism was the product of precisely the kinds of local struggles over control analyzed in Chapter 3; early vigilante movements in the United States clustered in Southern frontier counties in response to conditions where enclosed authority could no longer work to manage local order. For example, just as in Illinois in the early 1840s, the wild Attakapas parishes of southwestern Louisiana witnessed a rash of banditry in the late 1850s that involved some of the more influential members of local society. And, again, just as in Illinois, the factionalization of elite networks precipitated a multi-parish organization of vigilance committees to address the problem.[39] In New Orleans (a city experiencing the same transformation as Chicago), a vigilance committee emerged in the 1850s in response to the mobilization of an increasingly strident nativist movement in the city: the partition of the city

34 *Report of the Adjutant General of the Louisiana Militia to the Legislature for 1859* (January 1860), 4–6.

35 Reinders, "Militia in New Orleans, 1853–1861," 36.

36 Data on membership taken from Owen, *In Camp and Battle with the Washington Artillery of New Orleans*, 9–11; Augusto P. Miceli, *The Pickwick Club of New Orleans* (New Orleans: Pickwick Press, 1964); Stuart Omer Landry, *History of the Boston Club* (New Orleans: Pelican Pub. Co, 1938). Artificers, color guard, drivers and band members were not included.

37 NDD, September 2, 1851; NOP, July 6, 1855; November 5, 1858; NOC, July 7, 1859; Reinders, "Militia in New Orleans, 1853–1861," 40–41.

38 See Brown, *Strain of Violence*, 98–103.

39 Alexandre Barde, *The Vigilante Committees of the Attakapas: An Eyewitness Account of Banditry and Bakcklash in Southwestern Louisiana*, ed. David C. Edmonds and Dennis Gibson, trans. Henrietta Guilbeau Rogers (Lafayette, LA: The Acadania Press, 1981), 2–3; NOC, September 20, 1859; October 15, 1859; NOP, September 28, 1859.

in distinct spheres of influence was increasingly compromised by a growing immigrant population, which blurred the old distinction between the French and American centers of gravity.[40] In both cases, vigilantism was essentially a struggle over control in conditions of increased physical mobility and social ambiguity.

Vigilantism in the antebellum South was uniquely shaped by both the threat posed by slavery and the experience of participation in slave patrols and local volunteer militias.[41] While slaves were economic resources (and therefore valuable property to be protected) they were also agents capable of (and often reasonably interested in) resisting their masters and other whites. As a result, patrolling slave populations in the South often involved conflicts between property owners and those afraid of slave revolts –the pervasive slave panics that gripped not just Louisiana, but also Texas, Tennessee, Kentucky, and elsewhere in the aftermath of John Brown's 1859 raid lead to vigilante mobilizations that reflected local struggles over political power and influence as much as they did fear of the slaves themselves.[42] Indeed, even as slaves were relatively defenseless in terms of their personal legal rights, they were still frequently subject to extra-legal and informal lynching.[43]

At the same time, antebellum vigilantism in the South was fundamentally sporadic and local – fears over slave panics and the organization of vigilance committees were part of the complex tradition of rough justice which pervaded the region, but they did not fundamentally challenge the militia as a state institution.[44] If anything, the need for constant vigilance against the slave threat usually propped up rather than undermined the efficacy of local militia institutions and provided a key point around which Southern yeomen and planters alike could mobilize against the North.[45] The link between vigilant citizenhood, race, legal populism, and militia service made organized coercion

40 NOP, June 3, 1858; NDD, June 4, 1858; John S. Kendall, "The Municipal Elections of 1858," *Louisian Historical Quarterly* 5, no. 3 (1922): 357–376.

41 Hadden, *Slave Patrols*, 146–150; Kantrowitz, *Ben Tillman and the Reconstruction of White Supremacy*, 28.

42 Donald E. Reynolds, *Texas Terror: The Slave Insurrection Panic of 1860 and the Secession of the Lower South* (Baton Rouge: Louisiana State University Press, 2007), 55–67; Harvey Wish, "The Slave Insurrection Panic of 1856," *The Journal of Southern History* 5, no. 2 (1939): 206–222. Vigilance committees were also established in contested areas in state like Georgia and South Carolina to create unanimity of local opinion over succession. See Stephanie McCurry, *Masters of Small Worlds: Yeoman Households, Gender Relations, and the Political Culture of the Antebellum South Carolina Low Country* (Oxford: Oxford University Press, 1997), 292–295.

43 Pfeifer, *The Roots of Rough Justice*, 32–46.

44 Pfeifer, *The Roots of Rough Justice*; Christopher Waldrep, *Roots of Disorder: Race and Criminal Justice in the American South, 1817–1880* (Urbana: University of Illinois Press, 1998).

45 Kantrowitz, *Ben Tillman and the Reconstruction of White Supremacy*, 30–34; Stephanie McCurry, *Confederate Reckoning: Power and Politics in the Civil War South* (Cambridge, MA: Harvard University Press, 2010), 46–49.

in the South a much more participatory affair than even the most isolated frontier regions of the North. The basic notion of a public interest best served by white men in the militia was only rarely called into question.

Reconstruction changed these patterns of vigilantism. Now, they did not merely reflect crisis of local control, but rather systematic shifts in the authority whites had over freed African Americans generally and elites had over employees and laborers specifically. As such, groups like the Ku Klux Klan and the White League were qualitatively different; they, too, reflected the decoupling of day-to-day forms of social control relations from the order provided by political institutional rules (just as in the local forms of vigilantism), but they were organized across counties and parishes (often at the behest of wealthy residents) to shape the politics of the state as a whole.[46] In other words, these groups basically involved the conversion of the state militia and slave patrol into something quite different – a private, entrenched system of racial terror which could be used to help perpetuate the political economy of African-American subjugation under conditions where the older form of representative authority no longer worked.[47]

The kinds of vigilantism associated with the White League and other movements of the late 1860s and early 1870s thus built on the organizational template of the militia – they involved the public, and organized and coordinated efforts of communities across the state to use private violence to pursue a shared public aim. But they were used in a context in which the older basis of representational authority – the exclusion of particular groups from the political process – was under attack. The older militia no longer worked because what counted as the people had changed.

The war also transformed the public role of the militia. Militia – both units involved in the larger military as well as home guards – were a key part of the mobilization strategy of the Confederacy, but the complexities of Northern occupation and the viciousness of what frequently turned into a guerrilla struggle heightened the paranoia and fears of many Southern residents who were increasingly unable to determine friend from foe and who organized highly coercive vigilance committees and home patrols to detect Union sympathizers.[48] Participating in the militia now often meant joining sides

[46] Eric Foner, *Reconstruction: America's Unfinished Revolution, 1863–1877* (New York: Harper & Row, 1988), 424–432; Trelease, *White Terror*.

[47] Hadden, *Slave Patrols*, 211–216.

[48] Michael Fellman, *Inside War: The Guerrilla Conflict in Missouri during the American Civil War* (Oxford: Oxford University Press, 1990), 23–29, 132–192; Herman M. Hattaway, "The Civil War Armies: Creation, Mobilization, and Development," in *On the Road to Total War: The American Civil War and the German Wars of Unification, 1861–1871*, ed. Stig Förster and Jörg Nagler (Cambridge: Cambridge University Press, 1997), 173–198; McCurry, *Confederate Reckoning*, 118–124; Stephen V. Ash, *When the Yankees Came: Conflict and Chaos in the Occupied South, 1861–1865* (Chapel Hill: University of North Carolina Press, 1995), 125–126; 208–211.

in a feud or a partisan fight, since more than one militia was often active in a contested region.[49]

Moreover, the manpower requirements of the war forced Confederate states to change the parameters of who, exactly, could participate in armed violence. In Louisiana, a group of free Creoles established a Native Guard, which was organized to help defend New Orleans and, after the city fell to the Union troops in 1862, allied themselves with the infamous regime of Benjamin Butler.[50] Moreover, free people of color were also enlisted to help patrol slaves in places like St. Landry parish.[51]

After the Union occupied Southern states, they also made adaptations to the representative forms of control inherent in the antebellum militia. In 1867, responding to an outbreak of violence throughout the South, Congress passed a rider to an Appropriation Act demobilizing militia in the Southern states.[52] One year later, as it gained control over Reconstruction policy and Republican governors complained about crime and disorder, Congress changed course, granting allied governors in North Carolina, South Carolina, Florida, Alabama, Louisiana, and Arkansas the right to organize home militias. By 1870, they extended this privilege to Texas, Virginia, Mississippi, and Georgia, the governorships of which had passed into Republican hands.[53] These militias, crucially, were made up, in part, of African Americans, reflecting the sea change in political rights accruing to freedmen by the Reconstruction Era Congress, and fundamentally challenging the white dominance over coercive organization found in the antebellum South. The upshot, however, was that the official militias increasingly were the tools of Reconstruction governors and the target of resistance on the part of many Southern whites.[54]

The fragmentation of the militia created a crisis in what, exactly, organized violence would look like. Coercive groups like the Ku Klux Klan, a Tennessee social association for unreconstructed Democrats which expanded throughout the South in 1868 and 1869, built on the model of secret societies by using many of the same essential tactics of the slave patrol (especially

49 Emberton, *Beyond Redemption*, 88–91. Governor Warmouth, interestingly, had himself served in a militia company in Missouri, the seat of the most intense guerrilla fighting. Henry Clay Warmoth, *War, Politics, and Reconstruction: Stormy Days in Louisiana* (New York: Macmillan, 1930), 13–17.

50 Donald E. Everett, "Ben Butler and the Louisiana Native Guards, 1861–1862," *The Journal of Southern History* 24, no. 2 (1958): 202–217; NOP, April 21, 1861; April 23, 1861; NDD, October 7, 1862.

51 *An Ordinance Organizing and Establishing Patrols for the Police of Slaves in the Parish of St. Landry* (Opelousas, LA: Opelousas Patriot, 1863), 4.

52 Otis A. Singletary, *Negro Militia and Reconstruction* (Austin: University of Texas Press, 1957), 4–6.

53 ibid., 8.

54 Foner, *Reconstruction*, 437–444; Kantrowitz, *Ben Tillman and the Reconstruction of White Supremacy*, 58–64.

mounted night-riding in African-American areas).[55] The KKK vaguely resembled a kind of volunteer militia; it was exclusive, organized at the county or parish level but incorporated into statewide organizations, often composed of well-to-do young white men, and heavily reliant on spectacle to achieve their coercive effect.[56] The same volunteer militia logic appealed to many African Americans, particularly those with recent military experience in the war; with the aid of the freedmen aid groups like the Union League, former soldiers created voluntary militia companies that engaged in drilling and target practice in states like Alabama and Mississippi.[57]

As a result of these changes in militia policy and the inclusion of African Americans into what had previously been a closed circle of organized coercion, the link between the public and private security was broken. State militia continued to function, but public security seemed explicitly fractured into various private interests – or, more precisely, various particularist claims to representing the public. At its root, the fragmentation of the militia provided the seedbed for a systematic form of vigilantism, precisely because it provided an organizational template for how to secure such public security. Just as with previous forms of decoupling, older traditions of mobilization, personal drill and participation, and ritual were not abandoned; instead they had very different effects when used in new conditions. Private effort now became associated with factionalism, and non-representativeness rather than the securing of the public interest.

To explore what how this fragmentation played out and how powerful members of society, who had traditionally used the slave patrol and the voluntary militia as forms of coercion, adapted to a world in which they were largely excluded from political control and were under economic attack, I now turn to a closer examination of Reconstruction in Louisiana.

LOUISIANA AND THE WHITE LEAGUE: VIGILANTISM, RACE, AND REFORM

Louisiana's Reconstruction was longer and more complex than that of almost any other state. It was also likely more violent. Louisiana went through a uniquely tumultuous period of vigilante political mobilization in 1866 and 1868, during which hundreds of people died in a series of riots that rocked New Orleans, Bossier, St. Landry, and other parishes. Before unpacking how the militia changed in Louisiana through the organization of the White League

55 Emberton, *Beyond Redemption*, 149–150; Trelease, *White Terror*, 29–33.

56 Elaine Frantz Parsons, *Ku-Klux: The Birth of the Klan during Reconstruction* (Chapel Hill: University of North Carolina Press, 2015), 34–71.

57 Michael W. Fitzgerald, *The Union League Movement in the Deep South: Politics and Agricultural Change during Reconstruction* (Baton Rouge: Louisiana State University Press, 2000), 66–71.

in 1874, it is first necessary to understand the state's experience with Reconstruction more generally.

Louisiana's political crisis started during the Civil War, when the Constitution of 1864 (passed during the occupation of the state by Northern forces) included provisions ensuring the abolition of slavery and paving the way for future African-American suffrage; under the relatively firm control of occupation officials, the constitution was seen as a major step forward in the protection of newly freed populations. In the direct aftermath of the surrender, however, local towns and parishes, many of which remained firmly under the control of anti-Unionist politicians, began enacting a series of stringent Black Codes intended to limit African-American mobility and economic autonomy and to re-assert police power over a population many whites believed could prove disorderly. In St. Mary and St. Landry parishes, for example, both in the Sugar Bowl region of south-central Louisiana, African-Americans were forbidden from owning guns or staying out on the streets after 10:00 PM.[58]

The traditional elites in Louisiana – the planter and commercial class – had been desperate to gain some semblance of political control for years.[59] During the Civil War, the economy of the state had been crippled; Benjamin Butler, the occupying general who managed affairs in New Orleans after the surrender of the city in April of 1862, instituted a harsh policy against the financial and commercial elite of the city, most of whom had been supportive of secession and had attempted to use a cotton embargo to coerce England and France to join the war on the sides of the Confederacy. This included requiring banks to use US currency or specie, in deeply short supply, confiscating property (including slaves), censoring the press, and targeting Confederacy-allied commercial enterprises with taxes.[60] The cotton trade collapsed and a large number of merchants and bankers fled the city.[61] Of the $24 million in capital held by banks in New Orleans in 1861, only $7.67 million remained in 1865.[62]

Moreover, the question of labor loomed large. Not only had emancipation destroyed a huge amount of capital value, but it also called into question the underpinnings of the industrial organization of slavery. Initially, many in the planter community sought for other ways to coerce African Americans to participate in the harvest, including state-mandated labor.[63] This, of course, was opposed by the Freedman's Bureau, which had largely taken over economic management of ex-slaves. Planters desperately sought out ways to cope with the new economic reality, including importing labor from abroad and developing

[58] Taylor, *Louisiana Reconstructed*, 98.

[59] To a large extent, the many debates over banking policy and the rivalry between the Creole and Anglo-American communities plaguing the 1840s and early 1850s had been papered over by the boom years of the 1850s and the Civil War. Indeed, many merchants (largely associated with the Anglo-American faction) were also large landowners. See Marler, *The Merchants' Capital*, 45–52, 64–65, 122–127.

[60] ibid., 154–162. [61] ibid., 159–160. [62] ibid., 209. [63] ibid., 185.

new forms of short- and long-term contractual labor, such as sharecropping.[64] Gaining control over political office and enforcing the Black Code were thus integral to the survival of the commercial class, which had seen itself as the vanguard of protecting the city against the supposedly deleterious effects of free labor.

The threat of black suffrage was intertwined with this question of free labor: "in an instant," wrote the *Shreveport South-Western* in 1865, the "political status" of freed African-Americans "was changed, and they were thrust upon the world to take care of themselves as they could, with the vague idea running through their heads... that emancipation meant freedom from labor." This, of course, was untenable, when voting also might lead to redistributive policy: "the first thing to be done is to educate them in the arts of labor and the various occupations" so the "tens of thousands ... supported by the government" would "become sufficiently advanced and educated in the various avocations of industry."[65] When compounded with the fiscal problems of the Southern states, whose debts were seen by many as a Northern conspiracy to keep them compliant and to rob them of their property, the suffrage of the African Americans would have created an untenable political economy for traditional elites in the South.[66]

The political goals for Southern landowners and merchants was clear – restrict African-American suffrage and regain control over taxation and economic policy. A major victory by anti-Union forces in a series of contested New Orleans elections of 1866 seemed to portend a chance for them to achieve all of these objectives, at least in the state capitol.[67] In the aftermath of the election, however, a group of liberal Unionists and African Americans (many of whom were members of the city's well-entrenched free black population) called for the reopening of the 1864 constitutional convention. The reaction on the part of the city government, which saw the proceedings as illegitimate, was fierce; on July 30, the police stormed the Mechanic's Institute, where the convention was being held, and at least forty people (mostly African American) were killed.[68] A large number of those attacked were part of a procession of former African-American Union soldiers, at least thirty-four of whom had served with the Native Guard after defecting to work with General Butler.[69]

The actual attack on the convention was not publically supported by the merchant elite, though approximately 30% of those participating in the white

[64] NOP, November 5, 1867; *Morning Star and Catholic Messenger*, December 29, 1879; *South-Western*, July 23, 1869.

[65] July 26, 1865. [66] NOP, June 30, 1865.

[67] Gilles Vandal, "The New Orleans Riot of 1866: the Anatomy of a Tragedy" (PhD diss., College of William & Mary, 1978), 137–143; Justin A. Nystrom, *New Orleans after the Civil War: Race, Politics, and a New Birth of Freedom* (Baltimore: Johns Hopkins University Press, 2010), 63–67.

[68] Vandal, "The New Orleans Riot of 1866," 214–225. [69] ibid., 261.

mob accompanying the police were clerks and much of the commercial classes had opposed the calling of the convention.[70] The event, did, however, shock many Northern Republicans; in concert with another disturbing episode of collective race violence in Memphis several months earlier, the events of July 30 catalyzed a newfound resolve to impose radical political reforms on occupied states and to counter what appeared to be the Confederacy reorganizing itself in a different form. In addition to launching a series of investigative committees into Southern violence and shoring up military control over disorderly regions, Congress also began laying the groundwork for the Fourteenth and Fifteenth Amendments.[71] Moreover, a new convention in 1867 and 1868 drew up a constitution which became one of the most progressive in the South, and Henry Warmouth, committed to a much more radical form of republicanism, took the reins of state power.[72]

This upswing in radical reform, however, was met by an equally profound resistance on the part of many conservative Southern whites. In 1867 and 1868, the Democrats began to regroup as a force in Southern politics with an aim toward undermining Republicans in state government in the 1868 elections. This mobilization was a very complex process, involving the reorganization of those county Democratic central committees thrown in disarray in the post–Civil War years. But, most significantly, it also involved widespread, coordinated vigilante organization at a scale never seen before. Specifically, white supremacist groups launched what can only be described as a campaign of terror directed against Unionists and African-American voters in the spring and summer of 1868 in states all across the South, including, in particular, Louisiana. The Louisiana campaign, one of the most intense in the nation, included explicit attempts at voter intimidation in the April elections in the northwestern portion of the state (the Red River parishes), night-riding in Claiborne, St. Mary, St. Landry, and other central and western parishes throughout the summer, and, most significantly, a series of riots and massacres in New Orleans, St. Bernard, Caddo, and Bossier in the fall before the national elections.[73]

The mobilizations of 1868 lay the groundwork for what would become a sustained, systematic White League movement of 1874. A huge variety of

70 NOP, July 25, 1866; ibid., 174–178, 254; Marler, *The Merchants' Capital*, 195–196.

71 Taylor, *Louisiana Reconstructed*, 138–144; Ted Tunnell, *Crucible of Reconstruction: War, Radicalism, and Race in Louisiana, 1862–1877* (Baton Rouge: Louisiana State University Press, 1992), 106–107.

72 Taylor, *Louisiana Reconstructed*, 151–155.

73 Tunnell, *Crucible of Reconstruction*, 153–157; Gilles Vandal, "'Bloody Caddo': White Violence against Blacks in a Louisiana Parish, 1865–1876," *Journal of Social History* 25, no. 2 (1991): 373–388; Carolyn E. Delatte, "The St. Landry Riot: A Forgotten Incident of Reconstruction Violence," *Louisiana History* 17, no. 1 (1976): 41–49; US House of Representatives. 41st Congress, Second Session, *Testimony Taken by the Sub-Committee of Elections in Louisiana*, Misc.Doc.154.Part.1 (1870), 28–39; 125–126. Hereafter HMisc154P1.

groups participated in this campaign – in rural areas, the Knights of the White Camelia (KWC), the Swamp Fox Rangers, and even (in the parishes adjoining Florida) the Ku Klux Klan, which was imported from Alabama and Tennessee in late 1867 and early 1868. Most were highly local, organized only informally in conjunction with the local Democratic committees, though the KWC, which was responsible for the brutal St. Landry massacre of September 1868 (in which at least one hundred freed people died), was the most prominent and had a statewide organization.[74] It was organized at the parish or ward level and its activities were coordinated through a central committee.[75] Moreover, this upswing in violence had, at least in part, an economic logic; as Alcibiades DeBlanc, the organizer of the St. Landry KWC, claimed, "[W]e are ruined; every branch of industry is cramped and paralyzed" because of an "intolerable ... spoliating tax" levied by the tyrannical Reconstruction regime. The only answer was to "struggle with an unbroken, indefatigable, fearless spirit ... until you defeat the speculators in negro suffrage" and restore "the title of 'American Citizen.'"[76]

In urban areas like New Orleans and surrounding parishes, the key groups were ward clubs like the Seymour Legion and the Blair Sentinels, both named after the Democratic candidates in 1868. The ward clubs engaged in a systematic campaign of intimidation aimed at suppressing Republican turnout and converting African-American voters to support the Democratic ticket. In late September of 1868, several African-American members of a Republican clubs were killed by Blair and Seymour supporters, while on the night of October 24, seven African Americans were killed in a clash with a the Workingmen's Club, the Broom Rangers and the Swamp Rangers. The next few nights witnessed more clashes, as members of a Democratic club called the Innocents attacked black residents and ransacked Republican meeting rooms.[77]

The militia tradition proved critical in the democratic mobilization of 1868. Although hard evidence is difficult to come by, there is no doubt that many of the members of the ward clubs and KWC had belonged to official and volunteer militia companies mobilized by Confederacy; the very names of the vigilance groups active in 1868 were highly evocative of militia service. Key leaders like Frederick Nash Ogden, head of the Crescent City Democratic Club and DeBlanc, for instance, were Confederate officers, and members of the Democratic clubs were able to access large stores of weapons easily,

74 Taylor, *Louisiana Reconstructed*, 162–164; Tunnell, *Crucible of Reconstruction*, 153; NOR, October 12, 1868.

75 HMisc154P1 294–295, 298, 300; US House of Representatives. 41st Congress, Second Session, *Testimony Taken by the Sub-Committee of Elections in Louisiana*, Misc.Doc.154.Part.2 (1870), 227–237. Hereafter HMisc154P2.

76 HMisc154P2, 322–323. Vandal, "'Bloody Caddo,'" 378.

77 HMisc154P1, 720–725; 743-753; NOR, October 26, 1868.

suggesting a connection to the military armories.[78] Members of one secret society, the Southern Cross Association Number 9, seem to have shared a military background in the voluntary companies; five of the groups thirty-four members had served with the Crescent Regiment (a unit organized by the Pickwick Club), while three or four had been members of the Washington Artillery.[79]

These groups were supported by or included many prominent New Orleans residents, including members of the Washington Artillery like Louis Prados and Edwin Jewell, as well as commercial figures like E. H. Fairchild and W. B. Schmidt.[80] Jewell, along with Frederick Ogden (a partner of the son of one of the city's most prominent cotton brokers, Michel Musson), organized the clubs at the neighborhood level and coordinated them through an executive committee, laying the groundwork for the White League movement a few years later.[81]

Both the KWC and the ward clubs were also built, in part, on another key institutional template in New Orleans – that of the secret society. Secret societies in New Orleans could be traced back to the growth of antebellum fraternal organizations that, emulating the revolutionary cabals of Enlightenment Europe, had become part and parcel of antebellum politics in New Orleans.[82] Groups like the Knights of the Golden Circle – a secret society dedicated to the expansion of slavery into Mexico and an important part of the infrastructure of militant secessionists in the run up to Confederate mobilization – were highly active in New Orleans, which they used as a base of operations.[83]

After the war, secret societies – particularly elite clubs, like the Pickwick and Boston Clubs – were an important avenue through which ex-Confederates could express their political agency in a context where official participation was often difficult. Indeed, the boundary between party clubs in the neighborhoods and fraternal association – especially those involved in New Orleans' rich Mardi Gras tradition – was very blurry.[84] For instance, the most important

[78] James G. Dauphine, "The Knights of the White Camelia and the Election of 1868: Louisiana's White Terrorists; A Benighting Legacy," *Louisiana History* 30, no. 2 (1989): 180; HMisc154P1 645–646.

[79] US House of Representatives. 39th Congress, Second Session, *New Orleans Riots*, H.Rep.16 (1867), 521. Hereafter HRep16. Military service identified through www.ancestry.com.

[80] NOP, September 22, 1868; October 3, 1868.

[81] HMisc154P1, 745; HMisc154P2, 227–228.

[82] Robert C. Reinders, *End of an Era: New Orleans, 1850–1860* (Pelican Publishing Company, 1964), 115–116; Leon Cyprian Soulé, *The Know Nothing Party in New Orleans: A Reappraisal.* (Baton Rouge: Louisiana Historical Association, 1961), 47–60. On the history of the secret society roots of antebellum anti-North organizations, see Mark A. Lause, *A Secret Society History of the Civil War* (Urbana: University of Illinois Press, 2011), 51–66.

[83] John Hope Franklin, *The Militant South, 1800–1861* (Urbana: University of Illinois Press, 2002), 122–128; David C. Keehn, *Knights of the Golden Circle: Secret Empire, Southern Secession, Civil War* (Baton Rouge: Louisiana State University Press, 2013), 47–49, 188–189.

[84] Nystrom, *New Orleans after the Civil War*, 63–64, 77, 115–119, 134–137, 164–165.

of the Mardi Gras societies, the Mistick Crewe of Comus and Rex, composed primarily of Pickwick and Boston members respectively, used processions to mock and harangue Reconstruction officials like Grant and Warmouth.[85] The Crescent City Democratic Club was made up of members of the Chalmette Club, another secret society with roots in the Mardi Gras tradition.[86]

Moreover, these groups were known for their violence; thugs affiliated with secret societies had been crucial in setting up a violent mobbing tradition in New Orleans in the 1850s, one rooted in nativism and a powerful local Know-Nothing movement.[87] By keeping their membership numbers confidential and adopting elaborate costuming rituals, the vigilante groups of 1868 were able to project the image that they had ubiquitous power, just like the secret societies which provided much of their manpower.[88]

The vigilante campaign in Louisiana in 1868, in short, was systematic in the sense that it involved a coordinated, widespread movement oriented toward regaining control over the political institutions of the state. Elite merchants and planters alike supported the movement, and participants drew from the twinned traditions of the militia and the secret society to operationalize their discontent.

At the same time, this campaign also represented a change in how many residents perceived the link between the militia and public security. Participants in these movements saw themselves as protecting the people, while at the same time creating terror within their own communities. Indeed, they frequently justified their activities as a precautionary move against Warmouth's regime, which many suspected of wanting to organize "negro militia" to patrol and coerce white citizens.[89] Because they no longer controlled political representation in government, however, advocates of the white counter-mobilization could also no longer successfully offer a coherent vision of who the people (or, more precisely, the public) actually were; as a result, when they acted like militia forces or patrols, trying to monitor and patrol the behavior of African Americans or Unionists, their use of private violence increasingly appeared as highly partisan and self-interested. As Governor Warmouth argued in a letter to the president, "[T]here is a secret organization throughout the state ... founded for the purpose of placing and keeping the colored people in

85 NOP, February 14, 1872; ibid., 115–119.

86 Stuart Omer Landry, *The Battle of Liberty Place: The Overthrow of Carpet-Bag Rule in New Orleans, September 14, 1874* (New Orleans: Pelican Publishing Company, 1955), 58.

87 The Know-Nothing party in New Orleans, just as in Chicago, was itself more or less a secret society, although the southern clubs seem to have been much larger and more successful than its northern counterpart. Soulé, *The Know Nothing Party in New Orleans*, 61–84; Earl F. Niehaus, *The Irish in New Orleans, 1800–1860* (Baton Rouge: Louisiana State University Press, 1965), 87–97.

88 HRep16, 520; HMisc154P1, 223–224; Elaine Frantz Parsons, "Midnight Rangers: Costume and Performance in the Reconstruction-Era Ku Klux Klan," *Journal of American History* 92, no. 3 (2005): 811–836; Tunnell, *Crucible of Reconstruction*, 101–103;

89 HMisc154P1, 42–43, 389–391, 546, 652; 685–686; HMisc154P2, 25–26, 397–398, 419.

a condition of inferiority, and with a view to this end contemplates and designs the precipitation to conflict between the two races ... I fully believe that there is mediated a bloody revolution, the certain fruit of which would be ... ruin to the State."[90]

The events in St. Landry parish in the summer of 1868 reveal the tenuous line between traditional notions of communal protection via the militia and vigilante violence. St. Landry, a parish in the sugar-producing region of the state with a large number of African Americans (including a small elite), was ground zero for Republican attempts to organize voters in the summer of 1868.[91] The state elections in April had revealed that African Americans in the parish were both willing to vote and could turn the parish toward the Republicans in the fall; as Democrats began their counter-mobilization, tensions escalated and Republicans were forced to begin holding their meetings outside the town.[92] In so doing, many Republicans began arming themselves, in response to a campaign of night-riding that had begun earlier in the summer.[93] Both groups began to speak about the need to have arms in order to secure protection from one another; as rumors flew that a group of African-American Republicans was marching on the town of Opelousas to burn it to the ground, white members of the local Democratic organization – the Seymour Knights – armed themselves, provoking a confrontation diffused only by a general agreement to attempt a disarmament. The initial mobilization of both African-American and white groups resembled the basic logic of the militia – community protection as a matter of private participation.[94]

A week later, however, the truce broke apart when a Republican newspaper editor was beaten in public and a general call was made to mobilize the black Republican population for its own protection.[95] This, in turn, was interpreted as preparation for attack by the white residents of Opelousas, whose own counter-mobilization led to a general battle among residents and an ensuing massacre; at least two hundred African Americans likely died in the slaughter.[96] In other words, what had begun as the seemingly straightforward mobilization of the community for its own protection became an extraordinary case of vigilantism, precisely because there was no shared vision of what counted as the people. Representational authority had effective fractured.

The political campaign of 1868 was a direct result of rules decoupling from relations. The expansion of the voting franchise and political membership to African Americans undermined the control of local whites over law enforcement and the militia, and made them fearful of the "bitterest hate and enmity

[90] HMisc154P2, 514. [91] HMisc154P1, 407–410

[92] Delatte, "The St. Landry Riot: A Forgotten Incident of Reconstruction Violence," 41–44.

[93] OC, September 5, 1868. [94] HMisc154P1, 408–409, 414–415, 416–417, 420, 461.

[95] ibid., 410–411. [96] ibid., 411; NOT, October 6, 1868.

for the whites" they believed lay at the heart of the Radical Republicanism.[97] This meant, in turn, that political disputes began to be interpreted in as a matter of race.[98]

F. Perrodin, deputy sheriff in St. Landry, a member of the KWC and a participant in the riot, revealed the contradictions that had emerged in public security; while he claimed that he had "sworn to protect and treat" the freedmen as "gently as possible" he also opposed "amalgamation" of African Americans with even democratic party organization and was prepared to use violence to protect himself against processions of armed black men, which he saw as a general danger.[99] Mobilization for self-protection reflected, almost by definition, particular rather than shared interests. The direct challenge to antebellum forms of political authority in general embodied in the Constitution of 1868 and the Fourteenth and Fifteenth Amendments also undermined the racial basis of the militia as an institution primarily for white men. As a result, the militia fragmented, becoming a focal point of the struggle of recalcitrant conservatives against the state. For as the Franklin *Planters' Banner* noted, "[W]hile we beg and pray our people to hurt none of these people except strictly in self defense ... we do not ask them to stand more than human nature can bear."[100]

The response of the state was two-fold. On one hand, as Congress granted authority to the US Army to engage in direct enforcement of the newfound voting and political rights. This often involved local army units in arrests or patrol, particularly around election days.[101] However, the importance of military activity, while substantial, was rarely up to the task of handling day-to-day disorder. Indeed, while Congress expected the US Army to engage in domestic enforcement, the Department of War had gradually reduced the size of manpower available to division commanders; during parts of the summer of 1874, for instance, there were only sixteen uniformed troops monitoring events in eight of the most troubled Red River parishes.[102] While 9,772 troops had been stationed in the state in January of 1866, by early 1875, federal troop levels rarely reached 1,000 except right before and after elections.[103] While the military's assistance could prove decisive – as it would in the days following the coup in New Orleans in 1874 and 1875 – its role was increasingly a signal

97 NOT, October 8, 1868.

98 Kantrowitz, *Ben Tillman and the Reconstruction of White Supremacy*, 45, 51–54.

99 HMisc154P1, 462–463, 468.

100 September 5, 1868.

101 Joseph G. Dawson, *Army Generals and Reconstruction: Louisiana, 1862–1877* (Baton Rouge: Louisiana State University Press, 1994), 129, 132–133.

102 US House of Representatives. 43rd Congress, Second Session, *Conditions of Affairs in the South*, H.Rep.261.Part.3 (1875), 317. Hereafter HR261P3. There were significant increases in troop levels in Louisiana in September and November, however, Dawson reports that almost 2,000 troops were stationed in nine posts across the state in November of 1874. See Dawson, *Army Generals and Reconstruction*, Appendix III.

103 ibid.

of Washington's commitment to propping up local political allies rather than a solution to the problems of violence in Louisiana.[104]

On the other hand, because local law enforcement institutions (many of which remained under the control of powerful local conservative whites) continued to be the primary form of protecting citizens in areas where the military was absent, the Reconstruction governors of Louisiana themselves began to try to reorganize the state's control over violence. First, in the summer of 1868, Governor Warmouth reorganized the New Orleans police, the only bureaucratic police force in the state, enlarging its jurisdiction, reorganizing its chain of command, linking parish and city administration together, and restaffing it with loyalists.[105] Initially, the force was underarmed and was unable to do much to prevent bloodshed on election day in November, but it did provide the core of a force that would be under the direct control of the governor.[106]

Second, in 1870, despite objections from the US commander in the region, Warmouth reorganized the state militia, placing it under the control of a former Confederate, General James Longstreet. Longstreet centralized control over the force by focusing its activities in New Orleans, which was becoming the main seat of Republican power in the state.[107] While most of the officers in the new force were white, the militia included a large number of African Americans (around two-thirds or so), many of whom were former Union veterans.[108] Both the militia and the Metropolitan Police, which itself could be mobilized as a militia (giving it statewide jurisdiction), provided Louisiana's executive with a great deal of independent control over how and when to use force.[109]

Initially some Democrats responded with fury to the changes sought by Warmouth. One set of complaints had to do with who would serve: "[A] well organised (*sic*) body of militia, composed of conservatives who have the good of the country at heart ... is not objectionable," noted the *South-Western*, "but when organised from the rabble, for partisan purposes, under officers who would take the advantage of their positions to gratify personal animosity, it is one of the greatest curses that can be inflicted upon a people."[110] Indeed, as a letter to Governor Warmouth from notables in Caddo, Boissier, and DeSoto parishes, which had witnessed terrible violence in 1868, claimed, "[T]he consequences of sending and undisciplined rabble of armed men to

104 Rable, *But There Was No Peace*, 141–143.

105 Hogue, *Uncivil War*, 66; Rousey, *Policing the Southern City*, 127–129.

106 Tunnell, *Crucible of Reconstruction*, 159–161.

107 Hogue notes that 78% of the companies created in the militia prior to 1872 were housed in New Orleans. Hogue, *Uncivil War*, 72.

108 Dawson, *Army Generals and Reconstruction*, 88–89; Hogue, *Uncivil War*, 73–74. Indeed, initially, a number of former Confederates joined the force along with Longstreet, including a future member of the White League, William J. Behan. See Nystrom, *New Orleans after the Civil War*, 89–90.

109 ibid., 105–108. 110 August 19, 1868.

repress outrage where none exists, will be to create the very evil they are sent to prevent."[111]

Another set of complaints, predictably, had to do with taxes; in 1870, the general assembly allocated $100,000 to the militia in 1870 and $150,000 the next year, a figure that many in Democrats found "preposterous."[112] Robert Nash Ogden, a cousin of Frederick Ogden and a senator in the general assembly, contended that this cost was unnecessary: "[A]re we threatened by foreign invasion? Do the hostile flags of an approaching enemy chill us into anxiety?" he asked. "Why is it desired now to encumber the resources of the State and trammel her by establishing a militia, thereby entailing constant and incessant taxation?"[113] And in 1872, a group of prominent attorneys (including a number of future members of the White League) promised to "engage themselves, without compensation" for any wishing to resist the "metropolitan-police tax," which they considered illegal.[114]

Still, the main issue with the militia and the reconstituted police force, from the standpoint of most conservatives, was not its existence, but who controlled it. This was particularly the case with the municipal police of New Orleans, which, when under the control of Democratic allies in 1866 was considered by much of the press to be indispensable and a key source of patronage.[115] During the violence of 1868, Robert Nash Ogden even tried to cut a deal with the United States to have Fred Ogden placed as chief of police.[116] But as Warmouth reorganized the police so that they fell under state rather than municipal control, these praises turned to attacks, particularly when he initially appointed a large number of African Americans to the force. The Metropolitan Police was seen as illegal and illegitimate, and the superintendent was forced to fire most of the black officers.[117] This was true even for some political allies. General Lovell Rousseau, head of the military departments of Louisiana and Arkansas, claimed in a letter to President Grant that the police had lost all credibility with "the community at large"; this perception "alone rendered the metropolitan police as organized practically worthless, and placed life and property at the mercy of the worst classes in the city."[118]

The militia was thus seen by many conservatives as potentially quite helpful, as long as Radical officials weren't in charge.[119] The willingness of a large number of ex-Confederates to serve within the reconstituted state militia – particularly the First Regiment, of which Washington Artillery veteran William M. Owen was colonel – indicated a desire to co-opt the institution from

111 *Shreveport South-Western*, July 27, 1870. 112 *Ouachita Telegraph*, February 3, 1872.
113 NOR, March 24, 1870. 114 HR261P3, 963.
115 Vandal, "The New Orleans Riot of 1866," 253–257.
116 Nystrom, *New Orleans after the Civil War*, 78.
117 NOT, July 9, 1869; NOP, November 29, 1868; January 19, 1860; May 23, 1869; Rousey, *Policing the Southern City*, 124–125.
118 NOC, December 4, 1868. 119 Hogue, *Uncivil War*, 68–69.

within.[120] Moreover, many naturally looked to the militia as a way for existing elites to coordinate coercion; one of the first responses for many communities at the end of the war was to try to organize a militia for the patrol of local disorder.[121] The problem, as with the police, was that conservatives wanted control over this mobilization.

Control over the militia became an acute problem since, from 1868 through 1874, Louisiana was in more or less a constant state of political turmoil. In addition to the deep resistance of conservative Democrats, a major driving factor behind this turmoil were the splits in the Republican ranks, which split into a faction propped up by federal patronage and a close relationship to the Grant administration (centered in the US Custom House and headed by Stephen Packard, US marshal, and collector James Casey, brother-in-law to the president) and one with roots in New Orleans and the state government (Warmouth and his supporters belonged to this faction). Both factions competed with each other more fiercely than they did with the Democrats, at times even agreeing to form fusion tickets with the conservative Democrats to oppose their ostensible party allies. Complicating the issue was the extraordinary power of the returning board certifying election results, which was almost completely under the control of the governor; since the board could (and did) throw out the results of any parish election on the basis of fraud, it became a focus of conservative complaints of illegitimacy of state election results.[122]

The election of 1870 passed with relative calm, but the Republican party soon found itself in shambles. In early 1871, a group of Republicans tied to the federal government tried to arrest Governor Warmouth on conspiracy charges, which led to an armed standoff between different companies of the state militia and only resolved through the intersession of the US Army.[123] This, in turn, set the stage for the election campaign of 1872, during which Warmouth and his allies (including, incidentally, George Sheridan), who had become increasingly attached to some of the conservative elements in the Republican party, ultimately threw their weight behind a Fusion party headed by John McEnery, a conservative Democrat.

The election itself was a fiasco: the returning board, still under Warmouth, divided into factions and produced conflicting election reports. Both William Kellogg, a close associate of President Grant and the Radical Republican candidate, and McEnery took oaths of office in January and organized competing legislatures; initially, Congress was unable to resolve the issue, which

[120] *Annual Report of the Adjutant General of the State of Louisiana for the Year Ending December 31, 1870* (New Orleans: Louisiana Adjutant General's Office, 1871), 8.

[121] OC, December 2, 1865.

[122] Tunnell, *Crucible of Reconstruction*, 160; Taylor, *Louisiana Reconstructed*, 209–252.

[123] NOP, January 5, 1872; January 6, 1872; Hogue, *Uncivil War*, 82–85.

lingered for several months despite Grant's preference for Kellogg.[124] Many white Republicans, both inside Louisiana and elsewhere in the South, viewed Reconstruction in terms of political opportunism, and both the Warmouth and anti-Warmouth forces traded increasingly barbed accusations of corruption and bias.

The militia played a key role in this conflict, as both McEnery and Kellogg turned to the traditional institution to enforce their claims to the office. By late 1872, the force included factions of both former Confederate McEnery supporters (including William Owen) appointed by Warmouth and those loyal to P. B. S. Pinchback, the lieutenant governor and an ally of the Custom House faction.[125] When Warmouth was impeached on December 9 and replaced by Pinchback, different elements of the militia took sides; a group of McEnery supporters mobilized to occupy armories scattered throughout the city, only standing down after Pinchback called for federal aid.[126] Meanwhile, Pinchback purged the upper ranks of the force, reappointing James Longstreet, a friend of Grant's and, by this point, an ally of the Custom House faction, and replacing Owen and other McEnery partisans.[127]

By early 1873, the fracture was complete. In February, McEnery began to organize his own force, appointing Frederick Ogden as brigadier general and making a call for "all citizens of the Parish of Orleans ... subject to and capable of militia duty" to report for militia duty under Major General Eugene Waggaman, one of Warmouth's appointees and an another ex-Confederate.[128] The next week, this force mobilized to try to take over New Orleans' municipal arsenals and police stations. In these efforts, McEnery had the firm backing of many of New Orleans' elites; for instance, a number of influential merchants and cotton factors, like John Phelps and John Sinnott, apparently offered to reimburse a gunsmith providing arms to the McEnery force.[129]

The Metropolitan Police force, itself now mobilized as a militia under the control of the state adjutant general, resisted and, with the aid of a detachment of US infantry officers, were able to secure Ogden's surrender.[130] General Longstreet, in turn, ordered the Metropolitans to arrest fifty-three of the McEnery force members and, the next day, forced the McEnery legislature to disband.[131]

[124] Hogue, *Uncivil War*, 102–103. Taylor, *Louisiana Reconstructed*, 241–249.

[125] Hogue, *Uncivil War*, 98–99 *Annual Report of the Adjutant General of the State of Louisiana for the Year Ending December 31, 1872* (New Orleans: Louisiana Adjutant General's Office, 1873), 36.

[126] NOP, December 15, 1872.

[127] *Annual Report of 1872*, 41–42; *Annual Report of the Adjutant General of the State of Louisiana for the Year Ending December 31, 1873* (New Orleans: Louisiana Adjutant General's Office, 1874), 81.

[128] NOP, February 27, 1873; February 28, 1873. [129] NOR, April 26, 1873.

[130] NOP, March 6, 1873. [131] Hogue, *Uncivil War*, 104–106.

The use of competing militia in what became known as the First Battle of the Cabildo demonstrated, as one scholar has put it, that one man's mob was another man's militia in Reconstruction Louisiana.[132] The battle over who could control offices in Louisiana was one that ultimately involved control over the means of force. But, as confusion over the 1872 election spread from parish to parish, concerns over self-protection and who counted as the people were interpreted, increasingly, as a matter not merely of corruption but also of race.

In part this was a result of the strategy of the Republican party in New Orleans, which was attempting to redraw jurisdictional boundaries – usually along racial lines – in order to stabilize their voting bloc and reward supporters. Nine new parishes were created between 1868 and 1871, for example – many of which were intended to secure local black majorities. Grant Parish, for example, had been carved out of surrounding areas in turbulent Red River Country in 1869 in order to provide a refuge of sorts for freedmen, whose benefactor, William Calhoun, owned a large plantation in the area and had become an ally of the Republican administration.[133] As a result of the machinations, Grant had a bare but significant black majority, one that the Republicans hoped could be used to dilute the significant Democratic strength in the area.

This very practice, however, made such parishes the object of a focused political struggle. After Grant Parish was formed, for instance, the *Louisiana Democrat* called "the whole concern ... a Radical bone to feed the loyal mendicants, who hang around Sweet Willie's domains ... gotten up for no other purpose than to rob and pillage the State."[134] Following a campaign in which intimidation on the part of the significant white minority in the community played a key role in Grant Parish, McEnery allies had occupied the key parish roles of judge and sheriff after the election, having gained their commissions by outgoing governor Warmouth and having claimed majority wins.[135] At the same time, Kellogg commissioned two other local political allies for the roles, who, with the aid of local state assembly representative William Ward, forcibly occupied the courthouse and took over the positions. This confrontation almost immediately proceeded along military lines, as both Kellogg and McEnery had called for the mobilization of militia.[136]

In the case of a parish like Grant, militia mobilization reflected race because the boundaries of the jurisdiction were partly drawn to reinforce rather than

132 Kantrowitz, "'One Man's Mob Is Another Man's Militia': Violence, Manhood, and Authority in Reconstruction South Carolina."

133 Keith, *The Colfax Massacre*, 63–64; Thomas Howell, "Finding the Line: The Origin of Grant Parish and the Recent Dispute over Its Boundary," *Louisiana History* 51, no. 2 (2010): 215–230.

134 March 17, 1869. 135 HR261P3, 895.

136 Keith, *The Colfax Massacre*, 86–87; NOR, April 26, 1873; HR261P2, 14–15.

cut against this cleavage. African Americans, reasonably concerned about their own safety, had marshaled to defend Kellogg's appointees in late March, and procured weapons and constructed fortifications around the city of Colfax, including building an earthworks defense and mounting several cannons.[137] In an eerie repeat of the scene in St. Landry in 1868, however, the substantial white population in Grant and the surrounding parishes became terrified of the prospect of armed African Americans. Witnessing the occupation of the courthouse in late March, which, according to R. H. Marr, a conservative Democratic lawyer, "assumed a semi-military character," white residents became "filled with apprehension and alarm" and quickly formed themselves into patrols.[138] The result was widespread regional panic; a large force of white men from surrounding areas gathered in Colfax in early April to capture the town. The result, as in Opelousas in 1868, was tragic – very likely a hundred or so blacks were killed as they surrendered or fled from the courthouse where they had been placed under siege.[139] All of this was justified by the white militia in traditional communal terms, as rumors of armed freedmen roaming the countryside and threatening homes and families rendered a political dispute into a large-scale social emergency for white residents.[140] The Colfax Massacre, as it was later termed, became a focal point for the mobilization of the White League in 1874.

THE AFTERMATH OF COLFAX: WHITE LEAGUE VIGILANTISM AND POLITICAL REFORM

The most tangible outcome of the Colfax Massacre was that it clarified the role of race and violence for many white conservatives. Specifically, by viewing the efforts of the white militias as a matter of public protection, they defined the opponents of public security as armed African-American Republicans. The controversy over the arming of the African-American militia members in Grant Parish became one of the most important defenses of the actions of the white militia at Colfax, a number of whom were arrested in the following months by the US Army under the provisions of the Enforcement Acts. It was this controversy that provided the seedbed for the organization of the White League in spring of 1874 and helped shape it into a combination of political party *and* statewide private militia group, organized along racial terms.

The main contention involved William Ward, the African-American captain of the Kellogg militia at Grant Parish; his commission had ended in late December of 1871 and he had, apparently, kept arms from the government against the command of James Longstreet, who was still serving as adjutant

137 US House of Representatives. 43rd Congress, Second Session, Conditions of Affairs in the South, H.Rep.261.Part.2 (1875), HR261P2, 15; *Louisiana Democrat*, April 9, 1873.
138 ibid. 139 NOR, April 18, 1873; NOT, May 4, 1873.
140 HR261P3, 895–899; *Louisiana Democrat*, May 14, 1873.

general of the state militia.[141] Ward had spent some of his time in 1870 and 1871 aiding the deputy US marshal in his pursuit of alleged Ku Klux Klan members in the Red River region, and had been involved in the killing of several white men in Natchitoches Parish in an arrest attempt in 1873.[142] This had made him extremely unpopular with conservative whites in the region. Moreover, his election to the state assembly in 1872 had tied him to the Republicans and made his participation in the militia activities in April of 1873 appear to Democrats like a thug imposing the dictates of the corrupt and illegitimate Kellogg regime.[143]

Most serious was Kellogg's use of the Metropolitan Police in a militia capacity. In the immediate aftermath of the massacre, Kellogg sent a force of metropolitans toward Colfax and these forces cooperated with a company from the 19th US Infantry to secure the scene and arrest any straggling participants.[144] Though the Metropolitan Police returned quickly from Grant Parish to New Orleans, over the next couple of months they were called out to address some problems with disorder in Tangipahoa Parish, and, more controversially, in St. Martin's parish to address problems with tax resisting.[145] The use of the Metropolitans outside the parish of New Orleans was considered by white conservatives to be a major breach of jurisdictional autonomy, in particular when used against those criticizing the Kellogg regime. Relying on traditional republican conceptions, the *Picayune* described the force as an illegal "standing army" and as a "body of armed janissaries."[146] And the *Lafayette Advertiser* blamed Kellogg's "usurpation of the war power" and his "invasion of remote parishes" by "white and black mercenaries" for the massacre. "The presence of this band of partisan emissaries," the editor claimed, "stimulates the negroes to violence and audacity, from a belief in their protection, and from an encouragement ... by their appearance in armed array."[147]

For some conservative whites, the solution was clear: "We will never permit another negro company to be armed and drilled by Mr. Kellogg or his government in Grant parish," wrote the *Alexandria Caucasian*. "If such a thing is attempted, we will meet it with open war, and appeal to the people of the North, by the blood of our ancestors ... for protection against a despotism more desolating than war."[148]

The indictments, pursuit, and ultimately trial of some of the Colfax Massacre perpetrators provided the key impetus for the organization of the White League in Spring of 1874. In the aftermath of the massacre, the district attorney of Natchitoches Parish, Ernest Breda, opted to try to arrest as many of the participants as possible, enlisting the aid of the US Army as well as state militia forces.[149] Many of the white participants in the massacre fled to Texas, while

141 HR261P3, 893; NOP, May 8, 1873.
142 Keith, *The Colfax Massacre*, 68–75; HR261P3: 514–515. 143 NOT, May 4, 1873.
144 Keith, *The Colfax Massacre*, 111–114. 145 Rousey, *Policing the Southern City*, 154.
146 NOP, April 2, 1873. 147 November 8, 1873. 148 AC, June 27, 1874.
149 Keith, *The Colfax Massacre*, 118–120.

others hid out with family and friends, becoming fugitives. In the eyes of many white conservatives – including elites across the state – these men were martyrs and refugees, persecuted for having defended their homes and families from the corrupt forces of the usurper, Governor Kellogg.[150]

To wealthy planters, cotton brokers, bankers, and other elites, the Colfax events confirmed that Kellogg's regime was an instrument to prop up African-American political agency, posing a direct threat to their economic and social power. Many influential white citizens began to treat the Colfax affair as a *cause célèbre*; the prisoners had appealed to a group of New Orleans notables for aid in "defraying the expenses of our trial," and a who's who of New Orleans society held a special benefit concert at the Varieties Theater to raise money.[151] A group of attorneys, mostly drawn from New Orleans' elite, represented the men.[152]

From the standpoint of the elite, the most pressing concern was that African-American military mobilization would began to affect the restiveness of labor. A violent uprising in Terrebonne over wages in early 1874, for instance, led the Democratic press to call for better protections for property and to accuse the Kellogg legislature of being behind the disturbance.[153] As the *Republican* put it, "without the immense motive power supplied by the one hundred thousand colored laborers, our planters would soon find themselves too poor to buy paper enough to write a mortgage on."[154] Both the planting and commercial classes understood this logic all too well, and began to contemplate ways of using economic coercion to help police African-American political opinion.

Celebrating the cause of the "Shreveport sufferers" (as the Grant Parish prisoners were known) was also part of an explicit political strategy aimed at unseating Kellogg regime through the opportunistic use of race. Kellogg's reliance on African Americans to staff key security positions made this a tempting target. By 1874, for instance, the hated Metropolitan Police force was approximately 28 percent African American and mixed-race (the city of New Orleans was 26% non-white in 1870).[155] Calculating figures for the militia is more difficult, since complete rosters do not exist, but, among the officer class, at least 65 percent of new officer commissions for the year 1874 were granted to African-American and mixed-race residents (around 50% of Louisiana's population in 1870 was non-white).[156] By shifting away from Warmouth's more

150 Keith, *The Colfax Massacre*, 116–117. 151 NOP, April 19, 1874; September 23, 1873.

152 Keith, *The Colfax Massacre*, 155.

153 NOT, January 14, 1874; NOP, January 15, 1874; January 16, 1874. A special committee investigating the affair found that a major precipitating factor was a wage-fixing scheme on the part of local planters. See NOR, January 21, 1874; NOP, January 25, 1874.

154 NOR, July 12, 1874.

155 Rousey, *Policing the Southern City*, 137. The figures for 1874 were calculated by using city directories and manuscript census data.

156 The list of new commissions was taken from *Annual Report of 1873*, 34, and race identified through manuscript census data.

cross-racial patronage strategy, Kellogg paved the way for opponents to make white supremacy a mobilizing strategy.

Elites had, in fact, experimented with other political coalitions in their opposition to Republican rule. There had been several attempts in 1872 and 1873 at forging a reform coalition based on cross-racial opposition to the Kellogg regime, but these had run against the rising tide of an invigorated white supremacy, which made it difficult for many conservatives to make any concessions to Republicanism.[157] By 1874, even those elites willing to dabble in these unification movements, like Michael Musson and W. B. Schmidt, had become firmly united with the more radical anti-Kellogg forces.[158]

Thus, when the White League was initially founded in April of 1874 in St. Landry Parish, it was to effect a counter-mobilization of whites and transform the election of November into a referendum on racial supremacy. In a letter to the *Opelousas Journal*, attorney Edward T. Lewis laid out the logic, claiming that cross-racial attempts at unification had failed and that it was time to look for another answer to the problem of attaining power in Louisiana. "On the question of race against race, there can be no doubt as to where the white man stands and none as to where the black man stands. Neither Democracy, Liberalism nor Republicanism can bridge the chasm lying between the two. We visit each other under flags of truce, each being conscious that the real contest is for the permanent ascendancy of the one over the other." What was needed was a political party capable of righting the many wrongs Lewis claimed had been done to the "public virtue" even at the "remote risk of shedding blood." After all, "the sooner the negro finds out that the white people are determined, as a race, to rule the government of the State, the better it will be for him."[159] Reform of the state was inextricable from establishing racial supremacy over its representative institutions.

Following Lewis's letter, a mass meeting of concerned citizens was held in Opelousas on April 27, and the White Man's Party was formed.[160] The idea of the White League quickly spread throughout the parish of St. Landry in the following weeks. From the outset, the party – soon christened the White League – was not only merely concerned with offering a political platform. The allegedly criminal nature of African-American rule in Louisiana mandated a potentially coercive response, but mobilization that might have to take place outside state law. The *Caucasian* was strident in its claims: "There is no respect for laws enacted by a bogus and fraudulent Legislature. There is nothing but contempt for the officers who pretend to administer them. They are regarded as usurpers and imposters, and without any legal authority to enforce order or afford protection." The only answer was self-protection – precisely according to the classic notion of republican citizenship: "Self preservation is the first law of nature, and if the thieves, burglars and other offenders, should wake up some

157 Nystrom, *New Orleans after the Civil War*, 120–121, 151–154, 158–159.

158 NOP, September 13, 1874. 159 April 17, 1874. 160 OC, May 2, 1874.

morning and find themselves suspended to a lamp post by an indignant people, they may attribute their ill-luck to the absence of any law or legal officers under the so called Kellogg Government."[161]

In addition to these calls of self-protection, White League platforms also included provisions intended to coerce African-American laborers who refused to comply with conservative wishes. Part of this included ostracizing whites who socialized or did business with politically active African Americans, but such coercion also included pacts to refuse to hire workers who voted for Republicans.[162] In New Orleans, for instance, a group of prominent steamboat line agents signed a card promising to try white instead of African-American laborers, while several Shreveport merchants publicly agreed to try to convince their employees to vote for the White League.[163] By simultaneously promising to reward whites and compliant African-American workers and punish political opponents, such elites hoped to make race a means of securing economic control.[164]

The message of race, economic coercion, and political reform was the foundation upon which the White League, as a statewide political and military organization, was built. White League branches sprouted up in neighboring St. Martin, St. Mary, and Lafayette parishes, intended to offer an alternative to local Democratic central committees, which many White Leaguers felt would simply activate older partisan animosities and undercut their attempt at racial organization.[165]

The growth of the League was fairly limited to these sugar parishes until the end of June, when the Crescent City Democratic Club of New Orleans, firmly under the control of Frederick Ogden and made up of a number of McEnery militia refugees (as well as influential cotton factors and merchants, like Harrison Watts and John Payne), decided to adopt the White League platform and name, now calling themselves the Crescent City White League (CCWL).[166] The new organization was clear about its aims: "[W]e are now drifting into a conflict ... which the men of Louisiana alone must settle ... It is a conflict between virtue and depravity – between between enlightenment and thick ignorance, between civilization and barbarism ... Having solely in view the maintenance of our hereditary civilization and Christianity menaced by a

161 AC, May 30, 1874.

162 George Frisbie Hoar, William P. Frye, and W. H. Wheeler, eds., *The White League in Louisiana: Examined by the Light of White League Testimony: The Occasion of Its Organization, the True Character of the Organization – Its Object and the Design of Its Originators and Leaders* (1875), 19–21; HR261P3, 172, 190, 250, 285–286, 866–867; NOP, June 19, 1874.

163 HR261P3, 465, 791.

164 Pressuring merchants and manufacturers who continued to hire African-American workers was also part of the mobilization strategy of the summer of 1874. See *New Orleans Bulletin*, July 5, 1874.

165 H. Oscar Lestage, "The White League in Louisiana and Its Participation in Reconstruction Riots" (master's thesis, Louisiana State University, 1930), 36–37.

166 NOP, June 24, 1874; Nystrom, *New Orleans after the Civil War*, 163–168.

stupid Africanization, we appeal to the men of our race … to unite with us against that supreme danger."[167] The CCWL, which quickly assimilated thirty-nine of the most notorious street-fighting ward clubs within its organization, made the White League message visible at the center of state power and created a center of gravity for the statewide organization of the movement.[168] In the following weeks – in particular in the days surrounding July 4 – the League or affiliated race-based parties spread all across the state, to St. Mary, De Soto, Lafayette, Red River, Iberia, Grant, and Natchitoches Parishes.[169]

The lines between the party and military dimensions of the White League were ambiguous. On the one hand, the League was a "non-partisan" alternative to the Democratic Party with an aim to attracting former Whigs fed up with the Republican regime but unwilling to vote for Democrats directly.[170] As such, it was identical to other party organizations: it was based at the parish level, with the aim of holding a common convention of delegates who would concur on a shared platform and would coordinate the party's activities at the state-level. Its plans initially went afoul of the Democrats, many of whom opposed the realignment of voting around race.[171] It was only after the Democratic Central Committee in New Orleans agreed to hold a convention at Baton Rouge (rather than in New Orleans, which would have advantaged the traditional party infrastructure) that the two groups made their peace. The outcome of this convention was a platform for a party calling itself the People's Party; this name was quite contested, particularly by inveterate White Leaguers, though most allies agreed that "People" clearly meant "white people."[172]

On the other hand, when the CCWL became associated with the movement, the White League took on a definite military cast. Not only did those entities that joined the White League platform in New Orleans include a number of former militia companies, but their incorporation into the White League reflected a military hierarchy. The group, founded on July 1, 1874, and composed, ultimately, of over 2,000 members, was organized along military lines and was, as Ogden acknowledged, for the purposes of self-protection against "a military brigade of police, backed by a negro militia, of which our Citizens were

167 NOP, July 2, 1874.

168 ibid. Many of the leaders of these clubs, like Henry Renshaw and Emile O'Brien, had ties to both New Orleans' social elite and the radical ex-Confederate movements of 1868 and 1872.

169 Lestage, "The White League in Louisiana and Its Participation in Reconstruction Riots," 37–38.

170 *New Orleans Bulletin*, August 21, 1874.

171 Lestage, "The White League in Louisiana and Its Participation in Reconstruction Riots," 37–42. Ironically, in St. Landry Parish, the place of its birth, the White League ran into strong resistance from local Democrats. See OC, August 15, 1874.

172 NOP, August 26, 1874. R. H. Marr, defender of the Colfax prisoners, was named president of the convention, which a number of notable New Orleans residents attended. See NOP, August 24, 1874; August 25, 1874.

in terror all the time."[173] Over the summer of 1874, the CCWL began importing rifles from New York, Pittsburgh, and Baltimore to arm its companies, while local committees organized drilling and musters.[174] In the parishes outside New Orleans, the White League branches never officially integrated themselves with Ogden's organization, but many (though not all) adopted an explicit willingness to link their political struggle to coercion.[175] Indeed, Ogden himself claimed that although "there are organizations 'of the League' in parishes throughout the state over which I have no control ... if I was to call upon them for assistance it would be rendered to me."[176]

The result of this ambiguous fusion of party and militia was that the League could simultaneously claim to merely be engaged in straightforward electoral politics while also engaging in a tacit policy of intimidation in the name of self-protection.[177] "While we counsel no man to join an organization having violence for its avowed and exclusive object," claimed the *Picayune*, "we nevertheless believe he should join none which proposes, in the event of an unavoidable conflict, to be overridden and suppressed."[178]

The White League drew on the republican conception most Americans possessed about the appropriateness of participation in self-defense while also claiming that their actions were not illegal (since the legal nature of the regime was itself in question). At the same time, they could (and did) plausibly claim that much of their activity was solely political in nature – indeed, even strident White Leaguers advocated an official policy of non-violence and non-intimidation, casting aside insinuations that they were simply a rebirth of the Ku Klux Klan.[179] Rather than a secret society, they openly adopted a public party platform, publishing the names of convention attendees in allied press outlets and heralding the establishment and expansion of party clubs.[180] Loosely coordinated through statewide conventions, the party was also able to exercise a great deal of local autonomy in regard to military and political mobilization.

173 Hoar, Frye, and Wheeler, *The White League in Louisiana*, 7; NOP, January 1, 1875; Landry, *The Battle of Liberty Place*, 60. Ogden noted that most of the command was vested in the company leader or Captain.

174 ibid., 65.

175 St. Martin Parish's White League, for instance, began procuring weapons and drilling in July and August of 1874. See ibid., 57.

176 Hoar, Frye, and Wheeler, *The White League in Louisiana*, 7.

177 For example, the *Caucasian* (by this time somewhat distancing itself from the more militaristic cast of the CCWL) nevertheless claimed that the nature of Republican leadership was itself threatening: "What can we do, what resource is left to us but to organize the white people upon the same issue which has so successfully united the negroes to a man? Not to wage any war upon him, but to protect ourselves against the war that he is waging upon us." AC, August 1, 1874.

178 July 3, 1874.

179 AC, August 1, 1874; September 26, 1874; OC, September 5, 1874

180 OC, August 22, 1874; September 5, 1874; *Lafayette Advertiser*, August 29, 1874.

Nevertheless, the effect of having the CCWL join the movement meant that, throughout the summer and early fall of 1874, the White League increasingly relied on its militia function to intimidate opponents. On July 11, for example, while a group of African Americans attempted to organize a Republican party committee in Claiborne Parish in the northern part of the state, rumors that a group of them were armed and ready to attack spread throughout the parish. This, in turn, led to a counter-reaction on the part of White League members, who quickly organized a *posse* and moved *en masse* to confront the Republican meeting. In turn, the Republicans themselves began "beating a drum" and organizing themselves in a military-seeming formation; the result was an armed standoff, which was only resolved when one of white allies of the Republicans, William Maxey, was able to get the black members to depart.[181] The pattern of attending Republican meetings armed in order to "protect" themselves from potential disorder continued through the summer; two Republicans were killed by some drunk White Leaguers following another organizing meeting later that month in Grant Parish, while accounts of armed *posses* attending or observing Republican gatherings became common.[182]

Some White Leaguers began using threats of disorder to seize local political power. The events near Coushatta in Red River Parish – which, like Grant Parish, was formed to help shore up Republican voting power along racial lines – were exemplary. A fatal confrontation between a small mob and a couple of black men in late August led White League militia units from surrounding parishes to mobilize and invade the parish in the name of public order, killing several more African Americans and arresting six local white Republican officeholders, whom they planned to force to abdicate. However, as they were being escorted out of Red River Parish, a group of rangers from nearby Shreveport took the men, held them captive and ultimately killed them. The event was greeted by the White League press as unfortunate but understandable in a context where the legitimacy of Kellogg allies holding office was in dispute; Republicans, though shocked and outraged, were equally disheartened that the Grant administration seemed less and less inclined to intervene directly in parish affairs.[183]

More important, however, were events transpiring in New Orleans, which revealed the growing coercive strength of the White League. By importing arms, continuing to drill as a militia, and linking these efforts explicitly to the fall elections, over July and August CCWL had become the target of much anxiety on the part of Governor Kellogg.[184] As a result, he directed the Metropolitan Police to be on the lookout for any activity that could pose an

181 HR261P3: 230–231. 182 ibid., 788.

183 NOP, August 30, 1874, September 3, 1874, September 8, 1874; HR261P3, 879–888, 903–906; Tunnell, *Crucible of Reconstruction*, 197–202.

184 Darrah A. S. Vaught, "The Origins and Activities of the White League in New Orleans (Reminiscences of a Participant in the Movement)," ed. Walter Prichard, *Louisiana Historical Quarterly* 23 (1940): 528–529.

explicit threat to the public order. In early September the police began seizing arms intended for the White League companies, an act the CCWL interpreted as a direct affront to not only their immediate aims, but also their republican rights to self-protection.[185] Because the Democratic press in the city had been spreading rumors of an armed Black League forming in New Orleans, the CCWL claimed that they were being disarmed in order to permit black coercion and intimidation.[186]

The issue came to a head on September 12, when a shipment of arms were seized from a steamship from New York called the *Mississippi*; this proved to be the last straw for the White League.[187] McEnery's interim governor (the loser in the Battle of the Cabildo had not formally abandoned his executive branch) called for a mass meeting of CCWL members to be held on September 14 and drew up a battle plan to retake the arms and demand Kellogg's removal. After meeting, the CCWL and its affiliates were met by a group of the Metropolitan Police under James Longstreet in downtown New Orleans; the result of the clash (which led to approximately twenty-seven deaths and over one hundred injuries) was one of the most unusual political events in American history; the Metropolitans were routed and Kellogg was forced to surrender his governorship to McEnery's stand-in, D. B. Penn, in what amounted to a *coup d'etat*.[188]

The party-militia hybrid structure of the League allowed branches across the region to try to shore up the gains made in New Orleans. White League groups in Richland, Franklin, East Baton Rouge, Livingston, Iberia, and St. Mary parishes mobilized their own local militia forces to seize the offices of Kellogg allies in the three days following what became known as the Battle of Liberty Place.[189] Eventually, Grant's reticence to act ended and he sent troops to New Orleans to demand the disbanding of the CCWL and the McEnery regime, but in the countryside, many Kellogg allies simply fled for their safety and left local government in the hands of an increasingly aggressive White League party.

Moreover, the White League, particularly in New Orleans, were able to shepherd what was increasingly looking like Northern exhaustion with reconstructing the South. Once again, in November, the returns from Louisiana were highly contested, as the returning board removed a large number of Democratic votes from the final tally. And once again, a group of enraged conservatives attempted to storm the state assembly in January of 1875, only to be repulsed by the US military.[190] But the CCWL did not disband and became a major focal point for reorienting the Democratic party in the coming years. Meanwhile, and

[185] Landry, *The Battle of Liberty Place*, 77–78.

[186] HR261P3, 668; 1007; NOP, July 1, 1874; ibid., 69–76. [187] HR261P3, 666, 677.

[188] NOP, September 15, 1874; Landry, *The Battle of Liberty Place*, 96–132; Hogue, *Uncivil War*, 131–138.

[189] HR261P3, 831–833; Landry, *The Battle of Liberty Place*, 177.

[190] NOP, January 6, 1875; January 7, 1875; Tunnell, *Crucible of Reconstruction*, 204; Hogue, *Uncivil War*, 148–154.

crucially, the Grant Parish administration grew disinterested in continuing to intervene in Louisiana to protect a highly polarized and ineffective Republican party. By 1876, when Rutherford B. Hayes began the withdrawal of military forces from the South, Louisiana had a robust opposition ready to take over the reins of state authority based, in part, on the unique political-military structure of the White League.

MOBILIZING FOR BATTLE IN NEW ORLEANS

Many whites in the state (and sympathetic observers elsewhere) viewed the Battle of Liberty Place as a product of the contested legitimacy of the Kellogg regime; like most vigilantism it involved competing claims to what counted as the public. But the ultimate choice to mobilize around the issue of race – to make, in other words, the public particularist – was also an elite response to a change in rules for political access. Cotton brokers, bankers, merchants and planters all recognized the danger of African-American suffrage to securing policies amenable to their interests; the threatened strike at Terrebonne in 1874 and the massive support for the Republican party among African Americans even at risk to their own lives and limbs indicated that reasserting both economic and political control was crucial.[191] Moreover, in New Orleans, the traditional commercial class was under assault from newcomers from the North, who aggressively moved into financial and commercial services in the aftermath of the war.[192]

To counter the changes in rules and the threat from newcomer competitors elites in New Orleans – like those elsewhere – drew upon their existing social and economic relations. But to do so also meant somehow using the traditional representative militia to depose the usurper force set up by Warmouth and Kellogg, "a corps of regularly enlisted, paid, armed and equipped and permanently organized body of men."[193] The White League was, in essence, the mobilization of elite networks into an armed force.

On September 13, a prominent group of merchants and bankers called for New Orleans businesses to close shop the next day and for residents to meet at the Clay Statue on Canal St. at 11 o'clock to "declare that you are, of right ought to be, and mean to be free."[194] This meeting – which would precipitate the battle later that day – was the clearest sign yet that a large number of the city's elite had decided that armed action was the only way forward.

The fifty-three firm representatives and individual business owners who signed the document included a number of inveterate opponents to Reconstruction government (such as John Payne and Harrison Watts), as well as a

[191] Rodrigue, *Reconstruction in the Cane Fields*, 160–165.

[192] Marler, *The Merchants' Capital*, 190–192. Marler estimates that over half of the commodities firms active in 1866 didn't exist before the war, most of which were founded by Northerners.

[193] NOP, April 2, 1873. [194] NOP, September 13, 1874.

small group of the most eminent financial and commercial elites in the city, some of whom (like Michel Musson and William B. Schmidt) had dabbled in the more moderate politics of unification. The majority were commercial merchants, cotton factors or wholesale grocers and retailers (66%).[195] Most were highly influential and well-connected in New Orleans society.

Several signees also had experience with the militia. Emile J. O'Brien and W. J. Behan had served in the Washington Artillery, with Behan going on to command the First Regiment Field Artillery under Warmouth.[196] Still others, including E. B. Briggs and John Payne had also been granted commissions in Warmouth's militia.[197] In addition, some, like William A. Bell and Michel Musson, were close associates of Frederick Ogden (who also claimed to have been a militia colonel under Warmouth).[198] In supporting the efforts of the CCWL, these civic elites were also drawing on first-hand experience with the republican notion of securing a public interest via private participation.

Elites not only supported the White League through public statements (and, crucially, financial contributions), they also joined it.[199] In his comprehensive work on the Battle of Liberty Place, Stuart Landry identified 492 members of the CCWL (including General Ogden), as well as another 742 members of other units participating in the events of September 14. Using 1874 New Orleans city directory, I was able to identify economic and residential information for 56% of the CCWL roster.[200]

A majority of the CCWL were professionals and businessmen (Table 11 lists the top fifteen occupations for members of the sample). Over 35 percent were clerks, while another 17 percent either owned their own firms or were independent professionals like doctors and lawyers. Moreover, as Table 12 demonstrates, CCWL members usually came from the wealthiest sections of New Orleans' society; they truly were, in the words of James Buckner, a commission merchant and member of the League: "the first young men of the city, merchants, doctors, lawyers – men of standing."[201]

CCWL members could be found throughout elite social and economic associations. Thomas S. Barton (one of W. J. Behan's business associates), served on the board of directors for a number of the city's largest banks and insurance

195 Appendix B (available at www.jonathanobert.com) contains a full list of these signees.

196 *Annual Report of 1872*, 17.

197 *Annual Report of the Adjutant General of the State of Louisiana for the Year Ending December 31, 1870*, 8, 13.

198 Nystrom, *New Orleans after the Civil War*, 150; NOP, January 1, 1875. I have been unable to verify Ogden's claim in the adjutant general reports.

199 HR261P3, 672.

200 *Soards' New Orleans City Directory for 1874* (New Orleans: L. Soards & Co., 1874).

201 HR261P3, 669. In her analysis of the White League mobilization, Jennifer Lawrence found that the non-CCWL participants in the Battle of Liberty Place were slightly more likely to be laborers than those in the CCWL, though this difference is not significant at the 0.05 level. Jennifer Lawrence, "The Crescent City White League, 1874" (B.A., Tulane University, 1992), Table 2.

TABLE 11. *Occupations of CCWL members**

Occupation	Number
Clerk	97
Firm owner	27
Bookkeeper	23
Laborer	13
Finisher	12
Broker	7
Collector	7
Salesman	6
Doctor	6
Machinist	5
Lawyer	5
Accountant	4
Carpenter	4
Warehouseman	3
Foreman	3

Only 15 most common occupations listed.
*Data from city directories and Landry (1955).

TABLE 12. *Class background of CCWL members**

Occupational prestige	Number	Percentage (%)
High	199	74
Medium	42	16
Low	25	9
Unknown	4	1

*Prestige derived from Hershberg and Dockhorn (1976).

companies and was an active member of the Pickwick Club. Samuel Logan, a prominent physician and member of the Boston Club and the Pickwick, also served on several insurance company boards and was a founding member of the Cotton Exchange, one of the most important commercial associations in the city. Both Barton and Logan, along with CCWL enlistee Hugh Rainey were involved in a long-simmering plan to build a railroad from New Orleans through central Texas.[202] Rainey (another Pickwick member), in turn, served on several bank and insurance boards himself, including one with Logan. In total, at least forty-eight past and future members of the Pickwick and thirteen members of the Boston joined the CCWL.[203]

202 NOT, October 21, 1874.

203 Landry, *History of the Boston Club*, 116; Miceli, *The Pickwick Club of New Orleans*, Appendix J.

TABLE 13. *CCWL employees across different industries**

Industry type	Number of CCWL employees	Percentage (%)
Commercial	64	30.6
Retail/wholesale	47	22.5
Heavy manufacturing	27	12.9
Agricultural services	20	9.6
Craft manufacturing	11	5.3
Legal services	8	3.8
Financial services	8	3.8
Transportation	6	2.9
Medical services	6	2.9
Government	3	1.4
Other services	2	1.0
Real estate	2	1.0
Hospitality	2	1.0
Utilities	1	0.5
Education	1	0.5
Construction	1	0.5

*Data from city directories.

The most prestigious voluntary militia units were also well-represented in the White League. According to James Hogue, eighteen of the officers of the League had belonged to the Washington Artillery, including Behan, E. I. Kurscheedt, and James Walton; indeed, at least 10% of Washington Artillery veterans from the Civil War participated, in some way, in the mobilization of September 14.[204] Moreover, as Hogue goes on to note, the fact that at least 88% of the officer corps in the White League militia had served in Louisiana-based units in the CSA is striking, given the amount of physical mobility seen in the South after the war.[205] The League, it is clear, was rooted in the political and social lives of the most stable and prominent families in the city.

Elite influence on the CCWL went beyond direct participation and public sponsorship. When we look at the economic affiliations of CCWL members, it becomes clear that many elites also worked behind the scenes, using their employees and social and political connections to aid the League's vigilante efforts.

I was able to identify employer information for about 75 percent of my sample of CCWL members (Table 13).[206] The majority of the employees worked in two types of industries – commercial operations (like cotton brokerages,

204 Hogue, *Uncivil War*, 130–131, Table 2.3. 205 ibid., 199.

206 These include only those employees working for an identifiable firm, those who are self-employed and those who are firm owners.

commission merchant firms, and factor houses) and retail (including hardware supply, wholesale grocery, and wine and liquor distribution) – although many others were involved in manufacturing and various professional services.[207]

The firms employing CCWL members, however, were also run by the crème of local society. I was able to identify 271 individuals who owned or operated firms for which CCWL members worked. This esteemed group included board members for many of the major financial and social institutions in the city; 75 percent of New Orleans' largest banks and 73 percent of the most important insurance companies had at least one employer of a CCWL member on its board of directors.[208] Almost 20 percent (twenty-three) of the 118 founders of the New Orleans Cotton Exchange ran firms employing the brokers clerks, bookkeepers, accountants, and salesmen populating the CCWL, including many of the most prominent, like John Phelps (president of the exchange in 1874).[209] Others whose employees joined the CCWL included New Orleans' financial elite, like William B. Schmidt, a wealthy wholesale grocer and financier, and Albert Baldwin, a well-known merchant and wholesaler.

Moreover, these elites were themselves highly interconnected. Using newspapers and other primary sources to identify affiliation data, I created a network dataset including all of the 271 employers of CCWL members (this dataset is described in Appendix B). Over 40 percent of these employers were capable of reaching each other through shared membership in clubs, executive boards, and commercial associations, a high rate considering the fact that New Orleans was the ninth largest city in the nation at the time.[210] In addition, slightly over one-fourth (seventy-two) of these employers had themselves participated directly in anti-Kellogg demonstrations or meetings. This was a mobilized, politically engaged, and cohesive group of elites, many of whom formed the backbone of resistance to Reconstruction government.

Indeed, many employers seem to have approved of the participation of their employees in the violence of September 14. In the days following the battle, a group of eminent merchants, bankers, and other notables wrote a telegram to President Grant requesting that he acknowledge the McEnery regime and claiming that with the battle "a load of degradation and oppression lifted from our people, and we are now hopeful and encouraged for the future."[211]

[207] With some deviations, Lawrence's analysis suggests that this basic breakdown in industrial sector holds for the non-CCWL in New Orleans as well. Lawrence, "The Crescent City White League, 1874," Table 2, Figure 2, Figure 4, 6–12.

[208] I. Smith Homans, ed., *The Banker's Almanac* (New York: Banker's Magazine & Statistical Register, 1874), 45 lists the largest banks by capitalization.

[209] NOP, February 21, 1871.

[210] This basic connectedness measure is defined in Stephen P. Borgatti, Martin G. Everett, and Jeffrey C. Johnson, *Analyzing Social Networks* (Los Angeles: SAGE, 2013), 154: $\frac{\sum_{i \neq j} r_{ij}}{n(n-1)}$, where n is the total number of nodes in a network and $a_{ij} = 1$ when i and j are tied in adjacency matrix A.

[211] NOP, September 16, 1874.

Approximately 30 percent of the named petitioners directly employed participants in the battle.

Other employers actually mobilized a significant number of their workforce to participate directly. For instance, at least twenty workers at the Leeds' Foundry, one of New Orleans' most important manufacturing centers and the provisioner for some of the artillery used in the conflict, participated in the battle. All these employees served in the same unit (Section D) and were largely organized after the hierarchy within the firm (firm superintendent Archibald Mitchell was also the unit's captain). Charles Leeds, the firm's owner, also participated in the battle and seems to have used the mobilization as a pathway to political power; he was elected the mayor of New Orleans several months later.[212] Other, smaller, firms, like Richardson & May and Folger & Co. (both commission merchant houses), contributed multiple employees to the CCWL.

Even though the CCWL publicized its membership, its organizational basis were the more closed-off secret societies and neighborhood ward clubs like the Southern Cross Association Number 9 (two of whose members, N. T. N. Robinson and Charles Dirmeyer, had employees who joined the CCWL).[213] The CCWL was organized as a militia body, with eight different companies and eight different sections. While firm connections were vital for some units in the CCWL – particularly Sections A and D, in which 10 percent and 20 percent respectively of the unit membership included coworkers – the key determining factor in participating was spatial proximity.[214] Those serving within a particular unit in the CCWL lived, on average, less than a mile away from another.[215] New Orleans wasn't an enormous city, by any stretch of the imagination, but the furthest any two members of the CCWL in the sample lived from one another was a comparatively minuscule 4.8 miles.

This type of spatial organization was markedly different from that of the police, who were responsible for patrolling the entire city and often worked with strangers rather than co-residents. Indeed, only about 54 percent of police officers listed in the 1874 city directory actually lived in the precincts they policed. Moreover, unsurprisingly, police tended to live much further apart from one another (nearly two miles on average) than members of the CCWL.[216] Where the CCWL was intimate, locally rooted, and embedded in overlapping economic, social, and political ties, the police force against whom they fought were essentially employees, some of whom shared kinship or neighborhood connections – but most of whom did not.

212 NOP, November 4, 1874.

213 Vaught, "The Origins and Activities of the White League in New Orleans (Reminiscences of a Participant in the Movement)."

214 The residential data is described in Appendix B (available at www.jonathanobert.com).

215 Using great-circle distance (specifically, the Haversine formula), those serving with the same unit lived, on average, 4,583 feet (or 1,397 meters) away from each other, while those not serving in the same unit lived an additional 699 feet (or 213 meters) apart.

216 9,967 feet, or 3,038 meters.

TABLE 14. *Class background of Metropolitan Police (1874)**

Occupational prestige	Number	Percentage (%)
Low	26	45
Medium	17	29
High	13	22
Unkown	2	3

*Data from manuscript census (1870) and city directory (1874).
Prestige derived from Hershberg and Dockhorn (1976).

The major differences between the police and the CCWL, of course, had to do with class and race. The Metropolitan Police – like most police forces of the time – were made up primarily of those from working class backgrounds.[217] Table 14 presents information about prior occupational prestige and class background for the 1874 force, focusing on those who held other occupations in the 1870 census. Seventy-five percent of the force or so held working-class or lower-middle-class occupations, while, of those holding high status jobs in 1870, approximately 38 percent were already public servants, working as clerks in government posts, Custom House officers, and so forth. Like Warmouth, Kellogg had used the police force as a form of patronage for republican supporters, most of whom were not native Louisianans; indeed, 79 percent of the white officers in the 1870 census were newcomers either from northern states or from overseas.[218]

More important, however, were the Metropolitan Police's black officers. As noted, African Americans and mixed-race Creoles – who possessed full arrest powers over white residents in the city – made up approximately 28 percent of the 1874 police force. Many of these officers, according to Dennis Rousey, were themselves among the elite within the black community in New Orleans; most held higher than average levels of property and a surprisingly large number participated in interracial marriages. But even though New Orleans' police was representative of its demographics – and, indeed, other Southern cities under Reconstruction governments had much higher percentages of African-American officers – their presence was obviously deeply contested.[219]

The police and the CCWL, in other words, represented two ways in which the militia had been repurposed in an era of changing political rules. The CCWL was an elite unit, deeply rooted in local social tradition and grounded in the antebellum logic of representative authority. Its members and sponsors, oriented toward controlling labor, limiting taxes, and relinking their considerable social and economic power to control over governance, tried to redefine what counted as a public in racial terms. The seeming victory of the League in the Battle of Liberty Place and its aftermath seemingly signified the

[217] Rousey, *Policing the Southern City*, 140–141. [218] ibid., 145. [219] ibid., 137–144.

TABLE 15. *Race and politics in White League parishes (1874)**

White League presence	Avg. % black	Avg. % democratic	% Parishes w/intimidation
Yes	52%	50%	64%
No	56%	36%	7%

*Data described in Appendix B (available at www.jonathanobert.com).

return of a "citizen soldiery" in which who counted as citizens would be deeply circumscribed.

The Metropolitan Police, on the other hand, were working class, multi-racial, and were part of an attempt by Warmouth and Kellogg to centralize political power within bureaucratic institutions.[220] When the police gained the capacity to serve as militia, this introduced the possibility of a semi-professionalized state guard to the coercive organization of Louisiana. At the same time, the militia and the police under Kellogg became a flash point for racial antagonism, precisely because of the crisis in what the public meant. In New Orleans, this took the form of the Battle of Liberty Place, but because the militia, ultimately, was a statewide institution organized on a local basis, parishes throughout the state were involved in the mobilization as well.

PATTERNS OF WHITE LEAGUE MOBILIZATION ACROSS THE STATE

At the statewide level, the White League resembled, in many ways, the antebellum Louisiana militia – parishes organized local, voluntary branches that were loosely incorporated into a larger organizational structure. As both the Metropolitan Police and Kellogg's more centralized militia became active in rural parishes and smaller towns, they were frequently met with counter-organization on the part of the White Leagues.

Those parishes most likely to have local White League branches were also those in which the changes in political rules were the most consequential. In Appendix B (available at www.jonathanobert.com), I present regression results demonstrating that in those parishes in which the population was most divided between African-American and white residents – where, in other words, uncertainty about electoral outcomes was most pronounced and traditional racial hierarchies were most unsettled – both White League mobilization and intimidation were more likely. Table 15, for instance, captures this logic in a snapshot – the more black and less Democratic, the less common the White League; these parishes, in turn, also witnessed less intimidation in the election of 1874.

220 Lawrence Powell, "Centralization and Its Discontents in Reconstruction Louisiana," *Studies in American Political Development* 20, no. 02 (2006): 105–131.

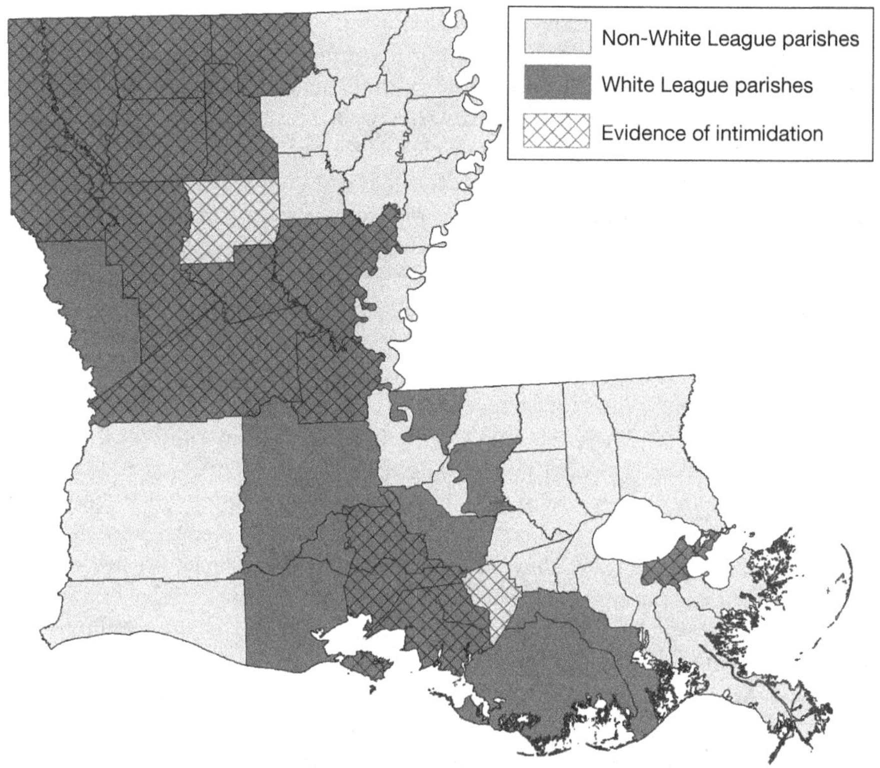

FIGURE 11. White League presence and political intimidation (1874)
Map shows 1870 parish boundaries.

As evident in the map in Figure 11, White League mobilization formed a band down the middle of the state made up of the Sugar Bowl region in the south, prairie and bluff land in the center of the state, and the remote Red River delta in the northwest, areas Gilles Vandal has argued were the most violent places in Louisiana in general during the post–Civil War era.[221] In these parishes, he contends, demographic divisions and labor problems made interracial interaction particularly troubled.[222]

The White League diffused into these areas for reasons similar to those in New Orleans: elites, opposed to Kellogg and confronting the consequences of new Reconstruction rules, organized their own networks into local militia to try to coerce African-American voters and regain political power. In the sugar region, for instance, several factors had made the challenge of Reconstruction

[221] Gilles Vandal, *Rethinking Southern Violence: Homicides in Post-Civil War Louisiana* (Columbus: Ohio State University Press, 2000), 48.
[222] ibid., 58–64.

particularly acute; unlike many cotton plantations, sugar plantations were often based on contract work rather than sharecropping, and the workers tended to be organized into larger gangs rather than being left to work their own small plots of land. This both allowed African-American workers on sugar cane plantations to mobilize more easily and made employers more susceptible to their demands when they did so.[223] Although, usually for reasons of economic necessity rather than ideology, some planters opposed the more extreme forms of White League violence, the group nevertheless successfully organized branches in parishes like Lafourche, Terrebonne, Iberia, and St. Mary.[224]

Although all of these parishes had suffered economically since the end of the war and the panic of 1873, Iberia had been hit particularly hard by its tax burden while experiencing a series of highly contested elections with unclear results.[225] A small group of white residents began organizing League units in July and August of 1874; a mass meeting of over 600 voters was held on July 25 to organize the local group. The leaders of this group and a central committee assembled several weeks later, including a number of prominent farmers, doctors, and merchants.[226] Not only were these men prominent, they were also wealthy: in 1870, they owned almost the three times the property as other residents of the sugar parishes on average.[227]

Indeed, just as in New Orleans, White League members in the rural parishes also reflected the militia tradition. For instance, one of the officers commissioned in McEnery's "rump" militia was Alcibiades DeBlanc, founder of the KWC and a prominent and wealthy attorney.[228] In early 1873, refusing to acknowledge Kellogg's election, DeBlanc organized a company to prevent the governor's appointees from being seated in St. Martin, as well as to resist attempts to collect state taxes. In response, Kellogg sent out a unit of Metropolitan Police to the parish, provoking a tense confrontation that ended with the arrest of DeBlanc and Alexandre DeClouet, one of the largest sugar planters in the region (and a former colonel of the 26th Louisiana Regiment), by a US deptuy marshal.[229]

The event made the men martyrs; they were greeted with wild applause and treated like celebrities when they were brought to New Orleans for their trial.[230] It also convinced them that using the infrastructure of local party clubs

223 Rebecca J. Scott, "'Stubborn and Disposed to Stand their Ground': Black Militia, Sugar Workers and the Dynamics of Collective Action in the Louisiana Sugar Bowl, 1863–1887," *Slavery and Abolition* 20, no. 1 (1999): 103–126; Rodrigue, *Reconstruction in the Cane Fields*, 176–177.

224 ibid., 166–168.

225 HR261P3, 613.

226 *Louisiana Sugar Bowl*, July 29, 1874; HR261P3, 614.

227 White men over the age of twenty-one in the sugar parishes held, on average around $1,370 dollars in real estate and personal property. The officers of the Iberia White League were worth over $4,200 that same year. These figures were derived from the manuscript census for 1870 and an IPUMS sample for the sugar parishes.

228 NOP, May 7, 1873. 229 NOR, May 10, 1873; May 15, 1873; NOP, May 16, 1873.

230 OC, May 31, 1873.

and militia units was critical. Such a combination, DeClouet argued, would mean that "the ball will roll from Parish to Parish. By organizing we will count our number and know our strength, and with energy and unity of action, with the manly determination to triumph, God in his mercy and justice, will permit us to save the honor of the state."[231]

When White League units began to organize in sugar parishes in late June and early July of 1874, DeClouet and DeBlanc made their way through southern Louisiana parishes giving speeches to rouse the faithful and lending a military cast to the proceedings.[232] Indeed, the two former Confederates, in addition to Edward T. Lewis (the lawyer and formulator of the original White League concept) and C. H. Mouton (a well-known judge), were catalysts for White League mobilization across Louisiana parishes in the first months of the group's existence (see Table 16).

As tensions ratcheted up over the summer, DeBlanc, in particular, began turning to action rather than rhetoric. In September, he organized a mass occupation of St. Martinsville and used a detachment of White Leaguers to force a local African-American minister to flee for his life.[233] His hope, apparently, was that by putting the local league on a "war footing" he could induce a conflict that would mobilize white men throughout the surrounding parishes and decisively defeat Kellogg's forces.[234] Though he failed in his short-term goals of provoking a confrontation, his strategy was intended to coordinate rural White League militia activity with that in New Orleans.

The Iberia White League, too, was willing to turn to violence. By the time of the election, the Iberia branch had grown to between 600 and 800 members, and during the election in 1874 League members could be seen riding through the parish attempting to intimidate African-American Republican voters.[235]. Other residents – suspected by republicans to be White Leaguers – organized a vigilance committee to pressure recalcitrant political foes to leave the parish.[236] And after the events of September 14 in New Orleans, the Iberia White League apparently was able to force remaining Republican officials out of office.[237]

Occasionally, Leagues from different parishes worked together; a large contingent from St. Martin's parish, for instance, came to New Iberia and threatened to lynch US Commissioner E. H. Riddell, who had testified before a congressional committee in late 1874.[238] And White Leaguers from St. Mary's worked with one of the local committees to try to lynch a local preacher "supposed to be objectionable to them."[239]

[231] "Address to the White Citizens of St. Martin," No Date, Box 1, Alexandre E. DeClouet Papers, Louisiana and Lower Mississippi Valley Collections, Hill Memorial Library, Louisiana State University; OC, June 20, 1874.

[232] *Lafayette Advertiser*, July 4, 1874; HR261P3, 875–887 [233] HR261P3, 779, 792

[234] ibid., 778. [235] ibid., 166–167, 334–335, 786–787 [236] ibid., 774.

[237] ibid., 831. [238] ibid., 334–335, 337. [239] ibid., 774.

TABLE 16. *White League meetings and speakers (April–July 1874)**

Parish	Town	Date	Key Speakers
St. Landry	Opelousas	4/27/1874	E. T. Lewis
St. Landry	Opelousas	6/13/1874	E. T. Lewis; A. DeBlanc
St. Martin	Beaux Bridge	6/14/1874	C. H. Mouton; A. DeClouet
St. Mary	Centerville	6/26/1874	
Natchitoches	Natchitoches	6/27/1874	
Lafayette	Vermillionville	6/28/1874	E. T. Lewis; A. DeBlanc; A. DeClouet
De Soto	Mansfield	6/30/1874	
Rapides	Pine Woods	7/4/1874	
St. Landry	Opelousas	7/4/1874	C. H. Mouton; E. T. Lewis
Red River	Coushatta	7/4/1874	
Grant	Colfax	7/25/1874	
Iberia	New Iberia	7/25/1874	R. H. Marr; A. DeBlanc; D. Caffery; C. H. Mouton
Natchitoches	Natchitoches	7/27/1874	D. Pierson; W. H. Jack; W. M. Levy; M. J. Cunningham

*Data from Opelousas Courier, Alexandria Caucasian, and HR261P3.

Sugar parishes were not the only locales in which local elites turned to the White League in an attempt to shore up their power. In Lincoln parish, far in the northern Red River delta, a popular local attorney and ex-Confederate colonel, E. M. Graham spearheaded the adoption of the White League.[240] And in nearby Red River Parish site of the Coashatta massacre, those behind the adoption of the White League framework were prominent planters and merchants like Thomas Abney and Ben Marston.[241] Just like other branches of the White League, these parish associations adopted a formal party platform while also creating ward clubs that could be used to mobilize coercion if need be.[242]

The party-militia hybrid structure of the White League provided it with a means both to contest elections openly and to engage in some of the intimidation techniques – otherwise known as bulldozing – that groups like the Knights of the White Camelia had pioneered years before. In those parishes confronting unsettled conditions, in which changes in political rules had accentuated the problem of social ambiguity, elites found precisely these kinds of organizations helpful. In other areas of Louisiana – with, for instance, very small or very large numbers of African Americans – the White League was not attractive. In these places, elite control would either require a full-scale system of racial terror, backed by the state (as in the cotton-growing Mississippi delta, where African Americans constituted a majority of the populace) or would take the form of class-based attempts to police banditry (as in the southwestern and Florida parishes).

At the same time, the White League was – like the Metropolitan Police and the Kellogg militia – based on antebellum traditions linking public service to private effort. While those agencies represented a form of state power that was independent of the people, however, the White League tried to reintroduce popular participation in contexts where the notion of the people was no longer secured by the representative authority of a relatively small, select group of white men.

While, initially, private vigilantism was opposed to the Republican state militia and police forces, after the collapse of Reconstruction in 1876, these traditions became uneasy partners. Conservative Democrats who earlier had castigated the police and militia reforms of the Reconstruction years did not abandon those reforms in *toto* after taking the reins of power. Instead, while a system of vigilantism became an integral feature of local social control in many Louisiana parishes, so too did the new, reformulated state militia.

240 David Rabb Cargill, "Reconstruction and the White League Movement in Lincoln Parish, Louisiana" (M.A., Louisiana Tech University, 1993), 101–106.

241 Ted Tunnell, *Edge of the Sword: The Ordeal of Carpetbagger Marshall H. Twitchell in the Civil War and Reconstruction* (Baton Rouge: Louisiana State University Press, 2001), 159, 190.

242 Cargill, "Reconstruction and the White League Movement in Lincoln Parish, Louisiana," 94–95, 108–109, 113–114, 119.

REDEMPTION AND BEYOND: VIGILANTISM, THE MILITIA, AND STATE REFORM

In the election of 1876, Republican rule in Louisiana came to an end, as did the political energy behind Reconstruction at the national level; although the results of the state election were, as in the past, legally contested, the Republican claimant, Stephen Packard, lost backing in Washington as President Hayes's administration began rolling back Reconstruction policy.[243] With that retrenchment came some important revisions in organized coercion in the state, including the reorganization of the Metropolitan Police and the state militia, and the withdrawal of US troops from most of Louisiana.[244]

The White League played a crucial role in the new order. It provided the infrastructure for Francis T. Nicholls, the Democratic candidate for governor in 1876, to occupy crucial state institutions with a minimum of disruption despite the fact that the returning board had declared his opponent, Stephen Packard, winner.[245] This, in turn, created a *fait accompli* rendering any revisions on behalf of Republicans costly to the federal government. Frederick Ogden and White League members physically took over police precinct stations and court buildings in a surprise maneuver on the 8th and 9th of January in 1877, while Nicholls appointed a new Metropolitan Police board of commissioners and supreme court (including as a member the ubiquitous Alcibiades DeBlanc).[246] As Nicholls consolidated his rule by building up new militia companies and borrowing money from sympathetic sources, machinations in Washington ensured that the military would no longer be able to play a political role in Louisiana.[247] This effectively ratified Nicholl's coup and ended military Reconstruction for good. It was also understood by many white conservatives as the true redemption of the state, reform in its most patriotic guise.[248]

In the post-Reconstruction period, the coercive apparatus of Louisiana underwent several changes. First, the Democratic legislature of the state placed the control of the Metropolitan Police back in the hands of the common council, sundering it from the militia and from control by the governor; this had the effect of allowing the mayor of New Orleans to restaff the force with allies and to eliminate most (though not all) of its African-American members.[249] It also allowed the city government to slash the funds delegated to the force; as Dennis Rousey points out, the New Orleans police suffered from a great deal

243 Taylor, *Louisiana Reconstructed*, 494–505.

244 Rousey, *Policing the Southern City*, 157–158; James K. Hogue, "Bayonet Rule: Five street Battles in New Orleans and the Rise and Fall of radical Reconstruction" (PhD diss., Princeton University, 1998), 185–194.

245 Taylor, *Louisiana Reconstructed*, 491–493.

246 NOP, January 10, 1877; NOT, January 10, 1877; Hogue, *Uncivil War*, 165–167.

247 Taylor, *Louisiana Reconstructed*, 501–502; Hogue, *Uncivil War*, 171–174.

248 See Emberton, *Beyond Redemption*, 206–208.

249 NOP, March 3, 1877; April 27, 1877; Rousey, *Policing the Southern City*, 156–161.

of corruption and infighting in the post-Reconstruction period and, along with most other Southern police forces, shrunk in size.[250]

On the surface, this would appear to be a reversion to a pre–Civil War mode of organizing force, but concomitant with the rollback in the police department was a centralization of the militia. In the aftermath of the takeover of state government, the CCWL's units provided the core for a new militia, allowing a seamless melding of vigilante mobilization with authorized state power.[251] Indeed, of the 176 New Orleans officers commissioned in the militia in 1878, over 25 percent (forty-five) had participated in the Battle of Liberty Place. A number of eminent Confederate veterans also took on crucial roles in the force, including sixteen members of the Civil War–era Washington Artillery. W. J. Behan, for instance, became was brigadier of the first division (that which included most of the former White League units), while P. G. T. Beauregard was named adjutant general. There was even a Crescent City Battalion of the new militia, suggesting Ogden's actual organizational hierarchy was adopted more or less wholesale by the state government.[252]

Most significantly, the Louisiana State National Guard was organized under the Militia Act in 1878 and was headquartered in New Orleans under the direct control of the governor. The force was composed not only of officers and companies selected by the governor, but was also given more of a priority in funds and armaments. Perhaps most significantly, the new guard was divided between the New Orleans–based state guard and a special militia, based in the rural parishes.[253] This would allow the governor to focus energy and resources on building a more organized and professionalized unit within the city that could then be used to supplement the special militia (which remained understaffed and undermanned).[254] The National Guard, which by the 1880s was receiving semi-regular payment for training activities, included all those independent companies that provided the backbone to the White League militia while incorporating them within the bureaucratic hierarchy established during Reconstruction; this provided the Governor with an opportunity to maintain and even expand coercive institutions while rewarding allies and returning the state to the appearance of an antebellum militia.[255]

250 ibid., 162–164. Just as with Chicago, a robust private security industry with close ties to the police force emerged in the 1880s and absorbed some of the protection business.

251 NOP, May 13, 1877.

252 *Annual Report of the Adjutant General of the State of Louisiana for the Year Ending December 31, 1878* (New Orleans: Louisiana Adjutant General's Office, 1879), 1–4, 24–29. 60% of the Battalion's officers were former White Leaguers.

253 *New Orleans Democrat*, April 1, 1877; *An Act to Enroll, Organize, and Equip the Militia of the State of Louisiana* (New Orleans: New Orleans Democrat, 1878).

254 In 1879, for instance, only 4 of 17 regiments and 10 of 206 commissioned officers were located outside the city. *Annual Report of the Adjutant General of the State of Louisiana for the Year Ending December 31, 1879* (New Orleans: Louisiana Adjutant General's Office, 1880), Table A.

255 Hogue, *Uncivil War*, 189.

In practice, the Guard continued to be used in some ways just as the Metropolitan Police had during Reconstruction – as an active means of ensuring executive control over the state. It was put on a relatively firm financial footing, it included provisions for regular target practice and mustering, and required regular reporting. The main difference was that it did not serve to protect the voting rights of African-American Republicans, but rather the interests of economic elites. This was particularly the case in the sugar-growing parishes, which were the site of much labor disorder in the 1880s. In 1887, for example, under the command of former White Leaguer and Confederate veteran William Pierce, the Louisiana State Guard was used to crush a strike coordinated by the Knights of Labor in St. Mary, Terrebonne, and Lafourche parishes.[256] The National Guard was also involved in breaking strikes in the sugar parishes of St. John the Baptist and St. Charles in the 1880s, confrontations usually (though not always) involving black workers and white overseers.[257]

The National Guard tried to counter African-American participation in other ways, often working in concert with local vigilance committees. In 1884, for instance, the militia were used to counter what appeared to be a coup attempt on the part of the Republicans in Iberia; ultimately, after allowing a local protective association to take over responsibilities for law and order in the parish, the Guard returned to New Orleans, only for a riot to break out right before the election that resulted in the deaths of around eighteen people.[258]

Despite being clearly used to help prop up the interests of planters, the National Guard nevertheless embodied the idea that the public was worthy of state efforts to protect it through a specialized and dedicated force rather than through the older republican notion that everyone should participate in their own protection through the militia. Whereas the Democratic press had decried Kellogg's militia as a standing army, they now began to argue that, in light of the labor problems of the day, "the natural and best method" to address social violence would be to use the National Guard. Properly drilled and disciplined, the soldiers of the National Guard should be as efficient as regulars in suppressing a riot, where only steadfastness and resolution can carry the day."[259]. This is a key change, one that many white conservatives championed: by redeeming the state, they had not abandoned some of the important changes made during Reconstruction. Rather, they simply repurposed them in a manner

[256] NOT, November 24, 1887; OC, November 19, 1887; November 26, 1887; *Annual Report of the Adjutant General of the State of Louisiana for the Year Ending December 31, 1887* (New Orleans: Louisiana Adjutant General's Office, 1888), 23–27; Hogue, *Uncivil War*, 190–192.

[257] NOP, March 19, 1880; March 20, 1880; April 2, 1880; Michael J. Pfeifer, "Lynching and Criminal Justice in South Louisiana, 1878–1930," *Louisiana History* 40, no. 2 (1999): 158; Vandal, *Rethinking Southern Violence*, 150–151.

[258] NOT, August 15, 1884; August 16, 1884; OC, November 8, 1884; Gilles Vandal, "Politics and Violence in Bourbon Louisiana: The Loreauville Riot of 1884 as a Case Study," *Louisiana History* 30, no. 1 (1989): 23–42.

[259] *New Orleans Daily Democrat*, June 22, 1879.

that could help reproduce white hegemony in a system that, on paper at least, had changed dramatically with the introduction of African-American voting.

Of course, private participation in coercion did not disappear. Many conservatives continued to insist on the public and private rollback of civil rights for African Americans, which led to extreme, racist "Bourbon" political movements within the Democratic party. Reinforcing this white hegemony not only involved the introduction of new black code restrictions, Jim Crow laws, and sharecropping indebtedness, but also the use of a private system of terror. This system was not only directed at African Americans, though they were always its main targets; rather it also served, in part, as a way of keeping economic and social power out of the courts and in the hands of the community. It hearkened back to an older system of justice in which private interests and public security could be linked, albeit in highly altered circumstances.[260] Now, however, with the more expansive punitive and coercive apparatus of the state, vigilantism was used to limit the access of undesirables to the protections afforded by those institutions and to create a system of justice that would remain firmly under the control of social and economic elites despite a modernizing state.

One form of vigilantism was directed specifically at workers. In the late 1870s, as prospects for political participation dimmed and African-American laborers in cotton-growing regions were subject to increased voting intimidation, some began to explore options for leaving Louisiana and heading north and midwest. In 1879, this "Kansas fever" reached a peak, and many planters and others became terrified that the agricultural backbone of the state would be broken.[261] While some whites called for the moderation of private violence and economic reform to induce potential migrants to remain, others tried to block their passage by intimidating them directly to remain or coercing steamboat and bridge operators to refuse to them on.[262]

Private violence also continued to play an important role in defending social and racial hierarchy. Lynching, in particular, was an important dimension of this control because it was spectacular; it demonstrated to that specific threats to the economic and social order would be addressed summarily.[263] Michael Pfeifer has counted over 400 lynching deaths in Louisiana between 1878 and 1930, arguing that the practice became most systematic and regularized in the north and northwestern parishes that had been the scene of extensive White League mobilization. Moreover, he also makes a compelling case that the patterns set up in the antebellum and reconstruction periods paved the way for future use

260 See Samuel C. Hyde Jr., *Pistols and Politics: The Dilemma of Democracy in Louisiana's Florida Parishes, 1810–1899* (Baton Rouge: Louisiana State University Press, 1996), 199–212; Samuel C. Hyde Jr., "Feuding Is Our Means of Societal Regulation: Elusive Stability in Southeastern Louisiana's Piney Woods, 1877–1910," *Louisiana History* 48, no. 2 (2007): 133–155.

261 NOT, April 22, 1879; *New Orleans Weekly Times-Democrat*, July 19, 1879.

262 *New York Times*, April 3, 1879; Peoples, "'Kansas Fever' in North Louisiana," 133–134.

263 Amy Louise Wood, *Lynching and Spectacle: Witnessing Racial Violence in America, 1890–1940* (Chapel Hill: University of North Carolina Press, 2009), 11–14, 34–41.

of private communal violence, and that we need to look back to the continuity of private violence over time to make sense of the rebirth of lynching late in the century.[264] It was in those areas that representative authority had been most unsettled – in other words, that lynching became most prevalent.

Pfeifer presents a highly useful way of discriminating amongst sporadic or demonstrative lynching events (e.g., those involving mass groups and/or *ad hoc posse* mobilizations gone awry) versus more systematic patterns.[265] He distinguishes between public spectacle events, private, small groups, and organized/militaristic terrorist entities (like the Ku Klux Klan); unlike the sporadic and relatively unpredictable public lynchings or summary justice events, these latter types indicate an entrenched system of private justice with highly targeted killing taking place over longer periods of time.

Table 17 depicts the growth of public lynching along with organized systematic vigilantism. The bottom panel of Table 17 reorganizes part of Pfeifer's data into five year increments to show how the constitutions of the group engaged in lynching changed over time (I only include data for which the constitution of the group is known). Through the 1880s, lynching was mostly the product of the same kinds of organizational dynamics characterizing the League: it was systematic and coordinated by small groups of dedicated violence experts who mostly exercised communal violence locally and privately.[266] Though the systematic form of vigilantism remained, it was soon complemented by a public face; by the mid-1890s, the relative numbers of sporadic and demonstrative lynching events outstripped systematic events, even as both increased in frequency.

Another means of interpreting the effects of systematic vigilantism is by examining who the victims of lynching campaigns actually were; the top panel of Table 17 provides this information. Specifically, it was only over time that vigilantism became associated exclusively with racial control — while vigilantism remained a residual practice of the antebellum militia, it was directed not only at African Americans, but also at those who offended communal norms more generally.[267] Even as lynching became more spectacular in the 1890s,

264 Pfeifer, "Lynching and Criminal Justice in South Louisiana, 1878–1930," 161–178; Michael J. Pfeifer, "The Origins of Postbellum Lynching: Collective Violence in Reconstruction Louisiana," *Louisiana History* 50, no. 2 (2009): 189–201.

265 Michael J. Pfeifer, *Rough Justice: Lynching And American Society, 1874–1947* (Urbana: University of Illinois Press, 2004), 38–44. For the original typology, see W. Fitzhugh Brundage, *Lynching in the New South: Georgia and Virginia, 1880–1930* (Urbana: University of Illinois Press, 1993), 19–47.

266 1876 witnessed the height of the vigilance committee movement in postbellum Louisiana, though they remained present through the early 1880s. Vandal, *Rethinking Southern Violence*, 93–97.

267 Jay Corzine, Lin Huff-Corzine, and Candice Nelsen, "Rethinking Lynching: Extralegal Executions in Postbellum Louisiana," *Deviant Behavior* 17, no. 2 (1996): 133–157; Mattias Smångs, "Whiteness from Violence: Lynching and White Identity in the US South, 1882–1915" (PhD diss., Columbia University, 2011).

TABLE 17. *Lynching in Louisiana (1876–1920)*

	Number of victims																	
	1876–1880		1881–1885		1886–1890		1891–1895		1896–1900		1901–1905		1906–1910		1911–1915		1916–1920	
Race of victim	N	%	N	%	N	%	N	%	N	%	N	%	N	%	N	%	N	%
Black	21	84	27	77	33	87	72	81	51	80	47	96	33	87	29	100	21	100
Other	4	16	8	13	5	13	17	19	13	20	2	04	5	13	0	0	0	0
Total (race known)	25		35		38		89		64		49		38		29		21	
	Number of Events																	
Vigilantism type																		
Systematic	15	83	10	56	19	66	29	41	25	47	7	20	11	52	17	65	8	62
Sporadic/demonstrative	3	17	8	44	10	34	41	59	28	53	28	80	10	48	9	35	5	38
Total (type known)	18		18		29		70		53		35		21		26		13	

Data from Michael J. Pfeifer, *Rough Justice: Lynching And American Society, 1874–1947* (Urbana: University of Illinois Press, 2004).

whites and foreign immigrants were frequently the target of private justice; by the time of World War I, however, lynching, though uncommon, was specifically racialized. I interpret this pattern to indicate that the White League, while paving the way toward a future of race-based private punishment, was also a transitional phenomenon attempting to create exactly the racial realignment that would later be par for the course for our understanding of Southern private violence.

The White League, in other words, represented one important link between the old, antebellum republican tradition of public–private coercive fusion and a new world where these different traditions co-evolved into bureaucratic and systematic vigilante violence. These public and private systems were not competitors, however, because they both drew on the republican tradition of militia service.

Moreover, maintaining racial control in the South meant that the two systems of violence often worked in concert. Of seventy-nine lynching events identified by Pfeifer for Louisiana in the 1880s, for example, I was only able to identify a single case, in Lafayette Parish in 1887, in which the state militia mobilized to address the crisis, and this was only due to an appeal by the sheriff for help in transporting the vigilante ringleaders.[268] Sugar-growing continued to involve gang labor, allowing workers to achieve some degree of organization and autonomy; these were precisely the areas seeing the most labor mobilization and, due to proximity to New Orleans and the spatial concentration of work, those to which the militia was most likely to come in aid of local economic elites.[269] In remote cotton-growing regions of the north and northwest, on the other hand, where labor discipline and decentralized surveillance were more necessary, the more diffuse and localized practice of vigilantism may have simply been more effective than the militia in countering individual threats.[270] In this sense, the National Guard and systems of private vigilantism divided coercive labor amongst themselves.[271]

CONCLUSION

To understand both post-Reconstruction patterns of racial violence *and* the adoption of an expert-led and bureaucratic coercive apparatus in the South, we need to look to the breakdown of the republican militia. The introduction of

268 *Annual Report of the Adjutant General of the State of Louisiana for the Year Ending December 31, 1889* (New Orleans: Louisiana Adjutant General's Office, 1890), 70–74; Major Winthrop Alexander, "Ten Years of Riot Duty," *Journal of Military Service Institution of the United States* 19 (1896): 10–11. Pfeifer notes that indifference to lynching was more or less an official policy of Louisiana governors through the 1890s, though this began to shift with the rise of Governor Newton Blanchard at the turn of the century. See Pfeifer, *Rough Justice*, 139–147.

269 Scott, "'Stubborn and Disposed to Stand their Ground'," 119–120.

270 Pfeifer, "Lynching and Criminal Justice in South Louisiana, 1878–1930," 160.

271 Vandal, *Rethinking Southern Violence*, 151–152.

political rights to previously disenfranchised African Americans created a threat to the racial order that had allowed white men to represent the public interest; as a result, the militia and other antebellum institutions of coercive enforcement became a target of the Redeemers. However, the conservative whites who had previously relied on the representative authority of antebellum state political institutions, like the militia, did not themselves abandon popular participation in violence. Instead they simply acted outside the confines of the law, creating a widespread, systematic form of political vigilantism in the White League. Socially powerful actors, in other words, responded as they often did – by trying to preserve older institutional rules in the midst of social change. But this had the effect of making American coercion appear schizophrenic – both private and public actors could claim rights over protection. The state really made no attempt to monopolize control over violence directly.

When those same Redeemers successfully regained control over state institutions after 1876, they did reorganize and reinforce state policing power by reforming coercive entities like the National Guard.[272] At the same time, they refused to abandon private violence; indeed, the widespread, systematic forms of vigilantism that plagued not only Louisiana but other southern states for years, often worked in concert with the racial order of the local state.

Louisiana was not alone. In South Carolina, for instance, conservative whites – who had used "rifle clubs" to intimidate black voters in 1874 and organized themselves into more coordinated paramilitary Red Shirts to provoke a series of confrontations with state National Guard – ultimately seized control over state government after bloody elections in 1876.[273] Following the overthrow, Governor Wade Hampton opted to reorganize (rather than disband) the primarily African-American National Guard and, in addition, create a new Volunteer State Troop force, which many Red Shirt units joined.[274] And, just as in Louisiana, state violence and private lynching often worked together to help enforce racial hierarchies, particularly in areas like the Upper Piedmont (a textile manufacturing center), which witnessed twenty-seven private lynchings and sixty-three state executions between 1881 and 1940.[275] States like Georgia, Arkansas, Texas, and Mississippi, among others, experienced violent codas to Reconstruction as well, codas involving the reconstruction of state

[272] While not a focus of this chapter, the growth of mass incarceration in the South largely followed this same Redeemer willingness to use the bureaucratic advances of Reconstruction to help reinforce the racial order via public institutions. See Loïc Wacquant, "From Slavery to Mass Incarceration," *New Left Review*, II, no. 13 (2002): 41–60.

[273] Kantrowitz, "'One Man's Mob Is Another Man's Militia': Violence, Manhood, and Authority in Reconstruction South Carolina," 72–74, 78–80.

[274] George Brown Tindall, *South Carolina Negroes, 1877–1900* (Charleston: University of South Carolina Press, 1952), 286.

[275] Terence Finnegan, *A Deed So Accursed: Lynching in Mississippi and South Carolina, 1881–1940* (Charlottesville: University of Virginia Press, 2013), 38.

government into more punitive and coercive agencies *alongside* the growth of a private system of terror.

In his vitally important revisionist account of Reconstruction, W. E. B. Du Bois provides a clear summation of the political economy of post–Civil War violence across the South: "First," he notes, violent conflict reflected "that kind of disregard for law which follows all war. Then it became a labor war, an attempt on the part of impoverished capitalists and landowners to force laborers to work on the capitalist's own terms. From this, it changed to a war between laborers, white and black men fighting for the same jobs. Afterward, the white laborer joined the white landowner and capitalist and beat the black laborer into subjection through secret organizations and the rise of a new doctrine of race hatred."[276] Racial violence was always, at least, in part, rooted in the attempt of economic elites to contain a threat to their social control over African Americans by trying to roll back the changes in rules instigated by Reconstruction. And the militia, as a repository of both public and private violence, became a key site for this struggle.

But there was another crucial factor at play in explaining post Civil War violence. As Du Bois goes on to point out, "it is always difficult to stop war, and doubly difficult to stop a civil war. Inevitably, when men have been trained to violence and murder, the habit projects itself into civil life after peace."[277] This "habit" of violence, however, was never limited to the South; indeed, it projected itself far into the trans–Mississippi West, where the end of the war brought opportunities for economic advancement and settlement and led to the emergence a new group of violence experts. These individuals, many of whom had first developed skills in violence during the war and Reconstruction, were, like other settlers, looking for a way to make a living in an environment rife with social change. At the same time, these experts – known colloquially as gunfighters – would both challenge this new project of territorial and market incorporation, as well as offer a private solution to firms, towns, and individuals in need of protection.

[276] W. E. B. Du Bois, *Black Reconstruction in America* (New York: Harcourt, Brace and Co., 1935), 670.

[277] Du Bois, *Black Reconstruction in America*, 670.

6

The Violent Careers of American Gunfighters

INTRODUCTION

James "Whispering" Smith's life was the stuff of legend. Although information about his early years is spotty, we do know that after a period of service for the Freedmen's Bureau in Louisiana and, most likely, time in the Union Army, Smith joined the New Orleans police department in 1868, by then a center for Republican patronage. During his years in New Orleans, Smith advanced quickly, being appointed a detective in the force in 1873, where he, along with other members of the force, became involved in the struggle against the White League. After participating in the Battle of Liberty Place and watching the city return to Democratic control several years later, Smith, like many others, began to drift west, making his way to Omaha in 1876.[1]

In Omaha, Smith's familiarity with law enforcement served him well; he attained a position as a railroad detective for the Union Pacific and was stationed in Cheyenne, Wyoming, where he concurrently held the position of special policeman, giving him access to powers of arrest. After several difficult years in Wyoming, Smith then moved into a position working for the Indian agent at Lone Pine Sioux reservation in the Dakota territory, where he made a name for himself tracking down horse thieves (especially members of the famed "Doc" Middleton gang) plaguing the area. On one occasion, a suspect arrested by Smith named "Lame Johnny" was suspiciously lynched while in his custody; weeks later, Smith shot another suspected thief in "self-defense."[2]

The reputation of Whispering Smith as a reliable and courageous fighter began to grow; he soon moved to New Mexico, where he began work as a chief of the Mescalero Indian Police in 1881. From here, his career followed

[1] Robert K. DeArment, *Deadly Dozen: Forgotten Gunfighters of the Old West, Volume 3* (Norman: University of Oklahoma Press, 2010), 58.

[2] DeArment, *Deadly Dozen Vol. 3*, 59–62.

the template of a western myth: he worked with local cavalry forces to hunt down and kill Apache fugitives in 1882 and 1883 and joined the Wyoming Stock Grower's Association in 1884 to work as a range detective, before serving, again, as a railroad detective through the 1880s and 1890s. In the process, he got involved in a large number of scrapes, fights, and chases with whiskey runners and railroad thieves, while also becoming acquainted with western law enforcement illuminaries like "Doc" Shores of Gunnison, Colorado, and "Quick Shot" Scott Davis, a well-known stagecoach guard based in the Deadwood area.

At the same time, Smith's reputation allowed him to pursue somewhat less savory economic opportunities as well. Most famously, he was hired by the *Denver Post* to intimidate another famous sporting gunfighter (and compatriot of Wyatt Earp), Bat Masterson, after a dispute between the paper and the promoter concerning a boxing match in 1900. And later in life, in desperation and poverty, Smith confessed (seemingly falsely) to running a bootlegging operation. Whatever the truth, Smith's end was ignominious; he killed himself in his Arapahoe County Colorado jail cell in 1910.[3]

Despite the mythological cast to his life, Smith's story was not really that exceptional. Instead, he was one of a significant number of gunfighters whose experiences in battle and war, as well as social connections with other fighters, allowed them to take advantage of a market for violence expertise that had emerged in the aftermath of the Civil War. The growth of the cattle trade, a booming railroad business, and the mining industry had completely transformed the trans–Mississippi West, turning territories into integral nodes in a national economic network.[4]

This kind of economic incorporation, however, led to a mismatch between the territorial rules imposed by the US government, which involved trying to outsource coercive enforcement to traditional local officers of the peace while keeping them local and underpowered (a kind of imperial "divide-and-rule" strategy of control), and the social relations induced by the market incorporation of the region, which allowed people to develop social connections to one another across enormous scales. As the end of the Civil War brought an explosion of territorial incorporation and settlement across the trans–Mississippi West, imperial forms of territorial control simply could not keep up; rustling, railroad banditry, and other threats that crossed jurisdictional boundaries made coordinating protection extremely difficult for local law officers like sheriffs and constables. The military, of course, was active in the area, but its main agenda was protecting national boundaries and managing the native population. For Anglo-American settlers and economic firms alike, local

3 DeArment, *Deadly Dozen Vol. 3*, 69–81.

4 I will use the word West to describe all the states and territories west of the Mississippi, excluding Louisiana, Arkansas, Iowa, and parts of Minnesota.

communities were forced to rely on often inadequate traditional republican forms of law enforcement to provide law and order.

Gunfighters, those American icons such as Jesse James, "Wild" Bill Hickok, and scores of others with wartime experience and skills in violence, took advantage of this mismatch, and began to sell their expertise on the open market to private actors like railroads and cattle barons, as well as to counties and towns as officers of the peace. Like the private detectives working in Chicago prior to the Civil War who were described in Chapter 4, these experts were entrepreneurs – they tried to make money however they could, by working as sheriffs and constables, serving as cattle detectives or stagecoach or railroad guards, or by going into business for themselves as bandits and thieves.

Like the White League vigilantes of Louisiana in Chapter 5, however, it was the experience of the Civil War and the shift in institutional rules that provided the impetus for this new class of experts. Indeed, the connection between vigilantism and gunfighting was quite deep – many early gunfighters were, like vigilantes, veterans of the war, and cultivated their initial skills in the partisan and violent atmosphere of the Reconstruction southwest. Some, in fact, have argued the gunslinger identity was deeply tied up in the alternative, guerrilla war of states like Missouri, Louisiana, and Texas, where the set-piece battles like Gettysburg and Bull Run were missing, and instead, the fight was deeply personal and communal.[5]

While participation in vigilante campaigns and communal warfare certainly did shape the careers of people like Jesse James (who cut his teeth in Missouri's vicious guerrilla war), for the most part gunfighters were private security entrepreneurs, committed to using their expertise in gunplay to make a dollar.

At first, the fighters were largely recruited in *entrepôt* boomtowns, places in which cattle were shipped via the railroad to eastern markets. Because they were key spots for the incorporating West, gunfighters active in boomtowns were able to cultivate and diffuse a reputation for their skills to potential buyers. Over time, patterns of fighting and partnering created a social network of gunfighters, which they used to share information and find new jobs. Amazingly, this social network connected a wide variety of fighters over space and time – figures like James Smith were just one of many who participated in these economic connections.

Before moving on to show how these connections worked and evolved over time, it is imperative to introduce the problem of the gunfighter and discuss the nature of incorporation in the western United States, showing how territorial administration based on divide-and-rule decoupled institutional rules from the market.

[5] Matthew Hulbert, *The Ghosts of Guerrilla Memory: How Civil War Bushwhackers Became Gunslingers in the American West* (Athens: University of Georgia Press, 2016), 15–42.

VIOLENT SKILLS AND THE US WEST IN THE LATE NINETEENTH CENTURY

In his fascinating work on American violence, Richard Maxwell Brown has done the most to demythologize gunfighters and treat them as economic and political actors in their own right.[6] Specifically, he has described a late-nineteenth-century Civil War of incorporation in the plains and far West between the powerful new business and state entities and between local interests he terms the "grassroots."[7] While focused on a variety of specific issues – railroad rights of way, the use of shared grazing land, local political autonomy and influence, and so on – what these conflicts had in common, Brown argues, is that they often turned violent, providing opportunity for enterprising actors to participate in fighting. Gunfighters were, in turn, the key players in this new war, representing different factions.[8]

There were actually *two* kinds of incorporation that followed the Civil War, when the blockage against Western expansion imposed by the battle between free states and slave states was broken. On one hand, the federal government renewed its attempts to gain control over Indian tribes, setting up and organizing new territorial jurisdictions for settlement, and paving the way for the construction of a national state. Like most state-building activities in the late nineteenth century, this expansion was a hybrid, a result of policies such as the Homestead Act, which allowed private citizens to gain cheap land in return for cultivation and economic growth.[9] This process, as I show in this chapter, was essentially imperial: while it depended on private actors, ultimately the federal government was in charge of most of the institutional development and tried to maintain a monopoly over control, if not actual resources.

6 Nineteenth-century gunfighting, of course, has been the subject of countless books and articles, most of which focus on specific fighters, feuds, wars, and battles. Most historians view gunfighting as the provenance of reckless, deinstitutionalized men living in isolated environments on the frontier, as a product of a cultural code of honor transmitted by southern migrants into new environs, or as a manifestation of postwar social banditry rather than as economic actors. See, for example, David T. Courtwright, *Violent Land: Single Men and Social Disorder from the Frontier to the Inner City* (Cambridge, MA: Harvard University Press, 1998); Daniel J. Herman, *Hell on the Range: A Story of Honor, Conscience, and the American West* (New Haven, CT: Yale University Press, 2010); Richard White, "Outlaw Gangs of the Middle Border: American Social Bandits," *The Western Historical Quarterly* 12, no. 4 (1981): 387–408. For a general bibliography of gunfighting in the United States, see Ramon F. Adams, *Six-Guns and Saddle Leather* (Norman: University of Oklahoma Press, 1969).

7 Richard Maxwell Brown, "Western Violence: Structure, Values, Myth," *The Western Historical Quarterly* 24, no. 1 (1993): 5–20; Richard Maxwell Brown, *No Duty to Retreat: Violence and Values in American History and Society* (Oxford: Oxford University Press, 1992), 43–46.

8 Brown also argues that Northern gunfighters tended to fight battles on behalf of incorporating interests, while those from the South – John Wesley Hardin from Texas, Jesse James from Confederate Missouri, and so on – were a local response to the attempt to consolidate US territory into shared economic market dominated by powerful and remote interests.

9 Heumann, "The Tutelary Empire"; Frymer, "Building an American Empire"; Frymer, "'A Rush and a Push and the Land is Ours': Territorial Expansion, Land Policy, and U.S. State Formation."

On the other hand, partly as a byproduct of these political changes, the West was also subject to an explicit and distinct *market* form of incorporation from powerful railroad and cattle companies, whose activities exploded in the 1870s and 1880s. The intersection of these two businesses was most pronounced in the Southwest, where cattle companies were transforming huge swaths of open plain into grazing land in postwar Texas, and railroad conglomerates were rapidly building connections across the continent. Later, the transportation and market links established by the postwar southwestern cattle industry grew to encompass the burgeoning copper and silver mining activities of Arizona and New Mexico, as well as those of Colorado and the northern Rockies. In this second, private form of market integration, concern for property rather than territory was paramount.[10]

Thus, the key to understanding how the strictures of the region's jurisdictional order decoupled institutional rules in the West from a system of social relations increasingly caught up in an incorporating market, means making sense of how territorial politics were supposed to work.

Territories, Empire, and the Market

Between 1861 and 1888, seven new territories were established in the trans–Mississippi West and Southwest, with four of them becoming states during that period. Territories – which always included a large number of political appointees – were a means both of providing patronage for allies, as well as a way for federal officials to increase their scope of authority in a manner that was simply not possible in the East, where the traditions of state autonomy and authority were strong and where sectional divisions inhibited administrative expansion. The result was that the federal government achieved an important role in managing the direct livelihoods of settlers that surpassed that of any other region in the nineteenth century, except for the South during the height of Reconstruction.[11]

The formal rules of the territorial system allowed the federal government to incorporate the trans–Mississippi West from a position of centralized control; appointees were responsible for the management of the residents of the territories, who themselves were politically infantilized and only allowed to possess local administrations and weak local assemblies.[12] This system was directed, in particular, at Native Americans; reservations and relocation had been part of the American strategy of managing native tribes beginning in the late 1840s.[13] But white settlers, too, were brought into a positions of subjugation to

[10] I thank Anne Holthoefer for this formulation.

[11] White, *It's Your Misfortune and None of My Own*, 176–177.

[12] Go, *Patterns of Empire*, 48; Heumann, "The Tutelary Empire," 8–9.

[13] The United States deployed spatial segregation and settlement as a means of trying to limit overt conflict between growing number of Anglo-American settlers and nomadic tribes. White, *It's Your Misfortune and None of My Own*, 91–93.

territorial administrators.[14] In terms of day-to-day social control, settlers and native tribes alike were able to organize their own local jurisdictions, but these jurisdictions lacked any direct conduit to the federal government that was not mediated directly by appointees from Washington. The US territorial system was imperial: it was a divide-and-rule system combined with local delegation and quasi-autonomy used to maximize the extraction of territorial resources at minimal cost.

Part of the imperial strategy was a local, bottom-up continuation of the settler colonial enterprise characterizing Anglo-American westward expansion since the colonial period. "Ordinary" citizens interested in conquering and cultivating land occupied by natives invariably became well-acquainted with personal violence. In Arizona in 1871, for instance, a group of Anglo-American and Mexican settlers, along with allied members of the O'odham, launched a vicious attack on a group of Apache women and children living at Camp Grant ostensibly under the protection of the US government. The attack, a product of retaliatory fears, economic uncertainty, and a basic desire to rid the land of the "wild" Apache, was another bloody reminder of a two-decade civilian struggle to appropriate native land in the Southwest borderlands.[15] Indeed, civilians and citizen militia – on their own and in cooperation with US Army troops – killed hundreds of Indians not only in Arizona, but also California, Colorado, Oregon, Idaho, Utah, and the Dakota Territory from 1850 through the end of the century.[16]

Even when they did not actually use violence, vigilance against native groups required Anglo Americans to be prepared to mobilize it if necessary. For example, on his way toward the Rocky Mountains in the 1858 to make his fortune in the Colorado gold rush, Thomas Aikens – a former member of the Banditti of northern Illinois who, escaping the Regulators in the mid-1840s, had made his way further west – encountered Niwot, a southern Arapaho tribal leader, and a band of about 200 of his followers near the St. Vrain River just outside the Boulder Valley. According to Aikens, a group of the Arapaho wanted to attack the settler and his small retinue, but he managed to convince Niwot that his intentions were peaceful by arguing that he was only interested in commercial relations with the tribe and by promising that he and his associates would stay only for a limited time on Arapaho land.[17]

Aikens, however, changed his mind and decided to establish a permanent home in Colorado. Undoubtedly well-versed in coordinating violence from his association with the criminal elements of Ogle and Lee, Aikens formed

[14] Go, *Patterns of Empire*, 48–49.

[15] Karl Jacoby, *Shadows at Dawn: An Apache Massacre and the Violence of History* (New York: Penguin, 2009), 2–3, 109–124.

[16] See Benjamin Madley, "Reexamining the American Genocide Debate: Meaning, Historiography, and New Methods," *The American Historical Review* 120, no. 1 (2015): 98–139.

[17] Taylor, "Captain Thomas Avery Akins and Margaret Ross Akins: Boulder Pioneers and Early Valmont Settlers (Part 1)," 105–106; Margaret Coel, *Chief Left Hand: Southern Arapaho* (Norman: University of Oklahoma Press, 1981), 65–67.

his band into a small militia company, which he used to defend a permanent settlement – the town of Boulder – they built near the nearby foothills.[18] The construction of towns like Boulder (and nearby Denver) considerably worsened relations with the Arapaho, despite Niwot's continued attempts to maintain peace. In 1861, a group of Arapaho elders (along with representatives of the southern Cheyenne), frustrated with the continual seizure of land and settlement, agreed to sign a treaty relegating them to a small reservation in the eastern portion of the territory. Others among the tribes, however, were unhappy, and a group of disaffected younger warriors started to make trouble, raiding stage stations on the Overland Route.[19] Following a failed attempt at parley at Denver, a Colorado militia detachment under John Chivington, organized as part of the territory's home guard during the Civil War, launched a surprise attack against Niwot, his followers, and a large group of Cheyenne on the banks near the Sand Creek in 1864. Dozens (possibly hundreds) of Indians were killed, many of them women and children.[20] Among those participating in the attack was the sergeant of Company D of the Third Regiment, Thomas Aikens.[21]

There was also, however, a top-down logic to this imperialism. Divide-and-rule politics meant keeping local communities politically and even socially distinct. The land policy of the US government in the nineteenth century tried to manage the problem of occupying and incorporating a vast expanse at minimal cost by pitting local groups against one another. Competition among towns would drive settlement while keeping the central government in charge. Moreover, Indian removal opened up space the government then hoped would be occupied by settlers – the Homestead Act, the Preemption Act, and so forth were actually part of a concerted policy of encouraging the growth of local settlements that would bear the brunt of the costs of defending and settling the frontier.[22] Overseeing the whole system was a small military, which would supplement the delegation of coercion to the masses of settlers and would patrol the boundaries of this spatial segregation. By linking the day-to-day governance of settler communities to a formal rule system of territorial governance in which communities were dependent on the center, the government could control the incorporation of new territories without expending the resources necessary to build coercive infrastructure.

Keeping these communities relatively isolated (at least from the Indians) and keeping their political interests funneled through Washington patronage

[18] Eugenie Cynthia Taylor, "Captain Thomas Avery Akins and Margaret Ross Akins: Boulder Pioneers and Early Valmont Settlers (Part 2)," *Boulder Genealogical Society Quarterly* 35, no. 4 (November 2003): 142.

[19] Coel, *Chief Left Hand: Southern Arapaho*, 181–194. [20] ibid., 251–291.

[21] Taylor, "Captain Thomas Avery Akins and Margaret Ross Akins: Boulder Pioneers and Early Valmont Settlers (Part 1)," 106.

[22] Frymer, "'A Rush and a Push and the Land is Ours': Territorial Expansion, Land Policy, and U.S. State Formation."

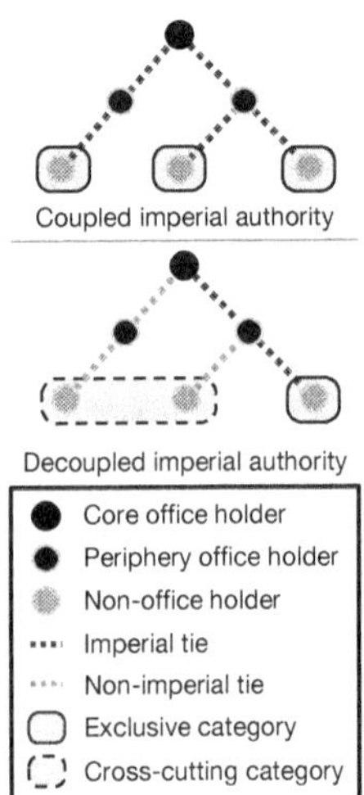

FIGURE 12. Imperial authority and jurisdictional coupling

networks helped prop up territorial governance for a couple of reasons. For one thing, as soon as settlers were able to organize themselves into states, they were able to make much more effective demands on Washington, demands that would undercut the patronage power and minimal infrastructure strategy of the federal government. This would include, for example, a much stronger demand that the federal government address threats from native groups. By forcing local settlers to organize, largely, on models adopted from eastern jurisdictions while also preventing them from having their own representation in Congress, the federal state could continue to rely on the republican link between private effort and public security to minimize these demands for more resources from the center.

Second, and more important, in the racial imaginary of the late-nineteenth-century United States, keeping the communities spatially distinct became important for ensuring that only the "right" kinds of settlers would eventually be able to organize themselves as states. In particular, this often meant ensuring that before territories were turned into states, they would need to have a majority white (preferably native Anglo American) population. Making such majorities often required spatially segregating other groups (Mexican Americans, Indians, and so on) and undercutting alternative forms of self-rule, such as tribal organization.[23]

Figure 12 depicts this system schematically. Imperial authority is built on the foundation of traditional law enforcement offices in local communities

[23] Frymer, "'A Rush and a Push and the Land is Ours': Territorial Expansion, Land Policy, and U.S. State Formation"; Heumann, "The Tutelary Empire," 390–392.

combined with the formal rules of divide-and-rule at the central level – only the imperial "core" connects all of the elements of the system together. Relations among exclusive categories of local community membership (e.g., membership in an Indian tribe, a settler community, and so on) were supposed to only be managed practically through relations to territorial administrators (peripheral officeholders), who themselves were only accountable to the imperial center. Authoritative imperial ties between the center and the periphery, in other words, depended on separation among local groups and settlements. Keeping these communities spatially and ethnically divided was a recipe to allowing a small military to manage serious conflicts at the border and bring reticent native groups into the fold, while outsourcing the provision of local order to local sheriffs, constables, and other republican institutions of self-government.

In a sense, then, this territorial system reflected the same kinds of republican assumptions other jurisdictions depended upon throughout the nineteenth century: private actors were assumed to be able bear the burden of public security responsibility, only the "best" citizens were supposed to gain access to any real political power, and large, state bureaucracies were viewed with suspicion. Moreover, traditional, local forms of republican law enforcement were expected to suffice for most kinds of protection in settler communities.

The problem for this system came when it encountered an unsettled world in which sheer advances in physical mobility made it increasingly impossible to actually map effective local political institutions onto the scale of emerging threats. Specifically, the end of the war not only brought about a change in political institutions in the new territories, it also unleashed a torrent of market incorporation, with transportation and economic integration increased dramatically, tying together jurisdictions that on paper were separate (in Figure 12 this is represented by the cross-cutting category linking two local communities together in the bottom panel). This decoupled the formal rules of imperial divide-and-rule from practical authority on the ground by creating interests like railroads and cattle firms whose property was not contained in a single jurisdiction.

This mobility was not a problem for all incorporating actors – the military, for example, was able to use the railroads to enhance their mobility relative to native tribes and to gain access to new supplies of food. But for economic actors, this was a problem: the scope of local jurisdictions like counties and towns that were in charge of much property rights protection – the stuff of local settlement in the trans–Mississippi West – were small, while the markets they were creating were large. Existing forms of coercive enforcement simply did not work as they once did in the midst of such large-scale economic change.

The Translocal Demand for Violence

The end of the Civil War was a mixed blessing in the Southwest: racial, economic, political, and personal animosities in Texas, Arkansas, and Missouri spilled over into a violent hothouse precisely at the moment the cattle industry was transforming itself into a translocal and very powerful regional player. This made coercion an important resource for those involved in protecting stock and railroads as well as for those interested in exploiting them. Moreover, while this demand originated in the Southwest, as mining and railroads expanded the scale of incorporation, the need for coercive services followed apace.

Settlement and incorporation of the southwestern United States (including New Mexico, Arizona, Texas, Oklahoma, and so forth) had been, with a few exceptions, stymied by sectional disagreements before the Civil War, as debates over slavery and native resistance had rendered economic returns tenuous. The end of the conflict and the turning of the US military toward the Southwest broke this impasse, providing the cattle industry with a new impetus to exploit the altered political situation and expand toward the northern railheads, where land-hungry settlers and the federal government established a strong presence in the 1860s.

As a result, despite the fact that the state was still reeling from a very difficult transition into Reconstruction, Texas ranchers like Charles Goodnight, Oliver Loving, and John Chisum took advantage of military buyers to explore new routes for moving cattle from remote regions in Texas to regional market centers. Of course, to some extent, this market activity had begun before the war. Not only had some pioneering cattle drivers been active before the war broke out, but the Atchison, Topeka & Santa Fe (AT & SF) Railroad, which was chartered in 1859, ensured that western agricultural goods would soon be able to reach much wider markets in the east, a continuation of a process of agricultural incorporation that had begun years before.[24] The size and scope of these cattle operations in the postwar period was unprecedented, however; while small scale family ranching continued (especially in areas around the Big Bend), the 1870s and early 1880s saw the consolidation of massive operations such as the XIT ranch, which reportedly covered nine Texas counties in 1882.[25]

The development of the cattle industry was rife with conflict. The new cattle barons confronted Comanche, Cheyenne, Arapahoe, Kiowa, and Anglo-American raiders, while also getting involved in squabbles government agents and, especially, with each other. Rustling and raiding, which had been part of the economy of the Comanche, continued in a newly invigorated form as organized bands of white rustlers, such as the John Kinney and Jesse Evans gangs, both active in southwestern Texas, got in on the game, leading to intense rivalries and driving demand for some form of protecting herds.

Rustling became a serious problem for ranchers in the early and mid-1870s, when profits for beef sales had sky-rocketed.[26] A congressional commission

[24] White, *Railroaded*, 466–482.

[25] Jacqueline M. Moore, *Cow Boys and Cattle Men: Class and Masculinities on the Texas Frontier, 1865–1900* (New York: New York University Press, 2009), 37–38.

[26] Moore, *Cow Boys and Cattle Men*, 92–101.

in 1872, for instance, reported that cattle-rustling by cross-border raiders had led to the loss of $27,859,363 in livestock, while one witness testified that between 1865 and 1872, 60,000 head of stolen cattle crossed into Mexico between Brownsville and Point Isabel.[27] Large-scale cowboy activity, in large measure, involved violence from the outset, as trail hands were expected to be prepared at any time to use force to protect the herds.[28] Conflicts between ranchers and their employees and smaller competitors also created a demand for protection. In particular, smaller-scale herdsmen organized in response to ranching consolidation, forming anti-fencing leagues which engaged in occasional property destruction of the barbed fences installed by large firms.[29] This led ranchers to turn to armed guards to help protect their herds from both their own employees as well as native, Mexican, and Anglo-American rustlers, while also forming Cattlemen's Associations to mediate disputes.[30]

One such guard was John Larn. Born in 1849 in Alabama, Larn moved west with his family in the late 1850s, and was hired as a cattle driver by the Reynolds and Matthews ranches in west Texas shortly after the war. Making his way through Colorado and New Mexico (and supposedly leaving several bodies behind him), Larn earned a reputation as a brave and brutal cattle guard.[31] After a particularly disastrous drive to Trinidad in Colorado, which involved a number of shootouts, confrontations with US cavalry, and suspected Mexican rustlers, Larn was hired by a rancher named John Hittson, who had been granted authority by the Texas governor to reclaim supposedly stolen cattle in New Mexico. After working with Hittson, Larn returned to Texas and settled near Fort Griffin, a wild frontier post and launching pad for the new cattle industry that was plagued by raiding and rustling. In 1876, Larn became sheriff but finding his official powers insufficient, he formed a gang of vigilantes known as the Tin Hat Brigade to serve as a protective agency for local ranchers.[32]

After a dispute with the Brigade, Larn teamed up with another local resident, John Selman, and became an official range inspector, where they apparently

27 US House of Representatives. 42nd Congress, Third Session, *Depradations on the Frontiers of Texas*, Ex.Doc.39 (1872), 3, 8, 18. To put the threat into perspective, the same commission reported that approximately 300,000 cattle were grazing in 1872 in eleven of the Texas counties bordering Mexico.

28 Paul Cool, *Salt Warriors: Insurgency on the Rio Grande* (College Station: Texas A&M University Press, 2008), 96–98, Robert V. Hine and John Mack Faragher, *The American West: A New Interpretive History* (New Haven, CT: Yale University Press, 2000), 308–310.

29 White, *It's Your Misfortune and None of My Own*, 344–346. Andrew R. Graybill, "Rural Police and the Defense of the Cattleman's Empire in Texas and Alberta, 1875–1900," *Agricultural History* 79, no. 3 (2005): 253–280.

30 William T. Hagan, *Charles Goodnight: Father of the Texas Panhandle* (Norman: University of Oklahoma Press, 2012), 72–78.

31 Robert K. DeArment, *Bravo of the Brazos: John Larn of Fort Griffin, Texas* (Norman: University of Oklahoma Press, 2002), 10–11.

32 ibid., 9, 27, 52, 65–66.

began to get involved in rustling themselves.[33] Indeed, by 1878, Larn himself had become a target of both the vigilantes and the new sheriff; while being held in jail in June of that year, he was killed by a group of masked men, supposedly in retaliation for the murder of several local residents but more likely because he knew secrets that could get members of the Brigade in serious legal trouble.[34] Selman, in turn, went to New Mexico where he organized a group of bandits known as Selman's Scouts, notorious for their brutality. Members of the Scouts (like Charles Snow and Roscoe "Rustling Bob" Bryant) had experience with other famous bandit outfits, including the Clanton gang in Arizona (known primarily for its confrontations with Wyatt Earp in the early 1880s) and the John Kinney gang, a key player in the famous Lincoln County War of 1878 that made Billy the Kid a legendary figure.[35]

John Larn was just one of the many range guards with an extraordinary history of violence. An important reason for this had to do with the complex experience of Texas in Reconstruction, which much like Louisiana, was subject to a great deal of racial and political unrest. Feuds, lynchings, and shootouts plagued the state in the years after the Civil War, and a number of gunfighters gained their first experiences using violence in this milieu.

John Wesley Hardin, a notorious outlaw and trail hand, is a prime example of the link between Reconstruction unrest and economic predation. Hardin was born to a strongly partisan Confederate family in north-central Texas in 1853. His entire youth was marked by fighting and, by 1868, had become a fugitive after killing one of his uncle's former slaves. Over the next few years, gambling and drinking his way across Texas, Hardin was involved in a number of other shootouts, including the alleged killing of a town marshal in Waco.[36] Joining many other restless young men, Hardin joined a cattle drive up the Chisholm Trail to Abilene in 1871, where, just like Larn, he served as a guard and was involved in several violent encounters with Mexican and Indian rustlers. In Abilene, Hardin joined the Texas faction of Ben Thompson, another notorious gunman and gambler from Texas, and his friend Phil Coe in opposing town marshal Wild Bill Hickok's efforts to police the rough and tumble boomtown, and supposedly was involved in yet another series of violent encounters, including a fanciful tale in which he killed a man for snoring too loudly.[37]

Returning to Texas, Hardin roamed for several years before finding refuge with relatives of his mother who, along with the Taylor family, was involved in a

33 DeArment, *Bravo of the Brazos*, 107–109. 34 ibid., 134–137.

35 Frederick W. Nolan, *The West of Billy the Kid* (Norman: University of Oklahoma Press, 1999), 155, 317.

36 Chuck Parsons and Norman Wayne Brown, *A Lawless Breed: John Wesley Hardin, Texas Reconstruction, and Violence in the Wild West* (Denton: University of North Texas Press, 2013), 1–22, 33–38.

37 ibid., 85–88, 99.

long-standing conflict with a local law officer, William Sutton, in the southern part of the state. Hardin quickly joined the Taylor faction and was involved in the killing of J. B. Morgan and Jack Helm, the sheriff of Dewitt County and former member of the pro-Reconstruction Texas State Police, in 1873. Following these murders, as well as the killing of another law officer, Deputy Sheriff Charles Webb in Brown County, Hardin and his gang went on the run. Several members of the outfit, including Joe Hardin (his brother) were lynched in retaliation for the murder of Webb. Finally, in 1877, Hardin was arrested in Florida, having made his way east via Alabama.[38]

For Hardin, violence was a way of life and expression of political animosity. But it was mostly a means of making money through rustling and guarding. And his experience was not unique. The Sutton-Taylor feud, the Higgins-Horrell War, the El Paso Salt War, as well as the banditry of "Simp" Dixon (Hardin's cousin), Cullen Baker Montgomery, and Ben Bickerstaff, and the countless other violent incidents pitted the small but vigorous pro-Union forces present in Texas against the more numerous and angrier Southern partisans. These wars continued through the tumultuous period of Reconstruction and state entities like the detested Reconstruction Texas State Police were often powerless to protect the Unionists and African Americans (a number of whom worked for the large ranches), who became easy targets for many of the most unforgiving partisans.[39]

Racial antagonism was one of the most important precipitating forces engendering violence in Texas during Reconstruction and played a crucial role in exacerbating political instability, further threatening the market. Hundreds of black residents lost their lives in what should be described as an assassination campaign, often for seeming complicity with the Texas State Police (approximately 30% of the force was likely composed of African Americans).[40] Not only did John Wesley Hardin, for example, target African Americans, but John Larn was equally vociferous in his hatred of Mexicans and Indians; on his

[38] ibid., 134–236. Interestingly, Hardin decided to become a lawyer while in prison. After seventeen years, he was released in 1894 and made his way to El Paso to set up his practice. Despite his age, Hardin's violent ways had not left him; in 1895, after a confrontation with a constable, the officer's father (also a constable) shot Hardin point blank in the back of the head. That father, in a stunning example of the interconnected nature of gunfighter life, was none other than John Larn's old rustling partner, John Selman. ibid., 342–371.

[39] James M. Smallwood, *The Feud That Wasn't: The Taylor Ring, Bill Sutton, John Wesley Hardin, and Violence in Texas* (College Station: Texas A & M University Press, 2008), 101–135; James M. Smallwood, Barry A. Crouch, and Larry Peacock, *Murder and Mayhem: The War of Reconstruction in Texas* (College Station: Texas A & M University Press, 2003), 73–82, 92–129; David Pickering and Judy Falls, *Brush Men & Vigilantes Civil War Dissent in Texas* (College Station: Texas A & M University Press, 2000), 129–136.

[40] Barry A. Crouch and Donaly E. Brice, *The Governor's Hounds: The Texas State Police, 1870–1873* (Austin: University of Texas Press, 2011), 176–177.

famous cattle drive to Trinidad in 1871, he reputedly shot and killed several Mexican cowboys and a shepherd he met on the trail simply out of spite.[41]

While racism, Reconstruction politics, border troubles, and cattle rustling were leaving Texas and parts of New Mexico in a condition of near anarchy, the railroads further north were also facing threats from organized bandits like the James-Younger gang. From 1866, when the Reno brothers of Indiana "invented" the modern train heist, other groups used the convenient, mostly predictable schedules of the railroad to plan their own increasingly elaborate robberies.[42] Given the role that railroad price-gouging played in the resentment of small-scale farmers in states like Missouri and Kansas, many of these robbers were seen as modern-day Robin Hoods; at the same time, the value of attacking railroads, particularly to Confederate sympathizers like Jesse James, was that it also served as an attack on the distant forces of Northern aggression.[43]

The West and Southwest were soon suffering an epidemic of train robberies and heists. The Sam Bass Gang, for instance, began robbing trains in the Southwest in 1877 and 1878, most famously making off with over $60,000 in the famous heist at Big Springs in Nebraska targeting the Union Pacific.[44] In the mid 1880s, the Rube Barrow gang picked up where Sam Bass left off, and began a long career robbing express deliveries in Texas, Mississippi, and Arkansas.[45] By the 1890s, trade periodicals began to keep track of the scale of the crimewave, much of which was centered in the trans–Mississippi West – while the *Express Gazette* recorded just twelve robberies nationally in 1890, that number increased fourfold, to forty-nine, just five years later.[46] Indeed, decrying the new kind of bandit, who "is reckless and abandoned, and will not hesitate to steal rob, and even kill," the *Gazette* even called for the transformation of Alaska into a penal colony, which would provide the felon "time for prayerful, solitary meditation over their sin and resolutions of reform" while "digging gold out of the mines for Uncle Sam."[47]

As this somewhat fanciful notion indicates, market incorporation in the post–Civil War West provided both opportunities for predation as well as protection. And gunfighters – masters in the new arts of personalized violence – became specialists in both.

[41] DeArment, *Bravo of the Brazos*, 15–16, 19.

[42] William A. Pinkerton, "Highwaymen of the Railroad," *The North American Review* 157, no. 444 (November 1893): 530–540.

[43] White, "Outlaw Gangs of the Middle Border"; T. J. Stiles, *Jesse James: Last Rebel of the Civil War* (New York: Knopf, 2002).

[44] Richard M. Patterson, *The Train Robbery Era: An Encyclopedic History* (Boulder, CO: Pruett Publishing Company, 1991), 14.

[45] ibid., 27–29.

[46] "Crimes of the Rail," *The Express Gazette*, January 15, 1903, Vol. 28, No. 1, p. 13.

[47] "Alaska as a Penal Colony," *The Express Gazette*, January 15, 1896, Vol. 21 (1), No. 1, p. 7.

Turning to Gunfighters

The risk of attacks from bandits and gangs affected cattle, railroad, banking, and mining interests most of all. To protect their property, they had, essentially, two options: they could trust the state, or they could try to protect their herds themselves. Many ranch outfits, particularly the larger companies, chose the second option.

Why didn't market actors turn to the government for protection? In part, of course, they did. Central state institutions did assume some responsibility for protecting market expansion; the military, as noted, was responsible for managing (though not necessarily fighting) much of the war of conquest against Native Americans in the Southwest, which many private parties agreed was critical for economic development. Moreover, state and territorial governments also organized constabulary police like the Texas and Arizona Rangers to patrol the plains.[48] And the constabularies, in particular, played an important role in the protection of property, serving, for example, as agents of the Texas & Pacific Coal Company during the strike of 1888.[49]

But several characteristics limited the effectiveness of central military and state police in providing protection and helped add to the demand for a private market in violence expertise. For one thing, government forces were both organized primarily to manage threats from outsiders – Indians, foreign nationals, and so on – rather than local threats. Consequently, they were subject to political actors that private interests (even powerful cattle barons) had a difficult time manipulating.[50] The US Marshals service, although offering crucial help in coordinating some policing efforts in the territorial west, remained politically contentious during the period (largely as a consequence of Reconstruction) and did not itself become a large presence in the region.[51]

Moreover, the actors involved in market incorporation were often involved in violent conflict with one another, making military intervention on behalf of private interests perilous.[52] The Army, for instance, increasingly evinced a

48 Graybill, "Rural Police and the Defense of the Cattleman's Empire in Texas and Alberta, 1875–1900," 12–16.

49 Andrew R. Graybill, "Texas Rangers, Canadian Mounties, and the Policing of the Transnational Industrial Frontier, 1885–1910," *The Western Historical Quarterly* 35, no. 2 (2004): 167–191.

50 Continual complaints about the military's effectiveness managing rustling threat (which was neither fully a native nor a Mexican problem) led to a number of congressional inquiries. E.g., US House of Representatives, 42nd Congress, Third Session, Ex.Doc.39; US House of Representatives, 45th Congress, Second Session, *El Paso Troubles in Texas*, Ex.Doc.93 (1878); US House of Representatives, 47th Congress, First Session, *Lawlessness in Parts of Arizona*, Ex.Doc.58 (1882).

51 Jonathan Obert, "A Fragmented Force: The Evolution of Federal Law Enforcement in the U.S., 1870–1900," *Journal of Policy History* 29, no. 4 (2017): 640–675.

52 This was true, for example, in the Lincoln County War of New Mexico, which involved commercial factions for control over local trade. When the event reached a dangerous standoff at Lincoln in the summer of 1878, the appearance of a unit commanded by Colonel Nathan Dudley ostensibly to "keep the peace" actually helped precipitate the shootout at the McSween house by dramatically shifting the balance of power, leading to a collapse in local order and

disinterest in becoming active in these kinds of squabbles, particularly after 1878, the year in which military forces were legally prohibited from participating in domestic law enforcement.[53] Such activity took them away from what they considered their core duty of territorial incorporation.[54] Finally, the military often had contentious relationships with local settlers that prevented them from acting as impartial arbiters of property crime.[55] While many local boosters in retail centers depended on railroad connections for access to eastern markets, local farmers and ranchers often resented the dominance of outside corporate *and* federal actors, whose power and connection to translocal networks of capital and resources created inequities in prices and political influence.

Most importantly, private corporate interests in the Southwest – like everyone else – operated in a context in which the traditional, local law enforcement institutions rather than the military were the most important locus of coercion in the United States. As with actors in the cities and states, territorial economic elites did not intentionally invent new forms of organizing coercion because they already *had* strong republican conceptions of how property was supposed to be protected by sheriffs and constables, whose role had carried over into territorial administration. These priorities often took precedence over centralized and bureaucratic approaches to violence, even in matters of statecraft. Indeed, it was law enforcement officials who often organized local responses to so-called Indian depredations, despite this being the explicit purview of the US military.[56]

a rapid increase in rustling and raiding by the independent groups of gunfighters brought in to work for the factions. Robert M. Utley, *High Noon in Lincoln: Violence on the Western Frontier* (Albuquerque, NM: University of New Mexico Press, 1990), 110–117.

53 Larry D. Ball, *Desert Lawmen: The High Sheriffs of New Mexico and Arizona Territories, 1846–1912* (Albuquerque: University of New Mexico Press, 1996), 235–237.

54 Clayton Laurie has argued that prior to 1878, the military was a fairly active and willing participant in local law enforcement on the frontier, acting as a kind of para-posse for local forces. Clayton D. Laurie, "Filling the Breach: Military Aid to the Civil Power in the Trans-Mississippi West," *The Western Historical Quarterly* 25, no. 2 (1994): 149–162. At the same time, General Sherman and other central elites, concerned with the possibility of lawsuits for wrongful arrest and preoccupied with ending Reconstruction, continually expressed their unease with this kind of activity. The military's growing professional ethos also meant that, on the whole, they did not necessary regret institutional occlusion from local *posse* service.

55 The US Army, for example, had been very active in suppressing the 1877 national strike, creating tense relationships with both industrial laborers and their antimonopoly homesteaders allies in the West, who suffered from the price-gouging of the railways and the complicity and occasional corruption of military officers. White, *Railroaded*, 291–292.

56 "Dangerous" Dan Tucker, for example, marshal of Silver City, New Mexico, organized a *posse* of local toughs (including future rustler John Kinney) to patrol the border during the conflicts of 1877 and 1878 on the Rio Grande. As usual, this adventure also led some of the participants to engage in rustling of their own. See US House, 45th Congress, 2nd Sess., Ex.Doc.93, pp. 4, 17, 64, 79.

From the standpoint of powerful market actors, the major problem was that despite holding legal authority to prosecute property crimes through arrest and physical force, traditional law officers for the small towns and settlements in the Reconstruction Southwest were not experts; indeed, they were precisely the kinds of republican amateurs found in counties and municipalities throughout the East.[57]

The translocal scale of the new threats in the Southwest, as well as the intense social mobility on the frontier, undermined the close relationship between public and private authority on which the territorial order was built. Moreover, the decentralized nature of these jurisdictions meant that translocal railroad and cattle interests would not necessarily be able to rely on equal levels of protection everywhere they operated. In particular, sheriffs and marshals were always, to some extent, local political actors, often elected by their constituents and more attentive to popular mood than the interests of translocal corporate interests.[58] In many jurisdictions, it was precisely the inability of large-scale mining and cattle interests to get cooperation by locals that induced them to rely on their own outside experts.[59] Hence, for larger, incorporating interests, the local solution of amateur participation in violence rarely worked as intended.

Thus, by the 1870s, many private corporations throughout the West began to try to field their own guards or hire guards provided by firms like the Thiel Detective Agency or the Pinkerton Agency.[60] The sheriff/constable system allowed such guards to be named special deputies and given legal powers of arrest despite the fact that their fees were paid for by private interests.[61]

Private firms and protective associations also needed to identify those with suitable skills and local knowledge. For example, the Pinkertons, who normally relied on a pool of young men from Chicago to manage large-scale strike-breaking and property guard activity in the West (as they did with the railroad strike in Wyoming in 1885), nevertheless also turned to more specialized experts in cases involving detection and infiltration.[62] This often posed a problem of identifying competent individuals; the firm, for example, seems to have had a difficult time finding experts capable of reining in the James gang in 1873 and 1874.[63] And Fred Dodge, a special officer for Wells Fargo (as well as a friend of Wyatt Earp's from Tombstone), had trouble finding reliable guards

57 Ball, *Desert Lawmen*, 43, 209–211.

58 This was often the source of intense consternation by large corporations, and was frequently invoked to justify the hiring of private guards. 52nd Congress, 2nd Sess., *Congressional Record*, 1280 (1893), 84, 129–130, 161–162, 242.

59 See Hagan, *Charles Goodnight*, 74, 78.

60 James David Horan, *The Pinkertons: The Detective Dynasty That Made History* (New York: Crown Publishers, 1968), 189–202, 360–394; Morn, *The Eye That Never Sleeps*, 78–79, 91–109.

61 Prassel, *The Western Peace Officer*, 132–133, 138–142.

62 52nd Congress, 2nd Sess., *Congressional Record*, 136–138.

63 Horan, *The Pinkertons*, 194–202.

for payroll shipments he knew were under threat from bandits in the aftermath of a wave of hold-ups in the first decade of the twentieth century. He wanted, in particular, an "out and out fighting man"; the problem was that the firm could "not secure that kind of a man unless we know something about him, see him and talk with him and know that he has been tried before."[64] Detective agencies and private firms relied on reputations earned via connections to the gunfighting system to hire experienced operatives for range and guard work. Charlie Siringo, for example, who later wrote several books chronicling his many adventures working for the Pinkerton agency, was hired by William Pinkerton after presenting references from Pat Garrett (the killer of Billy the Kid), who he had known in his cattle driving days.[65]

Some private security firms specialized in particular kinds of services. The Baldwin-Felts agency provided numerous guards to mining camps, for instance, while Thiel focused on the supervision of railway employees.[66] The Pinkertons, while involved in both labor and guard work, were also active in combatting railroad robbery. Pinkerton agents unsuccessfully tried to capture the James gang in the early 1870s, and coordinated the pursuit of the famed Butch Cassidy and Wild Bunch band of bandits active in the Rocky Mountain West in the late 1890s.[67] The agency was also involved in lesser-known cases, including the attempt to track down Marion Hedgepeth, a now forgotten train robbing specialist active during the same time in Missouri.[68] The firm held contracts with multiple railroad firms and its records – particularly those emanating from the Denver office, where famed former undercover operative James McParland was in charge – contain a great deal of correspondence with local law officers and private detectives, in addition to professional gunfighters like Tom Horn.[69] The Pinkerton brothers, particularly William, were well-known for cultivating extensive networks with underworld figures, who could be primed for information about heists and happenings in the world of organized crime.

[64] Fred J. Dodge to C. L. Mackenzie, September 3, 1909, Box 3, Folder 1, Correspondence (French, New Mexico: Robbery, J. B. Humphreys alias Arkansas, 1908–1915), Captain Fred J. Dodge Collection, The Huntington Library.

[65] Howard R. Lamar, *Charlie Siringo's West: An Interpretive Biography* (Albuquerque, NM: University of New Mexico Press, 2005), 135–136.

[66] Robert Michael Smith, *From Blackjacks to Briefcases: A History of Commercialized Strikebreaking and Unionbusting in the United States* (Athens, OH: Ohio University Press, 2003), 22–30; J. Anthony Lukas, *Big Trouble: A Murder in a Small Western Town Sets Off a Struggle for the Soul of America* (New York: Simon & Schuster, 1998), 84–85.

[67] James David Horan, *Desperate Men: The James Gang and the Wild Bunch* (Lincoln: University of Nebraska Press, 1997); Richard M Patterson, *Train Robbery: The Birth, Flowering, and Decline of a Notorious Western Enterprise* (Boulder, CO: Johnson Books, 1981), 133–137.

[68] William A. Pinkerton, "Train Robberies, Train Robbers, and the 'Holdup' Men," in *Annual Convention of the International Association of Chiefs of Police* (1907), 35–37.

[69] Beau Riffenburgh, *Pinkerton's Great Detective: The Rough-and-Tumble Career of James McParland, America's Sherlock Holmes* (New York: Penguin, 2013).

Another solution was to try to adapt older institutions to new demands by finding the right individuals to serve as more permanent law officers, or by expanding the power of those who were able to act translocally. The only law officer with any degree of territorial or trans-state authority was the US marshal, the policing official of the federal court system. US marshals had expansive territorial jurisdictional powers, but were limited in which crimes they could police; up through the Civil War, marshals were involved primarily in serving federal district court process, catching fugitive criminals and slaves, addressing counterfeiting, aiding in some customs/border issues, and dealing with illegal liquor trading.[70] While other crimes that affected interstate commerce, such as bank robbery and train heists, gradually came under the mantle of federal law, the service itself was initially minuscule – each state or territory had a single marshal and a small staff.

However, that staff could include deputies and, just as with local law enforcement, the deputization mechanism provided a means whereby individual citizens could be granted federal policing powers, with the advantages of being able to act within a larger territorial ambit.[71] While deputy marshals were accountable to the executive branch, by enforcing interstate commercial law, their activity helped protect private property interests. Moreover, the federal government relied heavily on a reward system for paying territorial deputy marshals that increased the incentives for professional trackers and gunmen to become involved in what had previously been an extension of *posse comitatus* law.[72] In short, operating within the context of extant legal institutions, the new private firms nonetheless tried to use traditional mechanisms like deputization as a means of allowing competent martial experts to protect their property.

By linking roles – by serving as sheriff in addition to deputy marshal, for example – violence experts could overcome the jurisdictional limits of the local institutions as well as the problems posed by local animosity to corporate interests.[73] By building a network of contacts to rely on to help mobilize force when needed, private companies and other interests would also get access to on-demand protection services. The real question was how to identify the right experts.

70 Frederick S. Calhoun, *The Lawmen: United States Marshals and Their Deputies, 1789–1989* (Washington, DC: Smithsonian Institution Press, 1990), 25–119.

71 Prassel, *The Western Peace Officer*, 223.

72 Rao, "The Federal Posse Comitatus Doctrine," 46–53; Stuart H. Traub, "Rewards, Bounty Hunting, and Criminal Justice in the West: 1865–1900," *The Western Historical Quarterly* 19, no. 3 (1988): 287–301. The US Marshal's office was considered an important patronage role not only for the marshal himself, but also deputies. See Larry D. Ball, *The United States Marshals of New Mexico and Arizona Territories, 1846–1912* (Albuquerque: University of New Mexico Press, 1978), 6–17.

73 Ball, *Desert Lawmen*, 34–35.

Gunfights and Skills in Violence

The decision by mining, railroad, and cattle firms to hire guards was simple and legally protected by robust republican traditions – but who was a likely candidate for such a position? Those who were able to handle themselves on the range had to, first and foremost, be good at fighting. And, in the aftermath of the Civil War, developing skills in violence had gone hand-in-hand with both the explosion of personally available firearms and the profusion of men who had had direct experience using weapons against others. These were the seedbeds for the gunfighting skill and those who could demonstrate such skills were much more likely to credibly sell themselves as experts to the cattle, railroad, and mining companies.

Gunfighting itself, of course, was not new. But the introduction of the Colt revolver in 1836 and the dramatic explosion of distributions of personal (and concealable) firearms during the Mexican-American and, especially, the Civil War, dramatically increased the likelihood that guns would be used in conflicts, particularly when liquor or romantic conflict were involved.[74] The uptick in use of firearms is noticeable, for instance, in the much noticed post–Civil War crime wave.[75] More importantly, however, easily available small firearms paved the way for more frequent encounters among actors carrying guns in day-to-day life than when the most ubiquitous weapons were hunting rifles.

Randall Collins has shown that situations that lead to violence are unusual, deeply uncomfortable, and often require explicit training to master in a skillful way. Such interactions involve an emotional connection between participants, one that increases levels of unease between participants, and raises the stakes involved in the contest until, ultimately, violence is the only way to dissipate this interactive tension.[76] Learning how to be violent, in other words, is not natural, but is a skill that must be learned, one entailing emotional competence and the mastery of fear.

One of the key ways this skill emerges is experience in warfare. In the case of the United States, the Civil War – one of the largest, most industrialized conflicts of the nineteenth century – acted as a prime mover for the sudden, mass cultivation of violence expertise. With the industrial scale of its slaughter, the Civil War fundamentally altered perceptions of mortality, fear, and bodily harm for participants and onlookers alike, as the deaths of nearly 700,000 soldiers upended traditional techniques of adapting to the consequences of violence in society.[77] In the process, wartime experience expanded the capacity for ordinary people to engage in brutal behavior they may have previously found unimaginable.

[74] John Walter, *The Guns that Won the West: Firearms on the American Frontier, 1848–1898* (London: Greenhill Books, 2006), 90–112.

[75] Edith Abbott, "The Civil War and the Crime Wave of 1865–1870," *Social Service Review* 1, no. 2 (June 1927): 212–234; Courtwright, *Violent Land*, 45–46.

[76] Collins, *Violence: A Micro-sociological Theory*, 399–409.

[77] Drew Gilpin Faust, *This Republic of Suffering: Death and the American Civil War* (New York: Knopf, 2008), 3–60.

Producing effective violence in the gunfighting milieu required a second skill as well: the capacity to cultivate a reputation. Using guns is quite easy, but the costs of not being skillful enough in an interaction in which personal firearms are used can be greater than with other technologies. Being skillful with a firearm thus also means *avoiding* contests in which one is likely to prove a less skillful participant – bullets are fast and deadly, and if one acts too slowly or with poor aim the chance of death is high.[78]

Indeed, the credibility of one's reputation as a skilled and dangerous adversary occasionally meant actually *demonstrating* those skills in a public way. Gunfights themselves played a key role in establishing this reputation. While fights themselves almost never followed the "walkdown" formula made famous in Western movies and were intense, sporadic, and incoherent affairs, in which ambushes were common and which frequently killed or maimed bystanders, the publicness of the gunfight was one of its most important characteristics.[79]

The reason for this had to do with American legal tradition, in which the "duty to retreat" found in English common law was revised to allow for the principle of standing one's ground. This meant, in practice, that as long as one could credibly (or sometimes incredibly) claim that an opponent also had a weapon and was threatening one's life, homicidal self-defense was legally justifiable. Hence, the trick for many specialists was to "get the drop" on one's opponent – surprising them with an attack while simultaneously eliciting a counterattack, rendering the proceedings legal. This also meant that the publicness of many gunfights could be a boon to the participants; witnesses who could testify that the interaction was a square meeting of equally armed individuals could provide a legal escape for fighters whose opponents met an unfortunate demise.[80]

The legality of fighting was itself an artifact of the republican conception of local protection undergirding imperial authority in the territories. Settlers were expected not only to defend aggressively their own property, but also to expand and settle new lands. Delegating law and order to local communities in areas surrounded by enemies implied an proactive and frequent use of violence on the part of regular citizens. As a result, the presumption of violence was integral to law enforcement in the territories.[81]

78 Thomas C Schelling, *Arms and Influence* (New Haven, CT: Yale University Press, 1966), 23–24.

79 Roger D. McGrath, *Gunfighters, Highwaymen, and Vigilantes: Violence on the Frontier* (Berkeley: University of California Press, 1987), 76–85.

80 Brown, *No Duty to Retreat*, 3–20.

81 This presumption animated not only gunfighting, but also the frequent recourse to lynching and vigilantism in territorial districts. Ken Gonzales-Day, *Lynching in the West, 1850–1935* (Durham, NC: Duke University Press, 2006); Ashraf H. A. Rushdy, *American Lynching* (New Haven, CT: Yale University Press, 2012). The number of gunfighters who participated in vigilantism – including Whispering Smith, Wyatt Earp, and others – is difficult to pin down, but there was undoubtedly a deep connection between the notion of communal protection and personal skill in gunplay within a market setting.

When fighting with guns therefore becomes widespread and legally protected, and participants in those fights survive and become known as powerful gunfighters, they are able, presumably, to avoid challenges to their expertise – at least from everyone except those who understand that vanquishing a well-known fighter would also provide a quick means to cultivating precisely such a reputation for one's self.

Indeed, in large measure, the gunfighters we know so well – Wyatt Earp, Doc Holliday, Wild Bill Hickok, Jesse James, and Billy the Kid – are famous precisely because of their careful management of their reputation as tough men of the West, many of whom had close relationships with the press, powerful political allies, or biographers who could spread the word about their dangerous capacities.[82] The post-frontier mythologization of the gunfighter is so important in American cultural history, it might be seen as a practical historical byproduct of the gunfighter's attention to matters of reputation and publicity as a form of marketing their skills.

How could a gunfighter develop a reputation, then? One way was to fight in places where employers were located or where news of the fights could travel easily. On the Western frontier, the expansion of the market lead to the development of boomtowns, places where the otherwise sparse transportation network intersected with local markets. Because these towns connected different kinds of markets – local markets with large, expanding national trading networks – I call them *entrepôts*, a term for ports of call or other places that specialize in the exchange of goods and services.

It was the high plains boomtowns of the cattle frontier – Dodge City (Kansas), Abilene (Kansas), Cheyenne (Wyoming), and others – where gunfighting became an actual career. While there were many other boomtowns (such as Fort Griffin) that played a similar role, these entrepôts were the main places where cattle trails intersected with railheads to Chicago, where many of the actual participants in gunfights in the 1860s through mid-1880s could meet with representatives of railroad and cattle firms (see Table 18 for a list of the cattle entrepôts used in this study, as well as information on which railroads and trails they serviced).[83] Over time, the connections forged in these towns provided a framework upon which a larger industry of private violence experts would be built, and diffusion of information and the making of the gunfighter career got tied up with the social network relations linking fighters together.

Many of the most famous gunfighters made their way through these entrepôts of the West. For instance, one such figure was Wild Bill Hickok,

82 Stiles, *Jesse James*, 210–211, 247–248, Brown, *No Duty to Retreat*, 84–85; Joseph G. Rosa, *They Called Him Wild Bill: The Life and Adventures of James Butler Hickok* (Norman: University of Oklahoma Press, 1974), 105–110.

83 Robert R. Dykstra, *The Cattle Towns* (New York: Knopf, 1968), 1–73; Hine and Faragher, *The American West*, 307–308. Other towns, of course, also played an important role in connecting gunfighters to potential employers, but I focus on railroad/trail entrepôts because they are the places we are most likely to observe this dynamic.

TABLE 18. *Entrepôt towns on the cattle frontier (1865–1890)*

Entrepôt	Peak years	Railroad	Trail
Abilene, Kansas	1865–1875	Kansas Pacific	Chisholm Trail
Ellsworth, Kansas	1870–1875	Kansas Pacific	Chisholm Trail
Wichita, Kansas	1870–1880	AT & SF	Chisholm Trail
Dodge City, Kansas	1875–1890	AT & SF	Western Trail
Ogallala, Nebraska	1880–1885	Union Pacific	Western Trail
Caldwell, Kansas	1880–1890	Chicago, Kansas & Nebraska	Chisholm Trail
Cheyenne, Wyoming	1880–1890	Union Pacific	Goodnight Trail

whose career as a law officer and gambler emerged out his experience with the Union Army in the vicious Kansas-Missouri theater during the Civil War. He had served as a US deputy marshal and town constable throughout the high plains in the 1860s and 1870s before becoming town marshal in Abilene, where he replaced another well-known gunfighter, "Bear River" Tom Smith, in 1871. Abilene was the center of a booming gambling and cattle industry and, while there, Hickok became familiar with a number of other frontier notables, including John Wesley Hardin. Hickok's most famous fight in Abilene – with Phil Coe in 1871 – involved the aforementioned dispute over wartime rivalries, as Coe and his friend Ben Thompson had grown resentful of Hickok's supposed pro-Union bias and comments. After killing Coe in one of the most stereotypical "walkdown" duels in Western history, Hickok became nationally known and went on to a career with Buffalo Bill's Wild West show, before being killed himself by Jack McCall in the mining boomtown of Deadwood in 1876. Throughout the rest of his life, Hickok's fights in Abilene made him an almost totemic figure with a reputation he was able to convert into economic gain.[84]

Entrepôts like Abilene helped make the gunfighter market by serving as a diffusion mechanism for marketable reputations. In such towns, a thriving local newspaper industry and informal rumor mill allowed information to spread quickly about comings and goings, particularly when events occurred that were bloody and sensational.[85] Moreover, the reputations of entrepôt fighters diffused regionally and beyond through a number of channels. The national press played an important role in this regard; cattle entrepôt affairs were nationally important, particularly during the boom years when even mundane saloon brawls were covered with some frequency in big-city newspapers.[86] Individual

[84] Rosa, *They Called Him Wild Bill*, 53–206.

[85] Werner J. Einstadter, "Crime News in the Old West," in *Media, Process, and the Social Construction of Crime: Studies in Newsmaking Criminology*, ed. Gregg Barak (London: Routledge, 1995), 49–68.

[86] For instance, I located 108 articles published in the *New York Times* and *Chicago Tribune* between 1865 and 1885 with the keywords "Dodge City," "Abilene," or "Wichita" in the title. Proquest Historical Newspapers Database, accessed July 4, 2013. These articles frequently dealt

entrepôt notables, such as Hickok, were profiled by serious periodicals such as *Harper's*, while John Wesley Hardin, Luke Short, and Bat Masterson first gained notoriety through sensationalist journals like *The National Police Gazette*.[87] As key economic locales in a very important new market, entrepôts were also central nodes in diffusing information translocally.

Dodge City, a classic Kansas cattle entrepôt, was a particularly important meeting ground for men interested in working as guards or range inspectors to develop a shared economic identity and to share information. The town became famous not only for its shootouts, but also for an assortment of gunfighting talent that could be made available to buyers.[88] For example, when he served as sheriff of Ford County, within which Dodge was located, Bat Masterson was asked by the AT & SF Railroad to gather a group of gunmen to protect railroad interests against the efforts of the Denver & Rio Grande (D & RG) to seize right of way in a prized Colorado mountain pass. Masterson (with the help of Doc Holliday) put together a mercenary band of Dodge denizens, who, after making their way to Pueblo, engaged in a short but violent struggle at the AT & SF roundhouse against the D & RG's men. Despite their willingness to work for Kansas interests in the Rocky Mountains, many of Masterson's colleagues (such as Dave Mather, Joshua Webb, and Hickok's old rival Ben Thompson) went on to careers as professional gunmen, selling their skills to a variety of bidders or, in the case of some, finding a life of occasional crime more profitable.[89] The town's reputation as a gunfighting emporium continued through the 1880s, when it served as the recruiting ground for the mercenary bands who participated in the county seat wars of Kansas, a group that included at least one former outlaw (Ben Daniels), one future US deputy marshal (Bill Tilghman), and Bat's brother James Masterson.[90]

Although railroads and towns only rarely hired entire armies of gunfighters, this example still demonstrates the importance of the communication network connecting these towns. It was also this network that allowed gunfighters who were physically distant to share information among themselves about more usual economic opportunities to serve in *posses*, collect rewards, or identify targets for banditry. Livestock associations like the Wyoming Stock Growers Association and the Protective and Detective Association of Texas issued circulars detailing rewards for stolen cattle, while the Rocky Mountain

with violent events, though they occasionally covered economic developments in the cattle industry as well.

87 "A Desperado's Declaration," *The National Police Gazette*, August 16 (1879): 3; "Dodge City's Sensation," *The National Police Gazette*, July 21 (1883): 5; George Ward Nichols, "Wild Bill," *Harper's New Monthly Magazine* 34, no. 201 (1867): 273–286.

88 Dykstra counted at least fifteen killings between 1876 and 1885 in Dodge, although there may have been more. Dykstra, *The Cattle Towns*, 144.

89 Gary L. Roberts, *Doc Holliday: The Life and Legend* (Hoboken, NJ: Wiley, 2006), 104–108.

90 Robert K. DeArment, *Ballots and Bullets: The Bloody County Seat Wars of Kansas* (Norman: University of Oklahoma Press, 2006), 38–40.

Detective Association, founded by Dave Cook in Denver in 1873, had affiliates throughout the Rocky Mountain West (including the cattle frontier) who shared photos and information about wanted criminals.[91] Cattle and mining associations began seeking out those who had good reputations as fighters-for-hire, while well-known lawmen like Whispering Smith's acquaintance Cyrus Shores and others became clearinghouses for information on identifying competent deputies and mining or railroad guards.[92] Sheriffs used the telegraph to mobilize *posses* composed of expert trackers with local knowledge in remote areas, while bandits used the same technology to coordinate stage and train heists.[93] The social organization of the gunfighting market depended, in other words, on the existence of towns embedded in a regional communications system.

Diffusion of information about job opportunities was also a matter of personal relationships forged in the entrepôt towns themselves, which continued to aid former residents as they moved throughout the Rocky Mountain West in the 1880s. Ben Daniels, for example, who had seen action as both a horse thief in Nebraska and a law officer in Dodge City, benefited from the network of former boomtown affiliates, including Jim Talbot, who helped him find work as a deputy in Lamar, Colorado, in the late 1880s.[94] After his experience with the Gray County seat war in Kansas in 1887 and 1889, he worked as an armed guard in the Cripple Creek struggle of 1893.[95] Former Dodge residents also organized a thieving ring in Las Vegas, New Mexico, in 1879, which drew heavily on the personal relationships forged in the saloons and gambling halls of the Kansas entrepôt.[96]

As a result of the information and social connections available in enrepôts, gunfighters increasingly began to regard all their employment options as violence experts – from law enforcement, to banditry, to private detection – as economic opportunities rather than commitments to a cause. Entrepôts fundamentally transformed the nature of all kinds of local coercive roles into a vibrant extension of the integrated postbellum market, one infused by experts who had more in common with each other than they did with either traditional peace officers or outlaws. They provided pathways for, say, cowboys

91 Traub, "Rewards, Bounty Hunting, and Criminal Justice in the West," 297–298; Prassel, *The Western Peace Officer*, 135–136; Newspaper Clippings, David J. Cook Papers, MSS 725, Stephen H. Hart Library and Research Center, Colorado Historical Society.

92 See, for example Box 1, Folder 3 (Miscellaneous Papers), Cyrus Shores Papers, Western History Collection, Denver Public Library. This file includes letters from those requesting Shores's help in finding work as deputies.

93 Mark R. Ellis, *Law and Order in Buffalo Bill's Country: Legal Culture and Community on the Great Plains, 1867–1910* (Lincoln: University of Nebraska Press, 2007), 66–68.

94 Robert K. DeArment and Jack DeMattos, *A Rough Ride to Redemption: The Ben Daniels Story* (Norman: University of Oklahoma Press, 2010), 10–21, 52–55.

95 ibid., 57–65, 70–71. 96 Ball, *The United States Marshals*, 95–97.

to become gunslingers, feudists to become bandits, and buffalo hunters to become stagecoach guards.

Indeed, over time, gunfighting activity in specific places became less important than the social structure linking gunfighters together. In the late 1880s and 1890s, for example, mining boomtowns developed in places like Leadville (Colorado) and Tombstone (Arizona), which served a similar function of connecting resources to eastern market interests. But by then, gunfighters developed other ways of establishing reputation and sharing information about expertise. In particular, the social connections linking gunfighters together had grown extensive enough to allow participants to network their way into jobs. The institutionalization of the gunfighting market, in turn, meant that the activity could spread beyond the narrow confines of the entrepôt towns. What had once been the idiosyncratic career choice of some violence experts, who used their skills in particular contexts, was becoming a full-blown social system. The next section begins to lay out this point empirically.

GUNFIGHTING AS A MARKET INSTITUTION: 1850–1930

Western gunfighting developed in four stages. The first, take-off stage lasted from just before the Civil War through approximately 1875 and was centered in Texas, Kansas, and Missouri. This period involved the organization of the James-Younger Gang out of the remnants of Quantrill's raiders, as well as the emergence of the first "Wild West" gunfighter characters in the buffalo hunting regions of the northern plains (e.g., Wild Bill Hickok) and the explosion of some of the most violent Reconstruction battles in Texas (e.g., the Lee-Peacock and Sutton-Taylor Feuds of the 1860s). Participants in these events were, in large measure, relatively disconnected from one another, but the convention of gunfighting was born in this period, as was the linking of other categories of violent actor (such as the desperado) to the larger category of the gunfighter. At the same time, a small network of individuals tied through entrepôts began to lay the groundwork for the transformation of random fighting into a means for diffusing skills and consolidating economic roles.

The second, professionalizing stage of gunfighting occurred from approximately 1875 to 1885 and expanded its reach into New Mexico, Arizona, and Colorado, while remaining focused on the cattle frontier; this was the golden age of gunfights in popular mythology (for example, this was the period when famous gunfights involving Wyatt Earp at the OK Corral and Billy the Kid in Lincoln County, New Mexico, as well as the martyrdom of Jesse James and Wild Bill Hickok, occurred). The key structural difference in this period was that what had, for the most part, been sporadic violent events now took on the cast of a larger system of social interaction, in which entrepôts played an important role in providing professional opportunities to savvy violence expert and diffusing their reputations. Indeed, this period has been mythologized for precisely this reason: what had appeared to be random violence could now be interpreted as a recognizable form of organized force.

The third, consolidating stage of gunfighting, from 1885 through the end of the century (the period of the large, organized gangs like the Dalton, Butch Cassidy and the Wild Bunch and Hole-in-the Wall gangs, as well as the development of a robust railroad and private detective industry), involved the partial polarization of gunfighting into camps of, broadly speaking, pro- and anti-incorporation forces. Though the social ties linked bandits and lawmen into a gunfighting network across the Rocky Mountain West, the focus of the system remained the Southwest – Oklahoma and the borderlands of Texas and New Mexico. This process by no means undermined the fundamental market logic of gunfighting, however, nor did it lead to any attempts at actually establishing a state monopoly over this pool of experts. Instead, gunfighters remained as mercenary as ever, often working for very powerful private interests like livestock and mine owners' associations rather than the state, but they also became more specialized in the kinds of skills employed. Railroad and range detectives, for example, were expert at tracking the highly organized train robbery gangs, which allowed some of them (like Tom Horn and Whispering Smith) to hire out as assassins or thugs for extra money.[97] During this stage, entrepôts became less important than the social relations among gunfighters themselves in diffusing information about opportunities.

The last stage of gunfighting, from approximately 1905 through the 1920s, was a period of rapid decline. Most of the old gunfighters died out and the political organization of violence in the United States was transformed by participation in the Spanish-American War and, especially, World War I. New forms of federal enforcement (such as the Border Patrol) made older forms of local enforcement obsolete and groups like the Rangers became increasingly professionalized and less dependent on the expertise of independent fighters. A few fringe figures held on, but the older traditions of banditry were altered by the introduction of the automobile and the advent of prohibition into a nationally organized set of criminal syndicates.

While these stages differed geographically, they were nevertheless linked together by the people who participated in them. Take the career of Frank Canton, for example. Born with the name Joe Horner in Indiana in 1849, Canton made his way to Texas after the Civil War, where, in addition to organizing a gang of rustlers, he got involved in a deadly dispute with African-American cavalry unit and became a fugitive, only to get caught by the Texas Rangers after robbing a bank in Comanche in 1877.[98] After escaping from the Rangers and changing his name, Canton made his way to the cattle frontier of

[97] Charles A. Siringo, *Two Evil Isms, Pinkertonism and Anarchism* (Chicago: C. A. Siringo, 1915), 43–57.

[98] Robert K. DeArment, *Alias Frank Canton* (Norman: University of Oklahoma Press, 1996), 21–46.

northern Nebraska and southern Wyoming, hiring on (like Whispering Smith) as a range detective with the Wyoming Stock Growers Association and working as a sheriff in the 1880s. In 1892, Canton played a key role in one of the most famous range fights in western history – the Johnson County War – where he developed a reputation as a skillful fighter and led a controversial invasion of the KC Ranch, the supposed refuge of a group of cattle rustlers. Moving to Oklahoma Territory in the mid-1890s, Canton served as a US deputy marshal under the jurisdiction of Isaac Parker at Fort Smith, where he was involved in the pursuit of the Dalton-Doolin Gang of train robbers who were plaguing the region.[99] By the late 1890s, Canton moved yet again, this time to Alaska where, in addition to pursuing mining interests, he continued his career with the marshals service (in another stroke of serendipity, Wyatt Earp and his wife, Josie, also in search of gold in the Yukon, rented the cabin Canton built in Rampart City in 1898).[100] After failing to strike it rich in Alaska, Canton moved back to Oklahoma and became the adjutant general of the Oklahoma National Guard in 1907.

Canton's life is a complex microcosm of gunfighter history. Moving through very different positions – on different sides of the law – Canton used his coercive skills to find work, at times for himself, at times for private interests, and at times for the state. He moved from the cattle frontier to the Indian territory to the mining frontier, and developed social and economic connections with a number of other prominent gunfighters, including Bill Tilghman, Scott "Quick Shot" Davis (Whispering Smith's old colleague from the Dakota territory), and Joe LeFors, a much-feared Wyoming law officer who, in addition to being one of the most prominent pursuers of the Butch Cassidy gang of railroad robbers, would go on to arrest the former Pinkerton agent Tom Horn for murder in 1903.[101] Although he apparently suffered intense pangs of guilt following the killing of several unarmed rustlers during the Johnson County War, Canton was ruthless in converting these connections and his reputation into opportunities to make money.

How did Canton's social world actually emerge? To explore this, I constructed a dataset of 255 participants in gunfights active mostly (though not exclusively) in the Southwest between 1850 and 1930, collecting information about their fights, their social connections, and their backgrounds.[102]

99 DeArment, *Alias Frank Canton*, 171–198. 100 ibid., 223.

101 Joe Le Fors, *Wyoming Peace Officer, an Autobiography* (Laramie, WY: Laramie Print. Co., 1953), 57–58; DeArment, *Alias Frank Canton*, 122, 190–191 .

102 Appendix C (available at www.jonathanobert.com) provides a list of these individuals and information about when their first and last gunfights occurred. The data are derived primarily from Bill O'Neal's *Encyclopedia of Western Gunfighters*, widely considered the standard reference work on the topic, though I supplement this work with several other sources. See Bill O'Neal, *Encyclopedia of Western Gunfighters* (Norman: University of Oklahoma Press, 1979); Robert K. DeArment, *Assault on the Deadwood Stage: Road Agents and Shotgun Messengers* (Norman: University of Oklahoma Press, 2011); Robert K. DeArment, *Deadly Dozen: Twelve Forgotten Gunfighters of the Old West* (Norman: University of Oklahoma Press, 2003);

These gunfighters compose just a sample of what was undoubtedly a much more extensive system of private violence specialists active in the trans–Mississippi West.[103] Nevertheless, the statistics for these group provide some important clues. In total, these actors fought at least 590 gunfights, ranging from 1854 (the earliest gunfight in the dataset) to 1928. Texas (165) had, by far, the largest number of gunfights in the sample, followed by New Mexico (81), Kansas (78), and Arizona (65).[104] These four states, in fact, represent two-thirds of the total number of gunfights in the system, not surprising given that these were the primary locations for the cattle and mining frontiers.

Moreover, while this represents a very small sample of the overall number of gun battles in southwestern states during this period, this data provide a rough approximation of the general trends in violence identified by other scholars.[105] Gunfighting exhibited a particular development – growing initially after the Civil War and then peaking in the mid 1880s before gradually declining. To begin, Figure 13 depicts the number of participants in the gunfighting system – that is, those who had fought at some point in the past and who would fight again. The slope of the line indicates that after a period of slow growth in the 1850s and early 1860s, the Civil War catalyzed a dramatic escalation in those who had had a gunfight or would have one in the future.

Robert K. DeArment, *Deadly Dozen: Forgotten Gunfighters of the Old West, Volume 2* (Norman: University of Oklahoma Press, 2007); DeArment, *Deadly Dozen Vol. 3*.

103 Ed Bartholomew has claimed that there were over 25,000 individuals participated in someway in gunfights in the West, a number that has never been independently verified. See Ed Bartholomew, "Review of *Encyclopedia of Western Gunfighters* by Bill O'Neal," *Arizona and the West* 22, no. 1 (1980): pp. 77–78. There were likely several thousand semi-professional and professional violence specialists active between the Civil War and the turn of the century.

104 Appendix C (available at www.jonathanobert.com) includes information about the aggregate numbers of fights in various states.

105 See, for example, Clare V. McKanna, *Homicide, Race, and Justice in the American West, 1880–1920* (Tucson: University of Arizona Press, 1997). Also see the table in *Journal of the Reconstruction Convention Which Met at Austin, Texas, June 1, A.D., 1868*, vol. 1 (Austin: Tracy, Siemering & Co., 1870), 194, which lists 939 fatalities associated with Reconstruction violence in Texas alone from 1865 to 1868. These were precisely the kinds of events in which many future gunfighters participated. In making this argument, of course, I am aware that I am directly contradicting a powerful strain of historical revisionism that contends that the postbellum US frontier was not actually an unusually violent place. However, recent scholarship has argued that firearm use and violence were relatively common in the West, the general view I adopt in this chapter. See Randolph Roth, "Guns, Murder, and Probability: How Can We Decide Which Figures to Trust?," *Reviews in American History* 35, no. 2 (2007): 165–175; Clare V. McKanna, *Race and Homicide in Nineteenth-Century California* (Reno: University of Nevada Press, 2002); McGrath, *Gunfighters, Highwaymen, and Vigilantes*; and especially Randolph Roth, *American Homicide* (Cambridge, MA: Harvard University Press, 2009), 354–385. For older revisionist views see: Robert R. Dykstra, "Body Counts and Murder Rates: The Contested Statistics of Western Violence," *Reviews in American History* 31, no. 4 (2003): 554–563; W. Eugene Hollon, *Frontier Violence: Another Look* (Oxford: Oxford University Press, 1974); Robert R. Dykstra, "Overdosing on Dodge City," *The Western Historical Quarterly* 27, no. 4 (1996): 505–514; Prassel, *The Western Peace Officer*.

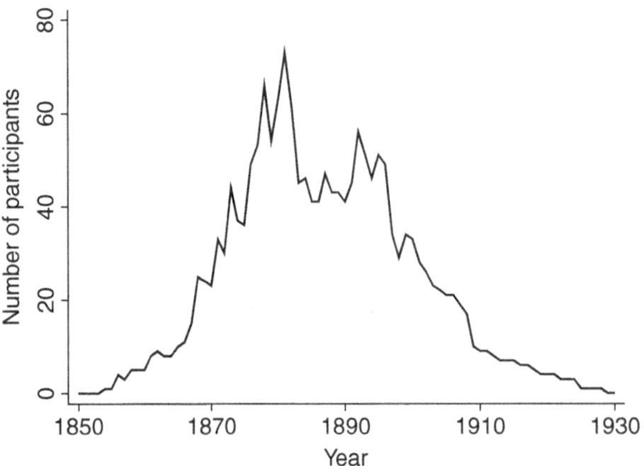

FIGURE 13. Gunfighting participants (1850–1930)

Indeed, participating in the war was a crucial experience for many gunfighters; at least 80% of those active in the mid-1860s were Civil War veterans, while even at the height of the gunfighting market in the mid and late 1870s, nearly 40% of the total gunfighting population had been active in the war.[106]

What about the fighting itself? Interestingly, the earliest period of gunfighting activity was also the most intense in terms of the likelihood that a participant would get involved in a fight. Between 1850 and 1875, there were approximately 0.43 fights per participant per year, while in the second stage (1875–1885) the number declined to 0.34. In the last two stages, the average number of yearly fights per participant was reduced to 0.27 (1885–1900) and 0.15 (post-1900) respectively. These proportions declined despite the fact that the aggregate number of fights per year actually *increased* until after the cattle boom declined in the late 1870s (in 1878, for instance, there were thirty-six fights, the most of any given year). In other words, even though overall levels of violence did not decline until the mid-1880s, individual gunfighters were increasingly able to go about their work without having to actually resort to force as frequently as they had previously. Some of this can be explained as simply a consequence of the net cumulation of system participants over time, but it also suggests, potentially, that reputations may have been beginning to substitute for actual fighting as a means of securing career opportunities. Later I show how more precisely the diffusion of reputations played out in the career pathways of professional gunfighters, but this trend illustrates the general point that the practices of gunfighters themselves changed over time in a manner consistent with the creation of a market.

[106] This decline is not simply a matter of mortality or professional disengagement; over 78% of gunfighting Civil War veterans were still alive in 1875, while over 60% of still living veterans were still working as professional violence experts in the later period. Indeed, as late as 1895, 40% of known veterans in the gunfighting system were sill alive.

Entrepôts, Reputations, and Employment Opportunities

What was the difference between the professional and amateur gunfighters? Professional gunfighters were not professionals in the sense of doctors or lawyers, with credentialing exams and professional associations; instead, they were violence experts whose jobs expected them to be able to engage in gunplay. This reliance on violence could be incidental but still critical to the success of their main source of income (e.g., gambling) or could involve taking a position in a role in which violence was the key function (e.g., law enforcement or guard work).[107] In both cases, the ability to use violence was critical to financial success, whether working for themselves or others. The employers of the gunfighters in this sample included at least thirty-four different firms, ranging from huge entities like the XIT Ranch in the Texas panhandle and national transport businesses like Wells Fargo and the Union Pacific, to smaller family ranches and local range associations. While most professional fighters worked for counties, towns, or firms, others, like Wyatt Earp, Bat Masterson, and Ben Thompson, occasionally went into business as saloonkeepers and gamblers on their own.

Even though only a few fights occurred in in entrepôt towns relative to the total number of fights, they were very important for the making of professional experts. Indeed, of the thirty-two gunfight participants in the sample who fought in the entrepôt locales listed in Table 18 between 1865 and 1885 (the height of the cattle boom), only four failed to become gunfighting professionals, while this was true for over a third of the non-entrepôt fighters – a statistically significant difference.[108] In other words, entrepôts were crucial in connecting fighters to job opportunities, forging links between employer and employee in those crucial years after the Civil War.

More strikingly, there is evidence that fighting in entrepôt towns also created more opportunities for career-development *over time*. That is, having experience in an entrepôt early in one's career offered advantage in later years, when the cattle trade had declined in significance. To measure this, I coded the number of moves made by professional gunfighters into new positions as violence experts in the years following their first professional experience with violence; those who fought in entrepôt towns made more such moves, on average, than those who did not.[109] In other words, entrepôt fighters

107 I exclude service in guerrilla militaries, as well as in militia, feuding, and vigilante groups, even if the experience involved some economic benefit, since these were primarily partisan commitments. I also exclude conventional military participation as professional work because such violence was not uniquely a matter of individual or small group effort. Instead, I try to identify those for whom individual competence in gunplay was remunerated.

108 There were ninety-one professionals and fifty-two nonprofessional active exclusively in non-entrepôt settings during this period. Fisher's exact test for this difference in outcomes (two-tailed) is significant at $p<0.05$.

109 Difference of means tests assuming unequal variances allow us to reject the null that the value of a one-tailed difference of means statistic is greater than zero with $p<0.05$; $t=-0.89$ with forty-seven observations of number of moves by non-entrepôt professionals (mean=2.45, s.d.=0.23) and twenty-three of number of moves by entrepôt professionals (mean=2.83, s.d.=0.36).

were significantly more flexible in their career trajectories than other kinds of professional gunfighters, exploiting multiple opportunities to use violence in order to earn money.

That they had more jobs, of course, could also mean that such entrepôt fighters were also less likely to keep jobs they did have, perhaps because they were the types of people who lived a more mobile life; the peripatetic careers of Wyatt Earp, John Wesley Hardin, and other famous entrepôt fighters, many of whom made their way from boomtown to boomtown, indicates that this factor likely played a role. But even if this is true, these entrepreneurial actors were still critical in the making of the actual market of gunfighters, since boomtown fighters were more likely to occupy violence expert positions and convert them into careers. Thus, regardless of whether the entrepôt difference in professional mobility is a selection effect of boomtowns, the underlying spatial effect is real: those who were active in places on the cattle frontier where large-scale capital interacted with the small-scale propensity for southwestern gunfighting were also pioneers in professionalizing a market for violence. They were, in essence, adapting traditional rules for self-protection in a world where social relations had been radically transformed by the frontier.

The Gunfighting Career and Opportunism

One of the key markers of a professional mercenary is opportunism; thus, if gunfighters were truly market actors, we should expect them to pursue money wherever it might be found. This means that, rather than acting as "good" guys or "bad" guys, most gunfighters were not really partisans; instead they pursued flexible careers.

Wyatt Earp's life is exemplary in this regard. Earp is best known for his work as a law officer in the 1870s and 1880s in Wichita, Dodge City, and, especially, Tombstone, where he and several allies (including Doc Holliday) were involved in the most famous gunfight of all: the battle at the OK Corral in 1881.[110] The fight itself was a result of a long-simmering dispute between the Earp brothers and the Clantons and McLaurys, the former of which were associated with the Cowboys, a group of suspected rustlers and bandits active in the border region. In it – and through the promotion of sympathetic biographers like Stuart Lake, who composed a myth-filled hagiography of Earp's life in 1931 – Wyatt gained a reputation as the quintessential incorporation gunfighter, fighting on behalf of business and Republican interests in a region that was plagued by a great deal of local resistance. Earp's post–OK Corral career was marked

110 The literature on Earp's life is quite complex and controversial. For the best accounts, see Allen Barra, *Inventing Wyatt Earp: His Life and Many Legends* (Lincoln: University of Nebraska Press, 2009); Andrew C. Isenberg, *Wyatt Earp: A Vigilante Life* (New York: Hill & Wang, 2013); Casey Tefertiller, *Wyatt Earp: The Life behind the Legend* (New York: John Wiley, 1997).

by adventures in Alaska and San Francisco (among other places), where he indulged in gambling and attempted to make his fortune with mining interests, all the while cultivating his reputation as a fierce and quick-witted fighter.

At the same time, as Andrew Isenberg has recently shown, this story is much more complex than the heroic narrative lets on – early in his life, Wyatt Earp had very likely been a bodyguard at a bordello and had been involved in several scrapes with the law, including an 1871 arrest in the Indian Territory for horse theft.[111] And the fight with the Clantons had as much to do with political opposition as it did rustling – the Clantons were Democrats, whose sometime ally Johnny Behan had defeated Earp in his bid for sheriff of Cochise County in 1881 and had refused to appoint Earp a lucrative position as deputy. Moreover, Earp was a frequent practitioner of private violence; after the gunfight – in which several of the Cowboys were killed – and an inconclusive trial, the Cowboys struck back, killing Morgan, Wyatt's younger brother, and wounding his older brother, Virgil. This lead Earp, now deputized as a US marshal, to organize a *posse* ostensibly to arrest the suspects in the killing, but that in reality served as an assassination campaign against several of the more notorious Cowboys.[112] The Vendetta ride made Earp and Doc Holliday temporary fugitives as they fled to Colorado, where they met up with Bat Masterson, who had started a gambling hall in Trinidad.

In other words, while professional gunfighters often did participate as partisans in specific feud or conflicts, they were also usually quite alert to the opportunities afforded on both sides of the law. Earp's work as a bouncer, law officer, horse thief, and vigilante depicts a complex career driven not only by partisan, but also by familial and pecuniary motives.

To capture this biographical complexity, I coded the roles of each professional gunfighter in the sample (there were 188 in total), noting whether or not they worked at any point for law enforcement or incorporation interests (e.g., private detectives, range detectives, and so on), whether they had any criminal behavior or activity in their careers, and whether or not they had combined both kinds of roles. I coded those whose biography only included the first kind of activity as "law and order" gunfighters; those whose biography only included the second, I call "bandits," while those whose pursued both are the "mixed" fighters.[113]

Figure 14 depicts the yearly proportion of professional gunfighters fitting each profile. The curves in the figure demonstrate two important things. First, the early period of gunfighting was characterized by a relative high level of banditry and a low level of law-and-order professionalism. This was, as

111 Isenberg, *Wyatt Earp*, 45, 62–63. 112 ibid., 113–169.

113 A few were unknown and hence excluded from the analysis. The commitments of nonprofessional gunfighters were also coded, though they play little role in the following analysis. In previous work, I have referred to the law-and-order and banditry roles as "incorporation" and "non-incorporation" respectively. See Obert, "The Six-Shooter Marketplace: 19th-Century Gunfighting as Violence Expertise," 67.

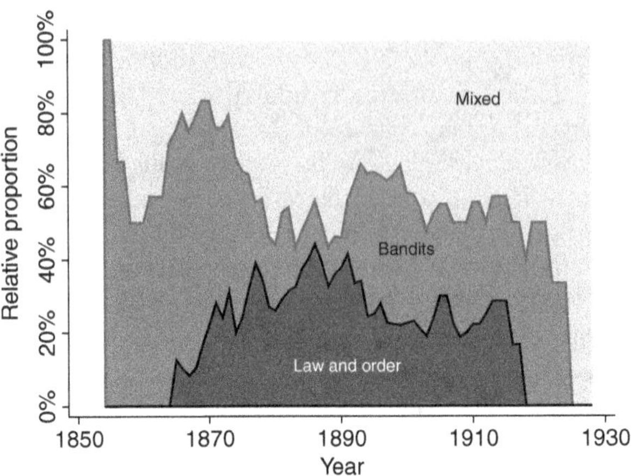

FIGURE 14. Professional gunfighter career types (1850–1930)

pointed out above, the result of the transformation of Civil War struggle into a campaign of predation on the part of groups like the Jesse James Gang, as well as generalized expansion of gunfighting techniques. It was only by the mid-1870s that a group of professionalized law-and-order gunfighters began to emerge.

Second, and more intriguingly, gunfighters in the mixed category were also an increasingly overrepresented proportion of the yearly gunfighting system, particularly after 1877 and 1878. These were the true opportunists, who moved back and forth between working on behalf of local governments and large firms while also participating in activities like banditry or rustling. The growth of this group introduces strong evidence that gunfighters had become market actors. Of the 188 members of the sub-sample, eighty-nine, or 47 percent, worked for a large-scale pro-incorporation interest like a private detective firm, a cattle association, or for the state or federal government at some point in their careers, a figure which included well over half of the total number of mixed fighters (58%).

The social milieu of entrepôt towns helped forge the mixed identity. Those who fought in the entrepôt towns identified in Table 18 in the early part of their careers were much more likely to move back and forth between law-and-order and banditry roles than those who did not. Overall, 119 of the 188 total professional fighters in the subsample were active during this period; of those who fought in entrepôt towns during this period, 57 percent can be categorized as mixed fighters, while only 30 percent of the non-entrepôt fighters pursued this kind of path – a statistically significant difference.[114]

[114] Fisher's Exact Test (two-tailed) is significant at the $p<0.05$ level for ninety non-entrepôt (sixty-three non-mixed; twenty-seven mixed) and twenty-eight entrepôt (twelve non-mixed; sixteen mixed) professional gunfighters.

In addition, just as with the emergence of private security in Chicago in the 1850s, a significant minority of law-and-order gunfighters (around 38%) moved between private and public employment, working as private detectives, cattle inspectors, bounty hunters, private guards, or special constables in addition to serving as law officers. Bob Paul, who was responsible for trying to chase down Wyatt Earp after the Vendetta Ride, had worked as a sheriff in both northern California and Arizona, as well as a Wells Fargo guard.[115] Fred Dodge, the associate of Earp's from Tombstone and Wells Fargo special officer, also worked as a constable and a member of a number of *posses* in Oklahoma, where he joined deputy marshals like Heck Thomas in the search for members of the Dalton and Doolin train robbery gangs.[116] Moreover, at least one-third of the incorporation fighters held both federal or state and local law enforcement roles at some point in their careers (the true proportion is likely higher, given the frequency with which deputy US marshal credentials were bestowed upon sheriffs and the scarcity of extant records), allowing them to maximize opportunities for earning fees. Though these actors were, undoubtedly, contributing to the law and order of the frontier, many were likely doing so with an eye first and foremost toward making money.

Social Connections over Space

Entrepôts provided opportunities for violence experts to spread information about their reputations for skill in gunplay. Over time, the opportunities they found in these towns allowed gunfighters to pursue careers using these skills. It is also, however, important to understand how social connections among gunfighters who often lived far from one another helped facilitate and build these careers.

Gunfighters were highly mobile, willing to pursue economic opportunities wherever they might be found. Figure 15 depicts this geographical opportunism, with the size of the circle indicating the number of gunfighters active in a particular state or territory and the width of the line connecting the jurisdictions the relative number of fighters moving from place to place.

This figure demonstrates, first and foremost, that the majority of fighters who were geographically mobile moved through the Texas-Oklahoma-Kansas and Texas-New Mexico cattle and mining corridors. John Wesley Hardin, for example, was active in Texas, Kansas, and the Indian Territory. John Selman – John Larn's partner in crime and Hardin's killer – moved through Arkansas, Texas, and New Mexico in his peripatetic career. Doc Holliday, who was born

[115] John Boessenecker, *When Law Was in the Holster: The Frontier Life of Bob Paul* (Norman: University of Oklahoma Press, 2012), 70–90, 94–100, 170–334.

[116] Fred Dodge, *Under Cover for Wells Fargo: The Unvarnished Recollections of Fred Dodge* (Norman: University of Oklahoma Press, 1998), 162–176.

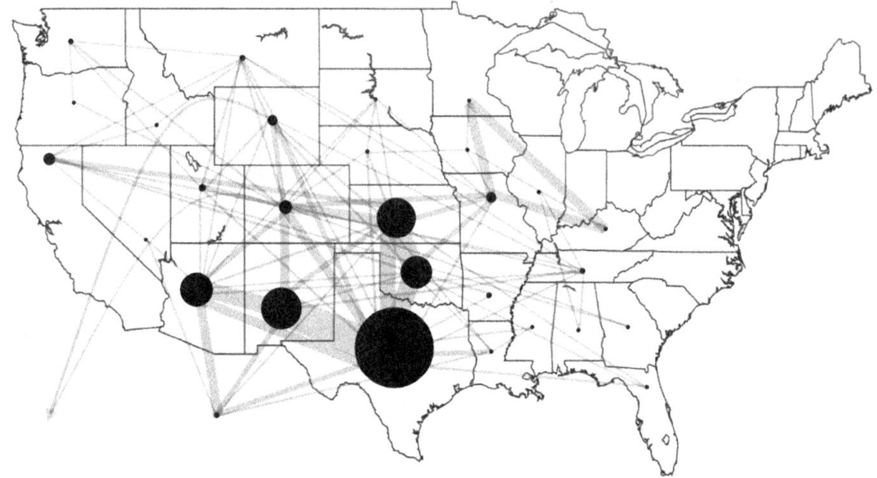

FIGURE 15. Flow of gunfighters between locales (1850–1930)
Map based on political divisions of 1890, with Indian Territory/Oklahoma combined for ease of contemporary interpretation. Width of line reflects number of gunfighters active in both locales. Diameter of circle is proportional to overall number of fights in a single locale.
Data from Bill O'Neal, *Encyclopedia of Western Gunfighters* (Norman: University of Oklahoma Press, 1979).

in Georgia, gambled and shot his way through Texas, Wyoming, Kansas, and New Mexico. And so on.

These violence experts, however, did not limit themselves to the range corridor itself, particularly after the cattle boom subsided in the 1880s and 1890s. Former Pinkerton agent and hired assassin Tom Horn, for instance, moved back and forth between Arizona, where he worked as a scout for the US army and as a hired gun in the Pleasant Valley range war of the late 1880s, and Colorado, where he was involved in detective work. Another participant in the Pleasant Valley War, Commodore Perry Owens, was a cowboy in New Mexico and Oklahoma before moving to Arizona, where, as a sheriff, he and several of his deputies were responsible for killing Ike Clanton, Wyatt Earp's old nemesis, in 1887.

More importantly, these careers involved crossing territorial and political jurisdictions. Texas and Kansas were, of course, states with traditional forms of local representation and policing authority. But the transport of cattle and rail involved crossing federally administered lands like Colorado (which became a state in 1876), New Mexico, Arizona, Wyoming, and, of course, the Indian Territories. The flow of gunfighters across these jurisdictions indicates precisely how the imperial rule of divide-and-control animating federal policy was undercut by well-established patterns of physical mobility. And this mobility, in turn, was generated by market incorporation.

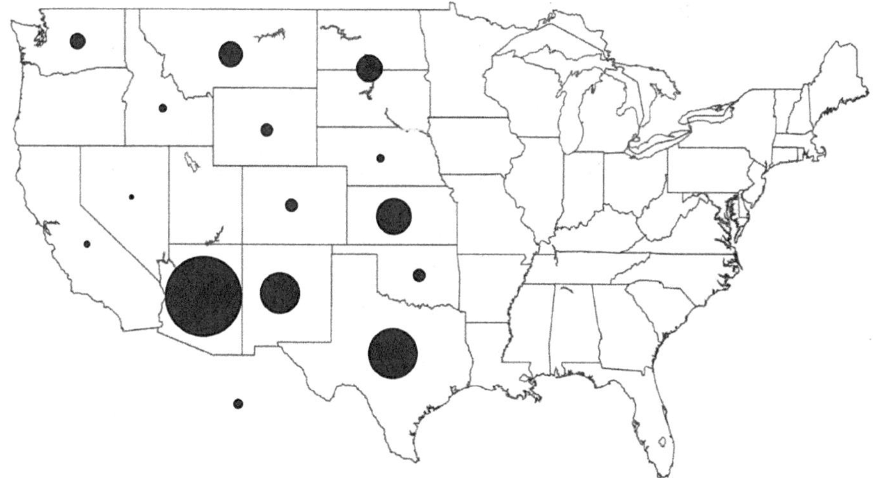

FIGURE 16. US military battle campaigns against Indian groups (1866–1891)
Map based on political divisions of 1890, with Indian Territory/Oklahoma combined and Dakota territory data aggregated into one measure for ease of contemporary interpretation. Diameter of circle is proportional to overall number of fights in a single state/territory/locale. Data from Susan B. Carter, Scott Sigmund Gartner, Michael R. Haines, Alan L. Olmstead, Richard Sutch, and Gavin Wrigh, eds., *Historical Statistics of the United States: Millennial Edition*, vol. 5, Series ED212-222 (Cambridge: Cambridge University Press, 2006), 382–402.

In other words, fighting clustered in specific places that were crucial in initiating social ties and building reputations, but the fighters themselves became highly mobile, moving from place to place as opportunities presented themselves. How, though, can this spatial pattern be distinguished from the activities of the state? That is, what does this actually tell us about an explicitly *market* form of organizing force that is distinct from that of political centralization and control?

To get a sense of these differences, I provide a spatial representation of the activities of the military during the same period. The map in Figure 16 depicts the distribution of US military battles with Indian communities across space following the Civil War. The first thing to notice is that, while settlers did indeed engage in anti-Indian violence, the federal government took over the primary role fighting the Indian Wars across the West the 1860s and 1870s. Though obviously not that surprising, this reinforces the general point made by scholars that the West was actually the site of a fairly profound expansion in state capacity in the postbellum era.[117] This capacity, however, was built on a small infrastructure of coercion: the US military in the West remained quite small throughout the nineteenth century and became increasingly focused on territorial incorporation.

[117] Heumann, "The Tutelary Empire."

On the other hand, market incorporation, which was linking together local communities into a regional and national system, also led to a different pattern of coercion across space, one focused on the cattle and mining extraction areas of the lower Rocky Mountain West and Southwest. Thus, while there was significant overlap between the presence of gunfighting and the military (in part because territorial incorporation often was a facilitating condition to market incorporation), the overall pattern still suggests important functional differences. In particular, the US Army was heavily involved in patrolling the Canadian border region in Montana and the Dakotas in the 1870s and early 1880s, an area where gunfighting was relatively scarce and population densities (and hence, market activity) were fairly sparse. This is what we would expect from a force engaged in trying to secure national borders and manage native populations. At the same time, gunfighters were more active in areas of the Rocky Mountain West where Indian pacification had been more or less accomplished by the late 1870s, but where mining interests grew considerably. Moreover, historically, we know that, although some gunfighters did, indeed, participate in anti-Indian campaigns (particularly at the famous battle of Adobe Walls in 1874), they did so independently and on an *ad hoc* basis; the military, conversely, was primarily engaged in precisely this kind of warfare during the postbellum period.[118] That is, whereas gunfighters were basically market actors, the military was involved in the protection of borders since enforcing political boundaries was the primary imperative of the territorial incorporation strategy pursued by the federal government.

The final piece of evidence for the market organization of southwestern gunfighting comes when we broaden our scope beyond the fights themselves to examine historically verifiable social interactions among these actors in general. To capture the relationships among gunfighting actors, I created a network including information for each of the 255 members of my sample in which ties capture who they fought against (conflict) and those with whom they were in league with during fights (alliance). Figure 17 depicts the main component of this network, with names removed for ease of viewing (solid lines are alliance, while dashed lines indicate conflict).

As it turns out, interactions among gunfighters were highly diffuse and widespread. Indeed, as evident in the figure, 196 of the 255 total gunfighters in the sample (approximately 77%), including most of the important figures in its history, were connected to each other in some way, through social alliance, kinship, or conflict with other members of the sample.

To give an example of how these networks played out on the ground, consider chain of relations tying Wyatt Earp and Henry "Billy the Kid" McCarty together, two actors who never met one another and never resided in

[118] For the identity of participants in the Adobe Walls conflict, see T. Lindsay Baker and Billy R. Harrison, *Adobe Walls: The History and Archaeology of the 1874 Trading Post* (College Station: Texas A & M University Press, 2001), 75–92.

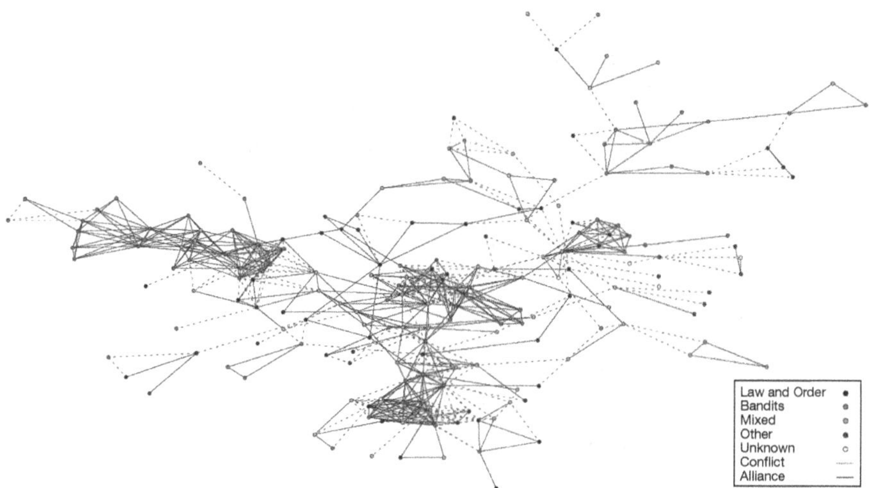

FIGURE 17. Gunfighter social network (1850–1930)
Main component only (*N*=196). Names removed for ease of viewing.

the same place. Billy the Kid, most famous for his participation in the Lincoln County War in New Mexico in 1878, had organized a rustling gang with a gunfighter named Dave Rudabaugh in 1880, who apparently had met one of the Kid's partners, Charlie Bowdre. Why was Rudabaugh able to join this gang? It turns out that before making his way to New Mexico, Rudabaugh had made his name as a (fairly unsuccessful) train robber in Kansas, where he had been captured by Bat Masterson in 1878. Masterson, in turn, was one of Earp's long-standing friends and both had participated in the hunt for cattle rustlers and train robbers in Kansas in the mid-1870s. Indeed, Earp himself claimed that he had tried to track down Rudabaugh the previous year, making it clear that these actors were likely quite aware of each other's reputations and capabilities.[119]

Moreover, there were multiple pathways through which information could spread. For instance, one of Earp's major targets during the famed "Vendetta Ride" was a rustler named "Curly Bill" Brocius (or Brosius) who had killed Tombstone Marshal Fred White in 1880 and was associated with the Clanton faction. Brocius and an friend named Bob Martin were known not only because of their work with the Clantons, but also because they had ridden with the John Kinney gang in Texas and New Mexico in 1878, an infamous group of gunfighters that later became involved in the Lincoln County War in opposition to Billy the Kid.[120]

[119] Frederick W. Nolan, *The Lincoln County War: A Documentary History* (Norman: University of Oklahoma Press, 1992), 482–483.

[120] Steve Gatto, *Curly Bill* (Lansing, MI: Protar House, 2003), 14–16. There are even more interesting and distant ways of connecting these actors. For example, Pat Garrett, who famously shot the Kid in Fort Sumner, New Mexico, in 1881, was later involved in the pursuit of Oliver

Another example demonstrating how these networks evolved over time involves Jesse James and Wild Bill Hickok, two other famous gunfighters not personally related in any way. Hickok, as noted, had a rivalry with gambler Ben Thompson in Abilene in the early 1870s; by 1876, Thompson had moved south toward Texas where he had become friendly with Bat Masterson, who hired him to participate in the famed railroad war on the side of the AT & SF in 1879.[121] At the same time, Masterson's brother James, who had frequently participated with Bat in search *posses* and arrest parties, had developed a reputation as quite a law officer as well; by the early 1890s, he was a Special U.S. Deputy Marshal and played a key role in the famous battle at Ingalls in Oklahoma in 1893, in which the original Dalton gang was decimated.[122] The Daltons, in turn, had a kinship link of their own; they were cousins of the Younger brothers, who had constituted the other half of the James-Younger gang.[123] The actual process of network formation in cases like these was likely driven by the knowledge that friends and relatives, too, were making money through skills in violence. These links provided access to newcomers and allowed them to quickly identify and exploit new market opportunities.

Countless other figures in the history of the gunfighting institution were connected through these chains of commerce, family, friendship, and rivalry both synchronously and diachronically. Indeed, as even this small sample demonstrates, the expansion of the market and the growth of physical mobility and communications infrastructure facilitated the wide and meaningful dispersion of these relational ties across the jurisdictional borders of the territories and states.

Moreover, despite the obvious importance of certain figures like Bat Masterson, who seems to have been connected to all sorts of gunfighting professionals, this network was not actually organized around a single hub or central individual.[124] Instead, it was diffuse and decentralized, just as we might expect with a vibrant, fluid market. When we include ties to individuals who were *not* themselves members of the sample, it is possible to trace connections

Milton Lee, a former deputy marshal accused of murdering Albert Jennings Fountain in 1896, who, in turn, had fought in a range war with another man named Tom Tucker in 1887, who that year was arrested by Commodore Perry Owens, whose deputy, Albert Miller, had killed Ike Clanton, a key figure in the shootout in the OK Corrall with Wyatt Earp. And so on. See DeArment, *Deadly Dozen Vol. 2*, 219–236; David Grassé, *"A Killer is What They Needed": The True, Untold Story of Commodore Perry Owens* (Santa Ana, CA: Graphic Publishers, 2013), 68, 88-90; Corey Recko, *Murder on the White Sands: The Disappearance of Albert and Henry Fountain* (Denton: University of North Texas Press, 2007).

121 Robert K. DeArment, *Bat Masterson: The Man and the Legend* (Norman: University of Oklahoma Press, 1979), 64–65, 150.

122 DeArment, *Bat Masterson*, 312–322.

123 Nancy Ohnick, *The Dalton Gang and Their Family Ties* (Meade, KS: Ohnick Enterprises, 2005).

124 Including both conflict and alliance ties, only 8% or so of the possible variation in the degrees of the 196 actors in the network was actually present in the network.

among at least 220 (or 86%) of the gunfighters examined in this chapter. This evidence demonstrates that famous gunfighters clearly knew each other both professionally and socially, through small groups of closely knit friends and relatives as well as through figures who bridged those more enclosed groups.[125]

This snapshot of a social network among gunfighters suggests that regardless of which "side" they were on, many gunfighters knew each other, fought against each other, and adopted a shared professional identity. They worked together in *posses*, on specific *ad hoc* jobs, and permanently for organizations like the Pinkertons. And, in the process, they created a form of organized violence that was driven by their distinctive status as entrepreneurial experts, one in which they would sell their skills to powerful buyers, whomever they might be.

CONCLUSION

Gunfighters, like vigilantes and private detectives, were private users of coercion who often collaborated with the state. They were also, however, an interconnected cohort of violence experts whose social lives and careers reflected a market that operated against the confines of territorial political institutions. The creation of new territories in the aftermath of the Civil War had led, indeed, to military deployments to manage native populations and police national borders; but they had also instituted a system of rules assuming that local communities of settlers could remain divided and separated and that law enforcement could remain a largely decentralized, republican endeavor. The reality of market incorporation, however, meant that these rules decoupled relations of control on the ground, which were confronted by threats like rustling and banditry that crossed jurisdictional boundaries. Civil War veterans, many with experience in the partisan conflicts of the Southwest, took advantage of this dilemma, and became entrepreneurs, supplementing the national strategy of military policing with a much more decentralized network of guns for hire. Indeed, in the expansive US West, bringing law and order has often really meant making a dollar.

[125] It is worth noting that the pattern of alliance and neutral ties within the main component of the direct inter-gunfighter network is highly clustered, implying that actors interacted mainly with those who also knew each other (the average weighted clustering coefficient for alliance/neutral ties within this component is 0.620, while the network density – the proportion of possible alliance/neutral ties present across the entire main component – was a mere 0.022, indicating strong neighborhoods among actors). This also, however, suggests that conflict was critical in forming the market, since over 64% of the nodes in the main component were unable to reach each other through alliance/neutral relations alone.

7

Conclusion

The first decades of the twenty-first century have renewed interest in the role of violence in American politics. The seemingly endless wars in Afghanistan and Iraq, the renaissance of the right-wing militia movement during the Obama presidency, the explosion of debate over the appropriateness and racial disparities of mass incarceration, questions of police brutality and surveillance, and the contentious protests surrounding issues like Black Lives Matter, Occupy Wall Street, and so forth, have brought to the fore once again questions of how the organization of violence have shaped core institutional activities and development.[1] These studies have begun to ask questions about the deeper interconnections between the private use of coercion and state-building, showing how, in ways often unexpected, these two faces of violence fundamentally shape each other.

This book has presented an institutional genealogy of this relationship, arguing that a common pattern of violence developed in the United States in the late nineteenth century across multiple scales and in multiple settings. On the one hand, the federal, local, and municipal state expanded directly, building the powerful interconnected bureaucracy of military, National Guard, and municipal police forces that have come to represent the violent arm of the contemporary American government. On the other hand, just as profoundly,

[1] e.g., Craig Calhoun, "Occupy Wall Street in Perspective," *The British Journal of Sociology* 64, no. 1 (2013): 26–38; Jeffrey C. Isaac, "The American Politics of Policing and Incarceration," *Perspectives on Politics* 13, no. 03 (2015): 609–616; Mayhew, "Wars and American Politics"; Lisa L. Miller, "The Invisible Black Victim: How American Federalism Perpetuates Racial Inequality in Criminal Justice," *Law & Society Review* 44, nos. 3–4 (2010): 805–842; Vesla M. Weaver and Amy E. Lerman, "Political Consequences of the Carceral State," *American Political Science Review* 104, no. 04 (2010): 817–833; Spencer D. Wood, Joseph T. Jakubek Jr., and Kristin Kelly, "You've Got to Fight to Be White: The Rural Foundation of the New Militia for Race Control," *Contemporary Justice Review* 18, no. 2 (2015): 215–230.

private actors began to innovate new ways of being violent: vigilantism *grew* rather than diminished with the consolidation of the National Guard and the militia in the South and North alike; a robust private security industry emerged, one that continues to exert a profound control over the protection of private property; and a system of gunfighting mercenaries adapted their skills in fighting to a market which demanded new forms of protection. In each case, these private and public forms of violence *complemented* and *coevolved* with one another: at the very moment the private security industry was born in Chicago, so were the police; just as the federal state made unprecedented advances in military incorporation in the West, so too were gunfighters professionalizing and transforming old law enforcement institutions.

Together these many developments led neither to a state monopoly on organized violence *nor* to a struggle of all against all, as many political economists and other proponents of the notion of the "Leviathan" as a centralized repository of violence and protection might predict. Instead, they broadened the notion of security past the notion that only anarchy or state control could suffice to protect people and property. Seemingly contradictory organizations committed to using force were instead linked together in a complex but coherent set of shared practices and personnel.

The dual emergence of public and private violence was largely the result of the transformation of traditional, early nineteenth-century republican institutions in which these private and public forms of violence had traditionally been indistinguishable from one another. As these republican institutions encountered unsettled frontiers – spaces of altered rules, social ambiguity, and/or physical mobility – they changed. The formal rules of social order on which they were built decoupled from practical day-to-day relations of social control on which they depended. At each jurisdiction in American government – counties, cities, states, and territories – the encounter between older republican ways of managing the peace and transformed rules or relations severed the link between public security and the private provision around which they were organized.

The dual transformation of the Market Revolution and the Civil War provided the main impetus for this shift in coercive enforcement. And, more importantly, this period also set in motion an institution trajectory with which we continue to live today. To understand the way that Americans seem to seamlessly integrate the "right to bear arms" with the need for a powerful military bureaucracy – something that would undoubtedly surprise the nation's republican progenitors, who feared both the anarchy of isolated, armed individuals as well as the tyranny of a powerful, coercive state – we need to look at how these institutions underwent such a transformation.

This book has also reconceptualized coercive institutions as reinforcing links between day-to-day forms of social control and the rules providing the ways people understand and make sense of social order. This helps rethink what we mean by institutional authority and collective action; I contend that actors cannot make choices about how to use violence outside of preexisting sets of social relations, and that rules are never simply reducible to the isolated decisions of individual actors. Stable forms of institutionalized enforcement, instead, arise when the rules to which particular actors are subject reinforce and are reinforced by patterns of social control they confront in their day-to-day relationships. The decoupling of rule from relation and vice versa, in turn, sets up the possibility for institutional change.

Organized violence is thus neither merely instrumental (in the sense that the causes of its organization depend solely on the cost-imposing effects of its use) nor solely expressive (in the sense that its causes are rooted in socially prior divisions and help to reproduce and enact those divisions). Instead, it is both: vigilantes, private detectives, and gunfighters were all involved in setting up protection "rackets" of a sort (thereby thinking of violence instrumentally), but those rackets rarely came into conflict with the prerogatives of the state because they are also embedded in preexisting systems of rules and relations (thereby producing violence expressively) that made private and public violence coextensive. Indeed, the very idea that private coercion *could* be distinct from public violence was, in other words, historically contingent; the divide between the two, at least in the context of the United States, only arose as republican forms of thinking about and organizing security fell apart. And as this book has shown, this divide was embedded in the lives of particular individuals like Wyatt Earp, Allan Pinkerton, and Frederick Nash Ogden, whose careers swerved between service in public and private coercive institutions alike.

THE INSTITUTIONAL LEGACY OF JURISDICTIONAL DECOUPLING

Several questions, however, remain unanswered. The first is simple: What came next? What, exactly, were the legacies of nineteenth-century jurisdictional decoupling for violence in the United States? The most immediate effects were, of course, institutional. And one of the most important was that core republican institutions of coercion – the shrievalty, the constabulary, and the militia – were not immediately abandoned. Instead they were transformed into public and private organizations that, in many ways, continue to be involved in protection.

Take, for example, the volunteer militia, which was active not only in Louisiana but also in places like northern Illinois in the 1840s and 1850s. In Elgin in Kane County, for example, a group of influential residents founded the Continentals, the premier private militia company in the county and one of the first northern Illinois units to be activated in the Civil War.[2] And Chicago had multiple independent companies in the decades before the war, including the Washington Guards, the Chicago City Guards, the Montgomery Guards (mobilized to add the special deputy force during the Beer Lager Riots),

[2] Joslyn, *History of Kane County (Vol. 1)*, 670–676.

and so forth.[3] Such groups became means for private individuals to establish themselves as socially distinctive, representing an important shift away from the notion of universal service in militia companies even before the war itself.

While the war and Reconstruction clearly reorganized militia into more centralized and bureaucratic bodies in Southern states, these effects were also felt in the North. By the mid-1870s, the National Guard Association movement made increasing the training and professionalism of citizen-soldiers a goal across the entire nation.[4] In Illinois, for instance, the although many different ethnic groups formed local units, the National Guard movement was most popular among wealthy and middle-class urban and suburban residents, who were deeply committed to protecting private property in a context of increasing labor mobilization.[5] Through the 1870s and 1880s, as with the Louisiana State National Guard reforms addressed in Chapter 6, the movement was able to secure governmental support and gain an official status in a number of states, ultimately becoming a formal and organized part of the national military establishment through the Dick Act of 1903, which made the each National Guard unit a component of the national defense establishment.[6]

By advocating for a military force, under the control of the state, but not dependent on participation of those who might be party to local disorder, the National Guard movement addressed the concerns of powerful economic actors in the North and South alike.[7] In the South, the new National Guard units helped, as noted, bolster the racial order and represented, as with the transformation of the White League into the Louisiana State National Guard, a triumph of conservative whites and southern military tradition. Indeed, the first vice president of the National Guard Association was P. G. T. Beauregard, a former Confederate general and supporter of Francis Nicholls's Redeemer government who had been named his adjutant-general in 1878.[8] In the North, in turn, the National Guard provided coercive power to industrial elites concerned with suppressing labor mobilization. Of the more than 300 instances in which governors mobilized National Guard between 1886 to 1895, for instance, over one-third involved quelling labor disputes.[9]

At the same time, often with close relationships to the local branches of the National Guard, private shooting societies also developed into powerful statewide and even national organizations. The key example of this is the National Rifle Association, which began as an adjunct to National Guard

3 Andreas, *History of Chicago (Vol. 1)*, 275.

4 Skowronek, *Building a New American State*, 92–95, 104–107. 5 Eleanor L. Hannah, *Manhood, Citizenship, and the National Guard: Illinois, 1870–1917* (Columbus: Ohio State University Press, 2007), 10–15.

6 For a history of the legal transformation of the National Guard, see Louis Cantor, "The Creation of the Modern National Guard: The Dick Militia Act of 1903" (PhD diss., Duke University, 1963), 165–262.

7 Skowronek, *Building a New American State*, 94–95. 8 Hogue, *Uncivil War*, 187.

9 Alexander, "Ten Years of Riot Duty," 26.

expansion in the mid-1870s. While these groups were distinct – part of the *raison d'être* of the formation of the National Guard was to establish a seemingly apolitical coercive agent which could be used to enforce public order and aid the military at the national level, while the shooting clubs were explicitly amateur and private entities – they grew together, sharing membership and even resources. Indeed, the first president of the National Guard Association – George Wood Wingate – was *also* the cofounder of the National Rifle Association in 1871. The shooting clubs used marksmanship contests (often sponsored by firearms makers like Winchester and Colt) to propagate a message of the need for an armed masculine citizenry.[10]

The growth of this more centralized, bureaucratic, elite-controlled militia, however, did not obviate other national developments in private violence. Perhaps most famously, a widespread plague of lynching and lynching clubs took hold in the years following Reconstruction.[11] Much of this vigilantism, of course, occurred in the South, where it took the form of establishing communal control over socially or racially marginalized people and forging a white identity.[12] But in the Midwest and, especially, the trans–Mississippi West, local actors waged deadly vigilante campaigns against Chinese, Mexican, and other "undesirable" workers and migrants through the early decades of the twentieth century.[13]

[10] Russell Stanley Gilmore, "The Crack Shots and Patriots: The National Rifle Association and America's Military-Sporting Tradition, 1871–1929" (PhD diss., University of Wisconsin–Madison, 1974); Larry Isaac, "To Counter 'the Very Devil' and More: The Making of Independent Capitalist Militia in the Gilded Age," *American Journal of Sociology* 108, no. 2 (2002): 353–405.

[11] Pfeifer, *Rough Justice*, 13–37, 149; Pfeifer, *Lynching beyond Dixie*, 1–12. As Pfeifer's important revisionist work on vigilantism has demonstrated, only the northeast seemed relatively immune to the lynching phenomenon. The reasons why the northeast never experienced widespread lynching are complex. Hindus, for instance, argues that New England's legal culture, its racial demography, the pervasiveness and effectiveness of social control institutions like penitentiaries, and powerful Reformer social movements help explain the difference, while Pfeifer stresses a popular culture of restraint and the growth of capitalist discipline. Pfeifer, *Rough Justice*, 36–37; Hindus, *Prison and Plantation*, 251–255. Because of the jurisdictional foci for much of northern life was centered in the municipality and because the social transformation of the antebellum market (rather than war) was the most profound source of social change in such towns, most north-easterners (like Chicagoans) funneled their private policing efforts through economic rather than vigilance movements. This is why the private security industry emerged in Northern rather than Southern cities.

[12] Roberta Senechal de la Roche, "Collective Violence as Social Control," in *Sociological Forum*, vol. 11, 1 (1996), 97–128; Mattias Smångs, *Doing Violence, Making Race* (New York: Routledge, 2017), 15–29.

[13] Gonzales-Day, *Lynching in the West, 1850–1935*, 23–60; William D. Carrigan and Clive Webb, *Forgotten Dead: Mob Violence against Mexicans in the United States, 1848–1928* (Oxford: Oxford University Press, 2013), 20–63; Scott Zesch, *The Chinatown War: Chinese Los Angeles and the Massacre of 1871* (Oxford: Oxford University Press, 2012), 81–150.

But the decoupling of private force from the public interest meant that other forms of vigilance began to appear in rural areas. In particular, local Anti–Horse Thief Associations, which had spread throughout the midwest and northeast in the 1860s and 1870s, created a national organization to help centralize information about stolen animals and to act as a kind of proto-neighborhood watch.[14] These groups were subscription-based, but provided important investigative services as well as, occasionally, personnel for participation in *posses*. The Anti–Horse Thief and other protective associations created a private infrastructure of security in rural counties that, though explicitly non-governmental, reflected the *transformation* of republican expectations about communal participation in coercion rather than its abandonment. Such groups were even encouraged and authorized explicitly by state legislatures in Indiana and Illinois.[15] Much like the claims societies of the 1830s and 1840s, these groups were primarily collective efforts at investigation and recovery, much like insurance agencies. Even though they did not necessarily reflect the kind of breakdown in enclosed authority found in actual quasi-legal vigilante enforcement, they did stem from the same realization that no longer were the security interests of particular groups identical to those of the shared community.[16]

The legacy of quasi-official private enforcement continued throughout the Progressive era and beyond. During World War I and the early 1920s, as Chris Capozzola and others have shown, groups like the American Legion took up the mantle of vigilant citizenship and played a key role in enforcing labor and racial standards, often with the tacit support of federal governmental actors.[17] And much of the mobilization behind and enforcement of prohibition of alcohol and prostitution was drawn from the rich tradition of private anti-vice associations like Anthony Comstock's New York Society for the Suppression of Vice, which had operated in a quasi-official capacity from the 1870s onward.[18] In New York, the Citizens Home Defense League gained police powers of arrest when

[14] John K. Burchill, *Bullets, Badges, and Bridles: Horse Thieves and the Societies That Pursued Them* (Gretna, LA: Pelican Publishing Company, 2013), Appendix 1; Cindy Higgins, "Frontier Protective and Social Network: The Anti-Horse Thief Association in Kansas," *Journal of the West* 42, no. 4 (2003): 63–73; Szymanski, "Stop, Thief! Private Protective Societies in Nineteenth-Century New England."

[15] At least thirteen states, all in the midwest or northeast, provided legal means for anti-horse thief associations to incorporate between 1850 and 1900. Eight of those were even able to secure police powers of arrest for members. Burchill, *Bullets, Badges, and Bridles*, 42.

[16] Gresham, *The Story of Major David Mckee*, 24–26, 74; Nolan, *Vigilantes on the Middle Border*, 126–171.

[17] Christopher Capozzola, "The Only Badge Needed Is Your Patriotic Fervor: Vigilance, Coercion, and the Law in World War I America," *The Journal of American History* 88, no. 4 (2002): 1354–1382.

[18] Lisa McGirr, *The War on Alcohol: Prohibition and the Rise of the American State* (New York: W. W. Norton, 2015), 121–155; Nicola Kay Beisel, *Imperiled Innocents: Anthony Comstock and Family Reproduction in Victorian America* (Princeton, NJ: Princeton University Press, 1998), 107–157.

transformed into New York Police Reserve in 1920, and members participated in a number of strike-breaking and public order efforts in the next few years.[19] Martin Greenberg, the foremost analyst of volunteer and citizen policing in the United States, has traced contemporary community policing initiatives, junior police programs, emergency response teams, and neighborhood watch groups to precisely these kinds of public-private partnerships.[20]

The institutional legacy of decoupled republicanism continued in other ways, however. For instance, the county shrievalty continued to exist as it always had – small, non-bureaucratic, and reliant on close community ties.[21] The office of the sheriff itself slowly became depoliticized and professional, and was reorganized into quasi-police departments within the slowly growing county administrations that emerged in the postbellum era.[22] Nevertheless, even in these areas, the sheriff and a small staff of deputies remained the key institution for *all* policing duties. Indeed, even the institution of the *posse comitatus* continues to play an important role in rural policing – in Colorado, for instance, attorney Dave Kopel argues that the deputization of volunteers under the *posse comitatus* legal framework remains essential to rural policing, particularly in emergency or crowd control contexts.[23] According to his inventory of state laws on deputization, only Maryland and New Jersey lack statutory ability to depute private citizens as temporary police officers.

In cities, most *posse comitatus* mechanisms have been supplanted by permanent coercive organizations. As Eric Monkkonen and many others have demonstrated, for instance, police departments were widely adopted by all sorts of American cities between 1860 and 1890.[24] Most scholars see these reforms as part of a general move toward a bureaucratic model of civil reform during the era of Progressivism, as well as a response to increasing labor struggle and disorder in the middle nineteenth century.[25] Nevertheless, by the end of the nineteenth century, almost every city in the United States with a population over 10,000 residents had a full-time, professional police force.[26]

19 Martin A. Greenberg, *Citizens Defending America: From Colonial Times to the Age of Terrorism* (Pittsburgh: University of Pittsburgh Press, 2005), 116–127.

20 ibid., 148–185.

21 John Lee Allaman, "Nineteenth Century Homicide in Henderson County, Illinois: A Study of Court Records and the Press Media as Reliable Sources for Writing Local History" (D.A., Illinois State University, 1989), 74–87.

22 Smith, *Rural Crime Control*, 48–74.

23 Kopel, "The Posse Comitatus and the Office of Sheriff," 812–823.

24 Monkkonen, *Police in Urban America*, 54–59.

25 Sam Mitrani, "Reforming Repression: Labor, Anarchy, and Reform in the Shaping of the Chicago Police Department, 1879–1888," *Labor* 6, no. 2 (2009): 73–96; Jon C. Teaford, *The Unheralded Triumph: City Government in America, 1870–1900* (Baltimore: Johns Hopkins University Press, 1984).

26 George Wesley Hale, *Police and Prison Cyclopaedia* (Cambridge: Riverside Press, 1892), 70–168.

TABLE 19. *Private detective agencies in select American cities (1870–1900)*

	Number of agencies listed			
City	1870	1880	1890	1900
Baltimore	1	1	1	10
Boston	1	11	14	15
Buffalo	0	2	2	6
Cincinnati	1	1	2	4
Cleveland	0	0	5	8
Dallas	0	0	1	2
Denver	0	1	4	2
Detroit	0	1	10	6
Indianapolis	0	0	3	1
Kansas City	1	1	1	6
Los Angeles	0	1	3	4
Louisville	0	0	2	2
Memphis	0	0	0	1
Minneapolis	0	0	3	10
New Orleans	0	0	4	2
Pittsburgh	0	1	4	7
Providence	0	0	1	1
San Francisco	3	7	5	5
St. Louis	1	3	2	6
Toledo	0	0	0	1

Data from city directories.

At the same time, the private market for experts in coercion exploded as well, demonstrating that public police were only one part of the solution to the problem of protecting private property. Table 19, for example, tracks the number of private security agencies identified in different city directories during the years in question.[27]

The same phenomenon also applied to the use of private guards. Firms continued to hire watchmen, with or without public deputization, in greater

[27] Much of this expansion was driven by the creation of national private security networks and branch offices. By 1890, for example, the Pinkerton Agency had branches in St. Paul, Chicago, New York, Denver, Boston, Philadelphia, and Kansas City, and expanded further into San Francisco, Portland, and Montreal by 1900. The agency also established patrol branches in Kansas City and Portland, in addition to Chicago. The Thiel Agency, one of Pinkerton's major late nineteenth-century rivals, had branches in St. Louis, New York, Chicago, St. Paul, Kansas City, Portland, Montreal, and Mexico City. Moreover, while New York and Chicago remained hubs for the national agencies, most major urban centers had local or regional firms providing detective services for private residents. These trends continued into the twentieth century, as the private security industry became more specialized and more diffuse; by 1935, the Pinkerton Agency had branches in twenty-seven different cities and annual revenues of over $2 million. City directory of Denver in 1890: 1346; City directory of Denver in 1900: 1406–1407; Morn, *The Eye That Never Sleeps*, 186.

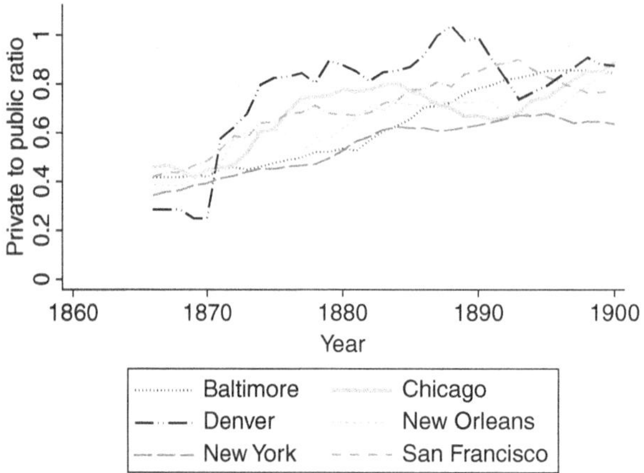

FIGURE 18. Ratio of watchmen to police in select cities (1865–1900)
Ratio of frequency of terms "watchman" to "police" in scanned city directories; data smoothed (five-year MA).

and greater numbers throughout the rest of the century. Moreover, this was not affected by the growth in police forces at the same time, which also were involved in protecting property through patrol. Indeed, there is some very provocative evidence that the ratio of private guards to police active in given cities actually *increased* throughout the rest of the century. Figure 18 provides a rough but very suggestive indication of this phenomenon.[28] The general upward slope in each of the cities' trend lines demonstrates the commitment of private corporations to providing for their own security.

Labor groups and reformers began to call for reform of the private security industry after the 1870s. This was primarily due to the increasing use of specialized firms to break strikes and control workers. Working against organized labor had become par for the course for private detective agencies in the aftermath of the Pinkerton agency's famous battle with the Mollie Maguires in Pennsylvania in the mid-1870s, but organized labor increasingly targeted "Pinkertonism" as an illegitimate mode of corporate control via coercion. Western states began outlawing the importation of outside deputies, while radical groups began organizing their own militia in response to private strikebreakers and gun thugs, an attempt to recapture the mantle of public cooperative violence in the context of deteriorating industrial relations.[29]

[28] Using digitized city directories, I performed key term searches intended to identify frequency of terms associated with private guards and public police and converted the raw data into yearly ratios of the two searches.

[29] J. Bernard Hogg, "Public Reaction to Pinkertonism and the Labor Question," *Pennsylvania History* 11, no. 3 (July 1944): 171–199.

Many of these efforts were short-lived or subverted by powerful corporate interests. Hearings by congress in the aftermath of the Homestead debacle of 1893 (which had involved a pitched battle between Pinkerton guards and striking workers) shook up the private security industry, leading the Pinkerton firm to limit (though not abandon) anti-labor activities and create legislative momentum to limit and monitor the activities of the private agencies at the federal level.[30] Still, private detective agencies were part and parcel of the American security sector in not only municipal and industrial areas by the late 1880s, but also throughout the nation. For instance, armed guards were hired countless times in Chicago by reform groups, citizen's associations, and even (in the case of the post-Haymarket investigation) by the police themselves.[31] Meanwhile, the Pinkertons and other private operations continued to expand their presence throughout the twentieth century, getting involved in investigative, espionage, and security guard work, while a specialized class of strikebreaking agencies emerged in the early twentieth century to manage industrial, mining, and agricultural labor disputes.[32]

All of these transformations find their point of origin in the mid-nineteenth century, as the Market Revolution and Civil War upended the link between rules and relations in older republican institutions in jurisdictions across the nation. While policy diffusion across states and cities, entrepreneurial activity by political elites, and federal legal coordination also undoubtedly played a role in the institutionalization of novelties like the municipal police, the private security industry, and the National Guard, this book has shown that the process of decoupling in local jurisdictions played perhaps the key role setting in motion a system in which both public and private forms of violence could coevolve and coexist.

THE LEGAL LEGACY OF JURISDICTIONAL DECOUPLING

The decoupling of republican forms of coercion in the nineteenth century also, however, shaped logic of American governance by helping to establish

30 Rhodri Jeffreys-Jones, *Violence and Reform in American History* (New York: New Viewpoints, 1978), 78–114.

31 For example, the Committee on Public Safety, a reform group organized ostensibly to combat electoral fraud, hired guards to shuttle poll-watching challengers from poll to poll in the municipal election of 1876. Investigations of electoral fraud by the manifold private reformer bodies also hired private detectives, particularly since the police were viewed by many early progressives as enablers of ballot-stuffing and ward mobilization; in 1883, for example, the Political Action Committee of the Union League budgeted over $1,000 dollars for private detective investigations into electoral corruption. See Sidney I. Roberts, "Businessmen in Revolt: Chicago 1874–1900" (PhD diss., Northwestern University, 1960), 34, 46. On the cooperation between the Pinkerton Agency and the police department's post-Haymarket investigation (led by Michael Schaack), see Mitrani, "Reforming Repression," 91.

32 Smith, *From Blackjacks to Briefcases*; John Walton, *The Legendary Detective: The Private Eye in Fact and Fiction* (Chicago: University of Chicago Press, 2015).

the legal basis for a state-controlled, powerful coercive bureaucracy. After all, one of the key concerns of republican political theory is a distrust of standing armies. What explains the seeming abandonment of this principle in the nation's constitutional tradition?

In fact, as this book has shown, this principle was never abandoned; instead, the collapse of the republican tradition allowed for *both* private and public forms of protection to thrive. Legally, this took the form of both a slow and highly controversial expansion in the private access to firearms as a matter of constitutional guarantee as well as a gradual legal acknowledgment that the police power of the local and federal government could expand bureaucratically.

One of the most important jurisprudential legacies of Reconstruction (particularly in Louisiana) is the legal edifice authorizing compatible public and private forms of violence.[33] Reconstruction involved, for the first time, massive federal participation in local law enforcement, as Congress passed a series of laws to curtail electoral intimidation of African-American and Republican voters by groups like the Ku Klux Klan.

This effort had involved, quite naturally, new claims to state power – particularly rights to control and monitor who might have access to firearms. Federal prosecutions against members of the Ku Klux Klan in other states (in particular, South Carolina) had made a novel argument that at least one of the violations perpetrated by the group was that it disbanded lawfully authorized state militia. By seizing weapons intended for African-American militia units, prosecutors argued, the KKK were interfering with the constitutional right to arm for self-protection.[34] The underlying claim of this argument was, in part, that the Second Amendment of the US Constitution was "incorporated" into the protections of the Fourteenth Amendment – that is, that the right to bear arms was, essentially, an individual civil right of self-protection which could be protected by the federal government. The defense, in contrast, argued that the Second Amendment referred to militia matters and hence was a matter of states' rights *not* an individual right.[35] Though legal historians have debated exactly the extent to which Republican lawmakers were willing to adopt an incorporation interpretation of the Second Amendment, by the time of the prosecution of the perpetrators of the Colfax Massacre in 1873, that

33 Determining the scope under which individuals (often as a substitute for an absent state) could use violence had been deeply embedded in highly local and often semi-formal kinds of law in the antebellum period, though in some places municipal courts broadened the conditions for an explicitly private right to use force in self-defense in the 1830s through 1850s. See Joshua M. Stein, "Privatizing Violence: A Transformation in the Jurisprudence of Assault," *Law and History Review* 30, no. 2 (2012): 423–448; Edwards, *The People and Their Peace*, 74–80, 226–238.

34 Saul Cornell, *A Well-Regulated Militia: The Founding Fathers and the Origins of Gun Control in America* (Oxford: Oxford University Press, 2006), 179–180.

35 ibid., 185–186.

precipitating moment in the history of the White League, the constitutional stakes centered around the issue of whether the right to bear arms was an issue vested in the authority the local state.[36]

Thus the two issues of local resistance to federal preemption of republican forms of participatory law enforcement and state control over the militia were linked by Louisiana White League conservatives into a unified legal opposition to the US government's Colfax prosecution, known as the *Cruikshank* case.[37] Initially, the government intended to prosecute ninety men in the Colfax case, but were only able to try nine of them on charges related to denying African Americans their civil rights to self-defense. After securing three guilty verdicts, the defense launched an appeal directed squarely at whether or not the Enforcement Acts were constitutional, which wound up in front of the Supreme Court.[38]

In its verdict, the court agreed with the defense that the Second Amendment was primarily a matter of state's rights and that the federal government could not effectively argue its case on the merits of a violation of the Fourteenth Amendment. The practical results of the case meant not only that the prosecution of Enforcement Act violations could no longer rely on an interpretation of the Fourteenth Amendment granting the federal government the right to protect the arming of militia, it also made the state's prerogative over who could bear arms according to the Second Amendment secure. Though the notion that individuals could still possess and use weapons for self-defense (which was part of the common law) was not affected by the ruling, the idea that the right to bear arms could be regulated by the state was reaffirmed.[39] In other words, in a moment of high irony, the police powers of the state to regulate firearms was reasserted in a ruling that was in favor of a group of vigilantes, explicitly operating outside the corrupt regime of the Kellogg government. But this capacity to regulate arms as a matter of militia policy was, at the same time, sequestered from the control of the federal government.

The *Cruikshank* ruling – reinforced in 1886 by the court's decision *Illinois v. Presser*, which undercut the individual right to arm in volunteer companies outside the authorized state militia – paved the way to a sea change in both how the state militias could be organized as well as power of the state as a holder of policing authority to regulate ownership and use of weapons.[40]

[36] Carole Emberton, "The Limits of Incorporation: Violence, Gun Rights, and Gun Regulation in the Reconstruction South," *Stanford Law & Policy Review* 17 (2006): 615–634.

[37] Carol Emberton argues that the best way to understand the Colfax case is not through the lens of the abstract debates of constitutional lawyers involved in the case but rather as a practical "struggle over who would legitimately wield the means of organized force in the South." The problem with much of the Constitutional debate is that it delinks the social context in which force was used from the legal heritage organizing its use. See ibid., 622.

[38] Cornell, *A Well-Regulated Militia*, 192. [39] Cornell, *A Well-Regulated Militia*, 195–196.

[40] Uviller and Merkel, *The Militia and the Right to Arms*, 14–16.

On the one hand, the ruling served the purpose of reaffirming to White League conservatives and other states' rights advocates the notion that the state could and should be the locus of law enforcement. It effectively shut down federal prosecution of the Enforcement Acts based on a proto-incorporation theory, while providing ammunition to those in Congress who hoped to limit the military's role in Reconstruction. Two short years later, in 1878, Congress approved the Posse Comitatus Act, which severely limited the military's capacity to intervene in local law enforcement matters and reaffirmed the priority of the state and local governments as the locus of policing power.[41] This brought Reconstruction to an end in ignominy, hamstringing the military's domestic role and effectively subverting federal protection for civil rights for years to come. Thus, white conservative elites tried to contain the radical challenge embodied in African-American political participation by limiting the possibility for them to get access to external aid.

At the same time, powerful economic and political players in the South used the opportunity provided by the end of Reconstruction to reassert their control over social order by building on some of the new institutions that had emerged during Republican government. Thus, by placing the militia firmly under the police power of the state, policy changes like the Militia Act of Louisiana in 1878 – which severely limited African American involvement in the active force – both gave the state a powerful new form coercion and directed it at preserving racial hierarchy.[42] The state's rights view of the Second Amendment provided a powerful mechanism to limit African American's access to firearms, since the state was now able to exercise a guaranteed police power over both organized military companies as well as firearms.[43] In effect, by forcing African Americans to require state assistance to secure organized protection, the systematic vigilantism of the White League, itself sustained through a close alliance with the Democrats with control over the state, could continue without any real opposition. Public and private faces of violence could coexist without contradiction.

Of course, the local state's control over more professionalized and centralized policing and military forces had an important effect on how political elites *thought* about the exercise of state power. This largely involved the rather radical task of simply abandoning the older militia and turning the

41 Sean J. Kealy, "Reexamining the Posse Comitatus Act: Toward a Right to Civil Law Enforcement," *Yale Law & Policy Review* 21, no. 2 (2003): 383–442.

42 Cooper, *The Rise of the National Guard*, 24, notes that nine former Confederate states (including Louisiana) did allow African-American units to continue after the end of Reconstruction, but as segregated and often margianlized units. In Louisiana, for example, the National Guard force does not appear to have had any African-American units in the 1880s, while local black militia units in country parishes were placed under severe restrictions. See Scott, "'Stubborn and Disposed to Stand their Ground,'" 112–113.

43 Robert J. Cottrol and Raymond T. Diamond, "The Second Amendment: Toward an Afro-Americanist Reconsideration," *Georgetown Law Journal* 80 (1991): 309–361.

National Guard units inherited from the Reconstruction government into a "modern" standing military. By exercising its police power, political officials began centralizing and consolidating organizational control over what had previously been a diffuse and locally organized republican militia system.

This process of legally transforming the militia culminated in 1903 with the Dick Act. As Saul Cornell explains, this act and the National Defense Act of 1916 (which elaborated the role of the Guard), "effectively nationalized the function and control of the militia," while also, he claims, "draining the Second Amendment of much of its remaining force."[44] The "draining of the Second Amendment" meant that, quite ironically, the federal government could claim to possess some of the same regulatory controls over militia and firearms regulation that the states had. And, indeed, early twentieth century legal scholars such as Lucillus Emery interpreted the Second Amendment as primarily explaining the federal government's responsibilities not to interfere with a form of militia that had become defunct.[45] The federal government, in turn, grew increasingly concerned with firearms regulation beginning with the National Firearms Act of 1934, which banned weapons used by criminal syndicates.[46]

The *Cruikshank* decision and, more indirectly, the White League movement in Louisiana itself, helped set in motion a legal process that made the organized protection across the nation a matter of the state, or at least fully dependent on state policies and priorities. This meant that there was not only a distinct public security interest, but also that interest could legally be provided for by the National Guard and state police.

The legal monopoly of the state over violence secured in these rulings had an important long-term effect on vigilantism as well. In particular, the notion that vigilantism was now a fully private kind of violence put it in stark contrast to the kinds of claims about protection now available to the state in the aftermath of the *Cruikshank* ruling. African Americans took notice both of the prevalence of vigilante social control as well as the seeming indifference of the state to do anything about it, even though the state now had not only the responsibility but also the means for protecting its population. Hence, the anti-lynching campaigns that started with activists like Ida B. Wells were born, as Kimberly Johnson has pointed out, in the notion that the Jim Crow state was failing to live up to its responsibilities to protect the population – since, as *Cruikshank* made clear, African Americans weren't supposed to protect *themselves* with counter-militia, calling on the state to do so was a clever and ultimately quite successful appropriation of a legal regime that had originally been used to allow vigilantism and state violence to coexist.[47] By making vigilantism in

44 Cornell, *A Well-Regulated Militia*, 196. 45 ibid., 198–199. 46 ibid., 200.

47 Kimberley S. Johnson, *Reforming Jim Crow: Southern Politics and State in the Age Before Brown* (Oxford University Press, 2010), 43–65. Johnson focuses on the post-WWI use of this strategy, but as other scholars, like Christopher Waldrep, have made clear, defining lynching as a form of disorder rather than a heroic and chivalrous expression of white virtue was an

general – and lynching in particular – activities emblematic of disorder, African American and other Reformers hoped to yoke the police power of the state to suppressing the very tacit system of social control that helped prop up Jim Crow segregation.

The National Guard in southern states therefore was used grudgingly by Democratic governors to counter lynching attempts in increasing frequency in the late 1880s and 1890s, though this did not become as common in Louisiana until after the turn of the century.[48] Though African Americans, for all practical purposes, were excluded from positions of much political influence statewide, as citizens under the constitutional provisions of the Fourteenth and Fifteenth Amendments they could now make a viable legal claim to belonging to the public; if they were unable to use private violence legally to protect themselves, then neither could vigilantes. Their interests had to be represented as well.

Of course, as historian Daniel Kato has demonstrated, the legacy of private violence persisted even within the expanded coercive powers granted to both state and federal governments in the aftermath of the Civil War. Thus, despite the fact that the Ku Klux Klan acts clearly put collective racial violence under its jurisdiction, the federal judiciary opted instead to create a zone of "constitutional anarchy" – that is, an informal arrangement through which vigilantism could continue unabated, even when recognized to be illegal.[49] Only after the Civil Rights movement of the 1960s did the long struggle of anti-lynching reformers find reliable support in federal courts.[50]

Another key effect of the decoupling of republican coercive enforcement involved changes in the law of self-defense. While *Cruikshank* and *Presser* carved out space for the states to regulate the ownership of guns as a matter of controlling the militia, the growth of incorporation theory as a general matter of constitutional interpretation increasingly called the actual capabilities of the state to protect the "right to bear arms" into question. Did the "draining" of the Second Amendment simply mean that all regulation was acceptable? Did some Second Amendment right to gun ownership "incorporate" or supersede the local state's ability to regulate firearms? And, if so, what exactly did the text *mean* for individual gun ownership?

important rhetorical strategy for earlier reformers like Ida B. Wells. See Waldrep, *The Many Faces of Judge Lynch*, 97–101.

48 Jerry Cooper notes that despite the high levels of industrial violence found during this period in the North and West, the Guard was actually more active in the South precisely because of the need to respond to racial conflicts; he has counted at least thirty-one cases in which the Guard was mobilized in response to these kinds of events across all states. Cooper, *The Rise of the National Guard*, 46–47.

49 Daniel Kato, *Liberalizing Lynching: Building a New Racialized State* (Oxford: Oxford University Press, 2016), 104–132.

50 ibid., 144–150.

These questions have yet to be answered fully. But for gun rights advocates – particularly those involved in the widespread effort in the 1980s and 1990s to produce a new "standard model" interpretation of the Second Amendment, in which the historical text supposedly was intended to apply not only to state militia policy, but also to individual gun ownership – *Cruikshank* and *Presser*, again ironically, provided a clear template for rolling back gun regulation.[51] That is, whereas the conventional interpretation of these findings was that both federal and local government could regulate ownership of firearms, these advocates instead saw an opportunity in the *Cruikshank* and *Presser* decisions both to expand incorporation to the Second Amendment and to reinterpret the amendment itself as a matter of individual protection.

The *Heller* decision in 2008, which overturned portions of a federal statute put in place in Washington, DC, to regulate the sales of handguns, provided a victory for the individual rights interpretation, though not that of incorporation. While the decision has been widely criticized as illogical and contradictory, it also represents perhaps the clearest statement yet that gun ownership is a legally protected status for individuals and that such a status could coexist with a robust state presence.[52]

In its ruling, the court not only held that original constitutional protections for individual gun ownership had not been invalidated by *Cruikshank* and *Presser*, but also that its decision was actually rooted in an "ancient" right of citizens to protect themselves and their property from invasion and attack.[53] In a sense, *Heller* updated the principle, found in a number of very early state constitutions, "which enshrined a right of citizens to 'bear arms in defense of themselves and the state'" by claiming that both private and public forms of violence could were protected and compatible under the US Constitution.[54]

On one hand, this interpretation has some merit. On the other, this book tries to point the way toward a more fundamental institutional rather than strictly legal understanding of private republican-inspired visions of self-defense through firearms ownership, with serious implications for how we think about private violence in the United States Much of the scholarly debate on the Second Amendment – including that cited by the justices in *Heller* – has been focused on trying to understand what the Constitution meant by the "militia" and what was involved in the "right to keep and bear arms." The result has been unending debates about original intent, creating plenty of heat and no light.

[51] See Stephen P. Halbrook, "The Right of Workers to Assemble and to Bear Arms: Presser v. Illinois, One of the Last Holdouts against Application of the Bill of Rights to the States," *University of Detroit Mercy Law Review* 76 (1998): 943. On the dubious intellectual genealogy of the "standard model," see Saul Cornell, "Commonplace or Anachronism: The Standard Model, the Second Amendment, and the Problem of History in Contemporary Constitutional Theory," *Constitutional Commentary* 16 (1999): 221–246.

[52] Adam Winkler, "Heller's Catch-22," *UCLA Law Review* 56 (2008): 1551–1578.

[53] Antonin Scalia, *District of Columbia v. Heller*, June 2008, 25. [54] ibid., 11.

I suggest that this debate has gone nowhere, in part, because it does not address the question of state formation, in which the institutions (rather than legal precepts alone) that are actually responsible for managing and coordinating force are put front and center. When we focus clearly on these institutions – particularly when those institutions are practical embodiments of the kinds of republican principles over which scholars argue – it is possible to see that both views of the legality of firearms ownership have institutional roots in a republican tradition which linked private effort to public security. Self-defense, as it is normally construed, is an individual legal matter. But this is not a timeless truth, but rather an historical result of the "self" becoming detached from the collective institutions that made self-defense inextricable from public security. Only now do we view as distinct what early Americans saw as inseparable.

THE CULTURAL LEGACY OF JURISDICTIONAL DECOUPLING

Widespread private gun ownership, the link between vigilance and citizenship, and public support for self-defense are not simply institutional and legal realities; they are also part of a cultural project in which the effects of institutional decoupling and the compatibility between public and private violence have become key dimensions of American self-understanding.

Take, perhaps, the most famous example: the gunfighter. The historical gunfighter, as analyzed in this book, was, in the end, really only a transitional figure. Because both market and territorial incorporation were so successful – the frontier, in the language of Frederick Jackson Turner, became "closed" – the role of guarding the new transportation infrastructure and large industrial cattle and mining operations ultimately settled into the same kind of public/private policing story that characterized eastern cities. Large, organized private security firms such as Baldwin-Felts increased the scale of their services to mining operations in states like West Virginia, Colorado, Idaho, and Montana, which suffered from increasingly violent demands from laborers in the first decade of the new century.[55] At the same time, as territories became states, politicians began to invest in new public policing agencies, such as state rangers and police departments found throughout the West by the early 1920s, both helping to manage disturbances in far-flung sections of the country while also keeping an eye on the burgeoning highway system.[56] These new centrally organized public and private forces were less interested in hiring freelance specialists in violence

55 Richard M. Hadsell and William E. Coffey, "From Law and Order to Class Warfare: Baldwin-Felts Detectives in the Southern West Virginia Coal Fields," *West Virginia History* 40, no. 3 (April 1979): 268–286; Thomas G. Andrews, *Killing for Coal: America's Deadliest Labor War* (Cambridge, MA: Harvard University Press, 2008), 244.

56 H. Kenneth Bechtel, *State Police in the United States: A Socio-Historical Analysis* (Westport, CT: Greenwood Press, 1995), 25–44.

than in jointly securing a means to counter the threat of class violence. The age of the gunfighter as a real-life, interconnected market actor, moving between law-abiding and law-breaking activities, was over.

But the age of the gunfighter as a cultural figure had just begun. Gunfighters in the market were just trying to make a living often unconcerned with the principled aim of bringing "law and order." As myths, constructed through the literary efforts of authors like Owen Wister and the nostalgic political rhetoric of Teddy Roosevelt, however, gunfighters became something more – good guys and bad guys, emblems of individual competence in violence that could be put in the service of new political projects such as imperialism. Hence, just as real gunfighters began to die off, the cultural valence of gunfighters became a means to help to push American state-building into new directions.[57]

Roosevelt's Rough Rider regiment in the Spanish-American War was a key moment in the transformation of the economic logic of gunfighting into political myth. He staffed his hand-picked unit with well-known Southwestern characters, including William Llewellyn, one of "Whispering" Smith's old mentors, as well as a number of gunfighting specialists like Bat Masterson's friend Ben Daniels. These men served alongside a number of Ivy Leaguers and other elites from the east, in an explicit attempt to link the raw frontier masculinity of the West to the political class of traditional America, which Roosevelt felt was in danger of losing its vigor. For Roosevelt, who had had experiences of his own with vigilantes in Montana, gunfighters were private citizens who nonetheless could be relied upon to serve with valor and individual merit in organized military units; as newly baptized members of the US Army, they could also be used to rethink the connection between masculinity, citizenship, and expanding American power overseas.[58]

In other words, the new myth of the gunfighter resolved the uneasy contradiction between national military power and old republican traditions of private action as the cornerstone of public security. As Richard Slotkin observes, the United States became a "gunfighter nation" – one in which the values of western legends informed self-identity, and in which personal protection and use of violence became fully compatible with state coercion.[59] This sensibility, he argues, was found in much of the popular cultural and political rhetoric of the twentieth century in the United States, and had major effects in how presidents like Eisenhower – for whom "Wild" Bill Hickok was a key childhood hero – spoke and thought about the use of violence.[60]

57 Robert Warshow, "Movie Chronicle: The Westerner," in *The American West on Film: Myth and Reality*, ed. Richard A. Maynard (Rochelle Park, NJ: Hayden Book Company, 1974), 64–75.

58 Sarah Watts, *Rough Rider in the White House: Theodore Roosevelt and the Politics of Desire* (Chicago: University of Chicago Press, 2003), 16–20, 121.

59 Richard Slotkin, *Gunfighter Nation: The Myth of the Frontier in Twentieth-Century America* (Norman: University of Oklahoma Press, 1992).

60 Also see Brown, *No Duty to Retreat*, 37–38.

At the same time, this myth had an effect on another dimension of political culture as well: gunfighters helped make it possible to make guns themselves important tokens of citizenship. A nation of gunfighters was one constituted by good guys and bad guys; as a result, possessing and knowing how to use guns was the only way to truly secure the self-protection of the good in a world full of crime and danger. In this sense, private gun ownership not only connected citizenship to a mythic past of gunfighters and frontier violence, but was also evidence of one's civic commitment.[61]

Decoupling is by no means solely responsible for the growth of the gunfighter myth, nor the reproduction and expansion of that myth by way of Hollywood, comic books, and pulp fiction. But the empirical manifestations of the breakdown of republicanism – such as the historical gunfighting mercenaries of the late nineteenth-century Southwest – have provided ample resources for those trying to make sense of the growing disconnect between a powerful organizational state and the power and autonomy of ordinary citizens. Because the gunfighter myth often involves a figure committed to a state-building project while also serving as an exemplar of the power of the ordinary man, many Americans find narrative ways to overlook the seeming incompatibility of a growing security state with traditional conceptions of an active, involved membership in a political community.[62]

The gunfighter, of course, is not the only cultural legacy of decoupling. Literary private detectives like Sam Spade and Philip Marlowe, as well as representations of vigilantism in film and fiction reveal the complex ways in which private Americans can both operate outside the state while contributing, in a more fundamental way, to law and order.[63] On one hand, these figures are clear heroes and state-builders: many literary gunfighters are sheriffs or private detectives (both close allies to city police), or are vigilantes (respectable and decent citizens). On the other hand, these figures often work privately, outside the law and sometimes with limited effect. Thus, those same gunfighting sheriffs often have sordid pasts or, like Clint Eastwood's western hero Josey Wales, choose to fight against a corrupt and tyrannical state in order to advance a more perfect union. The classic literary detectives like Spade and Marlowe, in turn, are always deeply cynical in the face of urban squalor, which they invariably fail to eradicate. Most interesting, perhaps, are vigilantes, such as the Ku Klux Klan or Batman's alter ego Bruce Wayne, who shield their identities in order to avoid calling the legitimacy of the state itself in question. In other words, these myths propagate the notion that, even in a world of political alienation, the private

61 Jennifer Carlson, *Citizen-Protectors: The Everyday Politics of Guns in an Age of Decline* (Oxford: Oxford University Press, 2015); Richard Hofstadter, "America as a Gun Culture," *American Heritage* 21, no. 6 (1970).

62 Robert B. Pippin, "What Is a Western? Politics and Self-Knowledge in John Ford's the Searchers," *Critical Inquiry* 35, no. 2 (2009): 223–253.

63 Michael Rogin, "'The Sword Became a Flashing Vision': D. W. Griffith's the Birth of a Nation," *Representations* 9 (1985): 150–195.

use of use of violence is dangerous, but can – under the right circumstances – provide a form of order. And in so doing, they contribute to a long tradition in the United States and elsewhere that private force helps sustain rather than challenge the state, particularly on the frontier.

DECOUPLING EVERYWHERE?

Decoupling thus led not only to the development of distinct but compatible public and private forms of violence within institutional settings, but also forged cultural and legal complexes recognizing and acknowledging this distinction. Most Americans seem to possess a clear sense of what the boundary separating public security from private efforts at control is, but many also treat this duality as compatible and even desirable, at least tacitly. This paradox is not so puzzling when we trace the alteration of republican institutional frameworks in particular historical settings, as this book has tried to do, but it does leave us with a different way of thinking about the state from that presented by many accounts.

Nevertheless, there remain a number of unresolved questions about the larger context of these legacies. What does this analysis tell us about the frequent claim that the United States is a particularly violent place? Is this account yet another example of exceptionalism by another name?

The United States, of course, was not the only state to experience the kinds of unsettled contexts I have described in this book. Australia, South Africa, Mongolia, and countless other states were marked by their own borderlands spaces, even as urbanization, transportation revolutions dislocated supposedly traditional forms of social life in many places, and the frequency and intensity of social interaction across place and time increased.[64] In this sense, I have treated the nineteenth century as a kind of world-historical critical juncture: it set in motion processes of transportation and interconnection that made social ambiguity and physical mobility common in many places. Colonialism and empire, the industrial revolution, the growth in nationalism and mass military conscription, and the making of market capitalism all contributed to making this juncture, spreading the experience of the frontier far and wide.

But in the United States, these unsettled frontier spaces were combined with a pervasive republicanism, both a conviction that the link between private effort and public security was the natural product of good citizens and a good government, and a series of institutional arrangements designed to implement this conviction. In eighteenth – and nineteenth-century Britain, which (as did most places) also possessed similar kinds of institutional arrangements, social transformations associated with industrialization led to dual public and private forms of coercion as well; a robust private security industry, the emergence

64 Wolfgang Schivelbusch, *The Railway Journey: The Industrialization of Time and Space in the 19th Century* (Berkeley: University of California Press, 1986), 33–44.

of private prosecution societies, and some residual forms of private collective punishment went hand-in-hand with the growth of professional policing.[65] But England and other British jurisdictions lacked the kinds of profoundly unsettled spaces, marked by levels of physical mobility, institutional instability, and social ambiguity, found in the United States, as Little and Sheffield have convincingly demonstrated.[66] The United States is not exactly exceptional, but even in states with similar institutional legacies, decoupling rarely led to anything approaching the bifurcated public and private response found in American life.

What was the relationship these new private and public patterns of coercion and the *levels* of disorder they addressed in the mid-nineteenth century? The nation as a whole *does* seem to have become more violent across the century: as Randolph Roth has shown, for instance, personal homicide rates seem to have increased dramatically in the late nineteenth century, which he attributes to a breakdown in civic consciousness.[67] But violence is an interactive process, and my contention in this book has been that explaining the frequency of violence depends on understanding its social context. In turn, there is no simple relationship between an increase in violence and an increase in coercive institutions. The two concepts are inseparable. Even if, for example, by hiring private detectives or gunfighters market actors were responding to a tangible increase in property crime just as the state was confronting other kinds of threats to the general peace, it is important to remember that the actors responsible for those increases in crime and disorder were, themselves, often responding to changes in how coercion was organized by the market and the state.[68] Thus, one important implication of this project should be that studying quantities of violence does not make sense outside the institutional conditions under which that violence is produced.

Curiously, many scholars have sidelined the political implications of seemingly exceptional levels of American violence. Years ago, Richard Hofstadter noted that the nation has "a history but not a tradition of domestic violence," by which he meant that most violence was and is directed by and at private actors rather than the state, therefore "lack[ing] both an ideological and a

[65] Joyce Lee Malcolm, *Guns and Violence: The English Experience* (Cambridge, MA: Harvard University Press, 2002), 90–115; Les Johnston, *The Rebirth of Private Policing* (London: Taylor & Francis, 1992), 3–48.

[66] Little and Sheffield, "Frontiers and Criminal Justice," 806–807.

[67] Roth, *American Homicide*, 297–385.

[68] This does not even touch the important issue of how actions that at one point may have been considered harmless or private were increasingly legally defined as threats to the peace or vice versa. A fall or rise in domestic violence, to take one prominent example, may not reflect a shift in actual frequency in the actions, but their redefinition as matters of private or public concern. On the effects of legal change regarding conceptions of privacy and crime in the family, see Ruth H. Bloch, "The American Revolution, Wife Beating, and the Emergent Value of Privacy," *Early American Studies* 5, no. 2 (2007): 223–251.

geographical center."[69] In this vision, violence in the United States is somewhat apolitical and conservative, only indirectly affecting – if at all – the actual governing process.[70] Such assumptions have allowed students of American politics to think of the state as a pluralist arena for political competition rather than one dependent on a vast apparatus of coercive enforcement.

Of course, a battery of recent scholarship has challenged this argument, showing how crucial systems of mass incarceration and policing have become to help preserve American institutional authority.[71] While broadly agreeing with this critique, this book insists we understand that enforcement is also private – and is recognized to be so. Americans have traditionally had an aversion to state violence, yet nevertheless have allowed their government to become a behemoth of coercion. Institutionalized private violence is a part of, rather than competitor to, this behemoth. But precisely because the traditional link between public and private violence has also helped shape conceptions of citizenship in the United States, the right of the state to enact deeply punitive social control policies is fully compatible with a conception that individuals, firms, and communities also have a right to protect themselves.[72]

Another related issue has to do with the role of guns themselves in the transformation of American security. That is, part of the expansion of the market in the mid-nineteenth century also involved a technological shift in the availability and pervasiveness of personal firearms as Colt, Winchester, and other gun-making entrepreneurs developed production techniques which made highly reliable and cheap small weapons available directly to private consumers in the 1850s and 1860s.[73] This, in turn, displaced (in part) the earlier system of gunsmiths, which was fundamentally a local craft industry oriented toward making hunting rifles that were sold in very small quantities. The availability of personal handguns after the Civil War, in particular, helped prop up the notion that the private individual could, indeed, act as a repository of violence in a manner that was previously impossible. In short, while the new weapons did

69 Richard Hofstadter, "Reflections on Violence in the United States," in *American Violence: A Documentary History*, ed. Richard Hofstadter and Michael Wallace (New York: Alfred A. Knopf, 1970), 3.

70 Hugh Davis Graham, "The Paradox of American Violence: A Historical Appraisal," *Annals of the American Academy of Political and Social Science* 391 (1970): 74–82.

71 Marie Gottschalk, *Caught: The Prison State and the Lockdown of American Politics* (Princeton, NJ: Princeton University Press, 2015); Naomi Murakawa, *The First Civil Right: How Liberals Built Prison America* (Oxford: Oxford University Press, 2014); Jonathan Simon, *Governing through Crime: How the War on Crime Transformed American Democracy and Created a Culture of Fear* (Oxford: Oxford University Press, 2007); Vesla M. Weaver, "Frontlash: Race and the Development of Punitive Crime Policy," *Studies in American Political Development* 21, no. 02 (2007): 230–265.

72 David Garland, *The Culture of Control* (Oxford: Oxford University Press, 2001), 17–18.

73 Pamela Haag, *The Gunning of America: Business and the Making of American Gun Culture* (New York: Basic Books, 2016), 45–91, 249–266, 317–339.

not cause the breakdown of the republican system into a dual organization of public and private forces, it likely promoted it.

Much work needs to be done to investigate these questions. This book, however, has demonstrated that unsettled frontier spaces played a key role in this transformation. They undermined the capacity for small, enclosed communities to simply link private power to public effort. Social, market, and state actors each, in their own way, continued to *use* those institutions, thereby transforming them. And in the profusion of organizations making up the public and private violence, the basic principle that a private right to force – by businesses, by partisans, or by individuals – was fully compatible with the state continues to shape the way Americans think about and organize self-defense. In the United States, public security is always, at some level, a private matter.

Index